The Language of Computer Graphics

The Language of Computer Graphics

A dictionary of terms and concepts

John Vince

Architecture Design and Technology Press
London

First published in 1990 by
Architecture Design and
Technology Press
128 Long Acre
London WC2E 9AN

British Library Cataloguing in Publication Data
A CIP catalogue record for this book is available from the British Library

ISBN 1 85454 147 1

Linotronic: Alphabet Set, London

Printed in Great Britain by The Bath Press

To Annie, Samantha and Anthony

preface

Twenty years ago – when computer graphics was starting to evolve – it seemed possible to understand the entire subject, as it was basically concerned with clipping, transformations and elementary shading. Today, this is no longer the case – one only has to open the latest SIGGRAPH proceedings to discover subjects such as radiosity, stochastic sampling, solid texture, global illumination models, parametric surfaces and inverse kinematics, to realize the enormous progress that has been made. However, as with all evolving subjects, computer graphics is having to introduce new words and terminology that are equally baffling for the newcomer.

My sole purpose in collecting these thousand or so words together was to provide the newcomer to this exciting subject with an introduction to the language of computer graphics using descriptions that are simple to understand and, where possible, without any supporting mathematics. The entries are not taken entirely from computer graphics, as I have wandered into various disciplines from optics to electronics, selecting terms that frequently surface within technical papers. I have considered each entry very carefully, anticipating the conceptual problems a reader will encounter in understanding the scope and significance of its meaning. Such descriptions have been limited by the total space available for this publication; consequently, I have had to balance the level of description with the perceived complexity of the entry. I only hope that I have succeeded in establishing this balance.

In the majority of entries, I have highlighted (using small capital letters) certain words that are explained elsewhere in the book, and might assist the reader in perfecting an understanding of the term – and to complete this cross-referencing I have also suggested other related entries that may be worth investigating.

Finally, a list of references has been provided which identifies doctoral theses, proceedings, scientific papers, patents and selected books that will take the reader into relevant areas of interest. I know that I wish such a resource had been available when I first became captivated by computer graphics; so perhaps you will randomly delve into the pages of this book and discover something new, or suddenly understand a concept for the first time. Hopefully, some of the entries will translate into 'mind pictures' and assist you in understanding some abstract terms, and enable you to comprehend this amazing world of synthetic imagery and, who knows, could stimulate you to explore an exciting avenue of research.

John Vince

acknowledgements

I am indebted to the colleagues I have pestered over recent months to clarify the meaning of certain terms and concepts, without whose help, this book would not have been possible. In particular, I wish to thank Gareth Edwards who read an early manuscript and revealed a wealth of extra terms I had overlooked or had not encountered, and sent me off investigating obtuse subject areas in SIGGRAPH proceedings. Similarly, I must thank Dr Tony Crilly at Middlesex Polytechnic, who innocently volunteered to read the manuscript, offered invaluable advice on many areas, and proposed alternative definitions and explanations. Paul Froggatt and Mark Schafer at Symbolics have also been of tremendous assistance in providing me with the terminology and explanations of terms used within the computer animation community. Alastair Horn actually volunteered to read the final draft and made some valuable suggestions, however, the extra terms he recommended will have to wait for a second edition. A special acknowledgement is due to Dietmar Saupe for providing me with the illustration on page 93 – and also an endless source of information from the book *The Science of Fractal Images*. William Latham of the IBM Scientific Research Centre generously provided the computer images on the cover. Finally, a global thank you to the authors of the books, articles and proceedings that provided the original source material for this book.

absolute coordinates
The term absolute coordinates is sometimes used in place of world coordinates, which form a basis for defining 3-D models and their positions, together with the positions of light sources and trajectory paths. (See also WORLD COORDINATE SPACE.)
[Gasson-83]

A-buffer
Loren Carpenter developed the A-buffer HIDDEN-SURFACE REMOVAL algorithm at Lucasfilm Ltd as part of the REYES renderer. It is a descendant of the Z-BUFFER and addresses the problems of ANTI-ALIASING, TRANSPARENCY and interpenetrating objects by maintaining lists of pixel bit masks, which records a polygon's impact upon a pixel. These bit masks, together with colour, Z-DEPTH, OPACITY and AREA PROPERTIES, enable a pixel's intensity to be computed. The algorithm's name is due to the Anti-aliasing being achieved through Area-Averaged Accumulation of intensities. (See also HIDDEN-SURFACE REMOVAL, PAINTER'S ALGORITHM, RADIOSITY, SCAN-LINE ALGORITHM, Z-BUFFER, and ZZ-BUFFER.)
[Carpenter-89]

achromatic light
Achromatic light is without colour and describes light consisting of varying degrees of grey from black to white, as found on monochrome CRT displays. (See also CHROMATIC LIGHT.)
[Gregory-86]

active list
In SCAN-LINE ALGORITHMS the active list maintains references to those facets that intersect the current scan-line. By exploiting EDGE COHERENCE, this active list can be updated for the following raster by dropping those facets no longer intersecting the raster and including new facets that do intersect. (See also EDGE COHERENCE, OBJECT SPACE ALGORITHM, and SCAN-LINE ALGORITHM.)
[Burger-89, Foley-90, Hearn-86, Rogers-85]

acuity
See VISUAL ACUITY.

acute angle
An acute angle is less than 90°. (See also OBTUSE ANGLE.)

adaptive clipping
Where many clipping algorithms operate upon single lines or polygons, adaptive clipping is sensitive to, or 'adapts' to, the existence of rotation/shear INSTANCE TRANSFORMS in a hierarchical DISPLAY FILE. (See also CLIPPING and CLIPPING DIVIDER.)
[Newman-79]

adaptive forward differences (AFD)
As a POLYNOMIAL can be evaluated using FORWARD DIFFERENCES, PARAMETRIC CURVES and surfaces can be rendered with the aid of this technique. But where conventional FORWARD DIFFERENCES uses fixed increments, adaptive forward differences dynamically adjusts the controlling parameter so that the PARAMETRIC CURVE or surface is evaluated at pixel sized steps. (See also ADAPTIVE SUBDIVISION, CRACKS, FORWARD DIFFERENCES, PARAMETRIC CURVE, PARAMETRIC SURFACE PATCH, and RENDERER.)
[Chang-89, Lien-87, Rockwood-87, Shantz-87, Shantz-88]

adaptive progressive refinement
Adaptive progressive refinement refers to the way an image is progressively refined until certain visual goals are obtained. (See also ADAPTIVE SAMPLING, ANTI-ALIASING, and STOCHASTIC SAMPLING.)
[Bergman-86, Cohen-88, Painter-89]

adaptive sampling
Adaptive sampling is an ANTI-ALIASING strategy in which additional samples are introduced between previous samples to improve the SAMPLING. (See also ALIASING, OVERSAMPLING, RAY TRACING, and STOCHASTIC SAMPLING.)
[Cook-86, Glassner-89, Whitted-79]

adaptive subdivision

adaptive subdivision

One way of rendering a SURFACE PATCH is to repeatedly subdivide it into smaller subpatches – adaptive subdivision halts the process when some flatness criterion is achieved. Because the subdivision occurs in PARAMETER SPACE – rather than OBJECT SPACE – linear edges in PARAMETER SPACE are assumed to create linear polygon edges, which is not always the case. This assumption can create small visual artifacts between the rendered polygons in the form of missing detail called 'CRACKS'. (See also ADAPTIVE FORWARD DIFFERENCING, AREA SUBDIVISION ALGORITHMS, CRACKS, DIVIDE AND CONQUER, IMAGE SPACE ALGORITHM, PARAMETER SPACE, PARAMETRIC SURFACE PATCH, and WARNOCK ALGORITHM.)

[Catmull-74a, Clark-79, Dippe-84, Lane-80]

adaptive tree-depth control

In RAY TRACING, adaptive tree-depth control refers to the process of dynamically adjusting the depth of the RAY INTERSECTION TREE traversed by ignoring rays whose intensity falls below some threshold. (See also RAY INTERSECTION TREE and RAY TRACING.)

[Glassner-89]

additive colour mixing

Additive colour mixing is the technique of creating colours by superimposing two or three light sources from the red, green and blue portions of the visible spectrum. The idea is attributed to Thomas Young (1723–1829) who proposed additive colour mixing as the key to human colour vision. See Figure A-1. (See also ADDITIVE PRIMARY COLOURS, SUBTRACTIVE COLOUR MIXING, SUBTRACTIVE PRIMARY COLOURS, TRICHROMATIC COLOUR SYSTEM, and TRI-STIMULOUS THEORY.)

[Boynton-79, Burger-89, Gregory-86, Hunt-75]

additive primary colours

The additive primary colours are red, green and blue, because the human retina contains three types of cone photopigments with peak sensitivities in the red (650 nm), green (530 nm) and blue (425 nm) portions of the visible spectrum. Thus a model of colour matching – the TRICHROMATIC SYSTEM – can be used to describe colours as the additive combination of three primary components. This is the basis of most television and computer graphics display technology. See Figure A-1. (See also ADDITIVE COLOUR MIXING, SUBTRACTIVE COLOUR MIXING, SUBTRACTIVE PRIMARY COLOURS, TRICHROMATIC COLOUR SYSTEM, and TRI-STIMULOUS THEORY.)

[Boynton-79, Burger-89, Gregory-86, Hunt-75]

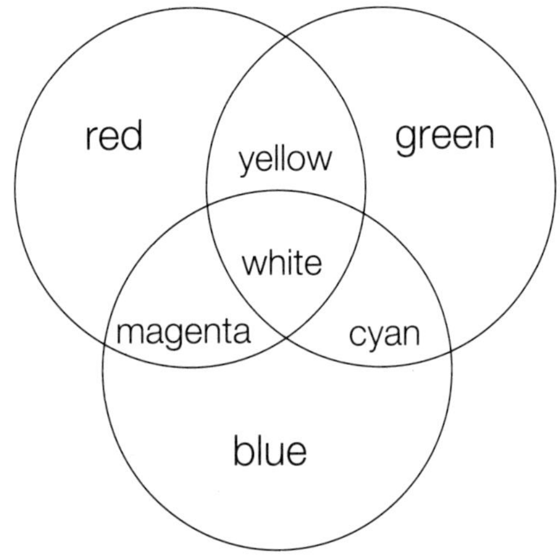

Figure A-1 *When the additive primary colours red, green and blue are combined together, they produce the secondary colours cyan, magenta and yellow. Furthermore, if equal amounts of red, green and blue are mixed together different intensities of grey result.*

AFD

See ADAPTIVE FORWARD DIFFERENCES.

affine transformation

Affine geometry and its associated transformations preserves the concept of parallelism, with the implication that any lines parallel before an affine transformation will

still be parallel after the operation. Examples of affine transformations are scale, reflection, rotation and shear. An affine transformation can consist of any number of linear transformations followed by a translation. A PERSPECTIVE TRANSFORMATION, for example, is not affine, as it does not preserve parallelism. (See also LINEAR TRANSFORMATION, MATRIX OPERATION, NON-LINEAR TRANSFORMATION, PERSPECTIVE TRANSFORMATION, and TRANSFORMATION.)
[Gasson-83, Rogers-89, Stevenson-74]

aim point

The orientation of the OBSERVER in WORLD COORDINATES can be effected by the EYE POINT and the aim point; the latter is the point at which the gaze of the OBSERVER is directed, and in general coincides with the centre of the VIEWPORT. See Figure E-2. (See also EYE COORDINATE SYSTEM, EYE POINT, LINE OF SIGHT, OBSERVER, VIEWPORT, and VIEW VECTOR.)

airbrush

(1) An airbrush is an air-driven paint gun which may be used to spray paint over a surface to achieve photo-realistic images.
(2) Airbrush is a paint mode in computer paint systems to imitate physical airbrushing. (See also PAINT SYSTEM.)

algebraic surface

An algebraic surface is a geometric representation of an equation describing in 3-D space the relationship between three variables. For example, the equation

$$z = 3x + y^2$$

relates together x, y and z, and by substituting values fo and y, one could identify the IMPLICIT SURFACE represented by the algebraic equation. Such surfaces are the basis of CONSTRUCTIVE SOLID GEOMETRY and RAY TRACING strategies. (See also EXPLICIT SURFACE.)
[Gasson-83, Glassner-89]

algorithm

A rigorous definition of an algorithm is: a mathematical or logical procedure for solving a problem composed from an indefinite number of steps, each step applying to the result of the one preceding it. Informally, it means a procedure used to solve a problem. The word algorithm is a corruption of Al Kworesmi, a ninth century Arabian mathematician. (See also DETERMINISTIC, HEURISTIC, and STOCHASTIC.)
[Earnshaw-85]

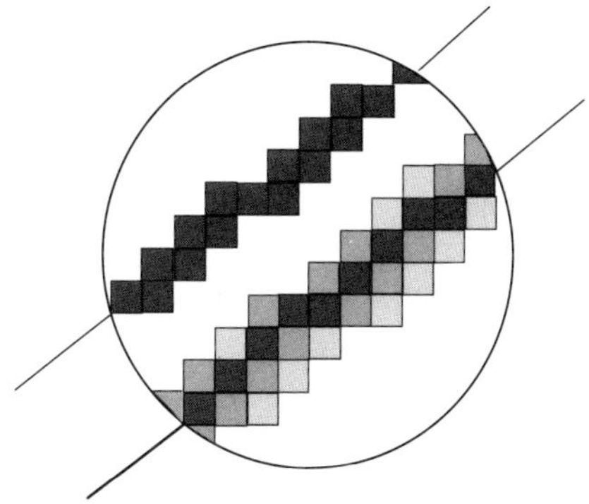

Figure A-2 *The magnified top jagged line can be improved by an anti-aliasing procedure which introduces neighbouring pixels of different intensities as shown in the bottom line.*

aliasing

(1) **Analytic**: When a complex signal is discretely sampled and a reconstruction is made from the samples, any frequency components in the original signal that exceed the NYQUIST LIMIT will appear as a low-frequency 'alias' in the reconstruction. The introduction of these extraneous artifacts is called aliasing.
(2) **Spatial**: In pixel-based display systems, visual artifacts such as jagged edges and MOIRÉ PATTERNS caused by insufficient spatial sampling are referred to as SPATIAL ALIASING. See Figure A-2.
(3) **Temporal**: Animation artifacts such as 'wagon wheels' apparently rotating backwards caused by the insufficient temporal sampling of moving objects is referred to as TEMPORAL ALIASING. (See also ADAPTIVE SAM-

PLING, ANTI-ALIASING, ARTIFACT, CONVOLUTION, FILTER, FILTERING, JAGGIES, NYQUIST LIMIT, POINT SAMPLING, SAMPLING, SPATIAL ALIASING, STOCHASTIC SAMPLING, and TEMPORAL ALIASING.)
[Blinn-89a, Burger-89, Foley-90, Gupta-81, Rogers-85]

alpha channel

The alpha channel is a video channel derived from a value called the ALPHA VALUE associated with each pixel in a video FRAME STORE. It is often used for storing MATTES when COMPOSITING images – and as each pixel may have a number of bits of KEY SIGNAL, the MATTE boundary can create an interpolated blend of intensities. (See also COMPOSITING and MATTE.)

alpha value

See ALPHA CHANNEL.

ambient light

ILLUMINATION MODELS employ a constant term to represent a background light level assumed to be caused by multiple DIFFUSE REFLECTIONS. This ambient light component allows surfaces not directly illuminated by light sources to receive some level of illumination. The ambient light level must be carefully adjusted in relation to the intensities of the other light sources, to ensure that surfaces are not saturated with light – a typical level might be around 25% of the total illumination level. (See also DIFFUSE REFLECTION, GLOBAL ILLUMINATION MODEL, ILLUMINATION MODEL, LIGHT SOURCE, and SPECULAR REFLECTION.)
[Burger-89, Foley-90, Glassner-89, Hearn-86, Rogers-85]

ambient reflection coefficient

The ambient reflection coefficient is a fractional value associated with a reflective surface that determines the level of ambient light it reflects. It is common to have a coefficient for each of the red, green and blue components. (See also DIFFUSE REFLECTION COEFFICIENT and SPECULAR REFLECTION COEFFICIENT.)
[Burger-89, Foley-90, Glassner-89, Hearn-86, Rogers-85]

analogue signals

Analogue signals vary continuously in time. Such signals are found in moving-coil microphones, gramophone pickups and loudspeakers. (See also ANALOGUE-TO-DIGITAL CONVERTER, DIGITAL SIGNAL, and DIGITAL-TO-ANALOGUE CONVERTER.)

analogue-to-digital converter

Analogue-to-digital converters translate an ANALOGUE SIGNAL into a DIGITAL SIGNAL by SAMPLING the waveform's amplitude at intervals and converting it to a binary number with a specified bit resolution. For example, the rotary controls on a FUNCTION BOX will employ an analogue-to-digital converter to translate rotational positions into DIGITAL SIGNALS for processing by a computer. (See also ANALOGUE SIGNAL, DIGITAL SIGNAL, and DIGITAL-TO-ANALOGUE CONVERTER.)

angle of incidence

The orientation of a source of illumination relative to a surface is measured by the angle of incidence, which is the ACUTE ANGLE formed by the SURFACE NORMAL and the incident ray illuminating the surface. For reflecting surfaces, the ANGLE OF REFLECTION equals the angle of incidence. See Figure A-3. (See also ANGLE OF REFLECTION and ANGLE OF REFRACTION.)
[Glassner-89, Jenkins-76]

angle of reflection

For a perfect reflecting surface, the angle of reflection is the ACUTE ANGLE formed by the SURFACE NORMAL and the reflected ray away from the surface. For such surfaces, the angle of reflection equals the ANGLE OF INCIDENCE. See Figure A-3. (See also ANGLE OF INCIDENCE and ANGLE OF REFRACTION.)
[Glassner-89, Jenkins-76]

angle of refraction

When light moves from one medium to another and undergoes a speed change, the direction of the transmitted light is also disturbed (refracted); this angle of refraction is the ACUTE ANGLE formed by the refracted ray

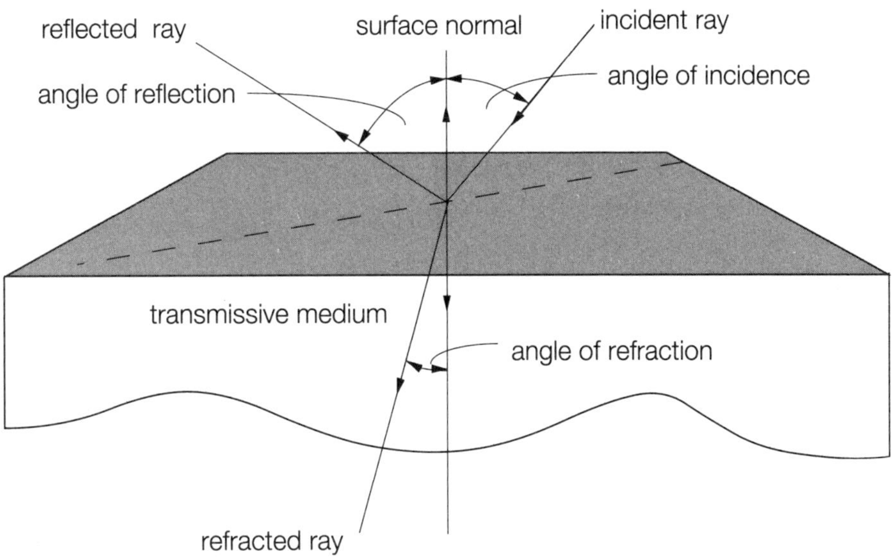

Figure A-3 *The first law of reflection states that the incident ray, the reflected ray and the surface normal at the point of incidence lie in the same plane; whilst the second law states that the angle of reflection equals the angle of incidence.*

and the reflected SURFACE NORMAL for a transmissive medium. The relationship between the ANGLE OF INCIDENCE and the ANGLE OF REFRACTION is defined by SNELL'S LAW. See Figure A-3. (See also ANGLE OF INCIDENCE, ANGLE OF REFLECTION, REFRACTION OF LIGHT, REFRACTIVE INDEX, and SNELL'S LAW.)

angle of view

The angle of view of a lens is the SOLID ANGLE of incident light transmitted by the lens. This may vary between 8° for a telephoto lens, through 50° for a normal lens, to 100° for a wide-angle lens. This optical phenomenon can be simulated in computer graphics. (See also APERTURE, DEPTH OF FIELD, F-NUMBER, and FOCAL LENGTH.)
[Glassner-89, Potmesil-81, Potmesil-82]

animation

Animation is the technique of creating continuously moving scenes by projecting a sequence of gradually changing discrete images in rapid succession to an observer. In computer animation, the computer is sometimes able to generate images in REAL-TIME, but frequently several minutes are required to create just one frame – and usually only when a sequence is complete can they be observed in an animated form. (See also BEHAVIOURAL ANIMATION, CELL ANIMATION, CHARACTER ANIMATION, COMPUTER ANIMATION, FLICKER, FUSION FREQUENCY, KEY-FRAME ANIMATION, and REAL-TIME.)
[Lasseter-87, White-86]

anisotropic

Anisotropic means varying as a function of direction. For example, SPECULAR REFLECTIONS are anisotropic as they can only occur over a limited angular range. (See also ISOTROPIC.)
[Kajiya-85]

anti-aliasing

In general, anti-aliasing encompasses strategies concerned with the removal or reduction of ALIASING ARTIFACTS arising from the insufficient SAMPLING of complex signals. In RASTER COMPUTER GRAPHICS this might be achieved by increased SAMPLING and averaging the result: this reduces aliasing by effectively raising the NYQUIST LIMIT. Unfortunately, no matter how many samples are taken, there will always be higher frequencies that will alias, so research effort has been expended in achieving better SAMPLING. See Figure A-2. (See also ADAPTIVE SAMPLING, ALIASING, ARTIFACT, BASIS FUNCTION, CONVOLUTION, FILTER, FILTERING, FOURIER WAVEFORM ANALYSIS, JAGGIES, NYQUIST LIMIT, OVERSAMPLING, PIXEL AVERAGING, POINT SAMPLING, POINT-SPREAD FUNCTION, SPATIAL ALIASING, STOCHASTIC SAMPLING, and TEMPORAL ALIASING)

[Abram-85, Blinn-89a, Blinn-89b, Crow-81, Crow-86, Dippe-85, Forrest-85, Glassner-89, Grant-85, Max-90a]

anticlockwise polygon

Polygons are an essential building block in modelling – and are constructed with an inherent 'sense', in that their boundary follows a clockwise or anticlockwise path: an anticlockwise polygon is defined as one whose interior is to the left and whose exterior is to the right when its boundary is traversed in the direction of its edges. The 'sense' of polygons can be critical to some algorithms, as they might assume that clockwise polygons represent solids and anticlockwise polygons represent holes. Similarly, a modelling scheme might require that all surfaces are constructed with a clockwise sense, to create outward-facing SURFACE NORMALS. A mistake in this scheme would produce an inward-facing surface normal, possibly creating problems in rendering and HIDDEN-SURFACE REMOVAL. (See also BACK FACE REMOVAL and CLOCKWISE POLYGON.)

aperture

Aperture is a measure of the physical area associated with a lens through which light can pass – and a conventional method of expressing this is by the F-NUMBER. Because lens systems are not 100% accurate, especially at large apertures, the DEPTH OF FIELD depends upon the F-NUMBER; this phenomenon can be simulated in RAY TRACING. (See also CIRCLE OF CONFUSION, DEPTH OF FIELD, F-NUMBER, and RAY TRACING.)

[Burger-89, Glassner-89, Jenkins-76, Potmesil-81, Potmesil-82]

approximating spline

Spline curves can be categorized into two simple types: those that intersect their CONTROL POINTS, and those that only approach them. Approximating splines are of the latter type, whilst the former are known as INTERPOLATING SPLINES. B-SPLINE CURVES are approximating splines. (See also BÉZIER CURVE, B-SPLINE CURVE, CATMULL–ROM SPLINE, CONTROL POINTS, INTERPOLATING SPLINE, NURBS, and SPLINE.)

[Bohm-84, Farin-88, Smith-83, Woodwark-86]

area coherence

Some algorithms are able to exploit area coherence by recognizing features that are consistent over ranges of area. For example, DIVIDE AND CONQUER algorithms or even the use of SPACE FILLING CURVES in IMAGE COMPRESSION exploit area coherence. (See also AREA SUBDIVISION ALGORITHMS, COHERENCE, DEPTH COHERENCE, DIVIDE AND CONQUER, EDGE COHERENCE, and QUADTREE.)

[Crocker-87b, Warnock-68, Warnock-69]

area coordinates

If the vertices P_1, P_2 and P_3 of a 2-D triangle have Cartesian coordinates $[x_1, y_1]$, $[x_2, y_2]$ and $[x_3, y_3]$ respectively, then any point P with coordinates $[x, y]$ which is inside the triangle can create three areas from the vertex sequences: (P, P_2, P_3), (P, P_3, P_1) and (P, P_1, P_2). If these areas are normalized so that they represent fractional values of the triangle's area and are labelled A_1, A_2 and A_3 respectively, then these area coordinates of P are related to its Cartesian coordinates as follows:

$$\begin{bmatrix} 1 \\ x \\ y \end{bmatrix} = \begin{bmatrix} 1 & 1 & 1 \\ x_1 & x_2 & x_3 \\ y_1 & y_2 & y_3 \end{bmatrix} \begin{bmatrix} A_1 \\ A_2 \\ A_3 \end{bmatrix}$$

As one can also define the areas A_1, A_2 and A_3 in terms of the triangle's vertices and *P*, it is possible to tell whether *P* is inside or outside the triangle, or whether it is located on an edge or a vertex. (See also BARYCENTRIC COORDINATES, CARTESIAN COORDINATES, and HOMOGENEOUS COORDINATES.)
[Jassen-83]

area filling curves
See SPACE FILLING CURVES.

area filling primitives
Area filling primitives refer to polygon filling modes allowed within GKS; this is normally in the form of a pattern and colour. (See also GKS.)
[Burger-89]

area infill
Area infill is the process of filling in regions of connected pixels on a display system with a colour or pattern. (See also BLEED, FLOOD FILL, and PAINT SYSTEM.)
[Burger-89, Dunlavey-83, Smith-79]

area properties
Modern RENDERERS include sophisticated illumination and reflectance models, which are central to PHOTOREALISM, but one consequence of these advances is the need to define parameters that provide control over the final synthetic image. Area properties are used to describe the physical attributes associated with an area such as AMBIENT REFLECTION COEFFICIENT, DIFFUSE REFLECTION COEFFICIENT, TRANSLUCENCY, TEXTURE MAPS, and TRANSPARENCY. (See also AMBIENT REFLECTION COEFFICIENT, ATTRIBUTES, BUMP MAP, COLOUR ATTRIBUTES, DIFFUSE REFLECTION COEFFICIENT, GLOSS COEFFICIENT, MATERIAL EDITING, OPAQUE SURFACE, TEXTURE MAP, TRANSLUCENT SURFACE, and TRANSPARENT SURFACE.)

area subdivision algorithms
Area subdivision algorithms follow the DIVIDE AND CONQUER strategy whereby an area is repeatedly divided into smaller elements until a condition is obtained capable of easy classification and analysis. The WARNOCK ALGORITHM is a typical example of this technique, as this repeatedly divides an area into four equal smaller squares until one of four possible conditions halts the process. See Figure A-4. (See also DIVIDE AND CONQUER, IMAGE SPACE ALGORITHM, QUADTREE, RECURSIVE ALGORITHM, and WARNOCK ALGORITHM.)
[Burger-89, Foley-90, Hearn-86, Rogers-85, Warnock-68, Warnock-69]

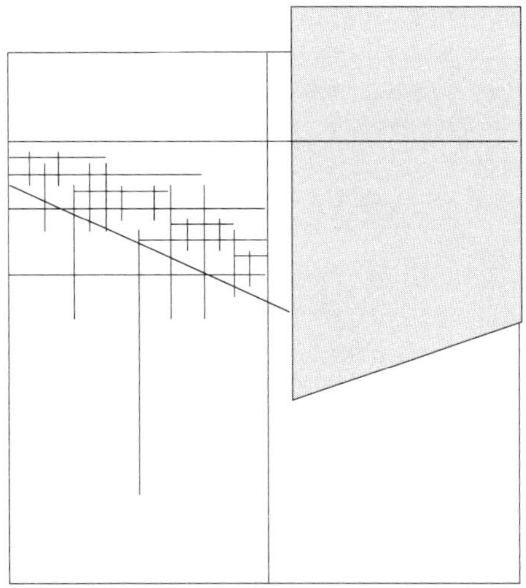

Figure A-4 *The lower left-hand corner of this image has been partially divided using an area subdivision algorithm. The process halts when a condition is reached that can be analyzed without the problems caused by the original complexity.*

arithmetic mean
See AVERAGE.

artifact
Artifacts refer to unwanted visual features introduced by a type of technology or an inaccurate algorithm. In raster displays, the discrete nature of the pixels causes ALIASING

artifacts in the form of jagged edges and flickering texture. See Figure A-2. (See also ALIASING, ANTI-ALIASING, FILTERING, FOURIER WAVEFORM ANALYSIS, JAGGIES, NOISE, NYQUIST LIMIT, POINT SAMPLING, QUANTIZING, SAMPLING, SPATIAL ALIASING, STOCHASTIC SAMPLING, TEMPORAL ALIASING, and UNIFORM SAMPLING.)
[Blinn-89a, Glassner-89]

ASCII

ASCII is an acronym for the American Standard Code for Information Interchange, and defines the bit patterns used to represent characters within a computer system. Seven bits are allocated to data and one bit for a parity check. (See also BINARY and BYTE.)

ASIC

ASIC is an acronym for Application-Specific Integrated Circuit, and relates to VLSI technology and the design of electronic circuits that undertake a specific operation such as LINEAR INTERPOLATION, square-root extraction or MATRIX OPERATIONS. (See also GEOMETRY ENGINE and VLSI.)

aspect ratio

The aspect ratio relates the vertical to the horizontal dimensions of an image or shape; in television this ratio is 3:4, but the recommendation for HDTV is 9:16.

asynchronous

An asynchronous process is not in step with another process: for example, the input signals from a keyboard are asynchronous events. (See also SYNCHRONOUS.)

atmospheric attenuation

The study of light transmission in the atmosphere is an extremely complex science and was an area of investigation long before the advent of computer graphics; however, models involving the sun and the atmosphere, and its associated attenuation, can only be approximated, as the attenuation is proportional to such things as slant angle, time of day, pollution and WAVELENGTH. The subject is treated at great length in the references below. (See also NATURAL PHENOMENA MODELLING, RADIOSITY, and RAY TRACING.)
[Glassner-89, Overington-76, Middleton-52, Willis-87]

attributes

Attributes are properties associated with various entities within a computer graphics system. They include parameters for intensity, colour, line style, text style, texture etc. (See also AREA PROPERTIES, MATERIAL EDITING, OPACITY, REFRACTIVE INDEX, TRANSLUCENCY, and TRANSPARENCY.)
[Burger-89]

auto-dimensioning

Auto-dimensioning is a feature of a CAD system which allows dimensions of a component to be derived from information already input. It also relates to the automatic calculation of dimensions when a scaling factor is introduced. (See also COMPUTER-AIDED DESIGN.)

average

The term average is the arithmetic mean of a set of variables and is expressed mathematically as

$$\bar{x} = \frac{x_1 + x_2 + x_3 + \ldots + x_n}{n}$$

or

$$\bar{x} = \frac{1}{n} \sum_{i=1}^{n} x_i$$

average normal

If $\boldsymbol{V}_1$, $\boldsymbol{V}_2$ and $\boldsymbol{V}_3$ are three different normal vectors

$$\boldsymbol{V}_1 = a\boldsymbol{i} + b\boldsymbol{j} + c\boldsymbol{k}$$
$$\boldsymbol{V}_2 = d\boldsymbol{i} + e\boldsymbol{j} + f\boldsymbol{k}$$
$$\boldsymbol{V}_3 = g\boldsymbol{i} + h\boldsymbol{j} + i\boldsymbol{k}$$

then the average normal $\boldsymbol{V}_n$ is given by

$$\boldsymbol{V}_n = r\boldsymbol{i} + s\boldsymbol{j} + t\boldsymbol{k}$$

where

$r = a + d + g$
$s = b + e + h$
$t = c + f +$

This may need normalizing to its unit form $\boldsymbol{V}_n$

$$\boldsymbol{V}_n = (r/w)\,\boldsymbol{i} + (s/w)\,\boldsymbol{j} + (t/w)\,\boldsymbol{k}$$

where $|w| = \sqrt{(r^2 + s^2 + t^2)}$

See Figure A-5. (See also GOURAUD SHADING, NORMAL VECTOR, SURFACE NORMAL, UNIT VECTOR, and VECTOR.)
[Burger-89, Foley-90, Rogers-89]

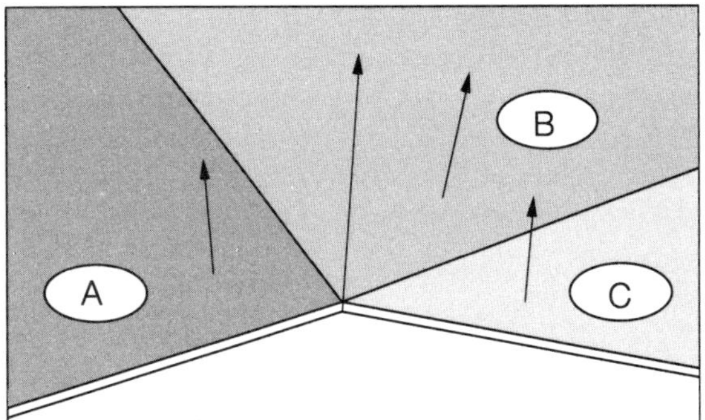

Figure A-5 *Facets A, B and C have separate facet normals, but at their common vertex an average normal vector can be computed, which is used in Gouraud shading.*

axis

(1) An axis is an arbitrary line in 2- or 3-D space about which operations such as reflection and rotation are performed.
(2) An axis is a line used to construct a system of axes as in Cartesian notation. (See also CARTESIAN COORDINATES, LEFT-HANDED AXES, and RIGHT-HANDED AXES.)

axonometric orthographic projection

The axonometric orthographic projection is a PARALLEL PROJECTION and shows more than one face of an object. Perhaps the most widely used example is the ISOMETRIC PROJECTION. (See also CAVALIER PROJECTION, ISOMETRIC PROJECTION, ORTHOGRAPHIC PROJECTION, PARALLEL PROJECTION, PERSPECTIVE PROJECTION, PROJECTION, and PROJECTION PLANE.)
[Foley-90, Gasson-83, Hearn-86, Rogers-89]

b

back clipping plane

The FAR PLANE, YON CLIPPING PLANE or the back clipping plane in the VIEWING PYRAMID controls the distance up to which objects are visible. See Figure C-5. (See also CLIPPING and FRONT CLIPPING PLANE.)
[Burger-89, Hearn-86, Foley-90, Rogers-85]

back face

The back face of a PLANAR polygon is defined as invisible when its SURFACE NORMAL is facing away from the observer, for when objects are constructed from polygons some display algorithms require to identify and reject back-facing polygons. However, with RADIOSITY and RAY TRACING, back-facing polygons are just as important as forward-facing polygons, because in RAY TRACING they could appear in a reflection and in RADIOSITY they receive and reflect light back into the environment. (See also BACK FACE REMOVAL, CLIPPING, FRONT FACE, HIDDEN-LINE REMOVAL, HIDDEN-SURFACE REMOVAL, and SURFACE NORMAL.)
[Burger-89, Hearn-86, Rogers-85]

back face culling

See BACK FACE REMOVAL.

back face removal

Back face removal, or BACK FACE CULLING, refers to the removal of all back-facing surfaces of a scene before it is rendered: this ensures that these invisible features do not impede the overall efficiency of a display algorithm. This can be accomplished by computing the angle between the SURFACE NORMAL and the observer's EYE VECTOR using the SCALAR PRODUCT rule; if this angle is equal to or greater than 90°, the surface is back facing. See Figure B-1. (See also BACK FACE, FRONT FACE, HIDDENLINE REMOVAL, HIDDEN-SURFACE REMOVAL, and SCALAR PRODUCT.)
[Hearn-86, Rogers-85]

backlight

A backlight is used to illuminate an object from behind to emphasize its SILHOUETTE EDGE. (See also AMBIENT LIGHT, DIRECTIONAL LIGHT SOURCE, INCIDENT LIGHT, LIGHT SOURCE, POINT LIGHT SOURCE, and SPOT LIGHT.)

back mapping

See INVERSE MAPPING.

back projection

In resolving HIDDEN-LINE and HIDDEN-SURFACE REMOVAL problems it is necessary to perform MAPPINGS between the IMAGE SPACE and the OBJECT SPACE. The back projection is used to relate points for a line on the PICTURE PLANE back to the original line in OBJECT SPACE. (See also PERSPECTIVE PROJECTION.)
[Burger-89]

backward ray tracing

Backward ray tracing is the strategy employed in RAY TRACING where, for every pixel, a light ray is traced backwards into OBJECT SPACE to determine its origins and its

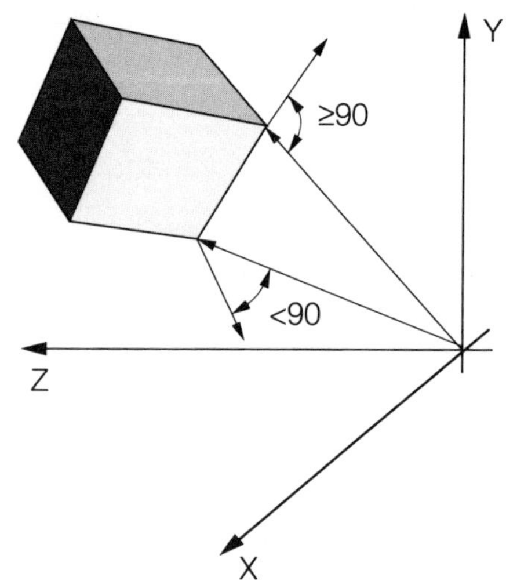

Figure B-1 *If the observer is located at the origin, then a surface is visible if the angle between the eye vector and the surface normal is less than 90 degrees, otherwise it is invisible.*

object intersections. (See also FORWARD RAY TRACING, OBJECT SPACE, and RAY TRACING.)
[Arvo-86, Burger-89, Glassner-89]

bandwidth

The maximum frequency range that a system is capable of transmitting without errors is specified by its bandwidth: in relation to display systems, this influences the highest level of detail that can be handled. In television, the PAL video bandwidth is 5.5 MHz, whilst NTSC is 4.2 MHz, with PAL providing a resolution of 625 lines at 25 Hz and NTSC 525 lines at 29.97 Hz. (See also HORIZONTAL SCAN FREQUENCY, RESOLUTION, and VIDEO FREQUENCY.)
[Hunt-75]

bar sheets

Bar sheets are used in animation projects as a reference document controlling dialogue, music and movements with frame numbers. (See also ANIMATION, COMPUTER ANIMATION, MODEL SHEETS, and STORYBOARD.)
[White-86]

Bartlett filter

A Bartlett filter can be approximated by a matrix of weights and convolved with an image to remove NOISE. It can also be used for reducing the resolution of an image; for example, an image computed to 1024 x 1024 can be filtered to 512 x 512 by using the weightings

1 2 1
2 4 2
1 2 1

where the central weight 4 is placed over an appropriate high-resolution pixel and the low-resolution pixel is formed by summing the weighted pixel intensities, and dividing the result by 16. The filter is then located along the same raster such that it shares one pixel horizontally; for the next raster the filter shares a common row. Similar weightings can be computed for (5 x 5), (7 x 7) etc., which incur a greater computational overhead. (See also ALIASING, ANTI-ALIASING, BASIS FUNCTION, BED-OF-NAILS, BOX FILTER, CONVOLUTION, CONVOLUTION FILTER, FILTER, FILTERING, FOURIER WAVEFORM ANALYSIS, GAUSSIAN FILTER, IMAGE PROCESSING, NYQUIST LIMIT, PIXEL AVERAGING, POINT SAMPLING, POINT-SPREAD FUNCTION, SAMPLING, SINC FILTER, STOCHASTIC SAMPLING, TENT FILTER, and UNIFORM SAMPLING)
[Crow-81, Gonzalez-87, Oppenheim-75, Pratt-78]

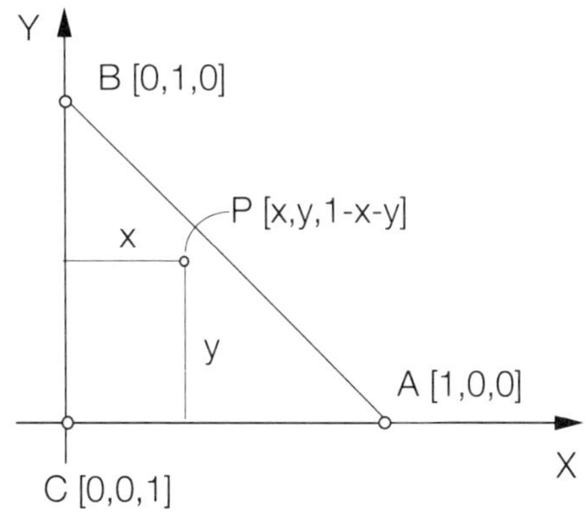

Figure B-2 *For any point P[x,y] the barycentric coordinates are the original Cartesian coordinates followed by 1-x-y.*

barycentric coordinates

Unlike CARTESIAN COORDINATES where two measurements are needed to locate a point on a 2-D plane, barycentric coordinates can relate a point with the three vertices of a triangle; this generates three measurements. For example, given three points **A**, **B** and **C** with Cartesian coordinates [1, 0], [0, 1] and [0, 0] respectively, then a point **P** with Cartesian coordinates [*x, y*] has barycentric coordinates [*x*, *y*, 1 – *x* – *y*], and the barycentric coordinates of **A, B** and **C** are [1, 0, 0], [0, 1, 0] and [0, 0, 1] respectively. They are of particular interest in INTERPOLATION schemes

especially in the manipulation of PARAMETRIC SURFACE PATCHES. See Figure B-2. (See also AREA COORDINATES, CARTESIAN COORDINATES, and POLAR COORDINATES.)
[Bohm-84, Burger-89, Farin-88, Hausner-65]

basis function
In creating BÉZIER CURVES and B-SPLINE CURVES, basis functions are used to generate the terms belonging to a PARAMETRIC POLYNOMIAL for weighting the influence of a CONTROL POINT. The functional form has the advantage that, given specific parameters, the terms can easily be evaluated by a computer algorithm. A typical example would be the BERNSTEIN BASIS FUNCTION. (See also BERNSTEIN BASIS FUNCTION, BÉZIER CURVE, BÉZIER SURFACE PATCH, B-SPLINE CURVE, B-SPLINE SURFACE PATCH, CONTROL POINTS, NURBS, and PARAMETRIC POLYNOMIAL.)
[Bohm-84, Farin-88, Gonska-83, Woodwark-86]

baud rate
The speed of digital data transmission is measured in units of bits/second; it is also generally known as the baud rate. The name comes from Baudot, who was instrumental in the development of the teleprinter in the 1860s. (See also BANDWIDTH.)

beam penetration CRT
A beam penetration CRT is a CRT construction where the screen's phosphor has two to four layers (normally red, green, orange and yellow), each excited by different electron energy levels. They are generally employed in FLIGHT SIMULATORS in night/dusk systems working in a CALLIGRAPHIC mode; this stroke mode provides the time to switch the anode voltage to achieve the phosphor penetration. (See also CALLIGRAPHIC, CALLIGRAPHIC DISPLAY, CATHODE RAY TUBE, RASTER DISPLAY, and RASTER SCANNING.)
[Schachter-83]

beam tracing
Beam tracing is a technique used in RAY TRACING where a coherent beam of rays in the form of a cone is used for estimating incident light and ANTI-ALIASING calculations. (See also RAY TRACING.)
[Amanatides-84, Glassner-89, Heckbert-84, Kirk-87, Shinya-87]

bed-of-nails
REAL-TIME IMAGE GENERATORS rely heavily upon special hardware to perform certain tasks at very high speed – and the bed-of-nails device undertakes spatial FILTERING by measuring a polygon's impact upon a pixel to subpixel levels. Typically, a sample is made at the centre of a (2 x 2) pixel zone, with each pixel represented by a (4 x 4) bit mask, i.e. the 'nails'. If the bed-of-nails is initially set to binary zero, a polygon's impact is registered by setting relevant bits to binary one. When used with spatial FILTERING circuitry, a number is created representing the fractional area of the polygon, which is subsequently used in the video mixing stage. (See also ALIASING, ANTI-ALIASING, BARTLETT FILTER, BASIS FUNCTION, BOX FILTER, FILTER, FILTERING, NYQUIST LIMIT, OVERSAMPLING, PIXEL AVERAGING, POINT-SPREAD FUNCTION, SAMPLING, SINC FILTER, SPATIAL ALIASING, STOCHASTIC SAMPLING, TENT FILTER, and UNIFORM SAMPLING.)
[Singer-86]

behavioural animation
Craig Reynolds' flocking animation software implements behaviour patterns such as flock centrering, collision avoidance and velocity matching; such simulation is known as behavioural animation. (See also ANIMATION, COMPUTER ANIMATION, DISPLACEMENT ANIMATION, DYNAMIC CONSTRAINTS, FORWARD DYNAMICS, FORWARD KINEMATICS, GOAL-ORIENTED ANIMATION, INVERSE DYNAMICS, KEY-FRAME ANIMATION, PROCEDURAL ANIMATION, and RIGID-BODY ANIMATION.)
[Reynolds-87]

Bernstein basis function
The Bernstein basis function is a POLYNOMIAL WEIGHTING FUNCTION of degree m defined by

$$W_i(t) = \frac{m!}{(m-i)!\,i!} t^i (1-t)^{m-i}$$

where i varies from 0 to m. For a QUADRATIC form (m = 2), the three terms are

$$W_0(t) = (1-t)^2$$
$$W_1(t) = 2(1-t)t$$
$$W_2(t) = t^2$$

whereas for a CUBIC form (m = 3), the four terms are

$$W_0(t) = (1-t)^3$$
$$W_1(t) = 3(1-t)^2\, t$$
$$W_2(t) = 3(1-t)\, t^2$$
$$W_3(t) = t^3$$

An essential property of the Bernstein basis functions is that the components sum to unity; this ensures that when they are used to modify CONTROL POINTS, say in a Bézier scheme, any intermediate point generated will always be within the CONVEX HULL of the CONTROL POINTS. (See also BASIS FUNCTION, BÉZIER CURVE, BÉZIER SURFACE PATCH, CONTROL POINTS, CONVEX HULL, MONOMIAL BASIS, and PARAMETRIC POLYNOMIAL.)
[Bohm-84, Burger-89, Farin-88, Gonska-83, Rogers-89, Woodwark-86]

Beta-spline

The Beta-spline is a development of the B-spline and incorporates tension and bias parameters, where tension refers to the general 'tightness' of the curve and bias controls how the curve is biased with or against the direction of the curve. These parameters provide users with two extra controls over a spline's shape. (See also B-SPLINE CURVE, B-SPLINE SURFACE PATCH, CATMULL–ROM SPLINE, NURBS, and SPLINE.)
[Barsky-81, Barsky-88, Barsky-90a, Burger-89, Farin-88, Goodman-86, Joe-87]

Bézier curve

A Bézier curve is generated by computing the spatial coordinates of a point on the curve from CONTROL POINTS weighted by terms from the BERNSTEIN BASIS FUNCTION. A

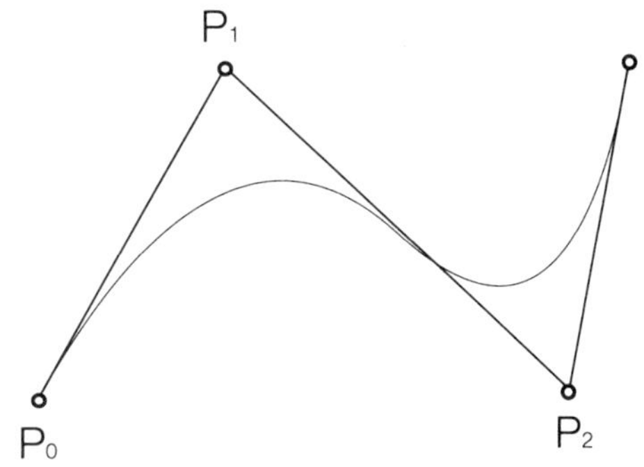

Figure B-3 *Any point on the above cubic Bézier curve is derived by summing the control points weighted by the Bernstein basis functions.*

second-order Bézier curve has the terms

$$\boldsymbol{P}(t) = (1-t)^2\boldsymbol{P}_0 + 2(1-t)t\,\boldsymbol{P}_1 + t^2\boldsymbol{P}_2$$

where $\boldsymbol{P}_0$, $\boldsymbol{P}_1$ and $\boldsymbol{P}_2$ are the CONTROL POINTS and t is a parameter varying between 0 and 1.
A third-order Bézier curve has the terms

$$\boldsymbol{P}(t) = (1-t)^3\,\boldsymbol{P}_0 + 3(1-t)^2\,t\,\boldsymbol{P}_1 + 3(1-t)t^2\,\boldsymbol{P}_2 + t^3\boldsymbol{P}_3$$

where $\boldsymbol{P}_0$, $\boldsymbol{P}_1$, $\boldsymbol{P}_2$ and $\boldsymbol{P}_3$ are the four CONTROL POINTS, and t is a parameter varying between 0 and 1. One weakness of the Bézier formulation is the global effect that changes in CONTROL POINTS have upon the curve or surface, which is not found in the B-spline approach. See Figure B-3. (See also BASIS FUNCTION, BERNSTEIN BASIS FUNCTION, BÉZIER SURFACE PATCH, B-SPLINE CURVE, CATMULL–ROM SPLINE, CONTROL POINTS, NURBS, PARAMETRIC POLYNOMIAL, and SPLINE.)
[Bézier-73, Burger-89, Farin-88, Foley-90, Forrest-72, Gasson-83, Hearn-86, Rogers-89, Woodwark-86]

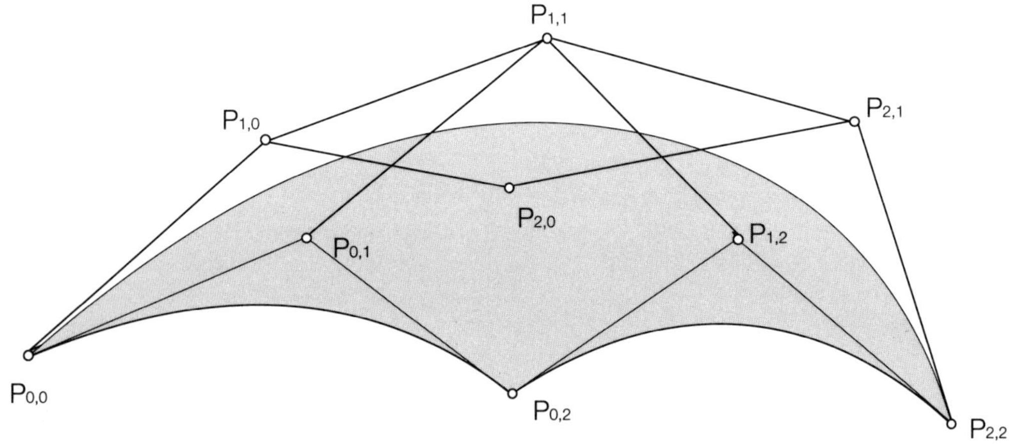

Figure B-4 *The quadratic Bézier surface patch is formed by summing the nine control points weighted by their respective Bernstein basis functions and if any point is altered, the entire surface patch will adjust to a new shape. Note that the patch only touches the control points at the four corners. For a cubic Bézier surface patch, sixteen control points are required.*

Bézier surface patch

Like BÉZIER CURVES, a Bézier surface patch requires CONTROL POINTS to form the overall geometry. By weighting the control points with a BERNSTEIN BASIS FUNCTION, any point on the surface can be expressed by the sum of the weighted CONTROL POINTS. A QUADRATIC Bézier patch requires (3 x 3) CONTROL POINTS, whereas a CUBIC Bézier patch requires (4 x 4) CONTROL POINTS. The patch always touches the four corner CONTROL POINTS and the patch's corner edges are coincident with the lines connecting the corner to their neighbouring edge control points. See Figure B-4. (See also BERNSTEIN BASIS FUNCTION, BIPARAMETRIC PATCH, B-SPLINE SURFACE PATCH, CARTESIAN PRODUCT PATCH, CONTROL POINTS, COONS PATCH, FERGUSON PATCH, HERMITE PATCH, NURBS, PARAMETRIC POLYNOMIAL, and PARAMETRIC SURFACE PATCH.)
[Aziz-90, Bézier-73, Bohm-84, Burger-89, Farin-88, Foley-90, Forrest-72, Gasson-83, Hearn-86, Rogers-89, Woodwark-86]

bicubic patch

A bicubic patch is a SURFACE PATCH definition employing CUBIC equations of two parameters to generate the coordinates of any point on the patch. Examples are a bicubic BÉZIER SURFACE PATCH or a bicubic COONS PATCH. (See also BÉZIER SURFACE PATCH, B-SPLINE SURFACE PATCH, CARTESIAN PRODUCT PATCH, COONS PATCH, FERGUSON PATCH, HERMITE PATCH, and PARAMETRIC SURFACE PATCH.)
[Farin-88, Woodwark-86]

bidirectional reflectance

Where simple reflectance models are unable to simulate the behaviour of light reflecting off structured surfaces, bidirectional reflectance employs a function to relate inci-

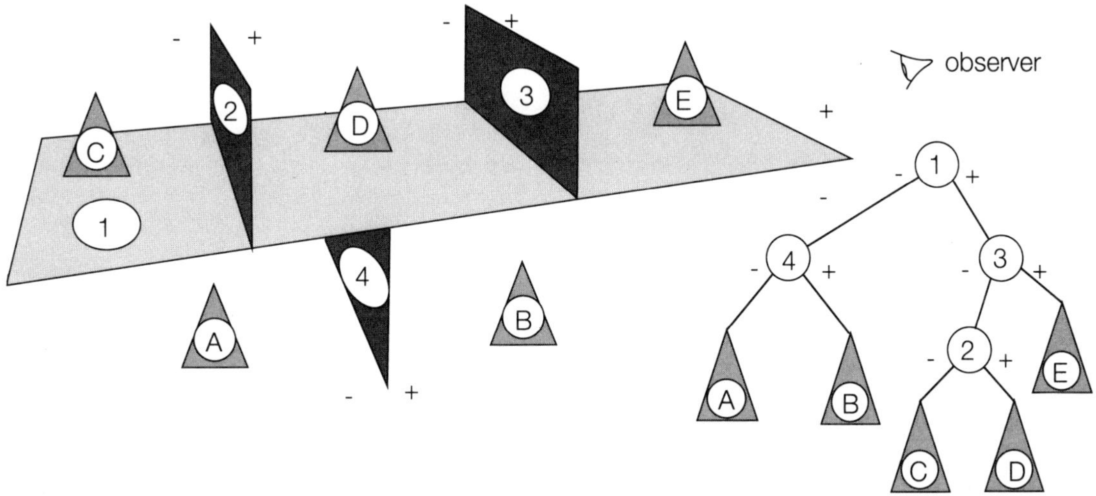

Figure B-5 *If the five objects A, B, C, D and E are partitioned by the four separating planes, a binary tree can describe their relationships with the signs of the half spaces created by the planes. If the observer is in the positive half-space of planes 1 and 3, then the tree traversal reveals a priority sequence of E, D, C, B and A, from the highest to the lowest. The objects can now be rendered in the sequence A, B, C, D and E.*

dent luminous intensity and reflected luminous intensity with direction, for small SOLID ANGLES. (See also ANISOTROPIC, ISOTROPIC, and REFLECTANCE MODEL.)

bi-level display

A bi-level display device registers a pixel image in two luminous states usually black on white. (See also BIT MAPPING.)
[Burger-89]

binary

The binary number system is a two-state code employed by electronic computer circuits for storing and manipulating data and instructions. (See also ASCII, BIT, BIT PLANE, BYTE, and DIGITAL COMPUTER.)

Binary Separating Planes (BSP)

The BSP technique is used in REAL-TIME IMAGE GENERATORS to resolve HIDDEN-SURFACE REMOVAL and shadow calculations. It was developed by Schumacker *et al.* where a polygonal database is processed OFF-LINE to include reference planes which partition or separate the polyhedra. The resulting planes and associated objects can be organized as a hierarchical binary tree which when traversed reveals the priority sequence of the objects from the observer. See Figure B-5. (See also DEPTH SORT ALGORITHM, HIDDEN-SURFACE REMOVAL, OBJECT SPACE ALGORITHMS, PAINTER'S ALGORITHM, SCAN-LINE ALGORITHM, Z-BUFFER ALGORITHM, and ZZ-BUFFER.)
[Chin-89, Schumacker-69, Sutherland-74b, Thibault-87]

biparametric patch

A biparametric patch is a surface patch whose geometry is controlled by two PARAMETRIC EQUATIONS. BÉZIER and B-SPLINE SURFACE PATCHES are typical examples. (See also BÉZIER SURFACE PATCH, BICUBIC PATCH, B-SPLINE SURFACE

PATCH, COONS PATCH, FERGUSON PATCH, PARAMETRIC EQUATION, and QUADRATIC SURFACE PATCH.)
[Farin-88, Woodwark-86]

bit
A bit is an individual element of a binary coded item; i.e. 0 or 1. It is synonymous with binary digit. (See also ASCII, BINARY, BIT PLANE, and BYTE.)

Bit-Blit
Bit-Blit or Bit-Blt operations are associated with Boolean operations performed upon rectangular areas of pixels. The operands for these operations consist of a source buffer and a pattern buffer which can be manipulated with a pair of Boolean functions (AND, OR or XOR) whose output is sent to a destination buffer. When associated with a video processor, Bit-Blit operations can be used to translate, rotate and animate images in BI-LEVEL DISPLAYS. (See also BI-LEVEL DISPLAY, BIT MAPPING, BLITTER, and RASTEROPS.)
[Burger-89, Foley-90]

bit-block transfer
See BIT-BLIT.

bit map
A bit map is a digital image of bits. (See also BIT PLANE.)

bit mapping
The technique of MAPPING a pixel-based image into individual bits of computer memory is known as bit mapping; this is the mechanism that enables PULL-DOWN MENUS temporarily to replace portions of a screen without permanent erasure of the image. (See also BIT-BLIT, BI-LEVEL DISPLAY, BLITTER and RASTEROPS.)
[Burger-89, Kornfeld-87]

bit mask
A bit mask is a sequence of bits arranged in a rectangular form, which can then be used to 'mask' or identify similar patterns in other bit streams. (See also A-BUFFER and BED-OF-NAILS.)

bit plane
The construction of a FRAME STORE can be imagined to be formed from layers of bit planes; the actual number determines the range of intensities the store is capable of registering for a pixel. If there are eight 1-bit planes, a FRAME STORE can effectively hold 256 GREY LEVELS, whereas a 24-bit plane system can provide 16.7 million intensities simultaneously. (See also BYTE, COLOUR TABLE, and FRAME STORE.)
[Hearn-86]

black light
See DARK LIGHT.

blanking
Blanking refers to the period of time when a CRT's electron beam is suppressed whilst it is repositioned for the start of a new FIELD or FRAME. (See also CRT, FIELD, FLYBACK, FRAME, GENLOCK, HORIZONTAL SCAN FREQUENCY, INTERLACING, RASTER SCANNING, SYNC, VERTICAL BLANKING INTERVAL, VIDEO FREQUENCY, and VIDEO SIGNAL.)

bleed
(1) Bleed describes the leaking of colour through a boundary hole during a FLOOD FILL. (See also AREA INFILL and FLOOD FILL.)
(2) Bleed refers to the colour bleeding that occurs when one coloured surface diffusely reflects light into another surface in close proximity. (See also RADIOSITY.)

blending function
A blending or interpolating function is used to blend together two or more numeric quantities. For example, a linear blend would be controlled by the functions

$$f(s) = 1 - s$$
$$g(s) = s$$

and a cubic blend might be

$$f(s) = 1 - 3s^2 + 2s^3$$
$$g(s) = \quad 3s^2 + 2s^3$$

The blended value is computed by

$$b(s) = f(s)A + g(s)B$$

where s varies between 0 and 1; A and B are the values to be blended. Note that the two functions sum to unity. (See also CUSHIONING, EASING, INBETWEENING, INTERPOLATION, LINEAR INTERPOLATION, PARAMETRIC EQUATION, PARAMETRIC POLYNOMIAL, and SLOW IN/SLOW OUT.)
[Burger-89, Weeg-66, Woodwark-86]

blend surface
A blend surface is a secondary surface that provides a smooth transition between adjacent surfaces. A blend attempts to interpolate surface geometry between these primary surfaces, where the interpolation characteristics are, perhaps, more important than the blend's own surface properties. (See also CONSTRUCTIVE SOLID GEOMETRY, INTERPOLATION, and SOLID MODELLING.)
[Farin-88, Middleditch-85, Woodwark-86]

blitter
A blitter is a hardware device associated with the manipulation of bit-mapped images. Blitters undertake the tasks of moving contiguous areas of bits about memory which is storing the bit-mapped image and of performing the BIT-BLIT operations. Blitters are also frequently found in microcomputers, arcade games and workstations incorporating windows. (See also BI-LEVEL DISPLAY, BIT-BLIT and RASTEROPS.)

body of revolution
See SWEPT SURFACE.

boil
When manually airbrushed images are animated, a visual 'boiling' effect occurs, as every frame is painted slightly differently from neighbouring frames. Computer-generated AIRBRUSHING does not exhibit this artifact, as it is so consistent. The same artifact can also be found in poorly computed STOCHASTIC SAMPLING. (See also AIRBRUSH, ARTIFACT, NOISE, PAINT SYSTEM, and STOCHASTIC SAMPLING.)

bounce light
Bounce light is synonymous with COLOUR BLEEDING. (See also COLOUR BLEEDING and RADIOSITY.)

boundary fill
A boundary fill operation alters the colour of all pixels connected to some specified pixel up to a boundary shape. If there is a hole in this boundary the colour will BLEED into surrounding pixels. (See also AREA INFILL, BLEED, and FLOOD FILL.)
[Burger-89]

boundary representation (B-rep)
The two major modelling strategies are CONSTRUCTIVE SOLID GEOMETRY and boundary representation, where the latter includes methods of modelling objects through a surface representation, rather than the volumetric approach of CONSTRUCTIVE SOLID GEOMETRY. Although B-rep techniques are still able to reveal surface and volumetric properties of objects, they must ensure that the integrity of surface geometry is maintained, which is why the WINGED-EDGE DATA STRUCTURE is employed. (See also CONSTRUCTIVE SOLID GEOMETRY, FREE-FORM SURFACES, GEOMETRIC MODELLING, NURBS, SCULPTURED SURFACES, SOLIDS MODELLING, and WIRE FRAME.)
[Farin-88, Woodwark-86, Woodwark-89]

bounding box
Like a BOUNDING SPHERE a bounding box is a minimum BOUNDING VOLUME in the form of a rectangular box associated with an object such that it completely encloses it. Consequently, when one requires to test for a collision condition between two objects, the test is first performed upon the bounding boxes; if this fails, further analysis is

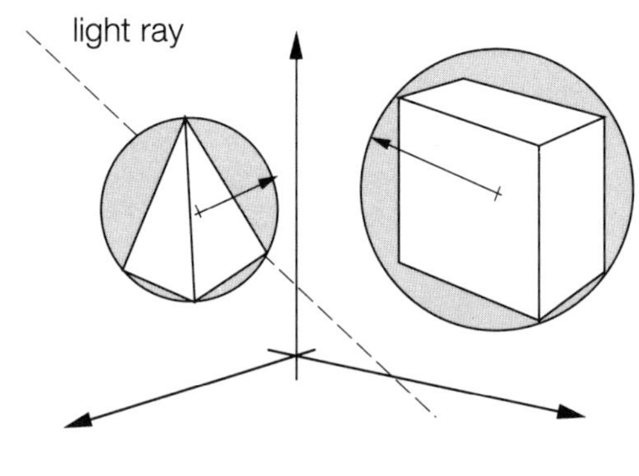

Figure B-6 *The sphere is a convenient bounding volume to associate with complex objects - and it is a trivial operation to test for a collision condition or for an intersection with a light ray.*

superfluous. But if the boxes intersect, then there is a possibility that the enclosed objects intersect and further intersection tests must be performed upon the objects. (See also BOUNDING SPHERE, BOUNDING VOLUME, and DEPTH SORT ALGORITHM)
[Burger-89]

bounding sphere
A bounding sphere is a minimum BOUNDING VOLUME in the form of a sphere. When a ray intersection or COLLISION DETECTION test is undertaken, it is first made using the bounding sphere's equation. If the result of the test is positive further testing with the enclosed object is pursued; otherwise it is ignored. See Figure B-6. (See also BOUNDING BOX, BOUNDING VOLUME, and COLLISION DETECTION.)
[Burger-89, Glassner-88]

bounding volume
Because computer graphics algorithms have to make repeated references to complex geometric objects, efficiency is greatly improved if the objects have an associated minimum bounding volume such as a sphere; consequently, tests for intersection, are first made using the sphere's equation rather than upon the object. If the result of the test is positive, further testing with the enclosed element is pursued; otherwise it is ignored.
[Burger-89, Glassner-89, Goldsmith-87, Rubin-80, Weghorst-84]

box filter
A box filter is a simple low-pass filter used in FILTERING and ANTI-ALIASING with a WEIGHTING FUNCTION the shape of a rectangular box of unit height and unit base. Although far from ideal – as it attenuates some useful low frequencies – it is easily implemented and provides acceptable results when convolved with an image. (See also ALIASING, ANTI-ALIASING, BARTLETT FILTER, BASIS FUNCTION, BED-OF-NAILS, FILTER, FILTERING, FOURIER WAVEFORM ANALYSIS, GAUSSIAN FILTER, JAGGIES, NYQUIST LIMIT, POINT SAMPLING, POINT SPREAD FUNCTION, SAMPLING, SINC FILTER, SPATIAL ALIASING, TENT FILTER, and UNIFORM SAMPLING.)
[Blinn-89a, Burger-89, Glassner-89]

boxing
Boxing refers to the substitution of a box for a BOUNDING VOLUME. (See also BOUNDING SPHERE and BOUNDING VOLUME.)

B-rep
See BOUNDARY REPRESENTATION.

Bresenham's algorithm
Jack Bresenham is known for his pioneering work in developing algorithms for displaying straight lines upon discrete display devices. These algorithms identify the pixels that form an optimum straight line between any pair of pixels by computing the error deviation from the required slope as the pixel line is generated. As the main loop of the algorithm relies upon additions, subtractions and two multiplications, its hardware implementation is extremely fast. He also developed complementary techniques for circles. (See also CIRCLE GENERATOR, DIGITAL DIFFERENTIAL ANALYZER, JAGGIES, and SCAN CONVERSION.)
[Bresenham-65, Bresenham-87, Bresenham-77, Pitteway-67]

brightness

Subjective terms have always been a source of confusion – and the term brightness is no exception. It is equivalent to the term LUMINOSITY which denotes the extent to which colours appear to emit more or less light. The eye's ability to discriminate between different levels of intensity depends upon many factors such as ambient light, surrounding coloured surfaces, age and the time allowed to adapt to the existing light levels. (See also COLOUR MODEL, COLOUR SPACE, HUE, LIGHTNESS, SATURATION, and VALUE.) [Boynton-79, Burger-89, Gregory-86, Hunt-75]

Brownian motion

Brownian motion describes the random movement of small suspended particles in a liquid caused by the kinetic energy of molecules; but in the context of FRACTALS it describes a class of noise called 'brown noise' described by the following function. If $B(t)$ is a one-dimensional function generating random variables for different values of time t, then the increment $B(t_2) - B(t_1)$ has a GAUSSIAN DISTRIBUTION and the VARIANCE of the mean square increments is proportional to the time difference; thus the average of

$$[B(t_2) - B(t_1)]^2 \propto |t_2 - t_1|$$

Brown noise can be generated by integrating WHITE NOISE or approximated by MIDPOINT DISPLACEMENT. A variation on the function provides the basis for creating random fractal terrains from so called FRACTIONAL BROWNIAN MOTION. (See also FOURIER FRACTAL, FRACTAL, FRACTAL CURVE, FRACTAL GEOMETRY, FRACTAL NOISE, FRACTIONAL BROWNIAN MOTION, MIDPOINT DISPLACEMENT, NOISE, and WHITE NOISE.) [Peitgen-88]

BSP

See BINARY SEPARATING PLANES.

B-spline curve

B-spline curves, especially their RATIONAL form as used in NURBS, are fundamental to many areas of computer graphics, from surface modelling to animation. Formally, they are described as a PARAMETRIC CURVE whose shape is determined by a series of CONTROL POINTS, whose influence is determined by BASIS FUNCTIONS. The 2- or 3-D spatial coordinates are computed separately from a PARAMETRIC EQUATION using a series of reference values called KNOTS, which control how various spans of the curve are influenced by different values of the generating parameter. A less formal definition, but one offering a model for visualizing the above description, is to imagine the task of a cyclist charged with steering a course through a network of obstacles (the control points). The latter radiate a force of attraction governed by smoothly changing equations (the basis functions). Now the cyclist's path is also influenced by a set of numbers (the knot vector) which apply a fine control to the journey, in that they influence when a control point is active or inactive and the degree of attraction. The cyclist's path can now be predicted by altering a number (the parameter) over the knot range and, for each value, adding together the forces from the active control points. This path must also ensure that the total force acting on the cyclist at any time remains constant at unity; this ensures that the curve followed by the cyclist is continuous. Whether the traced curve is a CUBIC or QUADRATIC is governed by the number of active control points. B-splines, unlike BÉZIER CURVES, have local span control which means that when a CONTROL POINT is adjusted its influence can be restricted to a local portion of the curve. (See also BASIS FUNCTION, BÉZIER CURVE, CONTROL POINTS, KNOT, KNOT VECTOR, NURBS, PARAMETRIC CUBIC CURVE, PARAMETRIC EQUATION, and SPLINE.) [Bohm-84, Burger-89, Foley-90, Hearn-86, Farin-88, Rogers-89, Woodwark-86]

B-spline surface patch

A B-spline surface patch is a PARAMETRIC SURFACE PATCH controlled by a matrix of CONTROL POINTS whose influence is determined by the product of two B-spline BASIS FUNCTIONS. As with curves, the B-spline formulation has advantages over a Bézier description in that the CONTROL POINTS have a local, rather than a global, influence over

surface geometry. (See also BÉZIER SURFACE PATCH, CARTESIAN PRODUCT PATCH, CONTROL POINTS, COONS PATCH, FERGUSON PATCH, HERMITE PATCH, NURBS, and PARAMETRIC SURFACE PATCH.)
[Bohm-84, Burger-89, Farin-88, Foley-90, Forsey-88, Hearn-86, Rogers-89, Woodwark-86]

bucket sorting
OBJECT SPACE ALGORITHMS frequently have to sort objects into various sequences. The technique of bucket sorting exploits the idea of a space or volume partition identifying those objects falling within each region; then the algorithm processes each 'bucket' in turn and sorts the associated objects into some desired sequence. This prevents having to sort every object into a coherent sequence. (See also DEPTH SORT ALGORITHM and OBJECT SPACE ALGORITHMS.)
[Burger-89, Rogers-85]

bump map
A bump map is a 2-D LOOK-UP TABLE holding intensity levels used to modulate a SURFACE NORMAL whilst rendering. The table is generally a photograph of some obliquely illuminated textured surface, and when this disturbs the SURFACE NORMAL the illusion of surface depth is created, even though the rendered surface is still completely smooth. (See also BUMP MAPPING and TEXTURE MAP.)
[Blinn-78c]

bump mapping
James Blinn developed bump mapping for creating a pseudo raised surface. Basically any source of numerical modulation, whether it be generated by a function or held within a BUMP MAP, can be used to perturb a SURFACE NORMAL by an amount controlled by the magnitude of the modulation. (See also BUMP MAP, DISPLACEMENT MAPPING, ENVIRONMENT MAPPING, OPACITY MAPPING, and TEXTURE MAPPING.)
[Blinn-78c]

business graphics
With the advent of low-cost personal computers, graphics packages are now available for creating business graphics where virtually any type of data set can be displayed as graphs, charts, pie charts and histograms.

byte
A byte is a group of 8 bits which is capable of encoding 256 unique binary patterns. (See also ASCII, BIT, and FRAME STORE.)

C

C
Although the majority of the pioneering work in computer graphics was undertaken in FORTRAN, the C language, which offers a rigorous logical environment to develop large structured programs, now appears to be the language for current and future research. It was designed and implemented by D. M. Ritchie of Bell Laboratories.
[Ammeraal-86, Kernighan-78]

C++
C++ is an extended version of C supporting OBJECT-ORIENTED PROGRAMMING concepts such as data abstraction (programmer-defined data types) and inheritance. (See also C.)

cabinet projection
Like the CAVALIER PROJECTION, the cabinet projection is a parallel OBLIQUE PROJECTION where lines perpendicular to the PROJECTION PLANE are foreshortened by a half; it is not widely used. (See also CAVALIER PROJECTION, ISOMETRIC PROJECTION, OBLIQUE PROJECTION, ORTHOGONAL PROJECTION, PARALLEL PROJECTION, PERSPECTIVE PROJECTION, PERSPECTIVE FORESHORTENING, and PROJECTION PLANE.)
[Foley-90, Gasson-83, Hearn-86, Rogers-89]

CAD
See COMPUTER-AIDED DESIGN.

CAD/CAM
See COMPUTER-AIDED DESIGN/COMPUTER-AIDED MANUFACTURE.

calligraphic
The term calligraphic has been borrowed from the domain of handwriting – and in the context of computer graphics it implies the ability to move freely in any direction, as found in CALLIGRAPHIC DISPLAYS. (See also BEAM PENETRATION CRT, CALLIGRAPHIC DISPLAY, RASTER SCANNING, and REFRESH CRT.)
[Hearn-86, Schachter-83]

calligraphic display
A calligraphic display, whether it is in the form of a display screen or a projector, is capable of controlling its display beam in an arbitrary manner. Unlike a raster device or projector, which repeatedly sweeps the display area on a raster basis, calligraphic projectors are able to address their display space randomly and dwell at any point or line to modulate the phosphor brightness. (See also BEAM PENETRATION CRT, CALLIGRAPHIC, RASTER SCANNING, and REFRESH CRT.)
[Hearn-86, Schachter-83]

canonical view volume
The six planes associated with the VIEWING PYRAMID in 3-D CLIPPING algorithms, form the canonical view volume when they are assigned orientations and ranges that create a unit environment, which can later be scaled to any required dimensions. For example, PARALLEL PROJECTIONS might have the CLIPPING PLANES set at $x = 0$, $x = 1$, $y = 0$, $y = 1$, $z = 0$ and $z = 1$, whereas a PERSPECTIVE PROJECTION would have $x = z$, $x = -z$, $y = z$, $y = -z$, $z = z$min and $z = 1$. Prior to CLIPPING against such a volume, WORLD COORDINATES must be normalized to this space. (See also ADAPTIVE CLIPPING, CLIPPING, CLIPPING DIVIDER, COHEN–SUTHERLAND ALGORITHM, DEPTH CLIPPING, NORMALIZED DEVICE COORDINATES, VIEWING PYRAMID, and WORLD COORDINATE SPACE.)
[Foley-90, Rogers-89]

cardinal spline
See CATMULL–ROM SPLINE.

Cartesian coordinates
Developed by Rene Descartes (1596–1650), Cartesian coordinates enable a point in 2-D space to be represented by two measurements, and a point in 3-D space by three measurements, relative to some defined origin and system of ORTHOGONAL axes. The notation permits the existence of LEFT-HANDED and RIGHT-HANDED AXES, although the latter is generally used in computer graphics. They are an essential tool in computer graphics as they provide a simple numerical mechanism for encoding shapes and objects. See Figure C-1. (See also AREA COORDINATES, BARYCENTRIC COORDINATES, HOMOGENEOUS

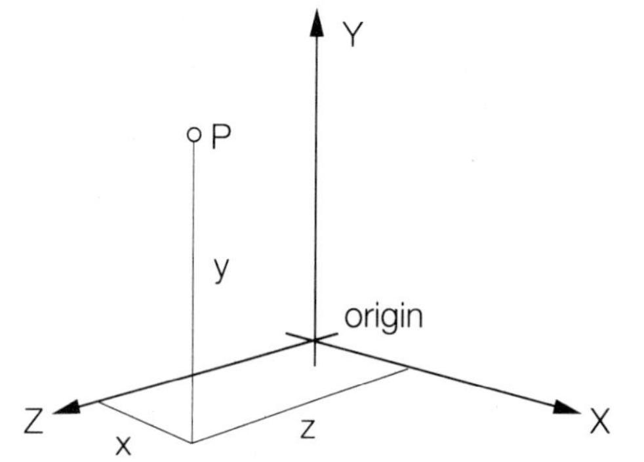

Figure C-1 *The position of the point P can be defined relative to the origin by the Cartesian coordinates representing the three distances x, y and z.*

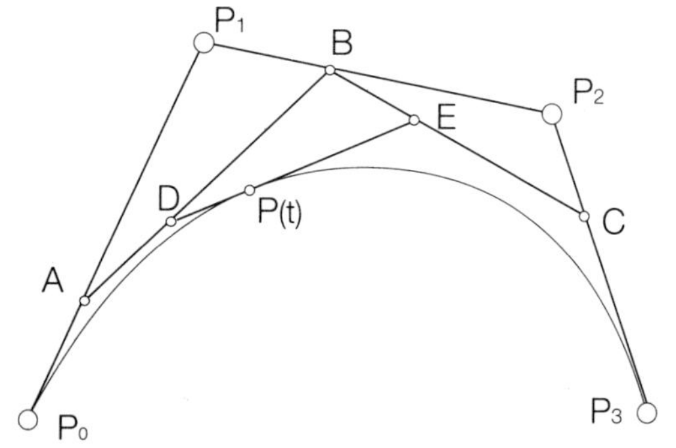

Figure C-2 *In de Casteljau's construction for a Bézier curve, the point P(t) divides the line segment DE into the ratio t : (1 - t), but the line DE is derived from the points A, B and C which also divide their line segments in the same ratio.*

COORDINATES, LEFT-HANDED AXES, POLAR COORDINATES, and RIGHT-HANDED AXES.)
[Gasson-83, Hearn-86, Rogers-89]

Cartesian product patch
When a surface patch is formed from two parametric cubics intersecting one another orthogonally, it is called a Cartesian product patch. Cartesian product patches can be specified by a (4 x 4) array of grid points using LAGRANGIAN INTERPOLATION, or a (4 x 4) grid of corner points, corner slopes and twist vectors using HERMITE INTERPOLATION. Either way, the patch geometry is derived from the product of terms from two sets of equations. (See also BÉZIER SURFACE PATCH, BICUBIC PATCH, B-SPLINE SURFACE PATCH, COONS PATCH, HERMITE PATCH, NURBS, PARAMETRIC SURFACE PATCH, and QUADRATIC SURFACE PATCH.)
[Farin-88, Ferguson-64, Woodwark-86]

Casteljau's algorithm
Paul de Casteljau's algorithm computes points on a BÉZIER CURVE by recursively dividing line segments formed between the CONTROL POINTS. See Figure C-2. (See also BÉZIER CURVE.)
[Burger-89, Farin-88]

catenary
Any heavy cable hanging freely under the influence of gravity forms a catenary curve. Power pylon cables follow a catenary shape, as do draped materials, which have been modelled and animated in computer graphics.
[Gasson-83, Terzopoulos-87]

cathode ray tube
A cathode ray tube is an evacuated glass chamber housing a modulated electron beam and a phosphor coated surface. By sweeping the beam in a regular RASTER fashion, the signal modulations are revealed as light intensities in the phosphor. If there are sufficient displayed points, and the screen is refreshed at least 25 Hz, the human visual system integrates this dot pattern into a stable continuous image. (See also BEAM PENETRATION CRT, CALLIGRAPHIC DISPLAY, COLOUR MONITOR, GAMMA CORRECTION, HIGH-RESOLUTION DISPLAY, LINEARITY, MONITOR, MULTI-SCAN-

NING MONITOR, REFRESH CRT, SHADOW-MASK COLOUR CRT, and STEREOSCOPIC DISPLAY.)
[Burger-89, Hearn-86, Hunt-75, Rogers-85]

Catmull–Rom spline
The Catmull–Rom spline belongs to the family of INTERPOLATING SPLINES and is also known as the CARDINAL SPLINE or the Overhauser spline. The cubic form can be specified by the following (4 x 4) matrix:

$$p = 0.5\,[u^3\ u^2\ u\ 1] \begin{bmatrix} -1 & 3 & -3 & 1 \\ 2 & -5 & 4 & -1 \\ -1 & 0 & 1 & 0 \\ 0 & 1 & 0 & 0 \end{bmatrix} \begin{bmatrix} \boldsymbol{P}_0 \\ \boldsymbol{P}_1 \\ \boldsymbol{P}_2 \\ \boldsymbol{P}_3 \end{bmatrix}$$

where u changes from 0 to 1, p will be a point on a spline approximately connecting points $\boldsymbol{P}_1$ to $\boldsymbol{P}_2$. $\boldsymbol{P}_0$ and $\boldsymbol{P}_3$ are two points before and after the centre segment respectively. (See also APPROXIMATING SPLINE, B-SPLINE CURVE, BETA-SPLINE, CONTROL POINTS, NURBS, OVERHAUSER CURVE, and SPLINE.)
[Barry-88, Brewer-77, Catmull-74b, Fletcher-90, Smith-85]

caustic
When light reflects against a curved surface, or is refracted through a curved object, caustic curves appear. For example, in a spherical mirror, parallel rays of light will not reflect into one focal point but will intersect one another near the focal point creating a locus of points called a caustic. This effect can be observed upon a tea cup illuminated obliquely by direct sunlight, which causes a caustic reflected curve to appear on the surface.
[Gasson-83, Ikanage-86]

cavalier projection
The cavalier projection is an OBLIQUE PROJECTION, where the direction of projection makes an angle of 45° with the PROJECTION PLANE; like the CABINET PROJECTION, it is not widely used. However, the terms Cavalier and Cabinet projections are used in North America to describe an oblique view with XYZ scales 1:1:1 and 1:1:0.5 respectively. (See also AXONOMETRIC ORTHOGRAPHIC PROJECTION, CABINET PROJECTION, ISOMETRIC PROJECTION, OBLIQUE PROJECTION, ORTHOGRAPHIC PROJECTION, PARALLEL PROJECTION, PERSPECTIVE PROJECTION, PROJECTION, and PROJECTION PLANE.)
[Foley-90, Gasson-83, Hearn-86, Rogers-89]

CCD
See CHARGE COUPLED DEVICE.

CCIR
CCIR is an acronym for Comité Consultatif International des Radio communications, which is a United Nations organization charged with developing standards for all forms of communication. (See also CCIR 601 and CCIR 656.)

CCIR 601
The CCIR 601 recommmendations cover the encoding parameters for digital television. (See also CCIR and CCIR 656.)

CCIR 656
The CCIR 656 recommendations cover interfaces for digital COMPONENT video signals.

cell animation
Traditional animation employs thin sheets of clear acetate called cell or cel, which are hand-painted and overlayed to create multilayered scenes. Some animation companies now employ computers to create the basic shape outlines on the cell which are then back-painted in the conventional way. (See also ANIMATION, BAR SHEETS, CHARACTER ANIMATION, COMPUTER ANIMATION, INBETWEENING, and KEY-FRAME ANIMATION.)
[White-86]

cell encoding
Cell encoding is an IMAGE COMPRESSION technique whereby an image is divided into cells (rectangular areas)

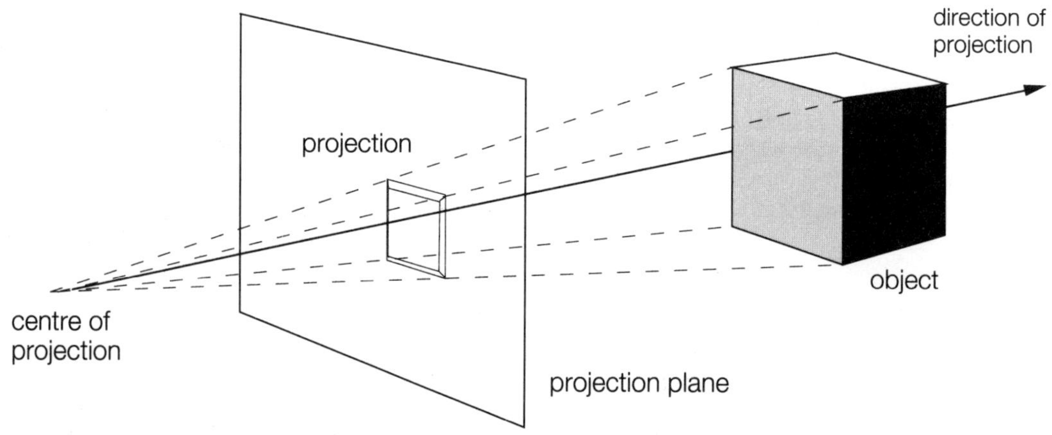

Figure C-3 *In creating a projection one requires a direction of projection, a projection plane and a centre of projection - and by tracing projection lines from the vertices of an object through the plane to the centre, a projection can be captured upon the projection plane. In perspective projections, the configuration is as illustrated, but for a parallel projection the centre is located at infinity with the plane usually orthogonal to the direction of the projection.*

of approximately 100 pixels. One or more bytes are then used to encode foreground and background colours and other colour features. (See also IMAGE COMPRESSION, LZW COMPRESSION, NAPLPS, and RUN-LENGTH ENCODING.)

centre of projection

In a PERSPECTIVE PROJECTION the centre of projection is the point through which all projection lines pass. In PARALLEL PROJECTIONS the centre of projection is positioned at infinity. See Figure C-3. (See also PARALLEL PROJECTION and PERSPECTIVE PROJECTION.)
[Burger-89, Foley-90, Gasson-83, Hearn-86, Rogers-89]

CGA

CGA is an acronym for Colour Graphics Adaptor which is a graphics board providing a maximum monochrome resolution of 640 by 200, and a four-colour resolution of 320 by 200. (See also EGA, HDA, HGC, MCGA, MDA, PVA, SUPER VGA, and VGA.)

CGI

CGI is an acronym for Computer Graphics Interface which defines a standard for computer graphics devices for the efficient implementation of GKS. (See also GKS and GKS-3D.)
[ISO-88a]

CGM

CGM is an acronym for Computer Graphics Metafile which defines a standard for archiving graphical descriptions within a file.
[ANSI-88, ISO-87a, Mumford-88, Mumford-89]

chaos theory

Chaos theory addresses the description and analysis of DYNAMICAL SYSTEMS that exhibit unpredictable and unstable behaviour patterns. Simple quadratic DYNAMICAL SYSTEMS have been used to create FRACTAL images by plotting the paths of chaotic ORBITS. (See also CHAOTIC BEHAVIOUR, DETERMINISTIC, DYNAMICAL SYSTEMS, FRACTAL, MANDELBROT SET, and ORBIT.)
[Barnsley-88, Burger-89, Devaney-86, Gleick-87, Peitgen-88]

chaotic behaviour

Chaotic behaviour can be associated with DETERMINISTIC systems that can behave unpredictably or randomly. For example, the function below, which may be interpreted as a model for population growth with P_n the population and k the rate of growth:

$$P_{n+1} = kP_n(1 - P_n) \text{ where } 0 \leq P_n \leq 1$$

can generate number sequences that can converge to zero, converge to some constant, or jump from one value to another in a chaotic manner. Such systems have been illustrated using computer graphics. (See also CHAOS THEORY, DYNAMICAL SYSTEMS, FRACTAL, JULIA SETS, and ORBIT.)
[Devaney-86, Gleick-87, Peitgen-88]

character animation

Where traditional character animation relies heavily upon the observational and drawing skills of animators to bring cartoon characters to life, computer character animation still requires the observational skills but depends heavily upon the software tools to translate an idea into synthetic images. (See also ANIMATION, BEHAVIOURAL ANIMATION, COMPUTER ANIMATION, FORWARD DYNAMICS, FORWARD KINEMATICS, GOAL-ORIENTED ANIMATION, INBETWEENING, INVERSE DYNAMICS, KEY-FRAME ANIMATION, and PROCEDURAL ANIMATION.)
[Lasseter-87, Schafer-89, Waters-87, White-86]

character generator

A character generator is a hardware device which has access to a ROM storing bit patterns or other descriptions (e.g. splines) of alphabets of symbols, which are mapped onto the screen of a display under software control.
[Burger-89]

characteristic roots

When square matrices are combined with a unit MATRIX to produce a characteristic equation and the DETERMINANT of this characteristic equation is equated to zero, a number of characteristic roots, or eigenvalues, emerges. If a characteristic root is unity, then the corresponding characteristic vector is called a fixed point of the matrix. (See also DETERMINANT, INVERSE MATRIX, MATRIX, MATRIX OPERATION, ORTHOGONAL MATRIX, and TRANSPOSE MATRIX.)
[Stevenson-74]

charge coupled devices (CCD)

Charge coupled devices are employed in modern cameras to convert the incident image into an electrical form. They are analogue devices and are capable of working under low levels of illumination without the disadvantages of tube burn or phosphor smear.

chroma

The MUNSELL COLOUR SYSTEM employs the term chroma to mean SATURATION, which measures the purity of a colour. (See also COLOUR, COLOUR MODEL, HUE, HUE CIRCLE, LIGHTNESS, MUNSELL COLOUR SYSTEM, PURITY, SATURATION, and VALUE.)
[Hearn-86, Hunt-75, Munsell-41, Rogers-85]

chroma keying

Chroma keying is a video process whereby a key signal which may be a single colour (often blue) or a group of colours is detected within an image and triggers control logic to substitute another video signal. A typical use is in television where an object is screened against a blue background; the blue is selected as the chroma key

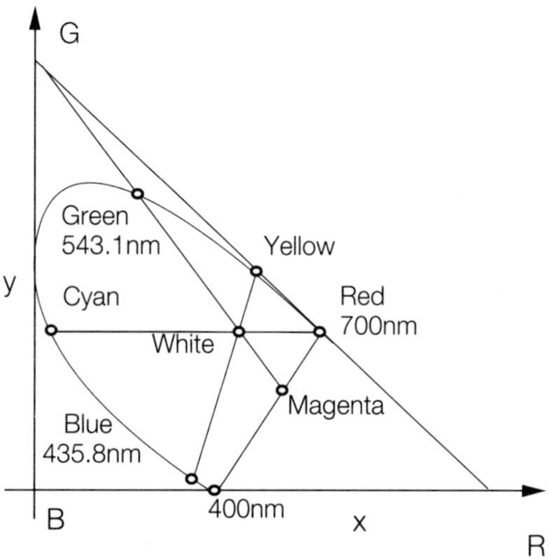

Figure C-4 *This chromaticity diagram plots y against x and shows the position of the primary colours and white. The phosphors employed in television have assumed (x, y) chromaticities of (0.64, 0.33), (0.29, 0.60) and (0.15, 0.06) for red, green and blue respectively.*

which in the VIDEO SIGNAL is replaced by another video signal at a corresponding position in the image. The final composition shows the original object superimposed upon another background. (See also COMPOSITING, DIGITAL CHROMA KEYING, KEYING, MATTE, and VIDEO MIXING.)

chromatic aberration

The degree of optical refraction not only depends upon the nature of the media forming the junction, but also upon the wavelength of the incident light. Therefore, if a lens is not 'corrected' to compensate for this sensitivity to wavelength, the transmitted image will include coloured fringes known as chromatic aberration. (See also ACHROMATIC LIGHT, CHROMATIC LIGHT, COLOUR, REFRACTION OF LIGHT, and REFRACTIVE INDEX.)
[Jenkins-76]

chromaticity diagram

As the *xyz* CHROMATICITY VALUES sum to unity, the chromaticity diagram only plots *y* against *x* because the value of *z* can be calculated from a knowledge of *x* and *y* . It is an extremely useful diagram for illustrating relationships such as shared DOMINANT WAVELENGTHS, GAMUT, COMPLEMENTARY COLOUR, and colour mixing effects. See Figure C-4. (See also ADDITIVE COLOUR MIXING, ADDITIVE PRIMARY COLOURS, CHROMATICITY VALUES, CIE PRIMARIES, DOMINANT WAVELENGTH, ILLUMINANT C, PURITY, and SATURATION.)
[Burger-89, Foley-90, Hearn-86, Hunt-75, Rogers-85]

chromaticity values

The PURITY of a light source is expressed in terms of its chromaticity values represented by the ratios:

$$x = \frac{X}{X+Y+Z}, \quad y = \frac{Y}{X+Y+Z}, \quad z = \frac{Z}{X+Y+Z}$$

where *X*, *Y* and *Z* are the weights applied to the CIE PRIMARIES. As $x + y + z = 1$, a graph relating these quantities can be produced by plotting *y* against *x*; this is known as a CHROMATICITY DIAGRAM. The [*x, y*] chromaticities [0.64, 0.33], [0.29, 0.60] and [0.15, 0.06] for red, green and blue respectively, relate to the colour CRT display phosphors used in television. See Figure C-4. (See also ADDITIVE COLOUR MIXING, CHROMATICITY DIAGRAM, CIE PRIMARIES, DOMINANT WAVELENGTH, ILLUMINANT C, PURITY, and SATURATION.)
[Foley-90, Hearn-86, Hunt-75, Meyer-88, Rogers-85]

chromatic light

Chromatic light is described by the attributes HUE, SATURATION and BRIGHTNESS; in essence it describes a coloured light. (See also BRIGHTNESS, COLOUR, HUE, and SATURATION.)
[Foley-90, Hearn-86, Hunt-75, Rogers-85]

chrome shading

Chrome shading can be created by using a LOOK-UP TABLE

addressed by computing a reflection vector from a surface along a SCAN-LINE. The result of this colour substitution is to cover a surface with graduated colour bands reminiscent of a chrome-plated object which move realistically when the surface is in motion. A much more natural approach is to employ ENVIRONMENT MAPPING. (See also ENVIRONMENT MAPPING and RAY TRACING.)

chrominance

The colour component of a VIDEO SIGNAL encoding the HUE and SATURATION but not the BRIGHTNESS is called the chrominance signal. The CCIR 601 digital standard allows 8 bits to encode the chrominance channel, which provides for 256 levels of chrominance, but this is not completely exploited by the standard. (See also COMPOSITE, LUMINANCE, VIDEO SIGNAL, YIQ, and YUV.)
[Hunt-75]

CIE primaries

Although the idea of ADDITIVE PRIMARY COLOURS works for many colours, experiments have shown that some colours cannot be matched without introducing the idea of subtracting a colour component. This complicates any attempt to represent this system graphically. Consequently, in 1931 the Commission Internationale de l'Eclairage (CIE), defined three hypothetical primaries X, Y and Z to represent the red, green and blue primaries that would allow a totally additive system to be used. The CIE primaries were defined as

$$X = 2.3646\,(R_0) - 0.5151\,(G_0) + 0.0052\,(B_0)$$
$$Y = -0.8965\,(R_0) + 1.4264\,(G_0) - 0.0144\,(B_0)$$
$$Z = -0.4681\,(R_0) + 0.0887\,(G_0) + 1.0092\,(B_0)$$

where R_0, G_0, and B_0 were light sources with wavelengths 700 nm, 546 nm and 436 nm respectively. When these CIE primaries are used for calculating CHROMATICITY VALUES the graph plotting the visible spectrum appears in the positive quadrant. (See also ADDITIVE COLOUR MIXING, ADDITIVE PRIMARY COLOURS, CHROMATICITY DIAGRAM, CHROMATICITY VALUES, COLOUR, GAMUT, ILLUMINANT C, and RGB COLOUR MODEL.)
[Burger-89, Foley-90, Hearn-86, Hunt-75, Meyer-88, Rogers-85]

circle generator

A circle generator is a hardware feature of a display device for computing and displaying a circle of any radius and position.
[Doros-79, Horn-76, Suenaga-79]

circle of confusion

A lens is unable to focus every light ray onto a FOCAL PLANE: some intersect before it, and others behind, but where they intersect the FOCAL PLANE, small circles of light are formed called circles of confusion. Small F-NUMBERS decrease their size and hence improve the clarity of the picture – and such effects have been simulated in RAY TRACING. (See also CHROMATIC ABERRATION, DEPTH OF FIELD, F-NUMBER, FOCAL PLANE, and RAY TRACING.)
[Burger-89, Glassner-89, Potmesil-81, Potmesil-82]

clipbox

A clipbox is a rectangular window in MASTER COORDINATE SPACE identifying a required viewing zone. Graphics shapes falling entirely or partially within this zone are transformed into the physical DEVICE COORDINATE SPACE for viewing. (See also CLIPPING, MASTER COORDINATE SPACE, NORMALIZED DEVICE COORDINATES, PHYSICAL DEVICE COORDINATES, VIEWPORT, and WINDOW.)
[Foley-90]

clipping

Clipping is the process of removing detail from a 2- or 3-D scene which is either invisible to the observer by way of projecting to a region of the viewplane not in the viewport, or not needed. To facilitate this process in 3-D, six mathematical planes are used to partition the EYE COORDINATE SPACE such that the detail on one side of the plane is rejected whilst the detail on the other side is retained. Detail behind or too close to the observer is partitioned

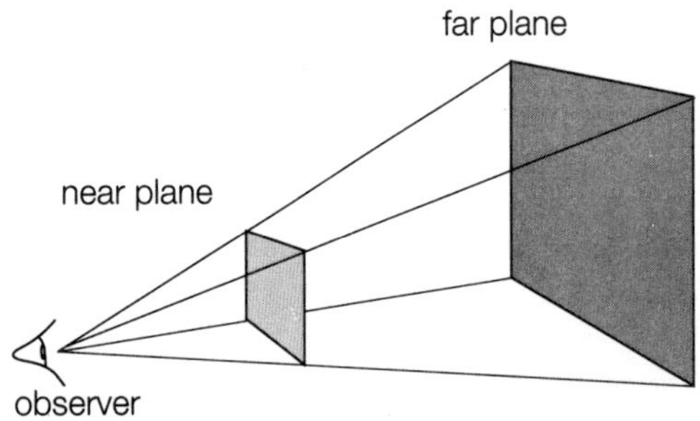

Figure C-5 *3-D clipping algorithms require six planes to define a volume of space visible to the observer: the left, right, top, bottom, near and far planes.*

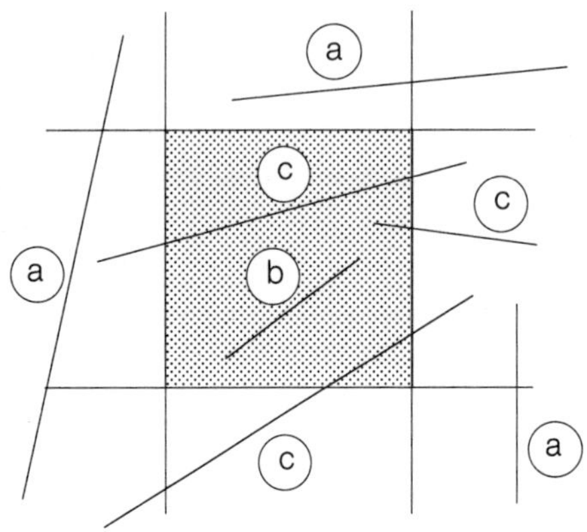

Figure C-6 *The Cohen-Sutherland clipping algorithm partitions space into nine zones such that all the lines labelled 'a' are invisible, the line 'b' is visible and the lines labelled 'c' require clipping. Given two codes defining the positions for the line's end points, a state table can store the action to follow.*

by a NEAR PLANE, whilst the YON or FAR PLANE controls the isolation of distant features. Top, bottom, left and right planes remove detail from the periphery. Although clipping is frequently undertaken by software, most workstations provide a hardware clipping feature which enables very high speeds to be achieved. Model clipping must not occur in a RAY TRACING environment as the entire geometrical model must always be available for illumination, reflection and shadow computations. See Figures C-5 and C-6. (See also ADAPTIVE CLIPPING, CLIPBOX, CLIPPING DIVIDER, COHEN–SUTHERLAND ALGORITHM, DEPTH CLIPPING, RAY TRACING, VIEWING PYRAMID, and WEILER–ATHERTON ALGORITHM.)
[Blinn-78a, Burger-89, Cyrus-78, Hearn-86, Liang-83, Nicholl-87, Rogers-85, Sutherland-74a]

clipping divider
Sproull and Sutherland developed a hardware 2-D clipping algorithm called a clipping divider. Central to the algorithm is a line division process which repeatedly divides a line into two segments until any visible portions are identified. (See also ADAPTIVE CLIPPING, CLIPPING, COHEN–SUTHERLAND ALGORITHM, and WEILER-ATHERTON ALGORITHM.)
[Hearn-86, Rogers-85, Sproull-68]

clipping plane
See CLIPPING.

clockwise polygon
A clockwise polygon is a polygon whose interior is to the right and exterior to the left when its boundary is traversed in the direction of its edges. (See also ANTICLOCKWISE POLYGON, HIDDEN-LINE REMOVAL, HIDDEN-SURFACE REMOVAL, and POLYGON.)

Clough–Tocher interpolant
The Clough–Tocher interpolating scheme is used to create surfaces that interpolate to positional and gradient values having a random rather than a regular distribution.
[Farin-85]

CMY

CMY is an acronym for Cyan, Magenta and Yellow, the SUBTRACTIVE PRIMARY COLOURS. (See also CMY COLOUR MODEL, CMYK, COLOUR MODEL, PRIMARY COLOURS, SUBTRACTIVE COLOUR MIXING, and SUBTRACTIVE PRIMARY COLOURS.)
[Hearn-86, Hunt-75, Rogers-85]

CMY colour model

Whereas the RGB COLOUR MODEL supports display technology, the CMY colour model is a Cartesian system of specifying the colours Cyan, Magenta and Yellow (CMY) for supporting hard-copy devices depositing coloured pigments onto paper. (See also CMY, CMYK, COLOUR MODEL, PRIMARY COLOURS, SUBTRACTIVE COLOUR MIXING, and SUBTRACTIVE PRIMARY COLOURS.)
[Hearn-86, Hunt-75, Rogers-85]

CMYK

CMYK is an acronym for Cyan, Magenta, Yellow and blacK – the colour separations used in half-tone printing. (See also GREY COMPONENT REPLACEMENT, SUBTRACTIVE COLOUR MIXING, and SUBTRACTIVE PRIMARY COLOURS.)
[Hunt-75]

Cohen–Sutherland algorithm

The Cohen–Sutherland clipping algorithm developed by D. Cohen and I. Sutherland partitions a 2-D space into nine (3 x 3) zones, where the central zone is the viewing window. By assigning binary codes to each zone, a line's end points can be allocated a pair of these codes from which it is possible to identify those lines requiring clipping. This technique can also be extended for the 3-D case. See Figure C-6. (See also CLIPPING, CLIPPING DIVIDER, and WEILER-ATHERTON ALGORITHM.)
[Foley-90, Rogers-85]

coherence

The efficiency of many computer graphics algorithms can be improved by identifying a coherent feature of a problem that minimizes repetitive calculations. For example, algorithms such as a SCAN-LINE RENDERER exploit span coherence to compute pixel intensities across a surface by a rendering technique that calculates one pixel's intensity from the span's start and end pixels. Similarly, the AREA COHERENCE properties of the PEANO CURVE enable certain images to be compacted more efficiently than RUN-LENGTH ENCODING. (See also AREA COHERENCE, DEPTH COHERENCE, EDGE COHERENCE, and RUN-LENGTH ENCODING.)
[Burger-89, Foley-90, Hearn-86, Rogers-85]

Collage Theorem

The Collage Theorem as proposed by Barnsley *et al.* provides a basis for describing certain images as a 'collage' of similar elements which have been transformed by a set of ITERATED FUNCTION SYSTEM codes. The Collage Algorithm provides the user with interactive tools to identify the IFS codes by examining polygonal outlines of the target image. The technique has been applied to create structured images of trees, leaves and flowers. (See also FRACTAL, FRACTAL GEOMETRY, ITERATED FUNCTION SYSTEMS, and SELF-SIMILARITY.)
[Barnsley-85, Barnsley-88, Horn-90, Peitgen-88]

collision detection

Collision detection refers to the mechanisms employed to identify those 3-D elements that have effectively touched or intersected one another; this is an essential system feature for FLIGHT SIMULATORS and RIGID-BODY ANIMATION. To speed up the process, objects are assigned a BOUNDING VOLUME, perhaps in the form of a sphere, and an intersection test is first made with the sphere before investigating more complex collision tests with the objects. (See also BOUNDING VOLUME, INTERPENETRATING OBJECTS, and RIGID-BODY ANIMATION.)
[Dai-89, Mirolo-89, Moore-88]

colour

The human visual system creates a sensation we refer to as 'colour' when a certain bandwidth of electromagnetic radiation is detected by the retina. Radiation with a WAVELENGTH of around 700 nm (nanometres) gives rise to a red sensation, whilst 400 nm causes a deep violet

one. The entire visual spectrum is a continuous transition from red, through yellow, green, blue, to violet. (See also ACHROMATIC LIGHT, ADDITIVE COLOUR MIXING, BRIGHTNESS, CHROMA, CHROMATICITY DIAGRAM, CHROMATIC LIGHT, COLOUR MODEL, COLOUR SPACE, COMPLEMENTARY COLOUR, GAMUT, HUE, HUE CIRCLE, LIGHTNESS, MUNSELL COLOUR SYSTEM, PURITY, SATURATION, SPECTRAL COLOUR, SUBTRACTIVE COLOUR MIXING, TRICHROMATIC COLOUR SYSTEM, VALUE, and WHITE LIGHT.)
[Boynton-79, Burger-89, Foley-90, Gregory-86, Hearn-86, Hunt-75, Rogers-85]

colour attributes
Before an object can be rendered, it must be assigned colour attributes in the form of numerical values encoding some surface feature. This might be in terms of levels of red, green and blue, HUE, SATURATION and VALUE, or commonly a LOOK-UP TABLE entry where colour codes are stored. Also, as ILLUMINATION MODELS tend to divide illumination into ambient, diffuse and specular components, reflection coefficients for the three ADDITIVE PRIMARY COLOURS may be used to control the way a surface absorbs and reflects light, which, by definition, is its colour. (See also ADDITIVE PRIMARY COLOURS, AMBIENT LIGHT, AMBIENT REFLECTION COEFFICIENT, COLOUR, DIFFUSE REFLECTION COEFFICIENT, GLOBAL ILLUMINATION MODEL, and SPECULAR REFLECTION COEFFICIENT.)
[Burger-89, Foley-90, Rogers-85]

colour bleeding
Colour bleeding occurs when one coloured surface influences the colour shading of another surface through DIFFUSE REFLECTIONS. This phenomenon is modelled effectively by RADIOSITY. (See also AMBIENT LIGHT, DIFFUSE REFLECTION, and RADIOSITY.)
[Baum-89, Cohen-88, Immel-86, Glassner-88, Rushmeier-87, Sillion-89, Wallace-87, Wallace-89]

colour enhancement
Colour enhancement is an IMAGE PROCESSING technique used in medical diagnosis and consists of increasing the SATURATION of pixels, with the result that different features having similar colours are easily differentiated.
[Burger-89]

colour gamut
See GAMUT.

colour interpolation
Colour interpolation is the process of interpolating between two colour values within a COLOUR SPACE. But as straight lines in the RGB COLOUR MODEL do not, in general, transform into straight lines in either HSV or HLS models, the interpolated colour values are different for each space. (See also ADDITIVE COLOUR MIXING, COLOUR, COLOUR MODEL, COLOUR SPACE, HLS COLOUR MODEL, HSV COLOUR MODEL, INTERPOLATION, and RGB COLOUR MODEL.)

colour map
See COLOUR TABLE.

colour model
A colour model is a convenient system for organizing and specifying colours within an application-dependent colour GAMUT. For example, computer graphics uses RGB and HSV, colour television YIQ and YUV, and hard-copy printing devices CMY. See Figure C-7. (See also CMY COLOUR MODEL, HLS COLOUR MODEL, HSV COLOUR MODEL, RGB COLOUR MODEL, YIQ, and YUV.)
[Burger-89, Foley-90, Hearn-86, Lindbloom-89, Rogers-85]

colour monitor
A colour CRT driven by unencoded colour signals is generally called a colour monitor. RGB monitors are driven by the three red, green and blue signals giving a high-quality image, whereas quality is sacrificed slightly when the signals are encoded into a COMPOSITE VIDEO signal as in a television receiver. (See also CATHODE RAY TUBE, COMPOSITE, MONITOR, MULTI-SCANNING MONITOR, REFRESH CRT, SHADOW-MASK COLOUR CRT, and VIDEO SIGNAL.)
[Burger-89, Hearn-86, Hunt-75]

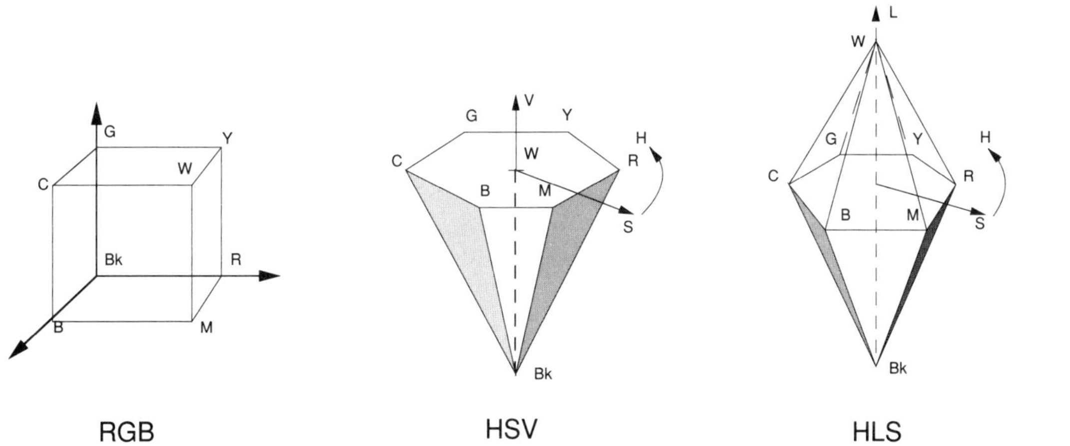

Figure C-7 *The RGB, HSV and HLS colour spaces provide three different ways of describing colour: whilst RGB identifies the additive primary components comprising a colour, HSV and HLS enable a colour to be described in terms of hue, saturation and value or lightness. In the three systems the following notation is employed: R=red, G=green, B=blue, Y=yellow, C=cyan, M=magenta, Bk=black, W=white, H=hue, V=value, S=saturation and L=lightness.*

colour space

A colour space is a 2- or 3-D method of organizing colour attributes. The RGB COLOUR MODEL can organize the three ADDITIVE PRIMARY COLOURS (red, green and blue) as a set of 3-D axes such that any colour can be visualized as a unique point within a unit cube of this space. Unfortunately, this does not provide a means for identifying families of colours sharing related attributes, which is why other colour spaces have evolved based upon the attributes HUE, SATURATION and VALUE. See Figure C-7. (See also ADDITIVE COLOUR MIXING, ADDITIVE PRIMARY COLOURS, COLOUR, COLOUR MODEL, HEXCONE, HLS COLOUR MODEL, HSV COLOUR MODEL, MUNSELL COLOUR SYSTEM, and RGB COLOUR MODEL.)

[Burger-89, Foley-90, Hearn-86, Joblove-78, Meyer-80, Rogers-85]

colour table

A LOOK-UP TABLE whose entries store colour descriptions, perhaps in the form of levels of red, green and blue, is also called a colour table; this could be associated with a FRAME STORE which addresses the colour table directly via its memory contents. This indirect addressing of colours enables the table entries to reference a set of viewable colours from perhaps a larger set of displayable colours. The colour table can also be used for GAMMA CORRECTION or even LOOK-UP TABLE ANIMATION. (See also FRAME STORE, GAMMA CORRECTION, LOOK-UP TABLE, and LOOK-UP TABLE ANIMATION.)

[Burger-89]

command language

A command language is a set of instructions available to a user to control an interactive interface. These could

involve creating, copying and renaming files, and creating, rearranging and transforming objects. (See also COMPILER, HIGH-LEVEL LANGUAGE, INTERPRETER, and LOW-LEVEL LANGUAGE.)
[Burger-89, Foley-90]

compiler
In computer language processing, compilers translate a high-level source program into a low-level object program, where the source program is constructed based upon a specific set of semantic and syntactic rules and the object program is associated with some target computer processor language. Languages such as PASCAL, FORTRAN and C, all require there own compilers. Compilers are also used in computer graphics to convert high-level descriptions of 3-D models into some other target format. (See also C, FORTRAN, HIGH-LEVEL LANGUAGE, INTERPRETER, LOW-LEVEL LANGUAGE, and PASCAL.)

complementary colour
In additive colour mixing, a colour when mixed with its complement produces colourless white light. For example, a blue-green (cyan) is the complement of red. (See also ADDITIVE COLOUR MIXING, ADDITIVE PRIMARY COLOURS, COLOUR, COLOUR MODEL, COLOUR SPACE, HUE, HUE CIRCLE, and MUNSELL COLOUR SYSTEM.)
[Burger-89, Hunt-75, Munsell-41]

complex number
Complex number notation is used to solve problems involving vectors and employ the concept of 'real' and 'imaginary' components. For example, a complex number can be represented by

$$z = x + \boldsymbol{i}y$$

where x is the 'real' component and y is the 'imaginary' component.This can be represented diagrammatically by using CARTESIAN COORDINATES, where the X-axis represents the 'real' component and the Y-axis represents the 'imaginary' component. The symbol $\boldsymbol{i}$ is interpreted as an operator meaning 'rotated anticlockwise through 90°'. Thus where $\boldsymbol{i}y$ identifies a point on the Y-axis, $\boldsymbol{i}$ identifies a point on the negative 'real' axis, which effectively makes the operation $\boldsymbol{ii}$ equivalent to a multiplication by −1. This in turn suggests that $\boldsymbol{i}$ is the square-root of minus one, which is meaningless – hence the use of the term 'imaginary'. As complex numbers can represent VECTORS (which are fundamental to computer graphics algorithms), they are frequently employed as an analytical tool in technical research papers. (See also CARTESIAN COORDINATES, QUATERNIONS, and VECTOR.)

component
In video technology, the term component refers to systems that process the LUMINANCE and CHROMINANCE signals as separate components. This ensures that the system BANDWIDTH is preserved, which is not the case when a COMPOSITE signal is created. (See also BANDWIDTH, CHROMINANCE, COMPOSITE, LUMINANCE, and VIDEO SIGNAL.)

composite
A composite VIDEO SIGNAL encodes the LUMINANCE and CHROMINANCE COMPONENTS into one of the coding standards such as NTSC, PAL or SECAM. (See also BANDWIDTH, CHROMINANCE, COMPONENT, LUMINANCE, NTSC, PAL, SECAM, and VIDEO SIGNAL.)
[Hunt-75]

composite curve
A composite curve is constructed from several individual segments normally having slope CONTINUITY preserved at their joins. See Figure C-8. (See also BÉZIER CURVE, B-SPLINE CURVE, CONTINUITY, NURBS, and PIECEWISE CURVES.)
[Burger-89, Farin-88, Woodwark-86]

composite video
See COMPOSITE.

compositing
Compositing is the process of superimposing one image upon another to create a single 'composite' image. Great

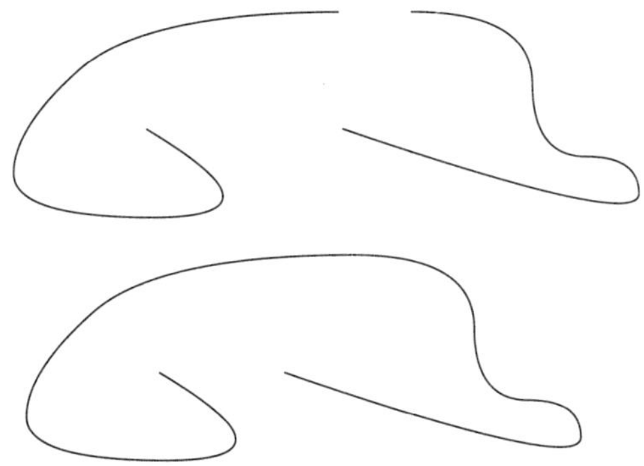

Figure C-8 *The bottom curve is a composite curve formed from the two top curve segments, but because slope continuity has been preserved at their boundary, no discontinuity is visible.*

care is needed to filter boundaries to disguise joins which otherwise could be visible – an ALPHA CHANNEL is used to control this in CHROMA KEYING. (See also ALPHA CHANNEL, CHROMA KEYING, DIGITAL CHROMA KEYING, DIGITAL MIXING, KEYING, MATTE, VIDEO MIXING, and VIDEO SIGNAL.)
[Duff-85, Nakamae-86, Nakamae-89, Porter-84]

computational geometry

Computational geometry concerns itself with the development of algorithms associated with geometrical problems, such as geometric searching, CONVEX HULLS, proximity testing and intersections.
[Gasson-83, Preparata-85]

computer-aided design (CAD)

Although, strictly speaking, computer-aided design does not imply the involvement of computer graphics, many CAD systems are concerned with the computerization of design activities associated with 2-D drawing and 3-D modelling. However, other CAD systems involved in acoustics, thermal modelling, gear design etc. may not involve any computer graphics at all, but visualization of numerical data will perhaps become a feature of all future computer design processes. (See also COMPUTER-AIDED DESIGN/COMPUTER-AIDED MANUFACTURE.)

computer-aided design/computer-aided manufacture (CAD/CAM)

CAD/CAM describes systems that integrate the features of CAD, such as modelling, engineering drawings, automatic dimensioning and physical properties, with those of CAM, such as CNC (Computer Numerically Controlled) machine interfacing, visualization of tool cutter paths and programmable contour offsets.
[Kochan-86, Rembold-86]

computer animation

Computer animation is concerned with the use of computers in creating animated synthetic images. The majority of such animation is achieved by constructing a series of scenes that are individually animated, rendered and stored, and then edited and composited into a final sequence. Computer animation exploits virtually every facet of computer graphics to assist animators in their task of bringing their synthetic forms to life. (See also ANIMATION, BEHAVIOURAL ANIMATION, CHARACTER ANIMATION, CUSHIONING, DISPLACEMENT ANIMATION, DYNAMIC CONSTRAINTS, ELASTICALLY DEFORMABLE OBJECTS, FORWARD DYNAMICS, FORWARD KINEMATICS, FREE-FORM DEFORMATION, GOAL-ORIENTED ANIMATION, INBETWEENING, INVERSE DYNAMICS, KEY-FRAME ANIMATION, PHOTOREALISM, PROCEDURAL ANIMATION, RIGID-BODY ANIMATION, and WALK-THROUGH.)
[Lasseter-87, Magnenat-Thalmann-85, Vince-85]

computer graphics

Computer graphics is concerned with the application of computers in generating synthetic images. In 2-D graphics, computer systems are available for developing layouts of line drawings and coloured painted images, with application areas including architecture, animation, television, engineering and electronics. 3-D graphics systems are available to create shaded perspective scenes of 3-D objects; these have areas of application in archi-

tecture, animation, medicine, CAD/CAM, product design, engineering and simulation.
[Burger-89, Foley-90, Kuni-83, Magnenat–Thalmann-87a, Rogers-85]

computer vision
Computer vision is concerned with the processing and understanding of real images. It is of particular relevance to robotics where computers are needed to interpret 3-D scenes in order to control the actions of the machine. (See also IMAGE PROCESSING.)
[Shirai-86]

concatenation
Concatenation refers to the multiplying out of matrices to produce one single MATRIX. (See also MATRIX and MATRIX OPERATION.)
[Blinn-87a, Gasson-83, Stevenson-74]

concave object
A line connecting any two points on the surface of a concave object cannot be guaranteed to be totally contained by the surface. (See also CONVEX OBJECT.)

concave polygon
A line connecting any two points on the boundary of a concave polygon cannot be guaranteed to be totally contained by the boundary; this is because one or more internal angles between two consecutive edges exceed 180°. (See also CONVEX POLYGON, IRREGULAR POLYGON, RE-ENTRANT POLYGON, and REGULAR POLYGON.)

concentration exponent
The concentration exponent controls the fall-off in light intensity over the CONE OF INFLUENCE of a SPOT LIGHT. As the fall-off can be represented by a COSINE FUNCTION, this can be raised to a power (the concentration exponent) to control the rate of decay. (See also CONE OF INFLUENCE and SPOT LIGHT.)

cone of influence
The cone of influence is the circular illuminated area produced by a SPOT LIGHT. (See also CONCENTRATION EXPONENT and SPOT LIGHT.)

cone of vision
The cone of vision or visual field is the SOLID ANGLE potentially visible to an observer. The unaided human eye has a cone of vision of approximately 100°, although its characteristics alter dramatically from the central fovea, where colour vision and ACUITY are maximum, towards the periphery where rod vision (night vision) and movement detection dominate. (See also ANGLE OF VIEW, DEPTH OF FIELD, and FOCAL LENGTH.)
[Gregory-86]

cone tracing
Cone tracing is a RAY TRACING technique where individual rays of light are replaced by conical beams of light rays. It has proved to be an effective method of computing INCIDENT LIGHT levels and improving ANTI-ALIASING. (See also ANTI-ALIASING, BEAM TRACING, and RAY TRACING.)
[Amanatides-84, Glassner-89, Heckbert-84, Kirk-87, Shinya-87]

conic sections
The conic sections are the shapes formed when a plane intersects a cone; these consist of the circle, ellipse, parabola and hyperbola.
[Gasson-83]

constant shading
Constant shading is a shading technique where single colours are assigned to surfaces which remain constant no matter how the object is manipulated or viewed. This is also known as flat shading. (See also COSINE SHADING, GOURAUD SHADING, PHONG SHADING, QUADRATIC SHADING, and SHADING MODEL.)
[Hearn-86]

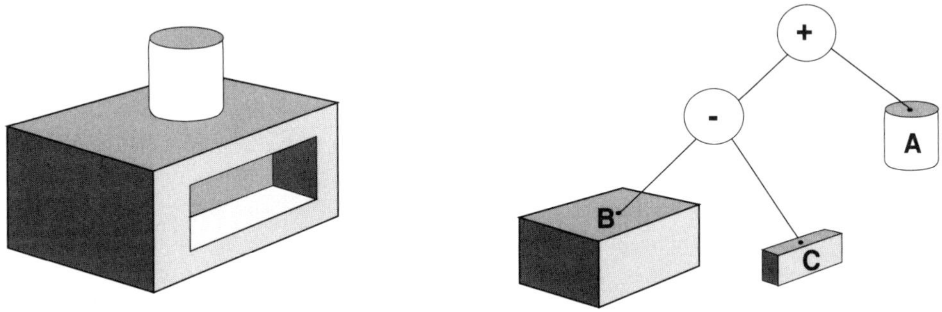

Figure C-9 *Constructive solid geometry requires that an object is built from a variety of graphic primitives, which themselves are built from planar, spherical, cylindrical and other simple surfaces. In this example, the assembly on the left can be described by the binary tree on the right, which confirms that the base of the object is the result of subtracting volume C from volume B; this in turn is added to the cylinder A. When the structure is rendered, a ray casting algorithm can use the half-spaces of the primitives to identify the boundary surfaces.*

constructive solid geometry (CSG)

Set-theoretic modelling or constructive solid geometry is a modelling strategy based upon HALF SPACES formed by planes, spheres, toroids and cylinders which can be related by the boolean operations of union, subtraction and difference. As opposed to B-REP strategies, CSG is concerned with the development of a space volume formed by the relationships between the above graphic primitives. See Figure C-9. (See also BOUNDARY REPRESENTATION, FREE-FORM SURFACES, GEOMETRIC MODELLING, HALF SPACE, MODELLING, NURBS, PARAMETRIC SURFACE PATCH, SCULPTURED SURFACES, SOLIDS MODELLING, and WIRE FRAME.)
[Atherton-83, Dobkin-88, Goldfeather-86, Goldfeather-89, Rochester-87, Laidlaw-86, Woodwark-86, Wyvill-85]

contained polygon

In AREA SUBDIVISION ALGORITHMS a contained polygon is totally enclosed by some reference rectangular window, and represents one of the possible conditions detected in the space division process. (See also AREA SUBDIVISION ALGORITHMS, DISJOINT POLYGON, INTERSECTING POLYGON, SURROUNDING POLYGON, and WARNOCK ALGORITHM.)
[Rogers-85, Warnock-69]

containment

Containment refers to the detection of whether a point is inside or outside some boundary. A conventional method of proving containment of a point is to construct a line with the given point and some known outside point and to compute the number of intersections it makes with the boundary contour. If the number of intersections is odd, then the point is contained (inside); if the number is even, the point is outside. Great care must be taken in handling the range of intersection conditions that can arise. (See also JORDAN CURVE THEOREM.)
[Burger-89, Rogers-89]

continuity
Because curve and surface representation techniques attempt to build complex forms from assemblies of simple elements, the nature of the joins at these boundaries is very critical. However, such joins can be hidden if slope continuity is preserved over the join – which is described very accurately by the first- and second-order changes in slope characteristics. For example, if a parametric cubic equation is differentiated, the resulting second-order equation provides the slope at any point; a further differentiation results in a first-order equation which provides the slope's rate of change at any point. These two equations supply the first- and second-order slope continuity parameters respectively. If now, a curve is to be constructed from a sequence of PARAMETRIC CUBIC CURVE segments, and one ensures that at the segment boundaries first- and second-order slope continuity is preserved then it will be impossible to visibly detect the join. This is fundamental to many piecewise modelling schemes. (See also BÉZIER CURVE, BÉZIER SURFACE PATCH, B-SPLINE CURVE, B-SPLINE SURFACE PATCH, COMPOSITE CURVE, COONS PATCH, DERIVATIVE, FERGUSON PATCH, HERMITE INTERPOLATION, LAGRANGIAN INTERPOLATION, NURBS, PARAMETRIC CUBIC CURVE, and PIECEWISE CURVES.)
[Barsky-90a, Burger-89, Farin-88, Woodwark-86]

contour
The term contour can mean anything from a constant height curve on a map to an arbitrary shape in space, but a PHIGS specification is much more rigid; here a contour is a polygonal line that is closed and planar and may even cross itself.

contouring
Contouring is the visible banding in an image normally caused by insufficient colour or intensity quantizing levels, or rounding errors. It is very noticeable when rendering surfaces coloured with a PRIMARY COLOUR, as all the intensity changes must be achieved perhaps within a resolution of 8 bits.
[Burger-89]

contrast
Contrast is the range of light values in an image from the darkest to the brightest.

control points
Bézier and B-spline curves and surfaces are constrained by a sequence of geometric control points that guide the shape's geometry. In the case of a cubic BÉZIER CURVE, four control points are required for its construction – and if any one is repositioned, the entire shape is affected. However, in the case of a B-SPLINE curve employing several control points, their adjustment is restricted to a local span of the curve. See Figures B-3 and B-4. (See also APPROXIMATING SPLINE, BASIS FUNCTION, BERNSTEIN BASIS FUNCTION, BÉZIER CURVE, BÉZIER SURFACE PATCH, B-SPLINE CURVE, B-SPLINE SURFACE PATCH, CONVEX HULL, and INTERPOLATING SPLINE.)
[Burger-89, Farin-88, Hearn-86, Rogers-89, Woodwark-86]

convex
Convex curves or surfaces partition space such that they never intersect with any line connected between any two enclosed points. The convex property is found frequently within computer graphics perhaps restricting a CLIPPING, TRIANGULATION or AREA INFILL algorithm to CONVEX POLYGONS. (See also CONVEX POLYGON and CONCAVE POLYGON.)

convex hull
Given any set of 2-D points, their convex hull is a closed CONVEX polygonal boundary such that the points are either within or on this boundary. The term describes a feature of Bézier and B-SPLINE CURVES and surfaces that are always created within the convex hull of their CONTROL POINTS. See Figure C-10. (See also BERNSTEIN BASIS FUNCTION and CONTROL POINTS.)
[Burger-89, Farin-88, Hearn-86, Rogers-89, Woodwark-86]

convex object
A convex object has the property that a line connecting

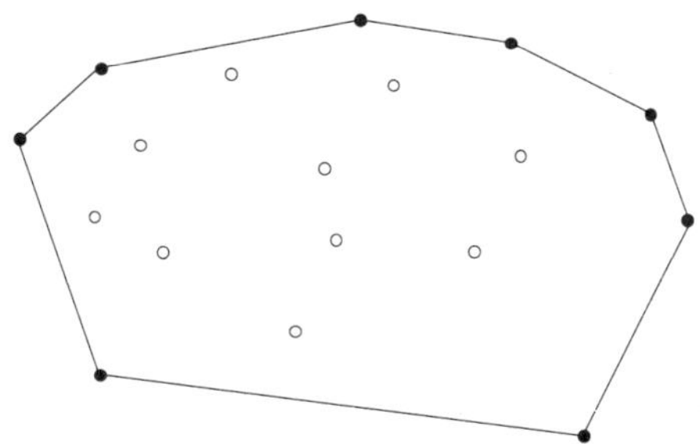

Figure C-10 *The convex hull of this random collection of points is the boundary connecting those points such that a line joining any two points, will never intersect this boundary. The concept of the convex hull is found in Bézier and B-spline curves and surfaces.*

any two points on the surface, is always completely within the volume. This could be exploited in RAY TRACING where, for example, if all objects were convex it would only be necessary to compute one entry and one exit point for a ray, whereas a CONCAVE OBJECT could give rise to any number of intersection pairs. (See also CONCAVE OBJECT.)
[Burger-89]

convex polygon

A line connecting any two points on the boundary of a convex polygon will always be contained by its boundary. (See also CONCAVE POLYGON.)
[Burger-89]

convolution

(1) **Continuous**: Given two functions *f*(*x*) and *g*(*x*), their convolution is defined as

$$\int_0^\infty f(u)\, g(x-u)\,du$$

which implies creating a third function using the following rules:
(a) reverse the direction of one of the functions, say *g*(*x*);
(b) slide the function *g*(-*x*) over function *f*(*x*) and compute the weighted average of the overlapping portions.
The resulting function is called the convolution of *f*(*x*) and *g*(*x*). This process effectively imprints one function upon the other.
(2) **Discrete**: Convolution is the process of placing a FILTER consisting of a multi-valued weighted pixel array at the sample points of a reference image and convolving (multiplying and summing) them together to form a filtered image. Convolution plays an important role in the understanding of ALIASING and its prevention through ANTI-ALIASING strategies by predicting the efficacy of FILTERS in removing unwanted high-frequency components. (See also ALIASING, ANTI-ALIASING, BASIS FUNCTION, CONVOLUTION FILTER, CONVOLUTION THEOREM, FILTER, FILTERING, FOURIER WAVEFORM ANALYSIS, NYQUIST LIMIT, POINT-SPREAD FUNCTION, and SPATIAL ALIASING.)
[Barrett-87, Blinn-89a, Blinn-89b, Burger-89, Gonzalez-87, Heckbert-86a, Naiman-87, Pratt-78, Rogers-85]

convolution filter

A convolution filter is a WEIGHTING FUNCTION or KERNEL used in IMAGE PROCESSING to filter images. The shape of the FILTER (box, tent, parabolic, Parzen etc.) determines the final visual effect. (See also BASIS FUNCTION, BOX FILTER, CONVOLUTION, CONVOLUTION THEOREM, FILTER, FILTERING, FOURIER WAVEFORM ANALYSIS, GAUSSIAN FILTER, IMAGE PROCESSING, SINC FILTER, SPATIAL ALIASING, and TENT FILTER.)
[Barrett-87, Blinn-89a, Burger-89, Gonzalez-87, Naiman-87, Pratt-78, Rogers-85]

convolution theorem

The convolution theorem states that if two functions *f*(*x*) and *g*(*x*) have FOURIER TRANSFORMS *F*(*u*) and *G*(*u*) respectively, then the CONVOLUTION of *f*(*x*) with *g*(*x*) is equivalent to *F*(*u*)*G*(*u*). Similarly, the CONVOLUTION of *F*(*u*) with *G*(*u*) is equivalent to *f*(*x*)*g*(*x*). This relationship between the SPATIAL and FREQUENCY DOMAINS makes for a powerful analytical tool in developing FILTERS. (See also ALIASING, ANTI-ALIASING, BASIS FUNCTION, BOX FILTER, CONVOLUTION, CONVOLUTION FIL-

TER, FILTER, FILTERING, FOURIER WAVEFORM ANALYSIS, FREQUENCY DOMAIN, GAUSSIAN FILTER, NYQUIST LIMIT, SINC FILTER, SPATIAL DOMAIN, and TENT FILTER.)
[Barrett-87, Blinn-89a, Blinn-89b, Blinn89c, Gonzalez-87, Pratt-78)

Cook–Torrance shading
The Cook–Torrance SHADING MODEL incorporates a classical approach to ambient and DIFFUSE REFLECTIONS, but computes the specular component using a term controlling the masking of light due to surface unevenness. It also includes a GAUSSIAN DISTRIBUTION of the SURFACE NORMALS, and a Fresnel term accounting for the change in WAVELENGTH that occurs with the ANGLE OF INCIDENCE. (See also COSINE SHADING, FRESNEL EFFECT, GAUSSIAN DISTRIBUTION, GOURAUD SHADING, PHONG SHADING, RADIOSITY, RAY TRACING, REFLECTANCE MODEL, RENDERING EQUATION, REYES, SHADING MODEL, SURFACE SHADOWING, and TORRANCE–SPARROW SHADING MODEL.)
[Burger-89, Cook-82b, Foley-90, Rogers-85]

Coons patch
A Coons patch is a SURFACE PATCH defined by four boundary PARAMETRIC CURVES and four corner vertices; these are then blended together to create the surface geometry, but if two patches share a common edge, the blending functions must be selected to provide the required degree of CONTINUITY. (See also BÉZIER SURFACE PATCH, B-SPLINE SURFACE PATCH, CARTESIAN PRODUCT PATCH, CONTINUITY, FERGUSON PATCH, HERMITE PATCH, NURBS, PARAMETRIC CURVE, PARAMETRIC SURFACE, PATCH, PATCHED SURFACE, and SURFACE PATCH.)
[Coons-67, Farin-88, Gasson-83, Woodwark-86]

coordinates
Coordinates are measurements locating a point within a COORDINATE SYSTEM such as CARTESIAN COORDINATES. In the Cartesian model they represent distances to a point parallel with each axis. See Figure C-1. (See also AREA COORDINATES, BARYCENTRIC COORDINATES, CARTESIAN COORDINATES, HOMOGENEOUS COORDINATES, and POLAR COORDINATES.)
[Gasson-83, Rogers-89]

coordinate system
A coordinate system is a geometric method for defining points in space in terms of various physical measurements such as Cartesian and polar notation. (See also AREA COORDINATES, BARYCENTRIC COORDINATES, CARTESIAN COORDINATES, COORDINATES, HOMOGENEOUS COORDINATES, and POLAR COORDINATES.)
[Gasson-83, Rogers-89]

co-planar vectors
Co-planar vectors coexist within a PLANAR region of space and in computer graphics allow for mathematical shortcuts to be applied in their manipulation.
[Burger-89, Gasson-83, Rogers-89]

CORE
CORE is a computer graphics standard developed in 1977 to address the problems of 2-D output such as line, text and polygon definition, and the simple attributes of line thickness, colour and pattern type. GKS, developed in 1978, now replaces it. (See also GKS, GKS-3D, and PHIGS.)
[Bergeron-78, Burger-89]

cosine
Angles can be either expressed as a swept rotation measured in DEGREES or RADIANS or be represented as a dimensionless ratio called a SINE, cosine or TANGENT. For example, the cosine of an angle formed by a pair of intersecting lines of lengths A and B is the ratio of the ORTHOGONAL projection of A onto B, divided by A. (See also SINE and TANGENT.)

cosine function
The cosine function generates a sinusoidal waveform identical to the SINE FUNCTION but displaced in the time domain by $-\pi/2$ radians. When the SINE of an angle Ø is known, the cosine can be computed from the relationship

$$\sin^2(\text{Ø}) + \cos^2(\text{Ø}) = 1$$

(See also SINE FUNCTION.)

cosine shading
Cosine shading is a simple shading model whereby the intensity of a surface is proportional to the COSINE of the angle between the INCIDENT LIGHT vector and the SURFACE NORMAL. Diffuse shading is often referred to as cosine shading, as it employs Lambert's observation that the brightness of a DIFFUSE SURFACE is independent of the observer's position but is a function of the illumination direction. (See also CONSTANT SHADING, DIFFUSE REFLECTION, DIFFUSE SURFACE, GOURAUD SHADING, INCIDENT LIGHT, LAMBERT'S COSINE LAW, and PHONG SHADING.)
[Burger-89, Foley-90, Hearn-86, Rogers-85]

cracks
When a SURFACE PATCH is rendered by rendering smaller sub-patches, small visual artifacts can appear at the sub-patch joins called cracks. Cracks can also occur between patches with insufficient CONTINUITY parameters. (See also AREA SUBDIVISION ALGORITHMS, ARTIFACT, CONTINUITY, IMAGE PLANE, PARAMETER SPACE, PARAMETRIC SURFACE PATCH, and RENDERER.)
[Rockwood-89]

critical angle
The critical angle is associated with a pair of transmissive media and defines an ANGLE OF INCIDENCE for the refracted ray into the second medium which, if exceeded, causes the refracted ray to undergo internal reflection. This phenomenon can be simulated in RAY TRACING. (See also ANGLE OF INCIDENCE, ANGLE OF REFLECTION, ANGLE OF REFRACTION, REFRACTION OF LIGHT, RAY TRACING, and SNELL'S LAW)
[Glassner-89, Jenkins-76]

cross-dissolve
A cross-dissolve is a video or animation effect where one scene is faded out whilst another is faded in.

crosshair
Crosshairs are a pair of thin intersecting lines displayed on a graphics display screen to identify a specific position.

cross product
See VECTOR PRODUCT.

cross-section rendering
Cross-section rendering is associated with the rendering of a space volume defined by VOXEL data. The data are organized in slices or cross-sectional surfaces and rendered, perhaps employing TRANSPARENCY. (See also G-OCTREE, OCTREE, TRANSPARENCY, and VOXEL.)
[Sabella-88]

CRT
See CATHODE RAY TUBE.

CSG
See CONSTRUCTIVE SOLID GEOMETRY.

CSG tree
A CSG tree describes a 3-D model constructed from primitive volumes with the boolean operators intersection, union and difference in a hierarchical binary tree structure. This DATA STRUCTURE is then processed by a RENDERER to realize a view of the model. (See also CONSTRUCTIVE SOLID GEOMETRY.)
[Burger-89]

cube
A cube is a PLATONIC OBJECT constructed from six squares. Within the nomenclature of polyhedra the cube is also known as a hexahedron. (See also PLATONIC OBJECTS.)
[Critchlow-69, Gasson-83]

cubic
A cubic is a POLYNOMIAL equation with no terms with a power greater than three. For example, the following is a cubic POLYNOMIAL in x:

$$y = ax^3 + bx^2 + cx + d$$

(See also BLENDING FUNCTION, LINEAR, MONOMIAL BASIS, PARAMETRIC EQUATION, POLYNOMIAL, and QUADRATIC.)

cubic curve

A cubic curve can be defined by a third-degree POLYNOMIAL and is the simplest curve to contain a point of inflection. The cubic also tends to be a popular curve in SURFACE MODELLING schemes, as fourth-degree curves and above can introduce further points of inflection that become difficult to control. (See also LINEAR, PARAMETRIC POLYNOMIAL, POLYNOMIAL, QUADRATIC, and RATIONAL POLYNOMIAL.)
[Blinn-89d]

culling

Culling is a term applied to any process that removes specific elements from a scene, such as BACK FACE REMOVAL. (See also BACK FACE REMOVAL.)

cursor

A cursor is a shape which can be displayed upon a display screen as part of a locating or pointing device in interactive systems. (See also CURSOR-CONTROL KEYS, MOUSE, PICK DEVICE and LIGHT PEN.)

cursor-control keys

Cursor-control keys are special keys on a computer keyboard used for positioning the display's CURSOR, or for similar positioning tasks in interactive applications.

curves of constant parameter

Curves of constant parameter, or isoparametric curves, are curves existing on a PARAMETRIC SURFACE PATCH where one of the parameters changes whilst the other remains fixed. (See also PARAMETER, PARAMETRIC CURVE, and PARAMETRIC SURFACE PATCH.)

cushioning

In traditional animation the terms EASING, SLOW IN/SLOW OUT and cushioning are used to describe the action of smoothing one movement into another. In COMPUTER ANIMATION it is implemented by using BLENDING FUNCTIONS that may be sensitive to the current frame or an equivalent parameter. (See also EASING, INBETWEENING, and SLOW IN/SLOW OUT.)
[Lasseter-87, Magnenat–Thalman-85]

cyclical overlapping polygons

Cyclical overlapping polygons occur when two or more polygons partly mask one another in a cyclic fashion. For example, given three polygons A, B and C, A could be slightly covering B, which in turn could be partly masking C, which itself could be masking part of A. This arrangement can cause problems in priority sequences in HIDDEN-LINE and HIDDEN-SURFACE REMOVAL ALGORITHMS. (See also DEPTH SORT ALGORITHM, HIDDEN-LINE REMOVAL, HIDDEN-SURFACE REMOVAL, PAINTER'S ALGORITHM, and Z-BUFFER ALGORITHM.)
[Foley-90, Rogers-85]

Cyrus–Beck algorithm

The Cyrus–Beck clipping algorithm exploits the DOT PRODUCT operation to determine points of intersection with a 2-D CONVEX POLYGON or a 3-D CONVEX OBJECT. At the heart of the 2-D algorithm is the idea that if a VECTOR is constructed from one edge of the clipping boundary, and a second VECTOR is formed from a vertex on this edge and a point on the line to be clipped, the angle between these vectors can be computed with the DOT PRODUCT operation. Furthermore, if the point on the line to be clipped is expressed in a PARAMETRIC form, the precise point of intersection (if any), can easily be detected when the angle is zero. (See also ADAPTIVE CLIPPING, CLIPPING, CLIPPING DIVIDER, and COHEN–SUTHERLAND ALGORITHM.)
[Burger-89, Rogers-85]

DAC
See DIGITAL-TO-ANALOGUE CONVERTER.

dark light
Dark light or BLACK LIGHT is an abstract concept employed in some renderers whereby 'dark light' sources subtract light instead of radiating. This is a convenient method of achieving subtle shadows in specific parts of a scene.

data base
A data base is a structure employed to organize large quantities of data such that it can be interrogated efficiently without necessarily having to investigate every item. A data base is a collection of data records which are associated with pointers that allow related items to be linked together in the form of lists, chains and trees, that provide the mechanism for the data base's traversal.

DataGlove
The DataGlove developed by VPL Research Inc. is a hand glove which monitors hand position and finger movements; these signals can be input to a computer graphics system and be used to manipulate elements within a 3-D virtual environment. (See also VIRTUAL REALITY.)

data structure
A data structure is a memory organization which maintains data in a format to ensure that individual items are easily accessed and processed. (See also GRAPHICAL DATA STRUCTURE.)
[Samet-88a, Samet-88b, Standish-80]

data tablet
See TABLET.

DDA
See DIGITAL DIFFERNTIAL ANALYZER.

degree
(1) A degree is a unit of angular measurement and by definition there are 360 to one complete circular rotation. 360° is also equal to 2π radians.
(2) The degree of a POLYNOMIAL refers to the highest power associated with its MONOMIAL terms. Equations with degree one to five are referred to as linear, quadratic, cubic, quartic, and quintic respectively.

delta form-factors
In RADIOSITY calculations the HEMI-CUBE is used in place of a hemi-sphere to identify the energy exchanges between a pair of sub-patches. The delta form-factors represent the micro FORM-FACTORS for the individual cells covering the hemi-cube, which are computed OFF-LINE. When the cells involved in an interchange of diffuse radiation between two sub-patches are identified, the relevant delta form-factors are summed to obtain the total FORM-FACTOR. Recent research has revealed that the hemi-cube approximation can lead to numerical instability. See Figure D-1. (See also FORM-FACTOR, HEMI-CUBE, PROGRESSIVE RADIOSITY, and RADIOSITY.)
[Cohen-85]

DEM
See DIGITAL ELEVATION MODEL.

depth buffer
See Z-BUFFER.

depth clipping
Depth clipping is the process of dynamically altering the position of the back CLIPPING PLANE to remove unwanted detail presented to the user. These features are generally found on high-performance graphics workstations. (See also CLIPPING, DEPTH CUE PLANES, and DEPTH CUES.)
[Foley-90]

depth coherence
SCAN-LINE ALGORITHMS exploit depth coherence to prevent unnecessary computations being made for each SCAN-LINE, for if the ACTIVE LIST references identical edges to the preceding line, and they are in the same order, then no changes in depth relationships can have occurred. (See

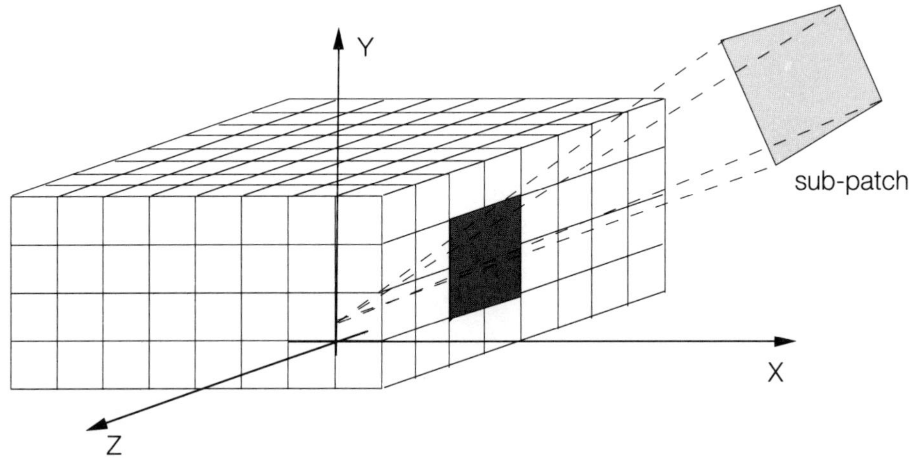

Figure D-1 *The above hemi-cube shows how the five surfaces are divided into pixels for which delta form factors are known. By projecting a sub-patch back to the origin of the hemi-cube, it is possible to identify those pixels that would intercept any energy exchange between the reference sub-patch and the one under investigation. If the delta form factors for these pixels is summed, an approximate form factor for the sub-patches is found.*

also ACTIVE LIST, AREA COHERENCE, COHERENCE, and EDGE COHERENCE.)
[Rogers-85, Romney-68]

depth cue planes
Depth cue planes are two reference planes ORTHOGONAL to the eye's Z-axis between which DEPTH CUE scaling factors operate. (See also DEPTH CUES.)
[Foley-90]

depth cues
Depth cues, which includes intensity modulation, increase our perception of spatial depth – for example, on VECTOR DISPLAYS the brightness of a vector can be attenuated according to its depth from the observer, which assists the user in interpreting the intersecting lines on a screen as lines imbedded in 3-D space. Intensity depth cueing is controlled by a pair of DEPTH CUE PLANES and is supported by PHIGS+. (See also DEPTH CUE PLANES.)
[Burger-89, Gregory-86]

depth map
A depth map is used for identifying SHADOW VOLUMES, and is actually the Z-DEPTHS created when a Z-BUFFER ALGORITHM is applied at the position of a light source. If the z-depths represent the nearest surfaces to the light source, any points beyond these values must be in shadow (for this light source); therefore, Z-DEPTHS with respect to the observer can be compared with depth maps for the light sources to discover whether the point is visible or in shadow. (See also SHADOWS, SHADOW VOLUME, Z-BUFFER, and Z-DEPTH.)
[Reeves-87]

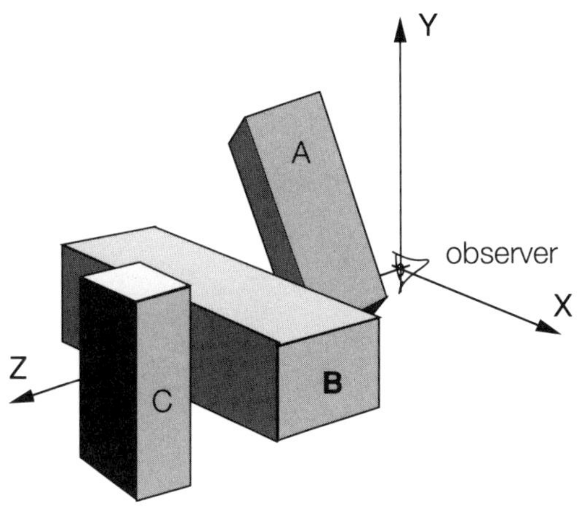

Figure D-2 *The depth-sort algorithm sorts objects into a z-depth sequence and renders them into a frame store in decreasing z-depth distance: eg C, B, A. Although this could overwrite pixels several times, it is effective and simple to implement.*

depth of field

The depth of field of a lens defines the distance range in its object space over which an in-focus image is created; outside these limits, the image appears blurred. The depth of field varies inversely with APERTURE and the ideal PINHOLE CAMERA has an infinite depth of field. Such optical effects can also be simulated within RAY TRACING. (See also APERTURE, CAUSTIC, CHROMATIC ABERRATION, CIRCLE OF CONFUSION, F-NUMBER, FOCAL PLANE, and RAY TRACING.)
[Burger-89, Chen-87, Glassner-89, Potmesil-81, Potmesil-82]

depth perception

Depth perception relates to the ability of the human visual system to recognize on an image elements of a scene that are more distant than others. Stereoscopic vision is a powerful aid to this process, as well as illumination, colour, shadows and cultural factors. (See also DEPTH CUE PLANES, DEPTH CUES, PARALLAX, STEREOSCOPIC DISPLAY, and STEREOPSIS.)
[Gregory-86]

depth sort algorithm

Newell, Newell and Sancha developed the depth sort algorithm as a simple method of achieving HIDDEN-SURFACE REMOVAL. It sorts polygons according to their largest Z-DEPTH and renders them in a descending depth sequence. As it is sensitive to relative Z-DEPTHS between polygons, CYCLICAL OVERLAPPING POLYGONS must be resolved into simple overlap conditions. See Figure D-2. (See also CYCLICAL OVERLAPPING POLYGONS, HIDDEN-SURFACE REMOVAL, and Z-DEPTH.)
[Newell-72]

derivative

The mathematical concept of the first derivative of a function identifies the slope at any point, whilst the second derivative describes the rate of change of the slope. Slope CONTINUITY of PIECEWISE CURVES and surfaces is achieved by maintaining first- and second-derivatives over boundaries. (See also CONTINUITY.)
[Burger-89]

desk-top publishing (DTP)

Desk-top publishing refers to computer-based systems that allow a user to interactively layout text and images often in a WYSIWYG environment. DTP systems provide facilities such as FONT selection, font scaling, page numbering, headers and footers, automatic index generation, illustrations, left, central and right justification, and mathematical and scientific notation. (See also WIMP ENVIRONMENT and WYSIWYG.)

determinant

Determinants arise naturally in the solution of linear equations and provide a compact way of expressing a numerical operation. For example, the expression ($ab - cd$) can be represented by the following 2 x 2 determinant

$$\begin{vmatrix} a & d \\ c & b \end{vmatrix}$$

which is evaluated by subtracting the cross-product of the diagonal terms. When the determinat evaluation is performed upon a square MATRIX , it is possible that the numerical result is zero – such matrices are known as singular. (See also CHARACTERISTIC ROOTS, MATRIX, MATRIX OPERATIONS, INVERSE MATRIX, and TRANSPOSE MATRIX.)

deterministic
The term deterministic means predictable and non-random in nature – a system whose future is determined by its past and current state. Many examples of DYNAMICAL SYSTEMS are deterministic, however they may nevertheless exhibit unpredictable CHAOTIC BEHAVIOUR. (See also CHAOS THEORY, CHAOTIC BEHAVIOUR, DYNAMICAL SYSTEMS, ORBIT, and STOCHASTIC.)

device coordinate system
The device dependent coordinate system in which a specific hardware device is addressed is called the device coordinate system. Device coordinates are normally computed from the device independent NORMALIZED DEVICE COORDINATES. (See also NORMALIZED DEVICE COORDINATES, PHYSICAL DEVICE COORDINATES, DEVICE DEPENDENT, DEVICE INDEPENDENT, and SCREEN COORDINATES.)
[Burger-89, Foley-90, Hearn-86]

device dependent
Device dependent systems reflect a dependence upon some specific hardware device, such as the number of pens on a graph plotter, or the number of available colours on a graphics screen. (See also DEVICE INDEPENDENT.)
[Burger-89]

device driver
Programs which interface peripherals to a computer system's application software are called device drivers; such drivers are needed for X–Y PLOTTERS, TABLETS and FRAME STORES.

device independent
Device independent systems reflect a degree of system independence from associated external hardware devices. Standards such as GKS and PHIGS attempt to isolate the internal computer graphics environment from the external hardware devices, thus making portability easier. (See also DEVICE DEPENDENT, GKS, GKS-3D, NDC, PHIGS, and PHIGS+.)
[Burger-89, Sproull-85]

dicing
Dicing is a term used in the REYES rendering system where polygons are 'diced' into MICROPOLYGONS, which are flat-shaded QUADRILATERALS with sides approximately half a pixel. (See also MICROPOLYGON and REYES.)
[Cook-87]

diffraction of light
When light is obstructed by an object(s) whose size is comparable with its WAVELENGTH, it undergoes a change of direction referred to as diffraction. Diffraction gratings are formed by a set of closely spaced objects (usually opaque lines) and may be used to mimic some of the optical effects performed by lenses and mirrors. As yet, the phenomenon has not been incorporated within RAY TRACING because the effect does not often occur in everyday scenes under normal illumination. (See also REFRACTION OF LIGHT.)
[Jenkins-76]

diffuse inter-reflections
Diffuse inter-reflections occur when two or more illuminated surfaces reflect diffusely between each other. To resolve this optical interaction, a steady-state condition relating the light energy exchanges for each surface must be computed, which is the objective of RADIOSITY. RAY TRACING is unable to compete with the RADIOSITY approach

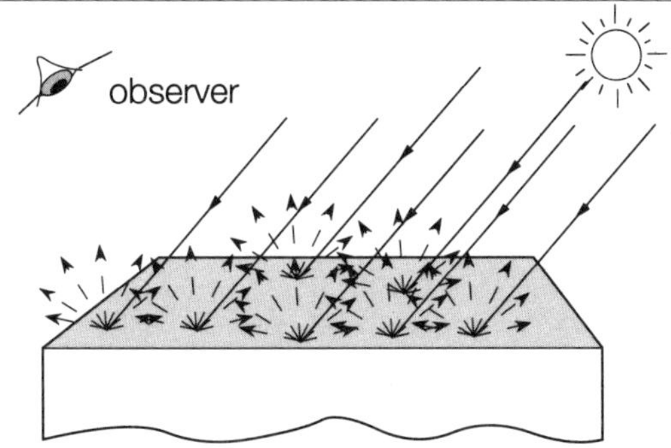

Figure D-3 *A perfect diffuse reflector reflects incident light away from the surface in random directions, with the result that the perceived brightness is independent of the view position, but dependent on the angle of incidence.*

in handling diffuse inter-reflections, in the same way that RADIOSITY finds difficulty in simulating the SPECULAR REFLECTIONS and REFRACTIONS handled so elegantly by RAY TRACING. (See also AMBIENT LIGHT, DIFFUSE REFLECTION, FORM-FACTOR, GLOBAL ILLUMINATION MODEL, ILLUMINATION MODEL, RADIOSITY, RAY TRACING, REFRACTION OF LIGHT, and SPECULAR REFLECTION.)
[Baum-89, Cohen-88, Immel-86, Rushmeier-87, Sillion-89, Wallace- 87, Wallace-89]

diffuse reflection
An illuminated perfect MATTE surface is a source of diffuse reflections, as any incident light is randomly reflected back into the illumination space. The intensity of a DIFFUSE SURFACE is dependent upon its orientation relative to the light source, but independent of the observer's position following LAMBERT'S COSINE LAW. See Figure D-3. (See also AMBIENT LIGHT, COSINE SHADING, DIFFUSE REFLECTION COEFFICIENT, DIFFUSE SURFACE, GLOBAL ILLUMINATION MODEL, GOURAUD SHADING, ILLUMINATION MODEL, LAMBERT'S COSINE LAW, MATTE, AND SPECULAR REFLECTION.)
[Burger-89, Foley-90, Glassner-89, Hearn-86, Rogers-85]

diffuse reflection coefficient
A fractional value called the diffuse reflection coefficient is used to control the amount of incident non-ambient light reflected from a MATTE surface. Three such coefficients are needed to control the three primary colour components that may be illuminating a surface. (See also AMBIENT REFLECTION COEFFICIENT, AMBIENT LIGHT, DIFFUSE REFLECTION, DIFFUSE TRANSMISSION, GOURAUD SHADING, MATTE, and SPECULAR REFLECTION COEFFICIENT.)
[Burger-89, Foley-90, Gouraud-71, Hearn-86, Rogers-85]

diffuse surface
A diffuse surface is one which reflects light equally in all directions and obeys LAMBERT'S COSINE LAW. See Figure D-3. (See also DIFFUSE REFLECTION, DIFFUSE REFLECTION COEFFICIENT, and LAMBERT'S COSINE LAW.)
[Burger-89, Foley-90, Hearn-86, Rogers-85]

diffuse transmission
Impurities in a transmissive medium can interfere with the transmitted light, causing it to be randomly disturbed on its journey through the medium. This phenomenon is called diffuse transmission and such materials are referred to as translucent. (See also TRANSLUCENCY and TRANSLUCENT SURFACE.)
[Burger-89, Foley-90, Glassner-89, Jenkins-76]

digital chroma keying
CHROMA KEYING is a video technique where one VIDEO SIGNAL can be superimposed upon another depending upon a chroma key, whereas digital chroma keying allows any colour or other digital attribute to become the key, without having to resort to a highly saturated colour such as the blue commonly used in television chroma keying. (See also CHROMA KEYING, KEYING, MATTE, and VIDEO SIGNAL.)

digital computer
A digital computer is an electronic processor capable of manipulating digitally encoded data under the control of a changeable stored program of instructions. (See also PROGRAM.)

digital differential analyzer (DDA)
A DDA is a technique for generating straight lines upon a raster display device and functions by specifying the equation of a line in its differential form (i.e. in terms of its differential slope). Unfortunately, it suffers from various limitations, the major one being its dependency upon floating point arithmetic. (See also BRESENHAM'S ALGORITHM.)
[Burger-89]

digital elevation data
Digital elevation data or height fields are data sets of geographical terrain which form the basis of 3-D terrain models. (See also DIGITAL ELEVATION MODEL and TERRAIN MODELLING.)
[Thiemann-89]

digital elevation model (DEM)
A digital elevation model is a block of DIGITAL ELEVATION DATA describing a specific area of the Earth. The United States Geographical Survey (USGS) provides blocks 7.5 minutes of arc square covering approximately 60 square miles, with data points spaced 30 metres apart. The Defence Mapping Agency (DMA) supplies blocks 1 degree square, with the data points spaced approximately 200 feet apart. Such HEIGHT FIELDS can be combined with satellite images to create realistic 3-D terrains, and ultimately used in FLIGHT SIMULATORS for military mission rehearsal scenarios. (See also DIGITAL ELEVATION DATA and TERRAIN MODELLING.)
[Thiemann-89]

digital mixing
Digital mixing refers to the combination of two digital streams representing the LUMINANCE and CHROMINANCE levels of a digital VIDEO SIGNAL. (See also CHROMINANCE, DIGITAL CHROMA KEYING, LUMINANCE, and VIDEO SIGNAL.)

digital signal
As opposed to an ANALOGUE SIGNAL, a digital signal can take on only a discrete number of levels. A binary signal only has two states, represented by the 1 or 0 symbols of the binary code. Digital computers function by manipulating such signals. (See also ANALOGUE SIGNALS, BINARY, BIT, and DIGITAL COMPUTER.)

digital signal processor (DSP)
A digital signal processor is designed specifically to undertake mathematical operations on digital signals. DSPs are useful in IMAGE PROCESSING and computer graphics to perform operations including MATRIX OPERATIONS, CONVOLUTION, FILTERING, and waveform analysis.

digital-to-analogue converter (DAC)
Continuous ANALOGUE SIGNALS are converted into a digital form by a device called a digital-to-analogue converter. A typical application for such converters is in the conversion of FRAME STORE data into RGB analogue signals to drive a colour monitor. (See also ANALOGUE SIGNALS, ANALOGUE-TO-DIGITAL CONVERTER, and DIGITAL SIGNAL.)

digitizer
(1) **2-D**: A digitizer is an active surface and control unit, which generates positional data for an associated pen or puck when in near or direct contact with the surface. Artwork attached to this surface can be manually converted into CARTESIAN COORDINATES by probing the individual contours in some ordered fashion. (See also CARTESIAN COORDINATES.)
(2) **3-D**: A digitizer can employ transducers or a robotic arm to probe a model and generate positional data. Such a device can be used to input the geometry of a complex form where it would be too difficult to model its surface by conventional modelling techniques. (See also CARTESIAN COORDINATES and MODELLING.)

digitizing
Digitizing is the process of capturing real-world data, either manually with a DIGITIZER or in the case of an image automatically with a video camera and FRAME GRABBER. (See also DIGITIZER, FRAME GRABBER, GRAPHICS TABLET, SCANNER, and TABLET.)

directional light source

(1) A directional light source is assumed to be located at infinity and emits light in only one direction; the sun is a good example if one only considers the light reaching the surface of the earth. (See also DISTRIBUTED LIGHT SOURCE, ILLUMINATION MODEL, LIGHT SOURCE, LIGHT SOURCE DIRECTION, POINT LIGHT SOURCE, and SPOT LIGHT.)

(2) In FLIGHT SIMULATOR computer graphics, a directional light source is used to simulate the visual approach slope indicators (VASI), which point into the sky and provide visual descent guidance to the pilot during the approach to a runway. The visibility of such light sources depends upon the relative orientation between the observer and the light.

[Schachter-83]

direction cosines

The components of a UNIT VECTOR are also known as direction cosines and are an essential mathematical concept in the analysis of rotation operations, and surfaces. See Figure D-4. (See also NORMALIZATION, POINT VECTOR, UNIT VECTOR, and VECTOR.)

[Burger-89, Gasson-83, Rogers-89]

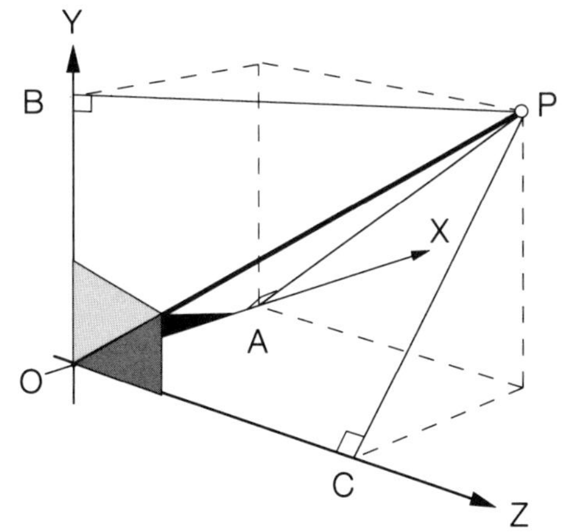

Figure D-4 *The cosines of the shaded angles between the axes and the vector OP are its direction cosines and are computed from the ratios OA/OP, OB/OP and OC/OP. When the vector is a unit vector, the direction cosines are simply the X-, Y- and Z-components of the vector.*

direction cube

Haines and Greenberg introduced the idea of a direction cube as part of their LIGHT BUFFER algorithm. It is used for accelerating shadow calculations, and effectively surrounds every light source so that different zones of the cube's surface can maintain lists of objects capable of creating SHADOW VOLUMES for light rays travelling through the zone. As this computation is undertaken prior to rendering, a RAY TRACING algorithm has much of its intersection testing considerably reduced. (See also HEMI-CUBE, LIGHT BUFFER, LIGHT SOURCE, RADIOSITY, RAY TRACING, SHADOWS, and SHADOW VOLUME.)

[Glassner-89, Haines-86]

discrete convolution

See CONVOLUTION.

disjoint polygon

In AREA SUBDIVISION ALGORITHMS a disjoint polygon is totally outside some reference rectangular window – and represents one of the possible conditions detected in the space division process. (See also AREA SUBDIVISION ALGORITHMS, CONTAINED POLYGON, INTERSECTING POLYGON, SURROUNDING POLYGON, and WARNOCK ALGORITHM.)

[Rogers-85, Warnock-69]

displacement animation

Displacement animation is a technique where an object constructed from facets can be animated into another object having a similar number of facets and vertices. The original and guiding secondary objects enable vectors to be constructed, along which the displaced vertices travel, with the displacement controlled para-

metrically. Intermediate objects with similar facet numbers may also be introduced so that the original object can be animated using the vector sum of the displacing objects. (See also COLLISION DETECTION, COMPUTER ANIMATION, ELASTICALLY DEFORMABLE OBJECTS, FREE-FORM DEFORMATION, PROCEDURAL ANIMATION, and RIGID-BODY ANIMATION.)
[Gourret-89, Schafer-89]

displacement mapping
Whereas BUMP MAPPING creates a pseudo surface finish by perturbing the SURFACE NORMAL, displacement mapping actually disturbs the geometry of a surface by the map value. (See also BUMP MAP, BUMP MAPPING, and DISPLACEMENT ANIMATION.)

displacement shader
The displacement shader is a feature of RENDERMAN and governs the rendering aspects of surfaces modified by SURFACE NORMAL displacements; i.e. BUMP MAPPING. (See also BUMP MAP, BUMP MAPPING, RENDERMAN, and SURFACE NORMAL.)
[Cook-87]

display file
A display file stores a DISPLAY LIST of graphical commands which are to be interpreted by some graphics processing environment. (See also DISPLAY LIST, PHIGS, and PHIGS+.)

display list
A display list is a sequence of graphics commands held within a DISPLAY FILE directing the display processor. Such lists will include commands instructing the processor to switch into different display modes and perform graphic operations undertaken in hardware. (See also DISPLAY FILE, PHIGS, and PHIGS+.)

distance
The distance or Euclidean distance between two points, is generally computed using the rule of Pythagoras. In the 2-D case, the distance between two points $[x_1, y_1]$ and $[x_2, y_2]$ is

$$\sqrt{(x_2 - x_1)^2 + (y_2 - y_1)^2}$$

whereas in the 3-D case the distance between two points $[x_1, y_1, z_1]$ and $[x_2, y_2, z_2]$ is

$$\sqrt{(x_2 - x_1)^2 + (y_2 - y_1)^2 + (z_2 - z_1)^2}$$

distributed light source
A distributed light source radiates energy over a defined area, rather than from a single POINT LIGHT SOURCE. This gives rise to shadow penumbrae which have been effectively simulated using DISTRIBUTED RAY TRACING. (See also DIRECTIONAL LIGHT SOURCE, GLOBAL ILLUMINATION MODEL, LIGHT SOURCE, POINT LIGHT SOURCE, and SPOT LIGHT.)
[Foley-90, Glassner-88]

distributed ray tracing
Distributed ray tracing or probabilistic RAY TRACING is concerned with the rendering of effects such as MOTION BLUR, DEPTH OF FIELD, PENUMBRA and TRANSLUCENCY within a RAY TRACING environment. In computing these fuzzy phenomena, light rays having a STOCHASTIC distribution are used to sample space and time to integrate approximately the optical effect at any one pixel. Because of the STOCHASTIC nature of the SAMPLING, ALIASING artifacts are considerably reduced and are replaced by a NOISE artifact, which is much more acceptable to the human visual system. For example, blurry reflections can be simulated by integrating the effect of light rays distributed according to some specular distribution function, and MOTION BLUR can be effected by integrating light rays distributed over some time interval. (See also ALIASING, ANTI-ALIASING, ARTIFACT, BEAM TRACING, CONE TRACING, DEPTH OF FIELD, MOTION BLUR, NOISE, PENUMBRA, PHOTOREALISM, RAY TRACING, STOCHASTIC, STOCHASTIC SAMPLING, and TRANSLUCENCY.)
[Cook-84, Cook-86, Glassner-89, Lee-85]

distributed rendering
Distributed rendering describes a rendering activity distributed over a network of processors where each processor has an identical copy of the RENDERER and returns

rendered whole or partial frames. (See also PARALLEL RENDERING and RENDERER.)
[Potmesil-87]

dithering
Dithering involves the addition of small random intensities (dithering noise) to an image to mask the ALIASING artifacts created by edges on BI-LEVEL DISPLAYS. (See also ALIASING, ANTI-ALIASING, BI-LEVEL DISPLAY, and HALFTONING.)
[Burger-89, Floyd-75, Pins-89, Pirsch-83]

divide and conquer
A popular strategy in algorithm design is called divide and conquer, and describes a process where a problem feature is repeatedly divided into smaller elements until it can be classified and processed to give an unambiguous result. AREA SUBDIVISION ALGORITHMS such as Catmull's and Warnock's display algorithms exploit this strategy. See Figure A-4. (See also AREA COHERENCE, AREA SUBDIVISION ALGORITHMS, COHERENCE, and WARNOCK ALGORITHM.)
[Catmull-74a, Catmull-75, Warnock-69]

dodecahedron
A dodecahedron is a PLATONIC OBJECT constructed from 12 HEXAGONS.
[Critchlow-69, Gasson-83]

dominant wavelength
When an observer perceives a dominant colour within a radiant light source, the spectral energy of the source will reveal a dominant wavelength causing this effect. It is also associated with purity and luminosity. (See also BRIGHTNESS, CHROMATIC LIGHT, COLOUR, HUE, PURITY, SATURATION, and SPECTRAL COLOUR.)
[Hunt-75]

dot-clock frequency
See VIDEO FREQUENCY.

dot product
See SCALAR PRODUCT.

double buffering
Double buffering is a strategy for improving processing efficiency when handling input–output devices such as printers, plotters and FRAME STORES. For example, in the case of a double-buffered FRAME STORE, one store would be used for holding the current image under construction, whilst a second store would be holding the previous constructed image being currently viewed. When the new image is formed, the system switches stores (sometimes called a 'ping-pong' arrangement), thus allowing the overlapping of two conflicting operations. Buffering also allows simple animation effects to be produced.

dragging
In INTERACTIVE COMPUTER GRAPHICS systems, dragging refers to the action whereby specific graphic elements can be physically 'dragged' (i.e. 'picked, moved and unpicked') across the screen to a new position. (See also HUMAN–COMPUTER INTEACTION and WIMP ENVIRONMENT.)
[Bier-86a]

drop-frame time code
SMPTE TIME CODE format is also referred to as a drop-frame time code, as it skips (drops) two frames per minute except on the tenth minute so that the time code stays in phase with real elapsed time. This is because the NTSC frame rate is not 30 Hz, but 29.97 Hz. (See also NTSC, SMPTE, and TIME CODE.)

dropshadow
A dropshadow is a graphical technique of introducing a shadow projected onto a plane beneath the original shape. It is a feature found in many PAINT SYSTEMS.

DSP
See DIGITAL SIGNAL PROCESSOR.

DST or D-STN
DST or D-STN is an acronym for Double-layer SuperTwist Nematic, as used in LIQUID CRYSTAL DISPLAY technology.

Such a display consists of two layers of liquid crystal material the rear layer called the 'driven' layer contains the active cells, whilst the front layer is a transparent liquid-crystal material to compensate colour-distortion originating in the driver layer due to birefringence.

DTP

See DESK-TOP PUBLISHING.

DXF

DXF is a language used by Autodesk for describing data models in Autocad. It has become a *de facto* standard.

dynamic constraints

The ANIMATION of physically constrained systems involving linkages, springs, gravitational fields etc. is governed by dynamic constraints. The technique of INVERSE DYNAMICS is used to compute the forces constraining the objects, so that these may be applied in the animation system to create natural movements. (See also COLLISION DETECTION, COMPUTER ANIMATION, DISPLACEMENT ANIMATION, ELASTICALLY DEFORMABLE OBJECTS, GOAL-ORIENTED ANIMATION, INVERSE DYNAMICS, RIGID-BODY ANIMATION, and PROCEDURAL ANIMATION.)

[Barzel-88, Moore-88, Platt-88, Wilhelms-85, Witkin-88]

dynamical systems

Dynamical systems are systems which evolve in time according to some rules (implicit or explicit) such as weather patterns, stocks and shares, international money exchanges, inter-cellular activity and magnetic storms on the sun. Describing and modelling dynamic systems on a computer has traditionally employed DETERMINISTIC approaches; however, CHAOS THEORY has transformed our understanding of dynamic behaviour by providing mechanisms for introducing instability without introducing randomness. (See also CHAOS THEORY, CHAOTIC BEHAVIOUR, JULIA SETS, and ORBIT.)

[Devaney-86, Gleick-87, Peitgen-88]

easing

The technique of altering the speed of an animated object is called easing. To achieve this, a BLENDING or CUSHIONING function is employed to control the speed. However, as motion plays a key role in convincing the observer to accept computer-generated images as real, unless the motion reflects the physical properties of the simulated object, the images remain unconvincing. FORWARD DYNAMICS overcomes these problems by computing acceleration values from a given set of forces, but such techniques are still impractical for many situations. Therefore the animator must resort to the use of B-SPLINE CURVES and adjusting its bias and tension to achieve a sense of realism. (See also BLENDING FUNCTION, B-SPLINE CURVE, CUSHIONING, and SLOW IN/SLOW OUT.)
[Lasseter-87, Magnenat-Thalman-85, White-86]

ECL

ECL is an acronym for Emitter Coupled Logic and refers to a type of integrated circuit fabrication capable of very high speeds. The technology is employed in the CCIR 656 interface where it is used in transmission distances over 100 metres. (See also TTL.)

edge

An edge is either part of the border of a shape or a line formed where two surfaces meet. It is either explicitly defined by specifying two end vertices, as supported by the WINGED-EDGE DATA STRUCTURE, or formed when two surfaces intersect as in CONSTRUCTIVE SOLID GEOMETRY. (See also CONSTRUCTIVE SOLID GEOMETRY, EULER'S RULE, HANGING EDGE, MODELLING, and WINGED-EDGE DATA STRUCTURE.)

edge coherence

Because facet edges generally intersect several RASTER LINES, SCAN-LINE ALGORITHMS exploit edge coherence by maintaining an active list of edges for the current raster. This IMAGE SPACE coherence enables edge intersections to be maintained on an incremental basis, when moving to the next raster, thus avoiding having to recompute the active facets for each raster. (See also AREA COHERENCE, COHERENCE, DEPTH COHERENCE, and SCAN-LINE ALGORITHM.)
[Burger-89, Foley-90, Rogers-85]

EGA

EGA is an acronym for Enhanced Graphics Adaptor and is a standard for a graphics board used in personal computers, with 16 colours from a palette of 64 up to a resolution of approximately 640 by 350. (See also CGA, HDA, HGC, MCGA, MDA, PVA, SUPER VGA, and VGA.)
[Burger-89]

elastically deformable objects

Elastically deformable objects such as flags, faces, tyres, curtains and plastic materials, demand special attention if their physical properties are to be modelled realistically. One method of deforming such objects is to divide surfaces into triangles or volumes into tetrahedra, and apply FINITE ELEMENT ANALYSIS techniques. But where objects interfere with one another, COLLISION DETECTION must also be investigated to prevent interpenetration. Another powerful technique is that of DISPLACEMENT ANIMATION, but this would require special procedures to animate the object as though it were obeying the laws of physics. (See also COLLISION DETECTION, DISPLACEMENT ANIMATION, DYNAMIC CONSTRAINTS, FINITE ELEMENT ANALYSIS, FREE-FORM DEFORMATION, and RIGID-BODY ANIMATION.)
[Terzopoulos-87, Terzopoulos-88b, Waters-87, Weil-86]

electroluminescent displays

Electroluminescent displays are flat screen devices exploiting the phenomenon of electroluminescence, where light is generated from a luminescent film when an electric field is applied. The film, which can be made from manganese-activated zinc sulphide, is only several atomic layers thick. These devices might eventually be employed in televisions and computer graphics workstations. (See also CATHODE RAY TUBE and LIQUID CRYSTAL DISPLAY.)

electrophotographic plotter

Electrophotographic plotters generate a tone-based output similar to an ELECTROSTATIC PLOTTER, the main difference being that a light source is used to charge selected areas of the paper, rather than an electrostatic writing head. (See also ELECTROSTATIC PLOTTER, FLATBED PLOTTER, and INK JET PLOTTER.)

electrostatic plotter

An electrostatic plotter utilizes the data in an image in raster format to control the modulation of the electrostatic nibs on a print head; These charge selected areas of the paper which attract the visible toner. (See also ELECTROPHOTOGRAPHIC PLOTTER, INK JET PLOTTER, and X-Y PLOTTER.)

emittance

The light energy emitted by a surface, or emittance, is a term employed in RADIOSITY calculations when describing the energy interchanges between illuminated surfaces. (See also FORM-FACTORS and RADIOSITY.)

environment mapping

Environment mapping is a rendering technique employing TEXTURE MAPS to create the impression of high-gloss surfaces such as mirrors and polished metal surfaces. One approach producing highly realistic effects is to surround the reference object with a six-sided box, whose sides will effectively hold the TEXTURE MAPS. These, perhaps, have been captured photographically using a wide-angle lens or have been created synthetically. A RENDERER can then determine which map is visible on any surface, and apply the reflected TEXELS to the relevant PIXELS. (See also BUMP MAPPING, CHROME SHADING, TEXTURE MAP, and TEXTURE MAPPING.)
[Cabral-87]

equilateral triangle

An equilateral triangle has sides of equal length, implying that internal angles are equal to 60°. (See also ISOSCELES TRIANGLE and TRIANGLE.)
[Gasson-83]

erosion models

Erosion models are associated with fractal terrain modelling schemes where they are used to improve realism by simulating phenomena such as weathering, drainage and sediment transport dynamics. (See also FRACTAL GEOMETRY and STOCHASTIC MODELLING.)
[Kelley-88, Mandelbrot-82, Musgrave-89]

Ethernet

Ethernet is a form of Local Area Network (LAN) used for interconnecting computers and terminals. A maximum of 1000 stations may be connected to a single coaxial cable up to 2 km long, transmitting data at a theoretical maximum rate of 10 Mbaud, but system overheads reduce this to a feasible 0.6 Mbaud.

Euclidean distance

Euclidean distance is a measure of DISTANCE as used in Euclidean geometry and is equal to the shortest distance between two points.

Euler angles

When rotating objects about a point, the rotation can be specified as three angular rotations about the X-, Y- and Z-axes; such angles are known as Euler angles. Although they can be very useful, they can lead to singularities when used to control the dynamics of an animated observer, especially when the observer is directed at the origin along one of the axes. QUATERNIONS are used to overcome these problems. (See also QUATERNIONS.)

Euler's rule

Euler's rule states that, for a POLYHEDRON without holes, the number of edges is always two less than the sum of the numbers of faces and vertices.This rule is maintained by the WINGED-EDGE DATA STRUCTURE. (See also POLYHEDRON and WINGED-EDGE DATA STRUCTURE.)
[Woodwark-86]

events

Interactive computer graphics systems respond to events, which are interrupts, usually user-generated, such as those caused by a MOUSE or STYLUS. Events may

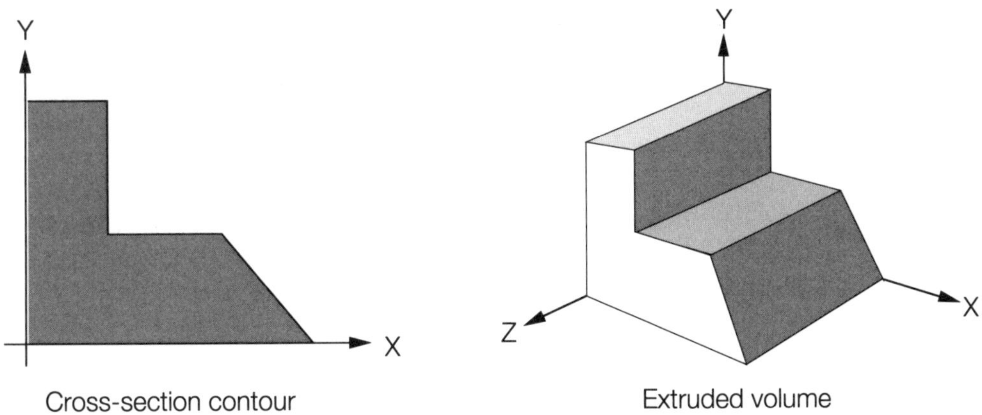

Figure E-1 *Extruding a cross-sectional shape through a distance is a basic modelling process and can be implemented by a procedure which only requires the extruding distance and the contour to build the final volume. In this example, there are 6 edges in the original contour, which generate the 8 facets in the extruded volume. A natural extension to this technique is to apply a degree of rotation to the cross-section at each stage of construction; this allows the building of screw threads and spiral-like forms.*

be SYNCHRONOUS and happen at predetermined times, or ASYNCHRONOUS and happen at any time.
[Burger-89]

expert system
An expert system is a computer system driven by a set of rules obtained from expert knowledge, which are then referred to during the processing of relevant data. Expert systems can be applied in any application where a decision is based upon evaluating complex choices against a set of rules describing the actions to take. (See also DATA BASE and DATA STRUCTURE.)

explicit surface
The geometry of an explicit surface is defined parametrically, for example a BICUBIC PATCH. The surface is 'explicit' as any point on the surface can be identified using two parameters, whereas ALGEBRAIC SURFACES only provide an IMPLICIT SURFACE which is obtained if solutions can be found to the algebraic equations. (See also ALGEBRAIC SURFACE, IMPLICIT SURFACE, and PARAMETIC SURFACE PATCH.)
[Bowyer-83, Rogers-89]

extents
The minimum and maximum spatial dimensions of an object are called its extents – which can be used to substitute a BOUNDING VOLUME for intersection tests in RAY TRACING. (See also BOUNDING VOLUME.)
[Burger-89, Glassner-88]

extruding
Extruding is a MODELLING technique where a 3-D volume can be created by specifying a 2-D cross-section contour and a path through which it is to be 'extruded'. The extruding algorithm may be used to create a BOUNDARY REPRESENTATION of the volume by creating the front and

eye coordinate system

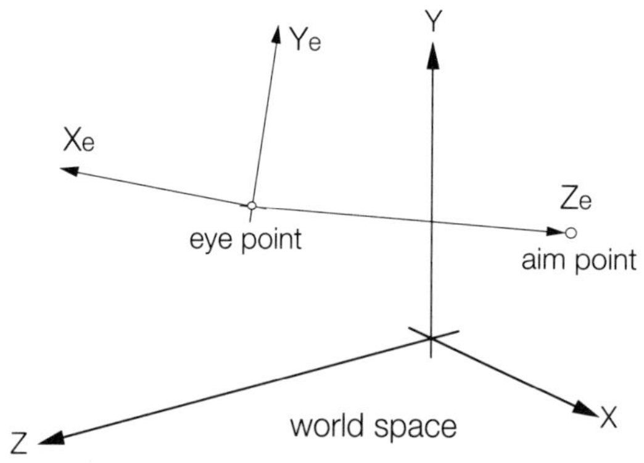

Figure E-2 *The XYZ world space is the frame of reference used for locating 3-D objects and their paths. To obtain a perspective view of these objects a pseudo observer must be located, which can be effected using an eye point and aim point; however, this assumes that the Xe axis is parallel with the world ground plane.*

back surfaces of the extrusion, together with the polygons formed when corresponding edges of these surfaces are connected. The technique can be extended by allowing the contour to be rotated and scaled around the path during the extruding. This enables complex forms such as screw threads, horns and springs to be modelled. See Figure E-1. (See also BOUNDARY REPRESENTATION, CAD, CONSTRUCTIVE SOLID GEOMETRY, MODELLING, SWEPT SURFACE, and WIRE FRAME.)
[Vince-85]

eye coordinate system

The eye coordinate system is a Cartesian set of axes associated with an observer positioned in WORLD COORDINATE SPACE. The eye coordinate system is necessary so that models which have a definition in world coordinates can be viewed from any arbitrary position as determined by the orientation of the observer. The latter is specified in a variety of ways, but one technique is to establish an EYE POINT and an AIM POINT: this aligns the Z-axis of the eye coordinate system. The horizontal X-axis is by default parallel with the ground plane of the WORLD COORDINATE SPACE, and the Y-axis is ORTHOGONAL to the X- and Y-axes. The eye coordinate system can be either left- or right-handed (either is used in practice) and one must be aware of the convention when designing the PERSPECTIVE TRANSFORMATION as coordinate sign changes can occur. A MATRIX OPERATION is used to transform world coordinates into eye coordinates before the PERSPECTIVE PROJECTION is performed. See Figure E-2. (See also AIM POINT, EYE POINT, LEFT-HANDED AXES, OBSERVER, ORTHOGONAL, PERSPECTIVE TRANSFORMATION, RIGHT-HANDED AXES, and WORLD COORDINATE SPACE.)
[Burger-89, Foley-90, Gasson-83, Hearn-86, Rogers-89]

eye point

The position of a 3-D observer in WORLD COORDINATE SPACE is called its eye point, whereas its direction may be fixed by using a Cartesian AIM POINT, or by POLAR COORDINATES fixing the VIEW VECTOR. See Figure E-2. (See also AIM POINT, EYE COORDINATE SYSTEM, OBSERVER, POLAR COORDINATES, VIEW VECTOR, and WORLD COORDINATE SPACE.)
[Burger-89, Foley-90, Rogers-89]

eye ray

In RAY TRACING the eye ray is the ray traced backwards from the EYE POINT through a sample point on the PICTURE PLANE connecting with the root of the RAY INTERSECTION TREE. This ray is assumed to be the sum of all the rays that could have arrived at this point in space following the classical laws of optics. (See also EYE POINT, PICTURE PLANE, RAY INTERSECTION TREE, and RAY TRACING.)
[Glassner-88]

eye vector

The eye vector is a VECTOR representing a 3-D line traced from the OBSERVER to some point in OBJECT SPACE.

facet

A facet is a PLANAR portion of some surface primitive. In the case of an arbitrary polygon, there is no guarantee that its surface is PLANAR; however, if it is triangulated, then each triangle can be treated as a facet, as triangles can only be PLANAR – apart from spherical triangles, which are not relevant in this description. Similarly, a PARAMETRIC SURFACE PATCH, which is to be rendered using a polygonal RENDERER, could also be triangulated to ensure planarity. (See also PARAMETRIC SURFACE PATCH, PLANAR, POLYGON, and TRIANGULATION.)

facet normal

The facet normal is an ORTHOGONAL VECTOR associated with a FACET. Where a surface has been triangulated to create a mesh of facets, these facet normals can be averaged to allow the surface to be rendered as a smooth continuous surface using GOURAUD SHADING. See Figure F-1. (See also AVERAGE NORMAL, GOURAUD SHADING, NORMAL VECTOR, ORTHOGONAL, and VECTOR.)
[Burger-89, Foley-90, Hearn-86, Rogers-85]

fade level of detail

In REAL-TIME IMAGE GENERATORS, fade level of detail is a technique for the dynamic management of polygonal models. This is because the number of polygons displayed is critical to the image generator's ability to work at REAL-TIME speeds; therefore, as distant small polygons – which are normally suppressed – are approached, they are introduced as TRANSPARENT SURFACES whose OPACITY reaches a maximum over several frames. Retreating polygons are handled in a similar way. This prevents new

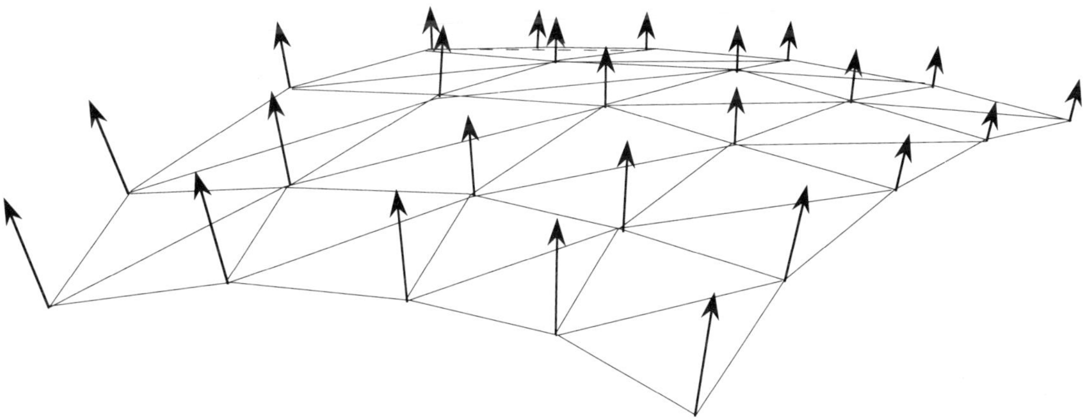

Figure F-1 *One way of rendering a patch is to divide it into a mesh of triangles to ensure planar facets. Then each triangle is individually rendered using the facet normals as shown above to control the surface intensity. For smooth Gouraud shading, the facet normals at common vertices can be replaced by an average normal, which effectively hides the edges forming the surface, although Mach bands may appear if the intensity changes either side of an edge are too great.*

level of detail from suddenly 'popping' into view. (See also IMAGE GENERATOR, OPACITY, REAL-TIME, and TRANSPARENCY.)
[Schachter-83, Vince-89]

fairing
See EASING.

far plane
See CLIPPING.

Fast Fourier Transform (FFT)
FFTs are fast algorithms for calculating the discrete FOURIER TRANSFORM. If N is the number of values in the discrete FOURIER TRANSFORM, the number of calculations is proportional to N^2, whereas the FFT reduces this to

$$N \log_2(N)$$

where N is expressed as a power of 2. (See also FOURIER TRANSFORM and FOURIER WAVEFORM ANALYSIS.)
[Barrett-87, Brigham-74, Walker-88]

fBm
See FRACTIONAL BROWNIAN MOTION.

FEA
See FINITE ELEMENT ANALYSIS.

feature extraction
Feature extraction refers to the automatic identification of features such as chamfer, round, fillet, bore and neck from computer graphics descriptions of components or assemblies, which may not refer to them explicitly but encode them implicitly within some modelling scheme. Such features may not be essential during the design phase, but may be vital to the manufacturing processes.
[Lee-87, Woodwark-89]

Ferguson patch
A Ferguson patch is based upon the CARTESIAN PRODUCT PATCH, where HERMITE INTERPOLATION is used to blend together four corner vertices, corner slopes and twist vectors, the latter having been set to zero. The reason for the zero twist vector is the difficulty in selecting reasonable values in the first place. Ferguson patches have been incorporated into APT, the numerical control language. (See also BÉZIER SURFACE PATCH, B-SPLINE SURFACE PATCH, CARTESIAN PRODUCT PATCH, COONS PATCH, PATCH, and SURFACE PATCH.)
[Farin-88, Ferguson-64, Gasson-83, Woodwark-86]

FFT
See FAST FOURIER TRANSFORM.

field
One television image FRAME consists of two interlaced fields which make up either all the odd or all the even SCAN-LINES. Many graphic displays are non-interlaced, and the concept of the field is not relevant. See Figure I-4. (See also FLICKER, FRAME, FUSION FREQUENCY, INTERLACING, PERSISTENCE, and REFRESH RATE.)
[Hearn-86, Hunt-75, Rogers-85]

4-field sequence
The NTSC colour coding system restricts coded video tapes from being edited to an accuracy better than four FIELDS without avoiding unwanted visual ARTIFACTS; this is generally known as the 4-field sequence. PAL is limited to eight FIELDS. (See also FIELD, 8-FIELD SEQUENCE, NTSC, and VIDEO SIGNAL.)

8-field sequence
The PAL colour coding system restricts coded video tapes from being edited to an accuracy better than eight FIELDS without avoiding unwanted visual ARTIFACTS; this is generally known as the 8-field sequence. NTSC is limited to four FIELDS. (See also FIELD, 4-FIELD SEQUENCE, PAL, and VIDEO SIGNAL.)

field size
The active width of sheets of cell or paper used by ani-

mators and graphic designers is known as its field size. (See also ANIMATION, CELL ANIMATION, and FRAME.)
[White-86]

filter
In IMAGE PROCESSING a filter can be represented by an array of numbers which when convolved with a pixel-based image perform signal processing tasks such as thresholding and edge detection. In computer graphics a filter may be used, for example, to prevent the introduction of ALIASING artifacts through incorrect SAMPLING. ALIASING can be avoided if the high-frequency terms can be filtered out before SAMPLING. When the frequency range of an ideal filter is expressed in the FREQUENCY DOMAIN, it has the shape of a square pulse, but in terms of the weights that must be applied to the samples made in the SPATIAL DOMAIN, the WEIGHTING FUNCTION is represented by the SINC FUNCTION. Unfortunately, this is impossible to implement due to its infinite width; therefore, other filter shapes are chosen that hopefully approach the efficiency of the SINC FILTER. These include the BOX FILTER, GAUSSIAN FILTER and TENT FILTER. (See also ALIASING, ARTIFACT, BARTLETT FILTER, BASIS FUNCTION, BED-OF-NAILS, BOX FILTER, CONVOLUTION, CONVOLUTION FILTER, FILTERING, FOURIER TRANSFORM, FREQUENCY DOMAIN, GAUSSIAN FILTER, NYQUIST LIMIT, OVER SAMPLING, POINT SAMPLING, SAMPLING, SINC FILTER, SPATIAL ALIASING, SPATIAL DOMAIN, TENT FILTER, and UNIFORM SAMPLING.)
[Blinn-89a, Blinn-89b, Blinn-89c, Gonzalez-87, Pratt-78]

filtering
Filtering is the action of processing an image with a FILTER to enhance or extract some visual information. In the context of computer graphics, this is achieved by selecting a FILTER (BOX, TENT, GAUSSIAN, SINC etc.) which will be used to compute the impact that a polygon (or any other geometric primitive) will have upon a pixel's intensity. At one end of the spectrum the BOX FILTER, which is simple to implement and produces 'reasonable' results, is still ineffective at filtering out all the high ALIASING frequencies; moreover, its FOURIER TRANSFORM reveals that desirable low-frequency information is attenuated. At the other end of the spectrum, the SINC FILTER (which is the ideal theoretical filter function) can only be implemented in some approximate form. Filtering is a computationally expensive process, but various strategies exist ranging from Crow's implementation of the BOX FILTER to Cook's STOCHASTIC SAMPLING technique. In IMAGE PROCESSING, filtering techniques are used to remove NOISE, smear edges and alter resolution. (See also ADAPTIVE SAMPLING, ALIASING, ANTI-ALIASING, ARTIFACT, BARTLETT FILTER, BASIS FUNCTION, BED-OF-NAILS, BOX FILTER, CONVOLUTION, CONVOLUTION FILTER, FILTER, FOURIER TRANSFORM, FOURIER WAVEFORM ANALYSIS, FREQUENCY DOMAIN, GAUSSIAN FILTER, JAGGIES, NOISE, NYQUIST LIMIT, OVERSAMPLING, PIXEL AVERAGING, POINT SAMPLING, POINT-SPREAD FUNCTION, SAMPLING, SINC FILTER, SPATIAL ALIASING, SPATIAL DOMAIN, STOCHASTIC SAMPLING, TEMPORAL ALIASING, TENT FILTER, and UNIFORM SAMPLING.)
[Blinn-89a, Blinn-89b, Blinn-89c, Burger-89, Cook-86, Crow-81, Fournier-88, Glassner-89, Gonzalez-87, Heckbert-86a, Naiman-87, Pavlidis-82, Pratt-78]

Finite Element Analysis (FEA)
Finite Element Analysis is a procedure for calculating the stresses and strains within computer representations of 2-D lamina or 3-D objects. To achieve this, a 2- or 3-D mesh has to be computed, which can be created automatically for simple structures but requires human interaction for complex forms. From this mesh, it is possible to apply forces at critical points and compute how the stresses and strains propagate throughout the model, causing it to deform. These deformations can be greatly exaggerated to emphasize how the structure would behave in reality.
[Gasson-83]

flatbed plotter
A flatbed plotter has the drawing or cutting medium attached to a flat surface, whilst a gantry holding the pen or cutter is moved over its surface. Plotter sizes generally vary between A3 and A0, but others also exist capable of plotting full-size drawings of cars. (See also ELEC-

TROPHOTOGRAPHIC PLOTTER, ELECTROSTATIC PLOTTER, INK JET PLOTTER, and X–Y PLOTTER.)
[Hearn-86]

flatter squarer tube (FST)

The spherical screens traditionally employed by CRTS are now being replaced by flatter squarer tubes; however, this development has meant that the electron beam has to be dynamically focused, as the distance between the electron gun and screen is not constant.

flicker

Flicker occurs when the frequency of a pulsating light source falls below the FUSION FREQUENCY of the human visual system. It can also occur when a CALLIGRAPHIC display device is unable to refresh its image before the previous one begins to decay. Flicker is also more apparent when an alternating source of light, such as a raster screen, is seen out of the corner of one's eye. This is due to special receptors in the human eye which are sensitive to changes in intensity rather than the observed signal strength. (See also FIELD, FRAME, FUSION FREQUENCY, PERSISTENCE, and REFRESH RATE.)
[Boynton-79, Gregory-86]

flight simulator

A flight simulator is a training environment where pilots are able to interact in REAL-TIME with 3-D computer graphics images produced by dedicated IMAGE GENERATORS. These generators employ traditional computer graphics techniques for producing coloured raster, CALLIGRAPHIC or vector images, but they are usually implemented in hardware for ultra high speed. (See also IMAGE GENERATOR and REAL-TIME.)
[Schachter-83, Vince-89]

flood fill

A flood fill operation changes all pixels connected to some given pixel to any specified colour. (See also AREA INFILL, BLEED, BOUNDARY FILL, FRAME STORE, and PAINT SYSTEM.)
[Burger-89]

flyback

The flyback or vertical retrace is the elapsed time between the end of a raster scan operation and the start of a new scan for a raster display, i.e. the time between one FIELD (or FRAME if non-interlaced) ending and the next one starting. (See also FIELD, FRAME, HORIZONTAL SCAN FREQUENCY, REFRESH RATE, VIDEO FREQUENCY, and VIDEO SIGNAL.)
[Hunt-75]

f-number

The f-number of a lens is its FOCAL LENGTH divided by its 'stopped' APERTURE. Increasing the f-number (normally by reducing the size of the aperture) increases the DEPTH OF FIELD, but image BRIGHTNESS is reduced. Although these terms are associated with photography, they could quickly become a familiar feature of computer graphics systems, as these optical effects have already been simulated using DISTRIBUTED RAY TRACING. (See also APERTURE, CHROMATIC ABERRATION, CIRCLE OF CONFUSION, DEPTH OF FIELD, DISTRIBUTED RAY TRACING, FOCAL LENGTH, and FOCAL PLANE.)
[Jenkins-76, Potmesil-81, Potmesil-82]

focal length

The focal length of a lens is the distance of the FOCAL PLANE to the lens when the INCIDENT LIGHT is from a distant source. As with other optical phenomena, the focal length parameter can be simulated within computer graphics. (See also ANGLE OF VIEW, APERTURE, CHROMATIC ABERRATION, CIRCLE OF CONFUSION, DEPTH OF FIELD, DISTRIBUTED RAY TRACING, F-NUMBER, FOCAL PLANE, and RAY TRACING.)
[Glassner-88, Jenkins-76, Potmesil-81, Potmesil-82]

focal plane

A lens creates a REAL IMAGE in sharp focus on a surface positioned at its focal plane. (See also ANGLE OF VIEW, APERTURE, CHROMATIC ABERRATION, CIRCLE OF CONFUSION, DEPTH OF FIELD, F-NUMBER, FOCAL LENGTH, REAL IMAGE, and VIRTUAL IMAGE.)
[Jenkins-76]

font

Font or fount describes a typeface style or a collection of graphics symbols, such as Times, Sans Serif and Helvetica. (See also DESK-TOP PUBLISHING and KERNING.)

form-factor

In RADIOSITY a form-factor represents the fractional radiant energy leaving one patch and arriving at another. A matrix of form-factors is required for RADIOSITY calculations to summarize how every patch relates to every other patch. See Figure F-2. (See also DELTA FORM-FACTORS, HEMI-CUBE, PROGRESSIVE RADIOSITY, and RADIOSITY.)
[Baum-89, Bu-87, Cohen-88, Wallace-89]

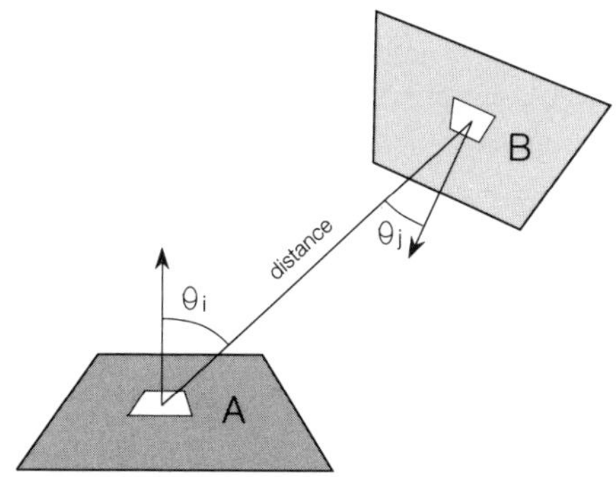

Figure F-2 *The radiosity technique computes for every sub-patch pair, the fraction of light energy leaving one sub-patch and arriving at another; these are called form factors. The nature of this energy exchange is a function of the distance between the two sub-patches, the angles between their surface normals and a line of sight and the areas of the sub-patches.*

FORTRAN

FORTRAN is an acronym for FORmula TRANslation – a scientific programming language used by many R&D laboratories in the past to develop computer graphics software. Today, the trend is towards the more rigorous environment offered by the C programming language. (See also C, C++, LISP, and PASCAL.)

forward differences

Forward differences permits the evaluation of successive points on PARAMETRIC CURVES through additions rather than multiplications. For example, when a QUADRATIC POLYNOMIAL is evaluated at regular intervals of its variable, the resulting values can be processed by subtracting neighbouring pairs. If this difference sequence is also processed in a similar manner, they will degenerate into a set of differences of constant value. This provides a mechanism for evaluating the POLYNOMIAL by working back from the difference values. Forward differences and ADAPTIVE FORWARD DIFFERENCES are also being employed in the rendering of SURFACE PATCHES. (See also ADAPTIVE FORWARD DIFFERENCES, PARAMETRIC CURVE, PARAMETRIC SURFACE PATCH, POLYNOMIAL, QUADRATIC, and SURFACE PATCH.)
[Burger-89, Lien-87]

forward dynamics

Forward dynamics is concerned with the calculation of a body's acceleration when an applied force is known. This data can then be used to determine its position in space at a future point in time and employed to produce realistic animation. (See also BEHAVIOURAL ANIMATION, COLLISION DETECTION, COMPUTER ANIMATION, DISPLACEMENT ANIMATION, DYNAMIC CONSTRAINTS, ELASTICALLY DEFORMABLE MODELS, FORWARD KINEMATICS, GOAL-ORIENTED ANIMATION, INVERSE DYNAMICS, KEY-FRAME ANIMATION, PROCEDURAL ANIMATION, and RIGID-BODY ANIMATION.)
[Barzel-87, Barzel-88, Isaacs-87, Miller-88a, Wilhelms-85, Witkin-88]

forward kinematics

Forward kinematics refers to the use of TRANSFORMATIONS in controlling the future position and motion of objects. TRANSFORMATIONS such as rotation and TRANSLATION can be employed by an animator to locate an object precisely between two extreme positions; however, this technique frequently creates unnatural movements, as the TRANSFORMATIONS ignore the inertial properties of the objects and the nature of the forces and torques controlling the motion. (See also BEHAVIOURAL ANIMATION, CHARACTER ANIMATION, COLLISION DETECTION, COMPUTER ANIMATION, DISPLACEMENT ANIMATION, DYNAMIC CONSTRAINTS, ELASTICALLY DEFORMABLE OBJECTS, FORWARD DYNAMICS, GOAL-ORIENTED ANIMATION, INVERSE DYNAMICS, KEY-FRAME ANIMATION, PROCEDURAL ANIMATION, and RIGID-BODY ANIMATION.)

forward ray tracing

Forward ray tracing is the inverse of BACKWARD RAY TRACING (conventional RAY TRACING), where rays of light are emitted by a LIGHT SOURCE and traced through the environment until they impact upon the IMAGE PLANE. This concept is not currently being pursued as a rendering technique because of its inefficiency. (See also BACKWARD RAY TRACING, IMAGE PLANE, LIGHT SOURCE, and RAY TRACING.)
[Glassner-88]

Fourier filtering

Spectral synthesis, or Fourier filtering, can be used for generating FRACTIONAL BROWNIAN MOTION, and is based upon the random selection of Fourier coefficients according to the distribution function

$$F[A(k)^2 + B(k)^2] \propto \frac{1}{k^{\beta}}$$

where A and B are the coefficients of the Fourier cosine and sine terms respectively, β is related to the FRACTAL DIMENSION and k is an index for the terms. This filter ensures that the spatial irregularities in the curve of the FBM follow a desired spectral density. (See also BROWNIAN MOTION, FOURIER FRACTAL, FRACTAL, FRACTAL DIMENSION, FRACTAL NOISE, FRACTIONAL BROWNIAN MOTION, and NOISE.)
[Peitgen-86]

Fourier fractal

A Fourier fractal is a FRACTAL set having a $1/f^{\beta}$ power spectrum, which appears to be very useful in the modelling of terrain and seascapes. A set of numerical values having a WHITE NOISE distribution, can be filtered with a $1/f^{\beta}$ filter to create the required power law distribution; the resulting height field can then form the basis of a 3-D surface. (See also BROWNIAN MOTION, FOURIER FILTERING, FRACTAL, FRACTAL CURVE, FRACTAL DIMENSION, FRACTAL GEOMETRY, FRACTAL NOISE, FRACTAL SURFACE, FRACTIONAL BROWNIAN MOTION, NOISE, SELF-AFFINE, SELF-SIMILARITY, and WHITE NOISE.)
[Peitgen-88, Voss-83]

Fourier transform

A Fourier transform computes the spectrum of harmonically related sine waves representing some complex waveform using the technique of FOURIER WAVEFORM ANALYSIS. (See also ALIASING, ANTI-ALIASING, CONVOLUTION, CONVOLUTION FILTER, CONVOLUTION THEOREM, FOURIER WAVEFORM ANALYSIS, FREQUENCY DOMAIN, NYQUIST LIMIT, SAMPLING, and SPATIAL DOMAIN.)
[Barrett-87, Blinn-89c, Brigham-74]

Fourier waveform analysis

Fourier waveform analysis relies on the fact that any complex periodic waveform can be represented by the sum of a series of harmonically related sine waves, differing in amplitude and phase. As an example, given a fundamental frequency F, the other components will have frequencies of $2F$, $3F$, $4F$ etc. Furthermore, Fourier analysis demonstrates that a square wave comprises an infinite series of odd-frequency sine terms. Now when a polygon edge is sampled for display on a pixel screen, the abrupt change from polygon to background can be thought of as a square wave edge-function. This generates an infinite series of high-frequency terms, which implies ALIASING as the NYQUIST LIMIT is fixed by the pixel sampling resolution. Although SAMPLING at sub-pixel resolution effectively increases the NYQUIST LIMIT, it can never provide for perfect ANTI-ALIASING. (See also ADAPTIVE SAMPLING,

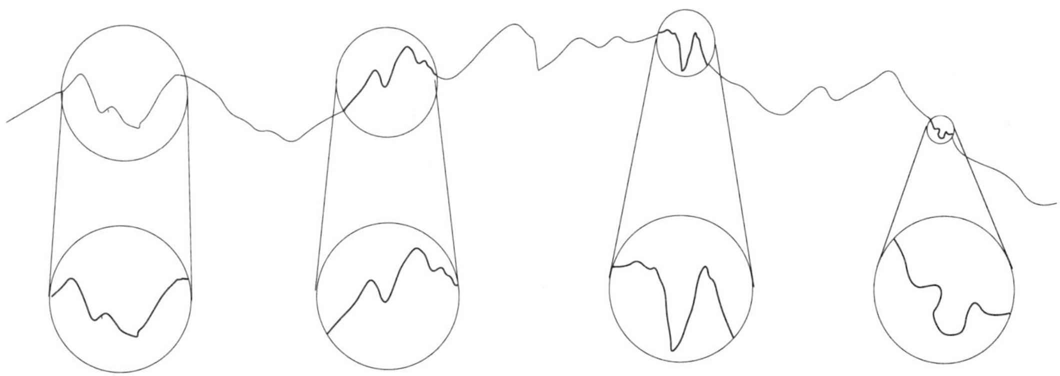

Figure F-3 *An important property of fractals is that of self-similarity: this describes the unusual characteristic that similar features of a fractal will always be discovered independent of the scaling factor. In the physical world this only occurs over limited ranges of scaling, for if one continuously magnified any natural object, one would discover different levels of detail. But there are mathematical systems where self-similarity is maintained. As an illustration, this diagram shows a pseudo fractal curve and four scaled portions, which all appear self-similar if one only considers the general roughness of the curve.*

ALIASING, ANTI-ALIASING, ARTIFACT, CONVOLUTION, CONVOLUTION FILTER, CONVOLUTION THEOREM, FILTER, FILTERING, FOURIER TRANSFORM, FREQUENCY DOMAIN, JAGGIES, NYQUIST LIMIT, OVERSAMPLING, PIXEL AVERAGING, POINT SAMPLING, SAMPLING, SPATIAL ALIASING, SPATIAL DOMAIN, TEMPORAL ALIASING, and UNIFORM SAMPLING.)
[Barrett-87, Brigham-74, Walker-88]

fractal
The term fractal was coined by Benoit Mandelbrot from the Latin *fractus* meaning 'broken' and is used to describe irregular data sets (numerical or graphical) that exhibit similar properties and features at different scales. The scaling property of fractals implies that detail observed at one level of magnification is still apparent at other levels of magnification. Naturally, the concept of infinite self-similarity only applies to a theoretical formulation, whereas fractals in the real world and in computer graphics can only be approximations. They can also be used in a relaxed form to describe phenomena occurring in the real world, such as coastlines, clouds, landscapes and some plants. Mathematical fractals exhibit high geometric complexity and low information complexity. See Figure F-3. (See also COLLAGE THEOREM, FOURIER FRACTAL, FRACTAL CURVE, FRACTAL DIMENSION, FRACTAL GEOMETRY, FRACTAL NOISE, FRACTAL SURFACE, FRACTIONAL BROWNIAN MOTION, ITERATED FUNCTION SYSTEMS, MIDPOINT DISPLACEMENT, and SELF-SIMILARITY.)
[Falconer-85, Mandelbrot-77, Mandelbrot-82, Peitgen-86, Peitgen-88]

fractal curve
A fractal curve is a curve exhibiting FRACTAL properties as defined by one of a number of dimension rules – an exam-

ple being natural coastlines which have a fractal dimension of approximately 1.3. Fractals can be, for example, a curve or surface having a fractional rather than an integer topological dimension. Synthetic fractal curves can be created using MIDPOINT DISPLACEMENT methods, MARKOV PROCESSES and INVERSE FOURIER TRANSFORMS; however, the first method is the simplest to implement. (See also FOURIER FILTERING, FOURIER FRACTAL, FRACTAL, FRACTAL DIMENSION, FRACTAL GEOMETRY, FRACTAL NOISE, FRACTAL SURFACE, FRACTIONAL BROWNIAN MOTION, ITERATED FUNCTION SYSTEMS, MIDPOINT DISPLACEMENT, and SELF-SIMILARITY.)
[Carpenter-80, Falconer-85, Mandelbrot-77, Mandelbrot-82, Peitgen-86, Peitgen-88, Voss-83]

fractal dimension
Fractal dimension is a feature of FRACTALS that measures their geometry in relation to familiar Euclidean elements which have integer topological dimensions of one, two and three. A measure of dimension D of a shape, fractal or otherwise, is given by

$$D = \frac{\ln(N)}{\ln(1/S)}$$

where N is the number of equal subdivisions that could be made on a curve or surface and S is the scale factor associated with each subdivision. For example, when a line segment is divided into 4 (N) equal segments, the scale factor S is 1/4: therefore, $D = 1$. And when a square area is divided into 4 (N) equal smaller squares, the scale factor S is 1/2: therefore, $D = 2$. But when a fractal shape such as a SPACE FILLING CURVE or a coastline is examined, its dimension might be 1.2619, which illustrates that the shape possesses subtle qualities, in that it is neither a simple contour or an area; it is a fractal. (See also FOURIER FRACTAL, FRACTAL, FRACTAL CURVE, FRACTAL NOISE, FRACTAL SURFACE, FRACTIONAL BROWNIAN MOTION, MIDPOINT DISPLACEMENT, and SELF-SIMILARITY.)
[Falconer-85, Mandelbrot-77, Mandelbrot-82, Peitgen-86, Peitgen-88]

fractal geometry
Fractal geometry is associated with the modelling of forms exhibiting the properties of FRACTALS. (See also FOURIER FRACTAL, FRACTAL, FRACTAL CURVE, FRACTAL DIMENSION, FRACTAL NOISE, FRACTAL SURFACE, FRACTIONAL BROWNIAN MOTION, ITERATED FUNCTION SYSTEMS, MIDPOINT DISPLACEMENT, and SELF-SIMILARITY.)
[Falconer-85, Mandelbrot-82, Peitgen-86, Peitgen-88]

fractal noise
Fractal noise describes a signal where the contribution of each frequency to the power spectrum is inversely proportional to the frequency. This is often called a $1/f^{\beta}$ power distribution. (See also BROWNIAN MOTION, FOURIER FILTERING, FOURIER FRACTAL, FRACTAL, FRACTAL CURVE, FRACTAL DIMENSION, FRACTAL GEOMETRY, FRACTIONAL BROWNIAN MOTION, MIDPOINT DISPLACEMENT, NOISE, SELF-SIMILARITY, and WHITE NOISE.)
[Mandelbrot-68, Mastin-87, Peitgen-86, Peitgen-88]

fractal surface
A fractal surface is a surface exhibiting FRACTAL properties. These surfaces have been used to model natural phenomena such as clouds, seascapes and mountain ranges, and they can be created by the techniques of MIDPOINT DISPLACEMENT, FOURIER FILTERING and MARKOV PROCESS. (See also FOURIER FILTERING, FOURIER FRACTAL, FRACTAL, FRACTAL CURVE, FRACTAL DIMENSION, FRACTAL GEOMETRY, FRACTAL NOISE, FRACTIONAL BROWNIAN MOTION, MIDPOINT DISPLACEMENT, NOISE, SELF-SIMILARITY, and WHITE NOISE.)
[Fournier-82, Mastin-87, Miller-86, Peitgen-86, Peitgen-88, Voss-83]

fractional Brownian motion (fBm)
Fractional Brownian motion is associated with the world of FRACTALS, and extends the idea of BROWNIAN MOTION to include a FRACTAL DIMENSION. Techniques for approximating fBm include MIDPOINT DISPLACEMENT, spectral synthesis and FOURIER FILTERING. (See also BROWNIAN MOTION, CHAOTIC BEHAVIOUR, FOURIER FILTERING, FOURIER FRACTAL, FRACTAL, FRACTAL CURVE, FRACTAL DIMENSION, FRACTAL NOISE, MIDPOINT

DISPLACEMENT, NOISE, SELF-SIMILARITY, and WHITE NOISE.)
[Mandelbrot-68, Mandelbrot-82, Peitgen-86, Peitgen-88]

frame

(1) **Animation**: A frame is a single image within an animation sequence. (See also ANIMATION, CELL ANIMATION, FIELD SIZE, and KEY-FRAME ANIMATION.)
(2) **Video**: A frame is two interlaced FIELDS forming a television picture. (See also FIELD, FUSION FREQUENCY, INTERLACING, and REFRESH RATE.)

frame buffer

See FRAME STORE.

frame grabber

A frame grabber is a video device for capturing a VIDEO SIGNAL for input into a computer graphics/video system. It enables images to be 'grabbed' from any video source and can provide images for PAINT SYSTEMS, and TEXTURE MAPS for RENDERERS. (See also FRAME STORE, SCANNER, and VIDEO SIGNAL.)

frame store

In RASTER COMPUTER GRAPHICS a frame store is a memory device used to hold a raster image, where each pixel is mapped into a specific number of bits. When 8 bits are assigned to a pixel, a LOOK-UP TABLE stores colour values to be substituted for the 8-bit codes, whereas when 24 bits are allocated for a pixel, the store can be effectively partitioned into three planes one byte deep for each ADDITIVE PRIMARY COLOUR, red, green and blue. The store can be scanned at video rates to reveal the internally held image upon a COLOUR MONITOR; and for animation applications, the image can be directly recorded onto a video recorder in a stop-frame mode. (See also ADDITIVE PRIMARY COLOURS, LOOK-UP TABLE, and RGB COLOUR MODEL.)
[Burger-89, Foley-90, Hearn-86, Rogers-85]

free form deformation (FFD)

Free form deformation is a powerful technique for distorting 2-D and 3-D structures. The underlying principle is to enclose the object to be deformed by a regular system of CONTROL POINTS which will control the deformation; these CONTROL POINTS perform a similar function in BÉZIER CURVES and BÉZIER SURFACE PATCHES. Any point in this control space will have its X-, Y- and Z-coordinates related to their EXTENTS to create fractional values ranging between 0 and 1; these are then substituted as the PARAMETER in the POLYNOMIALS associated with the CONTROL POINTS. As the CONTROL POINTS are moved, so the enclosed data points, when computed, are deformed. See Figure F-4. (See also BASIS FUNCTION, BERNSTEIN BASIS FUNCTION, CONTROL POINTS, MONOMIAL BASIS, PARAMETER, POLYNOMIAL, and POLYNOMIAL WEIGHTING FUNCTION.)
[Chadwick-89, Comninos-89, Sederberg-86]

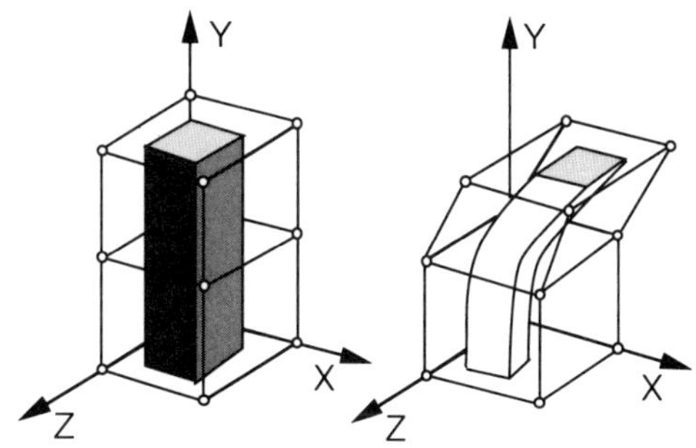

Figure F-4 *Free-form deformation operates upon a volume of space using a matrix of control points. Every point on the enclosed object can then be determined by the sum of the weighted control positions, such that when they move, the object is deformed.*

free form surfaces

Free form surfaces describe a class of surfaces that have no IMPLICIT geometric definition. The two popular strategies used in free form surfaces are cross-sections linked together into a surface by INTERPOLATION and SURFACE PATCH descriptions, which can be used to construct a

wide range of arbitrary surfaces. (See also BÉZIER SURFACE PATCH, B-SPLINE SURFACE PATCH, CONSTRUCTIVE SOLID GEOMETRY, COONS PATCH, EXTRUDING, FERGUSON PATCH, GEOMETRIC MODELLING, HERMITE PATCH, INTERPOLATION, NURBS, PATCH, PATCHED SURFACE, SCULPTURED SURFACES, SWEPT SURFACE, and WIRE FRAME.)
[Chiyokura-86, Chiyokura-87]

frequency distribution
A frequency distribution describes the occurrence of a particular quantity. For example, the numbers 2, 5, 7, 10, 6, 4, 1 could represent the frequency distribution of line lengths in an image: there are two lines 10 cm long, five lines 9 cm long, seven lines 8 cm long etc. Naturally, a frequency distribution can be represented graphically as a histogram, and it is possible to compute other characteristics such as VARIANCE and STANDARD DEVIATION. Frequency distributions are found in computer graphics, for example, in describing how micro-facets are oriented to simulate FRESNEL EFFECTS. (See also GAUSSIAN DISTRIBUTION, MEAN, MEAN DEVIATION, MEDIAN, POISSON DISTRIBUTION, STANDARD DEVIATION, and VARIANCE.)

frequency domain
The term frequency domain is associated with FOURIER WAVEFORM ANALYSIS when describing the frequency spectrum of a function. In ANTI-ALIASING schemes, a pixel WEIGHTING FUNCTION such as a BOX, TENT or SINC FILTER has a response described in the frequency domain, which is extremely useful in predicting the efficacy of the FILTER. The INVERSE FOURIER TRANSFORM of this function in the frequency domain translates to a weighting function in the SPATIAL DOMAIN. (See also ALIASING, ANTI-ALIASING, BASIS FUNCTION, CONVOLUTION, CONVOLUTION FILTER, CONVOLUTION THEOREM, FOURIER TRANSFORM, FOURIER WAVEFORM ANALYSIS, INVERSE FOURIER TRANSFORM, and SPATIAL DOMAIN.)
[Blinn-89a, Blinn-89b, Blinn-89c, Gonzalez-87, Pratt-78, Walker-88]

Fresnel effect
The Fresnel effect describes the shift in WAVELENGTH of specularly reflected light as the ANGLE OF INCIDENCE approaches 90°. The COOK–TORRANCE SHADING model implements an approximation of this effect, and it has also been incorporated in RAY TRACING. (See also ANGLE OF INCIDENCE, ANGLE OF REFLECTION, COLOUR, COLOUR BLEEDING, COOK–TORRANCE SHADING, GLOBAL ILLUMINATION MODEL, PHONG SHADING, RADIOSITY, REFLECTION OF LIGHT, SPECULAR REFLECTION, and SPECULAR TRANSMISSION.)
[Burger-89, Cook-82b, Glassner-89]

front clipping plane
The front, near or HITHER CLIPPING PLANE, delineates the minimum distance where points are visible in the 3-D VIEWING PYRAMID. See Figure C-5. (See also BACK CLIPPING PLANE, CLIPPING and VIEWING PYRAMID.)
[Burger-89, Foley-90, Hearn-86, Rogers-89]

front face
The front face of a polygon is classified as visible when its SURFACE NORMAL is facing towards the observer in EYE COORDINATE SPACE. (See also BACK FACE, EYE COORDINATE SPACE, FACET NORMAL, and SURFACE NORMAL.)

frustum
A frustum is a truncated pyramid representing the observer's VIEWING VOLUME in EYE COORDINATE SPACE. (See also CLIPPING, EYE COORDINATE SYSTEM, and VIEWING PYRAMID.)
[Burger-89, Foley-90, Hearn-86, Rogers-89]

FST
See FLATTER SQUARER TUBE.

function box
A function box is normally associated with a computer graphics workstation and consists of a collection of dials and keys which under software control provide the user with means for interactively setting values of attributes or system characteristics such as ZOOM, PANNING and SCROLL.

fusion frequency

The fusion frequency is the minimum frequency for an alternating source of light to appear constant to the human visual system – this is approximately 50 Hz, which is the frequency of the electricity mains supply in the UK. In the USA and some other countries, this mains frequency is 60 Hz. The fusion frequency depends upon the BRIGHTNESS of the source, with brighter images requiring refresh rates approaching 100 Hz. Television technology refreshes at 50 FIELDS/second (25 FRAMES/second) for PAL, and 59.94 FIELDS/second (29.97 frames/second) for NTSC, and cinema films are projected at 24 frames/second, although a three-bladed shutter interrupts each image, increasing the flicker rate to 72 Hz. Many computer display screens now operate between 60 and 72 Hz, non-interlaced. (See also FLICKER, NTSC, and PAL.)

[Boynton-79, Gregory-86]

g

gamma

Gamma is the exponent term in the equation relating output light intensity with the input electron drive signal for a REFRESH CRT. (See also GAMMA CORRECTION.)
[Blinn-89b, Burger-89, Catmull-79, Hunt-75]

gamma correction

The light intensity from PHOSPHOR when stimulated by electrons is a non-linear phenomenon: in fact, the intensity is proportional to the number of emitted electrons, raised to the power of a constant called GAMMA. Although display monitors may be gamma corrected to behave linearly, further gamma correction can be achieved via FRAME STORE LOOK-UP TABLES. (See also FRAME STORE, GAMMA, and LOOK-UP TABLE.)
[Blinn-89b, Catmull-79, Hunt-75]

gamut

The colour range that a device is capable of displaying is called its gamut, which can be identified with the CHROMATICITY DIAGRAM by plotting a triangular area from a knowledge of the primary phosphors or pigments. (See also ADDITIVE PRIMARY COLOURS, CHROMATICITY DIAGRAM, and COLOUR.)
[Foley-90, Hearn-86, Hunt-75, Robertson-88]

Gaussian distribution

A Gaussian distribution can be visualized as a hat-shaped function and typically describes a population having a dominant characteristic and a falling distribution on either side of this central feature, a typical example being the height characteristics of a group of people. It is described mathematically as

$$y = \mathrm{k}\, e^{\frac{-(x-\mu)^2}{2\rho^2}}$$

where
μ = the AVERAGE or MEAN of the distribution,
ρ = the STANDARD DEVIATION,
k = a normalizing constant to ensure that the area of the curve is unity and equals

$$\frac{1}{\rho\ \sqrt{(2\pi)}}$$

The STANDARD DEVIATION characterizes the FREQUENCY DISTRIBUTION by defining that there is approximately a 68% probability that a given value will be found within the interval $\mu - \rho$ to $\mu + \rho$. Markov proved the central limit theorem which states that the sum of a large number of independent random variables approximates to a Gaussian distribution. In computer graphics, the Gaussian function is encountered in FILTERING, FRACTALS, ILLUMINATION MODELS and JITTER. See Figure G-1. (See also AVERAGE, FREQUENCY DISTRIBUTION, MEAN DEVIATION, MEDIAN, POISSON DISTRIBUTION, STANDARD DEVIATION, and VARIANCE.)
[Blinn-89a, Glassner-89, Peitgen-88]

Gaussian filter

A Gaussian filter is used as an ANTI-ALIASING FILTER and has a shape in the SPATIAL DOMAIN in the form of a GAUSSIAN DISTRIBUTION – and although this contains a central shape somewhat like the ideal SINC FILTER, its FOURIER TRANSFORM (which is also a GAUSSIAN DISTRIBUTION) indicates that it filters out both high and low frequencies. (See also ALIASING, ANTI-ALIASING, BARTLETT FILTER, BASIS FUNCTION, BED-OF-NAILS, BOX FILTER, CONVOLUTION, CONVOLUTION FILTER, FILTER, FILTERING, FOURIER TRANSFORM, FOURIER WAVEFORM ANALYSIS, FREQUENCY DOMAIN, NYQUIST LIMIT, POINT-SPREAD FUNCTION, SAMPLING, SINC FILTER, SPATIAL ALIASING, SPATIAL DOMAIN, TENT FILTER, and UNIFORM SAMPLING.)
[Blinn-89a, Blinn-89b, Blinn-89c, Glassner-89, Gonzalez-87, Max-90a, Pratt-78]

GCR

See GREY COMPONENT REPLACEMENT.

GEM

GEM is an acronym for Graphics Environmental Manager and a trademark of Digital Research. GEM is a program that provides personal computers and microcomputers with a WIMP ENVIRONMENT. (See also WIMP ENVIRONMENT and WYSIWYG.)

genlock
When one video system is used to record the video images of a separate system without a common SYNC pulse, the recorded images could reveal a rolling frame bar, due to the slight frequency and phase differences in the two systems. Genlock is an electronic facility for synchronizing such systems. (See also HORIZONTAL SCAN FREQUENCY, INTERLACING, REFRESH RATE, SYNC, SYNC GENERATOR, VIDEO FREQUENCY, and VIDEO SIGNAL.)

geometric modelling
Geometric modelling encompasses MODELLING techniques that can be employed to represent objects accurately and satisfy the needs of CAD/CAM. Currently, there are two fundamental schemes, BOUNDARY REPRESENTATION and CONSTRUCTIVE SOLID GEOMETRY, and even these are far from perfect. With the increasing success of NURBS, SURFACE PATCH techniques are also important, but considerable research is still needed to integrate the number of disparate techniques into one integrated system. (See also BOUNDARY REPRESENTATION, CONSTRUCTIVE SOLID GEOMETRY, FREE FORM SURFACES, NURBS, SCULPTURED SURFACES, and WINGED-EDGE DATA STRUCTURE.)
[Farin-88, Hearn-86, Miller-89, Woodwark-86, Woodwark-89]

geometry engine
A geometry engine is a VLSI processor designed specifically to undertake geometric and MATRIX OPERATIONS at very high speed and is employed in state-of-the-art workstations. (See also ASIC, MATRIX OPERATION, VLSI, and WORKSTATION.)
[Clark-82]

GIF
GIF is an acronym for Graphics Interchange Format which is a colour-image transfer protocol developed by CompuServe in 1987. It supports images up to 64K pixels, with 256 colours from a 16.7 million colour palette, IMAGE COMPRESSION and decoding, and hardware independence. (See also CGM and IGES.)

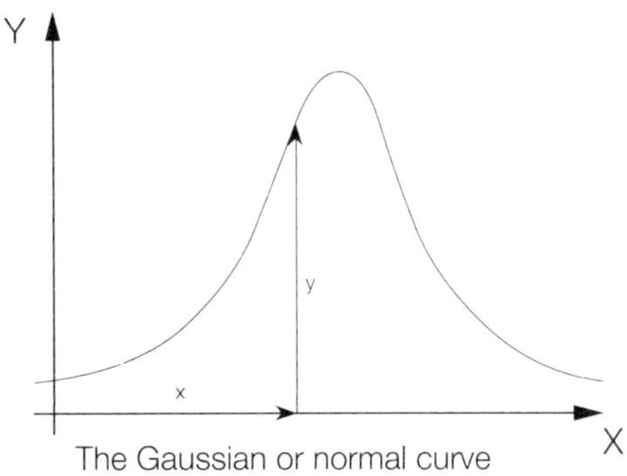

Figure G-1 *The Gaussian distribution is also known as the normal curve and is very useful in describing characteristics found in naturally occuring phenomena.*

GKS
GKS is an acronym for Graphics Kernel System which is an international 2-D interactive graphics standard intended to ease the design of computer graphics programs and provide a software environment to minimize hardware dependence problems. (See also CORE, GKS-3D, and PHIGS.)
[Bono-87, Burger-89, Herman-85, Hopgood-86, ISO-85, ISO-87d]

GKS-3D
GKS-3D extends GKS by including features addressing various aspects of 3-D computer graphics. (See also CORE, GKS, PHIGS, and PHIGS+.)
[Burger-89, ISO-87b, ISO-87e]

global illumination model
A global illumination model attempts to redress the limitations of the simple diffuse model proposed by Gouraud and the specular model due to Phong by incorporating the phenomena found within complex environments such as multiple reflections, shadow PENUMBRAE, COLOUR

BLEEDING, as well as DIFFUSE and SPECULAR REFLECTIONS. (See also COLOUR BLEEDING, COOK–TORRANCE SHADING, DISTRIBUTED RAY TRACING, FRESNEL EFFECT, ILLUMINATION MODEL, PENUMBRA, PHOTOREALISM, RADIOSITY, RAY TRACING, RENDERING EQUATION, RENDERMAN, REYES, and TORRANCE–SPARROW SHADING MODEL.)
[Buckalew-89, Burger-90, Foley-90, Glassner-89, Wallace-87]

gloss coefficient
A gloss coefficient controls the degree of gloss exhibited by a surface, and is the specular exponent term in PHONG SHADING calculations. (See also PHONG SHADING, SPECULARITY, SPECULAR REFLECTION, and SPECULAR REFLECTION COEFFICIENT.)
[Burger-89, Foley-90, Hearn-86, Rogers-85]

goal-oriented animation
Goal-oriented techniques can be used for animating articulated structures subjected to various physical constraints, where the structure can be given a goal in terms of a final position of one of its elements, and the orientation of the entire structure can then be computed. Similarly, PROCEDURAL ANIMATION can be expressed such that it is capable of realizing different goals under various conditions. For example, a procedure to animate a pair of walking legs can be given the task to walk over an uneven surface with the goal of preserving step distance. (See also BEHAVIOURAL ANIMATION, COLLISION DETECTION, COMPUTER ANIMATION, DYNAMIC CONSTRAINTS, FORWARD DYNAMICS, INVERSE DYNAMICS, PROCEDURAL ANIMATION, and RIGID-BODY ANIMATION.)
[Badler-87 Bruderlin-89, Girard-85]

G-octree
Mao coined the term G-octree which extends the OCTREE DATA STRUCTURE with a grey-scale level to facilitate its VOLUMETRIC RENDERING. (See also G-QUADTREE, OCTREE, QUADTREE, and VOLUMETRIC RENDERING.)
[Mao-87]

Gouraud shading
In 1971 Henri Gouraud proposed a rendering technique which computed pixel intensities for an illuminated surface by linearly interpolating colour intensities found at the two edges intersecting the same RASTER. These edge intensities are themselves interpolated from colour intensities calculated at their respective vertices. Gouraud shading creates a continuous transition of colour intensity across a facet, and it can also hide the edge boundaries between two facets by using the AVERAGE NORMALS to compute the initial light levels at the vertices. However, if the shading intensities change too much on either side of the edge, MACH BANDS are seen. (See also AVERAGE NORMAL, COLOUR INTERPOLATION, COSINE SHADING, DIFFUSE REFLECTION, DIFFUSE REFLECTION COEFFICIENT, INTERPOLATION, LAMBERT'S COSINE LAW, LIGHT SOURCE, MACH BANDS, and QUADRATIC SHADING.)
[Burger-89, Foley-90, Gouraud-71, Hearn-86, Rogers-85]

G-quadtree
Mao coined the term G-quadtree which extends the QUADTREE DATA STRUCTURE with a grey-scale level, to aid the display of encoded grey-level images. (See also G-OCTREE, OCTREE, and QUADTREE.)
[Mao-87]

gradation
Gradation is the blending of one colour into another, creating a colour gradient. (See also COLOUR INTERPOLATION.)

graph
A graph is a contour showing the relationship between several variables with reference to a system of axes and relevant scales.

graphical data structure
Data structures are extremely important in the design of computer graphics systems, as they must cope with an extraordinary range of data on a dynamic basis. Although some data can be held in a tabular form, much of the

data associated with a computer graphics system is variable in size, and grows and collapses during the running of a program. (See also DATA STRUCTURE.)
[Blinn-90a, Jansen-84, Kessner-85, Samet-88a]

graphic primitive
A graphic primitive is a shape or object which a graphic system uses as a building block for the construction of more complex scenes e.g. a line segment or a BIT-MAP.
[Burger-89, Foley-90, Hearn-86]

graphics package
A graphics package is a software system which undertakes a graphics task for a user, such as animation, modelling or painting.

graphics tablet
A graphics tablet is a small DIGITIZER frequently associated with a workstation for the input of graphical data, or controlling the screen's cursor. (See also DIGITIZER, DIGITIZING, and TABLET.)
[Burger-89, Hearn-86]

grey component replacement (GCR)
Grey component replacement is a technique for removing the grey level from a CMY colour definition and replacing it with a modified black level using a CMYK colour definition. (See also CMY, CMY COLOUR MODEL, CMYK, and SUBTRACTIVE PRIMARY COLOURS.)
[Lindbloom-89]

grey levels
Although a display device might be capable of displaying colour, the number of discrete intensity levels is often expressed in terms of the number of grey levels. (See also FRAME STORE and LOOK-UP TABLE.)
[Hearn-86]

grey-scale image
A grey-scale image has pixel values interpreted as different shades of grey.

h

half space
When the coordinates of a 3-D point are substituted into a surface equation, three conditions arise: if the equation is satisfied, then the point resides on the surface; otherwise the result creates a negative or positive value. These actually indicate that the point exists in one of the two space partitions created by the surface, which are called HALF SPACES. See Figure H-1. (See also ALGEBRAIC SURFACE, CONSTRUCTIVE SOLID GEOMETRY, and IMPLICIT SURFACE.)
[Bowyer-83, Burger-89]

halftoning
Halftoning is a technique that effectively increases the intensity levels of a pixel display by filling a small matrix (say 2 x 2 or 3 x 3) with patterns of dots of differing overall intensitites and replacing the original pixels by this matrix. (See also DITHERING and ORDERED DITHER.)
[Burger-89, Foley-90, Hearn-86]

hanging edge
A hanging edge is an edge that only is associated with one facet rather than two, as needed by the WINGED-EDGE DATA STRUCTURE – and arises when an object does not necessarily have to be geometrically sound but is graphically acceptable. An example could be in the modelling of a house where the floor is not included, for if the house is only seen from the outside then the floor polygon is superfluous. This means that the ground edges of the walls will not share two polygons. (See WINGED-EDGE DATA STRUCTURE.)

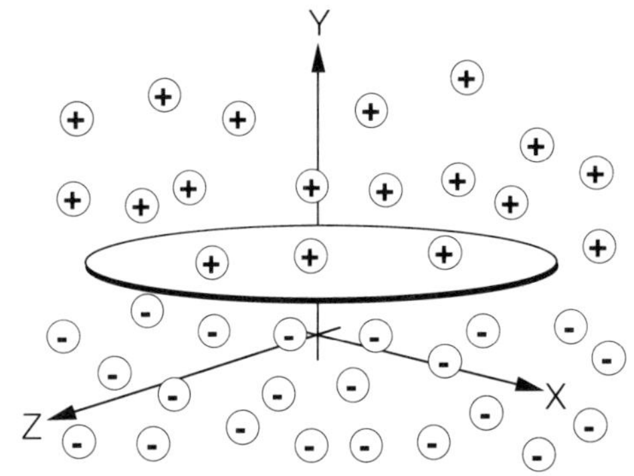

Figure H-1 *A plane equation effectively partitions space in two. Whilst points that satisfy the equation reside on the surface, the remaining points will exist in the negative or positive half spaces.*

HCI
See HUMAN–COMPUTER INTERACTION.

HDA
HDA is an acronym for Hercules Display Adaptor developed by Hercules to provide a graphics facility for personal computers with a screen resolution of 720 by 340. (See also CGA, EGA, HGC, MCGA, MDA, PVA, SUPER VGA and VGA.)

HDTV
HDTV is an acronym for High Definition TeleVision which has a proposed standard of 1125 lines at 60 Hz (FIELDS) interlaced, a 16:9 ASPECT RATIO, 30 MHz RGB and LUMINANCE BANDWIDTH.

head-up display (HUD)
Head-up displays employ display technology to reflect images into a viewer's eyes from a screen such that a VIRTUAL IMAGE is seen several metres ahead. HUD systems are currently used for displaying strategic flight information for fighter pilots, but similar systems are being developed for car instrumentation.

height field
A height field is a matrix of numerical values representing the vertical height of terrain above some reference surface; this could have been derived from a pair of stereoscopic satellite images, or even digitized directly from a map. The height field can easily be transformed into a 3-D surface by constructing a triangular mesh which can

be rendered with suitable colour data. (See also DIGITAL ELEVATION DATA, DIGITAL ELEVATION MODEL, and TERRAIN MODELLING.)

heliotropism

Plants grow and orient themselves according to the position of the sun in the sky; this behaviour pattern which is called heliotropism has been successfully simulated in computer models of plant growth.
[Greene-89]

hemi-cube

In RADIOSITY, the calculation of FORM-FACTORS is expressed geometrically in terms of solid angles and a hemi-spherical surface through which radiation transfers can be measured. An approximation of this hemi-sphere is the hemi-cube, which can be visualized as a cube cut in half to form a five-sided box which is placed over a reference sub-patch. The surface of the hemi-cube is divided into pixels, for which precomputed DELTA FORM-FACTORS are known. By projecting some other surface onto the hemi-cube, it is possible to integrate the DELTA FORM-FACTORS from the active pixels to produce an approximate FORM-FACTOR for the two surfaces. The accuracy of this technique depends on the number of hemi-cube pixels, and also assumes that the distance between the surfaces is large in proportion to their diameters. However, recent research has suggested that the hemi-cube can lead to numerical instability as its geometry does not reflect the symmetry of the hemi-sphere. See Figure H-2. (See also DELTA FORM-FACTORS, FORM-FACTORS, PROGRESSIVE RADIOSITY, and RADIOSITY.)
[Cohen-85, Greenberg-89]

Hermite curve

The Hermite curve is a PARAMETRIC CUBIC CURVE sensitive to the end point tangents. The curve is generated by interpolating between two end points and their associated tangents, which makes it useful for PIECEWISE CURVES. (See also APPROXIMATING SPLINE, BÉZIER CURVE, B-SPLINE CURVE, CUBIC CURVE, HERMITE INTERPOLATION, HERMITE PATCH, INTERPOLATING SPLINE, OVERHAUSER CURVE, and PARAMETRIC CUBIC CURVE.)
[Farin-88, Woodwark-86]

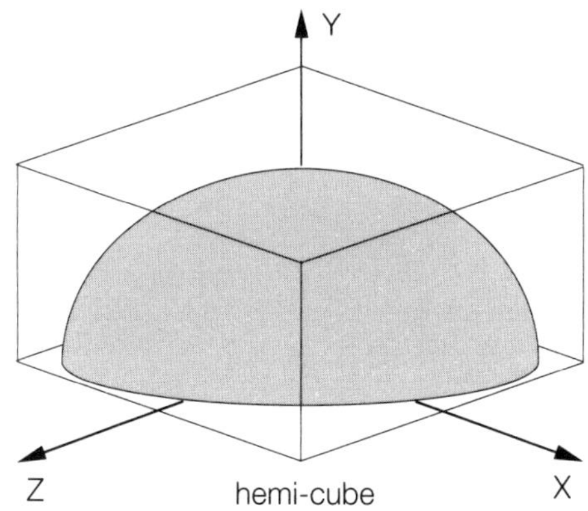

Figure H-2 *In radiosity calculations it is necessary to compute form factors between pairs of sub-patches, which involves integrating the light energy exchange over a hemi-spherical surface. As this is numerically complex, the hemi-cube provides a simple substitute, but unfortunately introduces errors.*

Hermite interpolation

Hermite interpolation uses PARAMETRIC POLYNOMIALS to interpolate between two points and their associated curve slopes. (See also HERMITE CURVE, HERMITE PATCH, HIGH-DEGREE INTERPOLANT, INTERPOLATION, and LAGRANGIAN INTERPOLATION.)
[Farin-88, Fletcher-87, Fletcher-90, Woodwark-86]

Hermite patch

A Hermite patch is a CARTESIAN PRODUCT PATCH employing a HERMITE INTERPOLATION between the corner points, corner slopes and corner twist vectors. As the latter can be difficult to fix, especially in a multi-patch application, they

can be given a zero value which produces the FERGUSON PATCH. (See also BÉZIER SURFACE PATCH, B-SPLINE SURFACE PATCH, CARTESIAN PRODUCT PATCH, COONS PATCH, FERGUSON PATCH, NURBS, PATCH, and PATCHED SURFACE.)
[Farin-88, Woodwark-86]

heuristic
In the analysis of problems where a goal is known but the precise technique of achieving it is not, a heuristic approach will attempt to apply certain strategies and measure the success of their efficacy in reaching the final goal, or some intermediate goal. By monitoring these attempts to reach the goal, the ALGORITHM improves, as it develops a history of past successes. Such procedures would be used in game playing, as in chess. (See also DETERMINISTIC and GOAL-ORIENTED ANIMATION.)

hexagon
A hexagon is a regular six-sided polygon.
[Gasson-83]

hexcone
A hexcone is a faceted cone with a six-sided polygonal base and is the geometrical form employed by the HSV COLOUR MODEL. See Figure C-7. (See also HLS COLOUR MODEL and HSV COLOUR MODEL.)
[Smith-78a]

HGC
HGC is an acronym for Hercules Graphics Card which is a MONOCHROME video adaptor card developed by Hercules, with a resolution of 720 by 348 pixels. (See also CGA, EGA, HDA, MCGA, MDA, PVA, SUPER VGA, and VGA.)

hidden-line removal
Hidden-line removal is a process for identifying edges that are invisible or partially occulted by surfaces and suppressing them before they are displayed. A first level of hidden-line removal is to remove back-facing surfaces: this is easily achieved by measuring the angle between the SURFACE NORMAL and the EYE VECTOR; the surface is invisible if this equals or exceeds 90°. Following this CULLING operation a variety of techniques are available, from the first known solution to the problem by Roberts in 1963, whose strategy consisted of first deleting edges and planes of an object hidden by its own volume and then comparing every edge with every other volume for obscuration, to the algorithm proposed by Jassen in 1983 who resolves the problem with the aid of AREA CO-ORDINATES and without the use of trigonometric functions and the need to compute 3-D angles. (See also BACK FACE REMOVAL and HIDDEN-SURFACE REMOVAL.)
[Burger-89, Hearn-86, Hedgley-82, Jassen-83, Rogers-85, Sutherland-74b]

hidden-surface removal
Hidden-surface removal is a hardware or software process for ensuring that the final rendered view of a 3-D scene has overlapping or penetrating surfaces correctly visualized. As with HIDDEN-LINE REMOVAL, the data structure storing the 3-D scene geometry must be processed to identify those surfaces invisible to the observer, and then the remaining surfaces are rendered to produce an acceptable image. Unlike HIDDEN-LINE REMOVAL, hidden-surface removal algorithms must not only resolve the spatial organization of surfaces but must also apply an ILLUMINATION MODEL to compute the surface illumination. (See also A-BUFFER, AREA SUBDIVISION ALGORITHMS, BACK FACE REMOVAL, BINARY SEPARATING PLANES, DEPTH MAP, DEPTH SORT ALGORITHM, DIVIDE AND CONQUER, IMAGE SPACE ALGORITHM, INTERPENETRATING OBJECTS, OBJECT BUFFER, OBJECT SPACE ALGORITHMS, PAINTER'S ALGORITHM, RAY TRACING, SCAN-LINE ALGORITHM, WARNOCK ALGORITHM, Z-BUFFER, and ZZ-BUFFER.)
[Atherton-83, Burger-89, Devai-87, Foley-90, Hamlin-77, Hearn-86, Lim-87, Myers-75, Newell-72, Rogers-85, Warnock-68, Warnock-69, Weiler-77]

hierarchical menu
A hierarchical menu is a family of menus organized as a tree structure, such that any menu is identified by some ordered route through the HIERARCHY. (See also HIERARCHY, HUMAN–COMPUTER INTERACTION, MENU, USER INTERFACE, and WIMP ENVIRONMENT.)

hierarchy

A hierarchy is an organization of things connected in such a way that a unique path exists between any two. Hierarchical structures are vital to computer graphics and computers in general, and are used in the form of trees to relate nodes referencing various types of data. OCTREES and QUADTREES are excellent examples of a data hierarchy. (See also DATA BASE, DATA STRUCTURE, OCTREE, QUADTREE, and RAY INTERSECTION TREE.)
[Burger-89]

high-degree interpolant

A high-degree interpolant is a POLYNOMIAL – perhaps fourth degree and higher – used for INTERPOLATION, but they can create spurious undulations between interpolant points. Most interpolants tend to employ CUBIC equations, as these satisfy the CONTINUITY criteria for PIECEWISE CURVE construction. (See also BLENDING FUNCTION, CONTINUITY, HERMITE INTERPOLATION, INTERPOLATING SPLINE, LAGRANGIAN INTERPOLATION, PARAMETRIC POLYNOMIAL, PIECEWISE CURVES, and POLYNOMIAL.)
[Weeg-66]

high-level language

A high-level language provides logical constructs for developing algorithms in terms relevant to some application area. (See also C, COMPILER, FORTRAN, LISP, LOW-LEVEL LANGUAGE, and PASCAL.)

high-resolution display

Unfortunately, this is a relative term as its definition moves with a rapidly changing technology. LCD technology is currently able to display in excess of 35 million pixels, combining raster and vector graphics in full colour. General-purpose graphics workstations display in excess of 1 million pixels, and other higher-resolution systems are of the order of 3 million pixels. (See also LIQUID CRYSTAL DISPLAY.)

hither clipping plane

See FRONT CLIPPING PLANE.

HLS colour model

W. Ostwald proposed the HLS colour model to associate Hue, Lightness and Saturation with a double HEXCONE, where HUE is represented by a rotational position about the central vertical axis, LIGHTNESS is a distance along the central axis, whilst SATURATION is the radial distance from the central axis. This, and the HSV COLOUR MODEL, have advantages over the RGB COLOUR MODEL in that colour definition is far simpler and intuitive and interactive colour selection is more efficient. Algorithms are available to convert RGB triplets into HLS triplets, and vice versa. (See also CMY COLOUR MODEL, COLOUR, COLOUR MODEL, COLOUR SPACE, COMPLEMENTARY COLOUR, HEXCONE, HSV COLOUR MODEL, HUE, HUE CIRCLE, LIGHTNESS, MUNSELL COLOUR SYSTEM, PURITY, RGB, SATURATION, and VALUE.)
[Burger-89, Foley-90, Hearn-86, Ostwald-31, Rogers-85]

hold

A single image frame repeated a specified number of times within an animation sequence is known as a hold. (See also ANIMATION, BAR SHEETS, FRAME, IMAGE SEQUENCE, SERIES, and SPACERS.)
[White-86]

hologram

A hologram is an image in which the interference fringes caused by direct light from a coherent light source (a laser) illuminating the plate and the same light source reflecting off some object are captured . When the hologram is viewed with a similar light source, a true 3-D image is observed of the original object. Holograms can be computed by computer using FFTs etc. and can be embossed on plastic or metal and may be viewed in white light.

homogeneous coordinates

Homogeneous coordinates extend CARTESIAN COORDINATES with an extra value such that, if $[x, y, z]$ are the existing Cartesian coordinates in 3-D, the homogeneous

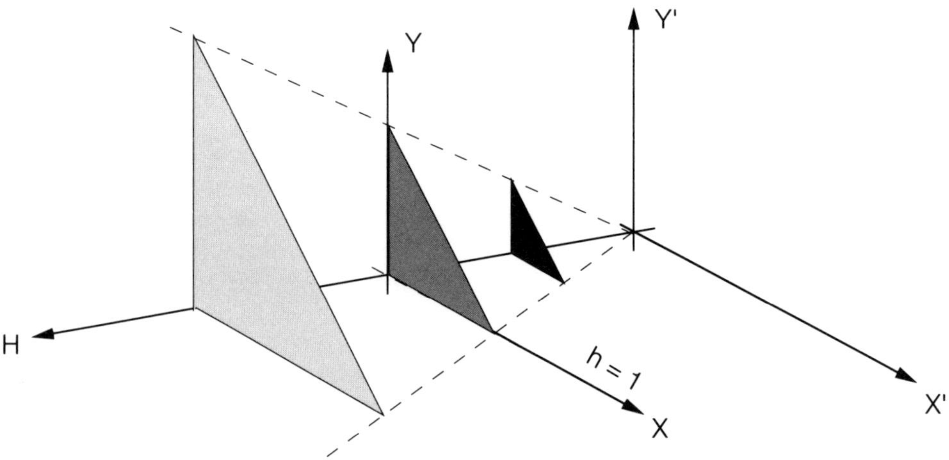

Figure H-3 *As an aid to visualizing the concept of homogeneous coordinates, imagine a 3-D space (homogeneous space) which contains an X-Y plane where h = 1, which in reality is the plane where all 2-D operations are performed. As one can see from the diagram, the plane's position is not important, as different values of h simply cause a change in scale, but when h = 1, homogeneous coordinates are equivalent to coordinates in the 2-D plane. This technique not only allows points at infinity to be located (i.e. h = 0), but its matrix form is also very useful.*

form is specified as $[x', y', z', h]$ where

$$x = x'/k$$
$$y = y'/k$$
$$z = z'/k$$

Thus when $k = 1$ the two forms are identical. The homogeneous form is convenient for handling points at infinity, where k is simply set to zero; furthermore, homogeneous coordinates can be treated as the original coordinates extended by an extra coordinate; thus they can be manipulated by MATRIX OPERATIONS in the normal way. The extra coordinate enables operations such as scaling, rotation and translation to be CONCATENATED within a single matrix. For example, in a 2-D transformation, the following MATRIX will translate (x, y) by (1, 2):

$$[x', y', 1] = [x, y, 1] \begin{bmatrix} 1 & 0 & 0 \\ 0 & 1 & 0 \\ 1 & 2 & 1 \end{bmatrix}$$

See Figure H-3. (See also BARYCENTRIC COORDINATES, CARTESIAN COORDINATES, COORDINATE SYSTEM, MATRIX, MATRIX OPERATION, ROTATION MATRIX, SCALING MATRIX, and TRANSLATION MATRIX.)
[Burger-89, Foley-90, Gasson-83, Hearn-86, Rogers-89]

horizontal resolution
The horizontal resolution refers to the number of pixels along one RASTER on a CRT display or a number of lines on a vector display. Other devices such as plotters and LCD screens etc. also have an associated horizontal resolution. (See also BANDWIDTH, CATHODE RAY TUBE, HIGH-RES-

OLUTION DISPLAY, HORIZONTAL SCAN FREQUENCY, RESOLUTION, VERTICAL RESOLUTION, VIDEO FREQUENCY, and VIDEO SIGNAL.)

horizontal scan frequency

The horizontal scan frequency or line frequency is the rate at which a CRT beam is stroked across a screen, and effectively controls the VERTICAL RESOLUTION. For the PAL system this frequency is 15.625 kHz and corresponds to 312.5 lines/field, although only 287.5 lines are visible, whereas for the NTSC system, the horizontal scan frequency is 15.734 kHz and corresponds to 262.5 lines/field, although only 241.5 are visible. (See also BANDWIDTH, CATHODE RAY TUBE, FIELD, FLYBACK, FRAME, INTERLACING, NTSC, PAL, REFRESH RATE, VERTICAL RESOLUTION, VIDEO FREQUENCY, and VIDEO SIGNAL.)

HSV colour model

Alvy Ray Smith proposed the HSV colour model where the attributes Hue, Saturation and Value are associated with a single HEXCONE, where HUE is represented by a rotational position about the central vertical axis, SATURATION is the radial distance from the central axis and VALUE is the distance along the central axis with black at the bottom and white in the centre of the top HEXAGON. This form of COLOUR MODEL is much more convenient than the RGB COLOUR MODEL when it comes to selecting and modifying colours at an interactive interface; nevertheless, as computer graphics hardware works with the RGB COLOUR MODEL, any HSV description must be converted into an RGB form, and simple algorithms are available for this conversion. See Figure C-7. (See also COLOUR, COLOUR MODEL, COLOUR SPACE, HEXCONE, HLS COLOUR MODEL, HUE, HUE CIRCLE, LIGHTNESS, MUNSELL COLOUR SYSTEM, RGB COLOUR MODEL, SATURATION, and VALUE.)
[Burger-89, Foley-90, Hearn-86, Rogers-85, Smith-78a]

HUD

See HEAD-UP DISPLAY.

hue

Hue is the attribute given to a COLOUR to describe its relative position within the spectrum, i.e. whether it is red-, orange-, yellow-, green- or blue-ish, and it plays an essential part in the HSV and HLS COLOUR MODELS. (See also BRIGHTNESS, CMY COLOUR MODEL, COLOUR, COLOUR MODEL, COLOUR SPACE, COMPLEMENTARY COLOUR, HLS COLOUR MODEL, HSV COLOUR MODEL, HUE CIRCLE, LIGHTNESS, MUNSELL COLOUR SYSTEM, PRIMARY COLOURS, PURITY, RGB COLOUR MODEL, SATURATION, SPECTRAL COLOUR, and VALUE.)
[Burger-89, Foley-90, Gregory-86, Hearn-86, Hunt-75, Rogers-85]

hue circle

A hue circle is a circular arrangement of HUES where red is positioned at a zero reference point, green is rotated 120° and blue 240°. Any hue can be specified either by an angle between 0° and 360° or by a fractional number. (See also ADDITIVE COLOUR MIXING, ADDITIVE PRIMARY COLOURS, COLOUR, COLOUR MODEL, COLOUR SPACE, COMPLEMENTARY COLOUR, HLS COLOUR MODEL, HSV COLOUR MODEL, HUE, LIGHTNESS, MUNSELL COLOUR SYSTEM, PRIMARY COLOURS, PURITY, RGB COLOUR MODEL, SATURATION, TINT-BUILD, VALUE, and WHITE LIGHT.)
[Munsell-41]

human–computer interaction (HCI)

Human–computer interaction is the aspect of computer system design that addresses the problems of communication between humans and computers. In INTERACTIVE COMPUTER GRAPHICS systems HCI design is vital to the effectiveness of the system, for the user must not only cope with text information but with 2- and 3-D graphics, which are often displayed at great speed. This raises problems of display, human interpretation, comprehension and reaction. Furthermore, manipulating 3-D forms with JOYSTICKS and mice viewed upon a 2-D screen can create some unusual HCI problems peculiar to computer graphics. (See also EXPERT SYSTEM, ICONS, INPUT DEVICE, INTERACTIVE COMPUTER GRAPHICS, MOUSE, REAL-TIME RESPONSE TIME, USER INTERFACE, WIMP ENVIRONMENT, and WYSIWYG.)

hypercube
In n-space (a space having n dimensions), a hypercube has $2n$ faces and 2^n vertices. It is a mode of connection for multiprocessor computers and ensures that any processor has at most $n - 1$ nodes between itself and another processor.
[Burger-89, Dew-89]

hypertexture
Ken Perlin and Eric Hoffert coined the term hypertexture for describing shapes of texture which are generated by object density functions and density modulation functions. Such techniques are useful in modelling phenomena such as fire, fractals, hair and fur. (See also BUMP MAPPING, DISPLACEMENT MAPPING, ENVIRONMENT MAPPING, PARTICLE SYSTEM, PHOTOREALISM, PROCEDURAL TEXTURE, SOFT OBJECTS, SOLID TEXTURE, and TEXTURE MAPPING.)
[Perlin-89]

icons

Icons are graphic objects symbolizing replacing actions or ideas – and they play an important role in simplifying the human–computer interface. By pointing with a MOUSE to specific icons displayed upon a screen, a user is able to communicate relatively complex procedures without the need to issue any explicit computer command. (See also HUMAN–COMPUTER INTERACTION, MENU, and MOUSE.)
[Burger-89]

icosahedron

The icosahedron is a PLATONIC OBJECT constructed from 20 EQUILATERAL TRIANGLES. (See also CUBE, DODECAHEDRON, OCTAHEDRON, PLATONIC OBJECTS, and TETRAHEDRON.)
[Critchlow-69, Gasson-83]

IFS

See ITERATED FUNCTION SYSTEMS.

IG

See IMAGE GENERATOR.

IGES

IGES is an acronym for Initial Graphics Exchange Specification which is a data exchange standard for CAD systems. It provides a neutral format for the representation of drawings and models, from which specific CAD formats can be generated. (See also CGM, COMPUTER-AIDED DESIGN, DXF, GIF, PAGE DESCRIPTION LANGUAGE, PRODUCT DATA EXCHANGE SPECIFICATION, and STEP.)
[Grabowski-87]

illuminant C

Illuminant C is a black-body radiator at 6504° K which represents white sunlight. (See also ADDITIVE PRIMARY COLOURS, CHROMATICITY DIAGRAM, CIE PRIMARIES, COLOUR, COLOUR SPACE, LUMINOSITY CURVE, PRIMARY COLOURS, PURITY, SPECTRAL ENERGY, and WHITE LIGHT.)

illumination model

To render a synthetic image, an illumination model is required to describe how light is emitted, reflected, transmitted and absorbed. Simple models may only address DIFFUSE and/or SPECULAR REFLECTIONS, whilst others, like RAY TRACING and RADIOSITY, attempt to simulate more complex physical phenomena. (See also ATMOSPHERIC ATTENUATION, BIDIRECTIONAL REFLECTANCE, COLOUR BLEEDING, COOK–TORRANCE SHADING, DIFFUSE REFLECTION, DIRECTIONAL LIGHT SOURCE, DISTRIBUTED LIGHT SOURCE, FRESNEL EFFECT, GLOBAL ILLUMINATION MODEL, GOURAUD SHADING, LAMBERT'S COSINE LAW, PHONG SHADING, POINT LIGHT SOURCE, POSITIONAL LIGHT SOURCE, RADIOSITY, RAY TRACING, REFLECTION OF LIGHT, REFRACTION OF LIGHT, RENDERING EQUATION, SNELL'S LAW, SPECULAR REFLECTION, SPECULAR TRANSMISSION, SPOT LIGHT, and TORRANCE–SPARROW SHADING MODEL.)
[Blinn-77, Blinn-82, Burger-89, Cook-82a, Cook-82b, Foley-90, Hall-86, Hearn-86, Tezenas du Montcel-85, Whitted-79]

image compaction

See IMAGE COMPRESSION.

image compression

Image compression relates to the techniques for reducing the memory storage for real or synthetic images. RUN-LENGTH ENCODING exploits SCAN-LINE COHERENCE, whilst PEANO CURVES and CELL ENCODING exploit AREA COHERENCE. The recent work of Barnsley *et al*. with ITERATED FUNCTION SYSTEMS may also provide a novel technique using fractals. (See also CELL ENCODING, COHERENCE, ITERATED FUNCTION SYSTEMS, LZW COMPRESSION, NAPLPS, PEANO CURVES, RUN-LENGTH ENCODING, and SPACE FILLING CURVES.)
[Cambell-86, Cole-87]

image generator (IG)

Image generators are computing systems dedicated to displaying REAL-TIME rendered images, and are generally employed in FLIGHT SIMULATORS. Image generators are capable of rendering, in approximately 20 milliseconds, a 1 million pixel image with a scene content between 500 and 5000 polygons, with TEXTURE MAPPING and ANTI-ALIASING. Generally, three to five systems are integrated to

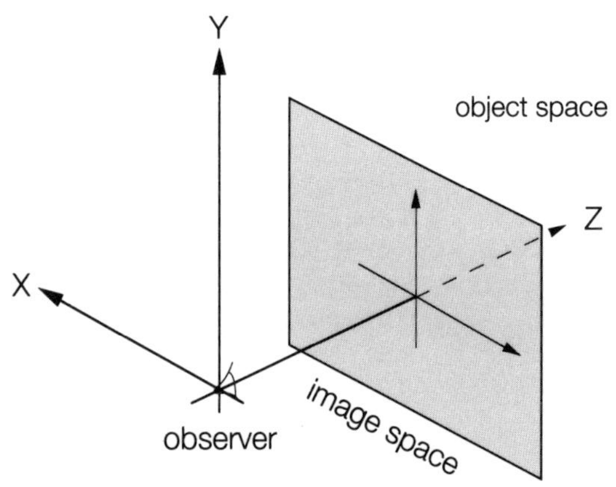

Figure I-1 *The picture plane used to capture a perspective image is also known as the image space - and some algorithms use this domain to perform their calculations. Another class of algorithms, such as ray tracing, perform their calculations in object space.*

provide sufficient pixel detail for panoramic displays.
[Schachter-83, Vince-89]

image plane
(1) **Optics**: A lens forms an in-focus REAL IMAGE at the image plane. (See also APERTURE, CIRCLE OF CONFUSION, F-NUMBER, FOCAL LENGTH, FOCAL PLANE, REAL IMAGE, and VIRTUAL IMAGE)
[Jenkins-76]
(2) **Computer graphics**: The image plane is synonymous with PICTURE PLANE. See Figure P-3. (See also PICTURE PLANE.)
[Burger-89, Foley-90, Hearn-86, Rogers-89]

image processing
Image processing is concerned with the analysis, manipulation and processing of synthetic and real images. Image processing techniques include operations such as FILTERING, edge detection, thinning and contrast enhancement.
[Gonzalez-87, Pavlidis-82, Pratt-78]

image sequence
A set of related images forming a SERIES within an animation sequence is called an image sequence. (See also ANIMATION, CELL ANIMATION, FRAME, HOLD, SERIES, and SPACERS.)

image space
Image space is the IMAGE PLANE where a PROJECTION of a 3-D scene has been captured: hidden-line, hidden-surface and rendering algorithms may undertake some of their work in this space, as well as using the OBJECT SPACE containing the original object definitions. See Figure I-1. (See also EYE COORDINATE SYSTEM, OBJECT SPACE, PERSPECTIVE PROJECTION, PICTURE PLANE, VIEWING PYRAMID, and WORLD COORDINATE SPACE.)
[Burger-89, Foley-90, Hearn-86, Rogers-85]

image space algorithm
An image space algorithm exploits the geometric and attribute information captured upon the IMAGE PLANE. As an example, a SCAN-LINE ALGORITHM creates a final rendered image by investigating the way polygons overlap when projected onto an IMAGE PLANE by using their PLANE EQUATIONS and other information; similarly, the WARNOCK ALGORITHM arrives at a final image by applying a DIVIDE AND CONQUER strategy on the projected polygons formed in the IMAGE SPACE. (See also AREA SUBDIVISION ALGORITHMS, CYCLICAL OVERLAPPING POLYGONS, DIVIDE AND CONQUER, IMAGE PLANE, IMAGE SPACE, OBJECT SPACE ALGORITHMS, SCAN-LINE ALGORITHMS, and WARNOCK ALGORITHM.)
[Burger-89, Foley-90, Rogers-85]

image store
See FRAME STORE.

implicit surface
An ALGEBRAIC SURFACE is an implicit surface as it describes

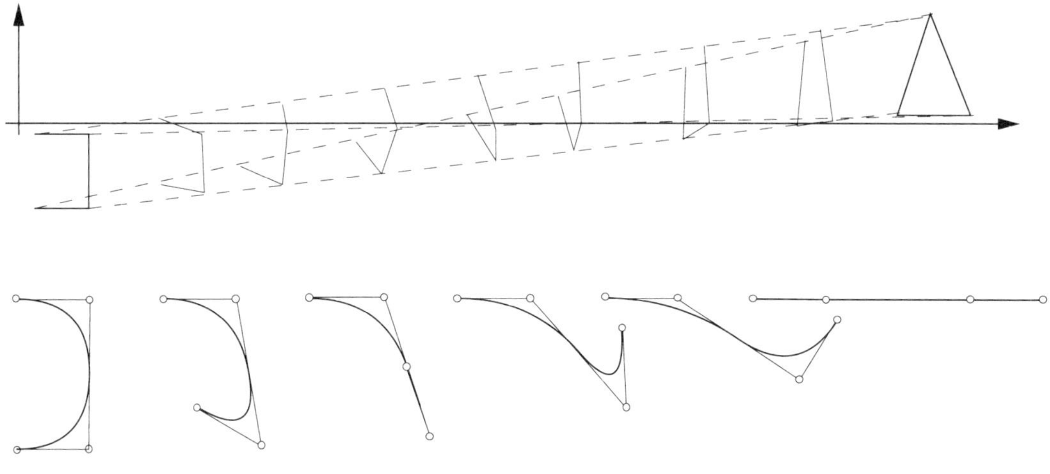

Figure I-2 *Although in traditional animation inbetweening refers to the creation of new images based upon a starting and final image, in computer graphics anything can be inbetweened. For example, in the top illustration, the vertices forming the shape on the left have been linearly interpolated with those on the right. However, in the lower illustration, angles between the line segments linking together a group of control points have been inbetweened and then used to form a Bézier curve.*

implicitly the relationship between three variables. By substituting values for the variables, one can identify whether the point is on the surface or to which half space it belongs. For example, a PLANAR surface may be described by

$$3x - 2y - z = 0$$

and the point $x = 2$, $y = 2$ and $z = 2$ satisfies the equation and is therefore on the surface; however, the point $x=1$, $y=4$, $z=1$, is in one of the HALF SPACES, and the point $x = 4$, $y = 0$, $z = 0$, is in the other HALF SPACE. (See also ALGEBRAIC SURFACE, EXPLICIT SURFACE, HALF SPACE, and PARAMETRIC SURFACE PATCH.)

impulse response

See POINT-SPREAD FUNCTION.

inbetweening

In the cartoon industry, a skilled animator draws the key frames for a short sequence, and an 'inbetweener' develops the inbetween images. Computer programs are available to undertake this work, although the term inbetweening is often used to describe the blending of parameters controlling size, colour, orientation, texture and light intensities. See Figure I-2. (See also ANIMATION, BLENDING FUNCTION, CELL ANIMATION, COMPUTER ANIMATION, and KEY-FRAME ANIMATION.)
[Reeves-81, Vince-85, White-86]

incident light

Incident light is the light actually arriving at a surface and is the basis for computing the reflected light seen by the observer. Frequently the incident light is represented as levels of red, green and blue, and shading calculations

are made individually upon these three components. Unfortunately, many ILLUMINATION MODELS do not investigate whether the incident light level corresponds to a real-world situation; they simply assume that light can travel uninterrupted from light sources, whereas in reality light is being continuously masked and reflected. RADIOSITY and RAY TRACING do attempt to address these problems, which is why their images are so realistic. (See also AMBIENT LIGHT, ANGLE OF INCIDENCE, ANGLE OF REFLECTION, ANGLE OF REFRACTION, RADIOSITY, RAY TRACING, REFLECTION OF LIGHT, and REFRACTION OF LIGHT.)
[Burger-89, Foley-90, Hearn-86, Rogers-85]

index of refraction
See REFRACTIVE INDEX.

ink jet plotter
An ink jet plotter creates an image by spraying charged droplets of coloured ink upon paper. The cyan, magenta, yellow and black inks can be applied on a continuous basis with droplets selected when needed (unwanted droplets returning to the reservoir) or on a demand basis, where an oscillatory piezoelectric crystal drives individual charged droplets from an ink reservoir. (See also CMYK.)
[Burger-89]

in point
An edit operation employs the terms in point and END POINT to locate the range of the edit. (See also 4-FIELD SEQUENCE, 8-FIELD SEQUENCE, FRAME, and OUT POINT).

input device
In computer graphics applications input devices include DATA TABLETS, TOUCH PANELS, keyboards and SCANNERS. (See also CURSOR-CONTROL KEYS, DIGITIZER, FUNCTION BOX, GRAPHICS TABLET, JOYSTICK, LIGHT PEN, MOUSE, SCANNER, STYLUS, TABLET, TOUCH SCREENS, TOUCH TABLETS, and TRACKBALL.)
[Hearn-86, Rogers-85, Vince-85]

input pipeline
The input pipeline is a data pathway within a computer graphics system starting at an event-creating device such as a MOUSE, button or keyboard, through to an application program which acts upon internally stored data.
[Foley-90, Hearn-86]

instance
When an image contains elements that are identical apart from size and orientation, it is only necessary to provide the geometry for one element, as it can be replicated as an instance of the original by defining an INSTANCE TRANSFORM. Consequently, this enables detailed structured scenes to be developed with a few geometric primitives, together with the relevant MATRIX OPERATIONS, without the storage overhead. See Figure I-3. (See also INSTANCE TRANSFORM.)
[Foley-90, Hearn-86]

instance transform
An instance transform is a MATRIX representing a scaling, rotation and translation operation to create an INSTANCE of an object. The homogeneous form provides a single MATRIX for these operations. (See also HOMOGENEOUS COORDINATES, INSTANCE, MATRIX, MATRIX OPERATION, ROTATION MATRIX, SCALING MATRIX, and TRANSLATION MATRIX.)
[Foley-90, Hearn-86]

intensity depth cueing
See DEPTH CUES.

intensity interpolation
See GOURAUD SHADING or PHONG SHADING.

intensity resolution
The intensity resolution of a display device is the maximum number of intensity levels, which is controlled by the number of bits allocated to each pixel. In HALFTONING processes, intensity resolution can be increased but at the sacrifice of spatial RESOLUTION. (See also FRAME STORE,

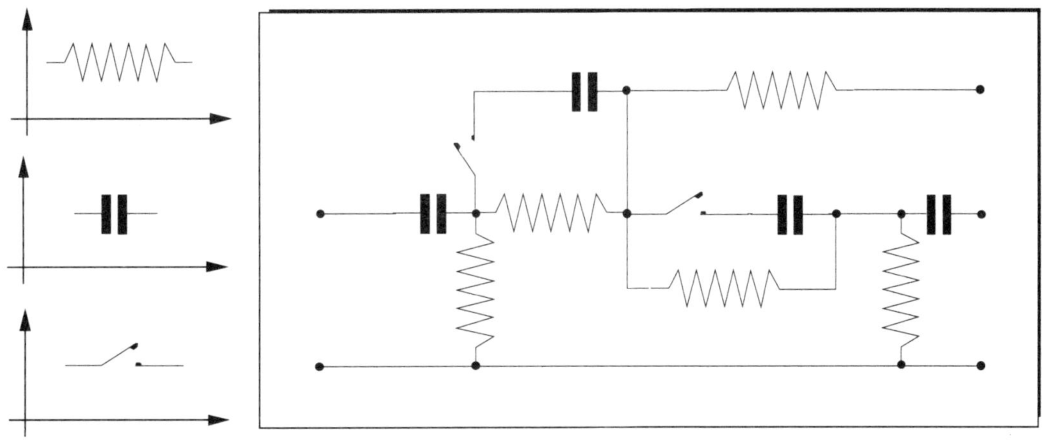

Figure I-3 *The circuit diagram on the right has been created entirely from the components displayed on the left using the technique of instancing. This involves storing the basic components in a reference master coordinate space, where, with the application of instance transforms in the form of a matrix, instances (or duplicates) can be repositioned, rotated and scaled in world coordinate space. Although this example demonstrates its use in two dimensions, it is also a valuable aid in building complex 3-D scenes.*

GREY LEVELS, GREY-SCALE IMAGE, and QUANTIZING.)
[Burger-89, Hearn-86]

interactive computer graphics

Interactive computer graphics is a generic term for computer systems providing users with REAL-TIME two-way graphical communication. Interactive systems are vital to activities such as MODELLING, COMPUTER ANIMATION, VLSI, and PAINT SYSTEMS.
[Burger-89, Foley-90, Haeberli-88, Hearn-86, Myers-86, Rogers-85]

interactive video

Interactive video is a computer system utilizing video laser disks for storing a DATA BASE of single and animated video images, which can be retrieved and displayed in REAL-TIME under computer control. (See also DATA BASE.)

interlacing

The BANDWIDTH of television systems is minimized by interlacing, which creates a FRAME from two interlaced FIELDS, where one FIELD consists of the odd RASTER lines and the other the even raster lines. The FIELDS are displayed alternately, which not only reduces the video BANDWIDTH but reduces FLICKER. See Figure I-4. (See also BANDWIDTH, FIELD, FLICKER, FRAME, FUSION FREQUENCY, HORIZONTAL SCAN FREQUENCY, NTSC, PAL, PERSISTENCE, REFRESH RATE, SECAM, VIDEO FREQUENCY, and VIDEO SIGNAL.)
[Hearn-86, Hunt-75]

interpenetrating objects

As computer graphics objects have a numerical definition, it is quite easy for one object to penetrate the 3-D space of another. A rendering algorithm such as the PAINTER'S ALGORITHM would not be capable of coping with

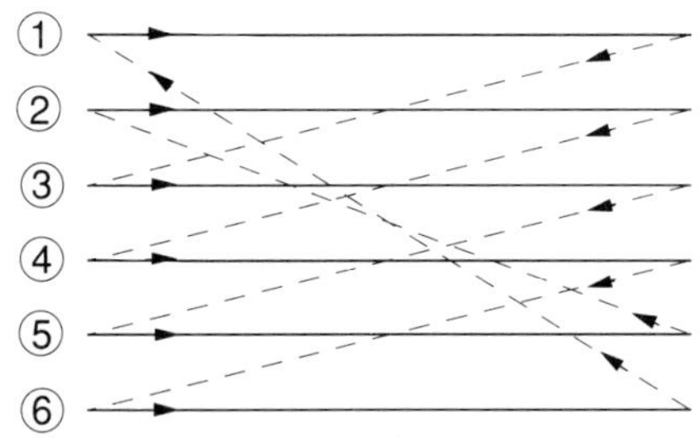

Figure I-4 *Television pictures are broadcast as sequences of fields which comprise the odd and even lines of one frame. This enables a high refresh rate to be achieved without increasing the bandwidth. In this illustration the frame consists of six raster lines which are broadcast in the sequence 1, 3, 5 (field 1) and 2, 4, 6 (field 2).*

interpenetrating polygons, whereas the Z-BUFFER resolves such conflicts. (See also CYCLICAL OVERLAPPING POLYGONS, DEPTH SORT ALGORITHM, OBJECT SPACE ALGORITHMS, PAINTER'S ALGORITHM, Z-BUFFER ALGORITHM, and Z-BUFFER.)
[Foley-90, Rogers-85, Segal-88]

interpolating spline
Unlike APPROXIMATING SPLINES, which only approach their CONTROL POINTS, interpolating splines actually intersect them. (See also APPROXIMATING SPLINE, BASIS FUNCTION, BÉZIER CURVE, B-SPLINE, CATMULL–ROM SPLINE, CONTROL POINTS, NURBS, and SPLINE.)
[Catmull-74b, Fletcher-90]

interpolation
Interpolation is the process of computing intermediate values between known values. It is extensively used in rendering, animation and surface modelling. Such schemes include LINEAR, QUADRATIC, CUBIC, HERMITE and LAGRANGIAN INTERPOLATION. (See also BLENDING FUNCTION, HERMITE INTERPOLATION, HIGH-DEGREE INTERPOLANT, INTERPOLATING SPLINE, LAGRANGIAN INTERPOLATION, LINEAR INTERPOLATION, and PARAMETRIC POLYNOMIAL.)
[Weeg-66]

interpreter
An interpreter is a computer program which accepts data in the form of stored commands and executes them. The commands are constructed from precise semantic and syntactical rules, and provide the user with logical constructs found in HIGH-LEVEL LANGUAGES. Unlike a COMPILER, which creates a translation of the source language in machine code, an interpreter 'interprets' the commands at execution time without any intermediate definition. (See also COMPILER, HIGH-LEVEL LANGUAGE, and LOW-LEVEL LANGUAGE.)

intersecting polygon
An intersecting polygon is partially contained within some reference rectangular window normally associated with AREA-SUBDIVISION ALGORITHMS, and represents one of the possible conditions detected in the space division process. (See also AREA SUBDIVISION ALGORITHMS, CONTAINED POLYGON, DISJOINT POLYGON, DIVIDE AND CONQUER, and WARNOCK ALGORITHM.)
[Rogers-85, Warnock-69]

inverse dynamics
One branch of COMPUTER ANIMATION is concerned with the realistic movement of physical structures – and inverse dynamics provides the numerical tools for determining the forces required to achieve these movements. Newton's laws of motion are central to these techniques and state that:
(1) Any body continues in a state of rest, or moves with uniform velocity in a straight line, unless acted upon by a force.
(2) The rate of change of momentum is directly proportional to the applied force.
(3) For every action force there is a reaction force, equal in magnitude but opposite in direction to the action.
These three laws form the basis of classical mechanics, where the first defines a force, the second measures a

force and the third describes the condition for force equilibrium. When these laws are included within an algorithm, they can be evaluated on a dynamic basis, perhaps using the Runge–Kutta method, to solve the equations of motion. (See also BEHAVIOURAL ANIMATION, COLLISION DETECTION, COMPUTER ANIMATION, DYNAMIC CONSTRAINTS, FORWARD DYNAMICS, FORWARD KINEMATICS, GOAL-ORIENTED ANIMATION, KEY-FRAME ANIMATION, PROCEDURAL ANIMATION, and RIGID-BODY ANIMATION.)
[Badler-87, Girard-87, Isaacs-87, Pentland-89, Wilhelms-87]

inverse Fourier transform
The inverse Fourier transform is the process of translating the FOURIER TRANSFORM of a function back into the original function. For example, a square wave pulse in the SPATIAL DOMAIN has a Fourier transform of a SINC FUNCTION in the FREQUENCY DOMAIN; however, the square wave can be reconstituted from the SINC FUNCTION by the inverse Fourier transform. (See also FAST FOURIER TRANSFORM, FOURIER TRANSFORM, and FOURIER WAVEFORM ANALYSIS.)
[Barrett-87, Gonzalez-87, Pratt-78, Walker-88]

inverse mapping
Inverse mapping or BACK MAPPING relates to the PROJECTION of a point in NORMALIZED DEVICE COORDINATES to WORLD COORDINATES. (See also DEVICE COORDINATE SYSTEM, NORMALIZED DEVICE COORDINATES, PERSPECTIVE PROJECTION, PROJECTION, and WORLD COORDINATE SPACE.)
[Foley-90]

inverse matrix
Given a non-SINGULAR MATRIX that performs some transformation upon an object, then there may exist another MATRIX called the inverse matrix capable of reversing this operation. When the MATRIX is an ORTHOGONAL MATRIX, its inverse is simply its transpose. (See also GEOMETRY ENGINE, HOMOGENEOUS COORDINATES, MATRIX, MATRIX OPERATION, ORTHOGONAL MATRIX, SINGULAR MATRIX, and TRANSPOSE MATRIX.)
[Gasson-83, Rogers-89, Stevenson-74]

inverse perspective mapping
In TEXTURE MAPPING, inverse perspective mapping is used to transform a point on the IMAGE PLANE back into the OBJECT SPACE from whence it came; this enables the pixel's footprint to be mapped onto the TEXTURE MAP so that its intensity can be accurately computed. (See also MAPPING, PERSPECTIVE PROJECTION, and TEXTURE MAPPING.)
[Gangnet-82, Hourcade-83]

inverse-square law
The inverse-square law is an empirical law stating that the intensity of illumination for a LIGHT SOURCE decreases as the square of the distance from the source. This is rarely taken into account within simple ILLUMINATION MODELS as it creates unnatural shading. (See also GLOBAL ILLUMINATION MODEL, ILLUMINATION MODEL, RADIOSITY, and RAY TRACING.)
[Glassner-89, Jenkins-76]

inverse video
An inverse video image is white on black.

irregular polygon
An irregular polygon has edges of different lengths.

isometric projection
An isometric projection is an axonometric projection where all three principal axes are equally foreshortened, thus allowing the same measuring scale to be associated with each axis. The isometric projection of a system of 3-D Cartesian axes creates an angle of 120° between any pair. It is a popular projection for engineering drawing. (See also AXONOMETRIC ORTHOGRAPHIC PROJECTION, CABINET PROJECTION, CARTESIAN COORDINATES, CAVALIER PROJECTION, ORTHOGRAPHIC PROJECTION, PARALLEL PROJECTION, and PERSPECTIVE PROJECTION.)
(Foley-90, Gasson-83, Hearn-86, Rogers-85]

isopachs
Isopachs or isopachytes are contours describing the differences between two surfaces. Their origin is in mining

where they are used to identify relative contours between two strata.

isoparametric curve

When one of the two parameters associated with a PARAMETRIC SURFACE PATCH is kept constant whilst the other is altered, an isoparametric curve is formed. (See also BÉZIER SURFACE PATCH, BIPARAMETRIC PATCH, B-SPLINE SURFACE PATCH, CARTESIAN PRODUCT PATCH, CURVES OF CONSTANT PARAMETER, PARAMETER, and PARAMETRIC SURFACE PATCH.)
[Gasson-83]

isosceles triangle

An isosceles triangle has two sides of equal length, implying that the angles formed by these sides with the third are also equal. (See also EQUILATERAL TRIANGLE.)

isotropic

Isotropic means invariant with respect to direction. For example a diffuse reflector is isotropic as it radiates light equally in all directions. (See also ANISOTROPIC.)
[Glassner-89]

Iterated Function Systems (IFS)

An Iterated Function System is an ordered set of TRANSFORMATIONS, with associated weights. IFSs have been used by Barnsley *et al.* to develop the COLLAGE THEOREM which enables complex images of leaves, clouds and trees to be constructed from very simple elements. IFSs also have applications in fractal interpolation, TERRAIN MODELLING and progressive rendering of PARAMETRIC CURVES and surfaces. (See also AFFINE TRANSFORMATION, COLLAGE THEOREM, FRACTAL, and SELF-SIMILARITY.)
[Barnsley-88, Demko-85, Horn-90, Peitgen-88]

jaggies

Jaggies is a popular name for the staircase stepping associated with pixel-based displays or graph plotters, when displaying lines or polygon edges. Their existence is an ALIASING ARTIFACT, but their removal requires an understanding of FOURIER WAVEFORM ANALYSIS and FILTERING. Although many workstations are able to display anti-aliased lines at very high speed, the ANTI-ALIASING of polygon edges and texture remains a feature of software renderers. However, current research indicates that automatic ANTI-ALIASING will rapidly become a feature of future graphics workstations. See Figure A-2. (See also ALIASING, ANTI-ALIASING, ARTIFACT, BASIS FUNCTION, FILTERING, FOURIER WAVEFORM ANALYSIS, NYQUIST LIMIT, OVERSAMPLING, POINT SAMPLING, SAMPLING, SPATIAL ALIASING, and UNIFORM SAMPLING.)
[Blinn-89a, Blinn-89b, Blinn-89c, Glassner-88]

jittering

Jittering is a method of ANTI-ALIASING by SAMPLING according to a POISSON DISK DISTRIBUTION. This is very effective as familiar ALIASING artifacts are replaced by NOISE which is much more acceptable to the human visual system. (See also ADAPTIVE SAMPLING, ALIASING, ANTI-ALIASING, ARTIFACT, BARTLETT FILTER, BASIS FUNCTION, BED-OF-NAILS, FILTER, FILTERING, NOISE, NYQUIST LIMIT, OVERSAMPLING, POINT SAMPLING, POISSON DISK DISTRIBUTION, SAMPLING, SPATIAL ALIASING, and STOCHASTIC SAMPLING.)
[Glassner-88, Shapiro-60]

Jordan Curve Theorem

The Jordan Curve Theorem states that a simple closed curve partitions a plane into two disjoint regions: an interior bounded by the curve, and an exterior without any boundary. This simple observation – which requires a complex mathematical proof – enables CONTAINMENT testing to be implemented in simple algorithms. (See also CONTAINMENT.)
[Rogers-85]

joystick

A joystick is an interactive pointing device associated with a graphics display and consists of a short moveable stick whose orientation can be adjusted manually. The stick's position is translated into vertical and horizontal components, which are translated by ANALOGUE-TO-DIGITAL COVERTERS into DIGITAL SIGANLS which eventually control the display's CURSOR.

Julia sets

Earlier this century Gaston Julia and Pierre Fatou investigated the behaviour of complex quadratic functions – and in 1980 their work was given a fresh impetus through the work of Benoit Mandelbrot. For example, the relation

$z \to z^2 + c$ (where z and c are complex)

is influenced by two values: the starting value z_0 and c. If one sets $z_0 = 0$ and examines the complex domain of c, the MANDELBROT SET is obtained, whereas, if the value of c is held constant and the complex plane of z_0 examined, the Julia set is found. Both sets have generated some of the most striking synthetic images ever created using computer graphics. (See also CHAOS THEORY, CHAOTIC BEHAVIOUR, FRACTAL, FRACTAL CURVE, FRACTAL SURFACE, MANDELBROT SET, and ORBIT.)
[Devaney-86, Hart-89, Julia-18, Peitgen-86, Peitgen-88]

K

kernel

See CONVOLUTION FILTER.

kerning

Kerning refers to the proportional spacing between letters in typesetting. In DESK-TOP PUBLISHING systems, the degree of kerning is under user control and requires sensitive handling, as it can destroy the readability and graphic quality of text if its influence is not appreciated. (See also DESK-TOP PUBLISHING and FONT.)

key-frame animation

Key-frame animation refers to the automatic process of generating images between selected key frames. By identifying parameters controlling features such as orientation and position of objects, attributes, position of observer and light sources, it is possible to interpolate these values and create the inbetween image. However, where a sequence of key-frames are involved, great care is needed to ensure that the BLENDING FUNCTION performing the interpolating does not introduce any discontinuities at the key-frames; one method of maintaining continuity is to employ B-SPLINE CURVES to control the complete blending operation. (See also ANIMATION, CHARACTER ANIMATION, COMPUTER ANIMATION, FORWARD KINEMATICS, FRAME, INBETWEENING, and INTERPOLATION.)
[Brotman-88, Burger-89]

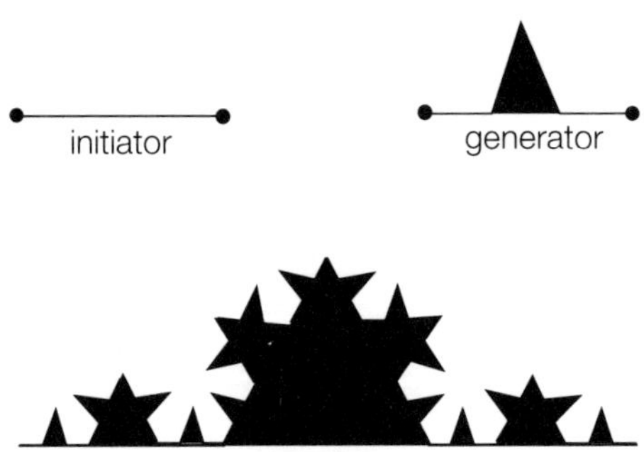

Figure K-1 *The Koch curve (or snowflake curve) can be constructed by recursively replacing an initiator segment by a generator segment. In the above example, the generator segment consists of four new initiator segments.*

keying

In video post production, keying is a process whereby two VIDEO SIGNALS are proportionally mixed depending upon the value of a KEY SIGNAL. This allows dissolves to be effected and provides a mechanism for handling MATTES. Two useful forms of keying are: CHROMA KEYING and alpha keying. (See also ALPHA CHANNEL, CHROMA KEYING, COMPOSITING, DIGITAL CHROMA KEYING, DIGITAL MIXING, MATTE, VIDEO MIXING, and VIDEO SIGNAL.)

key signal

See KEYING.

knot

A knot is the join between two curve segments forming a SPLINE and is represented by a PARAMETER value; these values are organized as a KNOT VECTOR which is used to control a B-spline generating algorithm. (See also BASIS FUNCTION, B-SPLINE CURVE, B-SPLINE SURFACE PATCH, CONTINUITY, CONTROL POINTS, KNOT VECTOR, NURBS, and SPLINE.)
[Burger-89, Farin-88, Hearn-86, Rogers-89, Woodwark-86]

knot vector

A knot vector is a sequence of non-decreasing PARAMETER values (KNOTS) used in the generation of B-SPLINE CURVES. The number of values stored depends upon the number of track points and the order of the curve, and their numerical spacing influences the control they have upon the curve; which is why NURBS have become so popular, as the knots can have non-uniform spacing. (See also BASIS FUNCTION, B-SPLINE CURVE, B-SPLINE SURFACE PATCH, CONTINUITY, CONTROL POINTS, KNOT, NURBS, and SPLINE.)
[Burger-89, Farin-88, Hearn-86, Rogers-89, Woodwark-86]

Koch curve
In 1906, Helge von Koch described a curve which now bears his name, although it is sometimes known as the 'snowflake' curve. It is constructed from two elements called the 'initiator' and the 'generator', where the initiator is a chain of line segments, and the generator is another chain, but generally only two or three segments long. If now the generator shape replaces every segment on the initiator and this process is repeated a few times, a snowflake effect is rapidly created. Because of the construction process, the curve exhibits the property of limited SELF-SIMILARITY and is a FRACTAL. See Figure K-1. (See also FRACTAL and SELF-SIMILARITY.)
[Koch-06, Prusinkiewicz-88b]

Lagrangian interpolation
Lagrangian interpolation is a parametric interpolant that passes through a given set of points. For example, to fit a QUADRATIC through three points, a parameter *t* would have values zero and one at the two end points, and an extra value of *t* must be specified for the intermediate point. Unfortunately, Lagrangian interpolation cannot be used for fitting curve sections together, as there is no mechanism for preserving slope CONTINUITY. (See also BLENDING FUNCTION, CONTINUITY, HERMITE INTERPOLATION, HIGH-DEGREE INTERPOLANT, INTERPOLATING SPLINE, INTERPOLATION, LINEAR INTERPOLATION, PARAMETRIC POLYNOMIAL, and QUADRATIC.)
[Bowyer-83, Burger-89, Weeg-66, Woodwark-86]

Lambert's cosine law
Lambert's cosine law states that the light reflected from a dull MATTE surface is proportional to the INCIDENT LIGHT and the COSINE of the angle between the incident light vector and the SURFACE NORMAL. This is the ILLUMINATION MODEL employed for DIFFUSE SURFACES. See Figure D-3. (See also COSINE SHADING, DIFFUSE REFLECTION, DIFFUSE REFLECTION COEFFICIENT, DIFFUSE SURFACE, GOURAUD SHADING, INCIDENT LIGHT, ILLUMINATION MODEL, MATTE, and SURFACE NORMAL.)
[Burger-89, Foley-90, Hearn-86, Rogers-85]

LCD
See LIQUID CRYSTAL DEVICE.

left-handed axes
A left-handed set of 3-D Cartesian axes is where one's left-hand thumb is aligned with the X-axis, the first finger with the Y-axis and the middle finger with the Z-axis. One must be careful when undertaking TRANSFORMATIONS between left- and right-handed systems as sign changes can occur. See Figure R-3. (See also CARTESIAN COORDINATES, RIGHT-HANDED AXES, TRANSFORMATION, and VECTOR PRODUCT.)
[Burger-89, Foley-90, Gasson-83, Rogers-89]

lerp
See LINEAR INTERPOLATION.

light buffer
In RAY TRACING, the light buffer is a strategy for accelerating shadow calculations, and employs a DIRECTION CUBE which contains a list of objects capable of forming SHADOW VOLUMES for a given LIGHT SOURCE. These lists are held for areas of the direction cube called cells, and can be processed for the current light ray to prevent the entire DATA BASE of objects from being processed. (See also DIRECTION CUBE, LIGHT SOURCE, RAY TRACING, and SHADOW VOLUME.)
[Glassner-89, Haines-86]

lighting model
See ILLUMINATION MODEL.

lightness
The attribute lightness is employed in the HLS COLOUR MODEL and is approximately equivalent to BRIGHTNESS. (See also HLS COLOUR MODEL, HUE, and SATURATION.)
[Foley-90, Hearn-86, Ostwald-31, Rogers-85]

light pen
A light pen is an interactive pointing device incorporating a photosensitive cell at its tip, and when it is used to probe a raster display screen it is possible for associated electronics to identify the raster and the pixel referenced by the pen. The pen has not proved to be a very popular device. (See also TABLET, JOYSTICK, MOUSE, STYLUS, and TRACKBALL.)
[Hearn-86]

light source
A light source is a virtual source of illumination upon which a RENDERER can make intensity calculations for surfaces. Light sources are typically AMBIENT, DIRECTIONAL, POINT and SPOT, and will be allocated attributes such as position, intensity, colour and direction. (See also AMBIENT LIGHT, DIRECTIONAL LIGHT SOURCE, DISTRIBUTED LIGHT SOURCE, GLOBAL ILLUMINATION MODEL, LIGHTING MODEL, LIGHT SOURCE DIRECTION, POINT LIGHT SOURCE, REFLECTANCE MODEL, RENDERER, SPOT LIGHT, SPOT SIZE, and SPREAD ANGLE.)
[Burger-89, Foley-90, Glassner-88, Hearn-86, Rogers-85, Verbeck- 84]

light source direction
A POINT LIGHT SOURCE radiates equally in all directions, whereas a VECTOR is needed to identify a light source direction for a DIRECTIONAL, DISTRIBUTED or SPOT LIGHT SOURCE. (See also DIRECTIONAL LIGHT SOURCE, DISTRIBUTED LIGHT SOURCE, LIGHT SOURCE, SPOT LIGHT, and VECTOR.)
[Burger-89, Foley-90, Glassner-88, Hearn-86, Rogers-85]

linear
A linear relationship is described by a POLYNOMIAL of DEGREE 1. For example, the following is a linear equation

$$y = ax + b$$

[Bowyer-83, Burger-89, Gasson-83, Rogers-89]

linear interpolation
Linear interpolation computes the values between two extreme values depending upon the status of some PARAMETER such that linear changes in the parameter produce linear changes in the interpolated values. For example, if A and B are two values to be interpolated, and t is a parameter, any interpolated value V can be computed from

$$V = (1-t)A + tB \quad \text{where } (0 \leq t \leq 1)$$

This is also known as the lerp function. (See also BLENDING FUNCTION, LINEAR, PARAMETER, and PARAMETRIC EQUATION.)
[Bowyer-83, Woodwark-86, Weeg-66]

linearity
In CATHODE RAY TUBES, absolute linearity is the maximum deviation of a raster from a reference line, and relative lin-

earity is the ratio of the absolute linearity to the line's length, expressed as a percentage. (See also CATHODE RAY TUBE.)

linear transformation

Linear transformations such as shearing, scaling, rotation and reflection ensure that when they operate upon a linear combination of vectors this linearity is preserved. (See also AFFINE TRANSFORMATION, HOMOGENEOUS COORDINATES, RIGID TRANSFORMATION, and TRANSFORMATION.)
[MacBeath-64, Rogers-89, Stevenson-74]

line equation

Although there are many methods for describing the line equation (parametric, implicit, homogeneous etc.) a familiar form is

$$y = mx + c$$

where m is the slope and c is the intercept with the Y-axis. But perhaps the most useful definition is

$$ax + by + c = 0$$

which avoids the problems of infinite slopes in the first example. (See also CARTESIAN COORDINATES, LINEAR, PARAMETRIC EQUATION, and PLANE EQUATION.)
[Bowyer-83]

line frequency

See HORIZONTAL SCAN FREQUENCY.

line of projection

In projection schemes, a line of projection is a line formed between a point on an object through the PROJECTION PLANE to the CENTRE OF PROJECTION. See Figure L-1. (See also AIM POINT, EYE COORDINATE SYSTEM, EYE POINT, LINE OF SIGHT, OBSERVER, PERSPECTIVE PROJECTION, PROJECTION, PICTURE PLANE, VIEWING PYRAMID, and VIEW VECTOR.)
[Burger-89, Foley-90, Hearn-86, Rogers-89, Rogers-85]

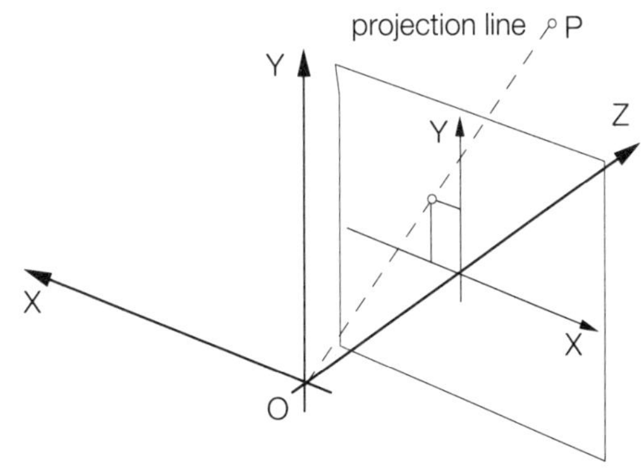

Figure L-1 *This diagram shows how projection lines are used to capture a projection upon the projection plane. Note that whilst the three-space is right-handed, the two-space is left-handed.*

line of sight

The orientation of the OBSERVER in WORLD COORDINATES can be specified by a line of sight joining the EYE POINT to the AIM POINT. The PICTURE PLANE is then ORTHOGONAL to this line and captures the final PERSPECTIVE PROJECTION. See Figure E-2. (See also AIM POINT, EYE COORDINATE SYSTEM, EYE POINT, OBSERVER, PERSPECTIVE PROJECTION, PROJECTION, PICTURE PLANE, VIEWING PYRAMID, and VIEW VECTOR.)
[Burger-89, Foley-90, Hearn-86, Rogers-89, Rogers-85]

line test

In animation, a line test is frequently performed whilst the images are still in vector form to confirm the fluidity of the animation. Some workstations are able to perform this in REAL-TIME by storing the images in memory or on disk, and displaying them sequentially. (See also ANIMATION, COMPUTER ANIMATION, and REAL-TIME.)

Lipschitz constant

The Lipschitz constant is associated with the Lipschitz condition relating to bounding curves and surfaces. The condition, when related to a parametric curve $F(u)$ where $0 \le u \le 1$ states that

$$|F(u_1) - F(u_0)| \le K\,|u_1 - u_0|$$

where K is the Lipschitz constant, and u_0 and u_1 are in the interval $0 \le u_i \le 1$. The concept appears in ITERATED FUNCTION SYSTEMS and TRIANGULATION algorithms. (See also COLLAGE THEOREM and ITERATED FUNCTION SYSTEMS.)
[Peitgen-88, Herzen-87]

liquid crystal display (LCD)
Liquid crystal displays are capable of changing their state from transparent to opaque when a voltage or laser pulse is applied. They are employed in portable computers and very high-resolution full-colour displays.

LISP
LISP is a HIGH-LEVEL LANGUAGE developed for processing lists of items and has been pioneered by Symbolics as a complete computer software environment. One of LISP's strengths, especially in COMPUTER ANIMATION, is that the program and data share one common environment, which allows modifications to be made to both code and data and the impact upon the system to be observed without compiling delays. (See also HIGH-LEVEL LANGUAGE, LOW-LEVEL LANGUAGE, and OBJECT-ORIENTED PROGRAMMING.)
[Winston-84]

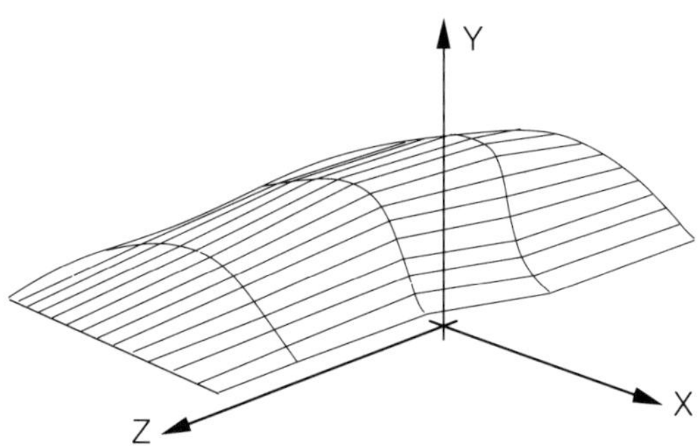

Figure L-2 *This simple lofted surface has been created by linearly interpolating between four contours representing cross-sections through the desired surface.*

lofted surface
A lofted surface or ruled surface is formed by linearly interpolating between several offset 3-D curves. See Figure L-2.
[Rogers-89]

lofting
Lofting is a traditional technique in the design of ship's hulls where SPLINES (thin strips of wood) are used to blend a series of cross-sections into a smooth surface. It is interesting to note that a constrained thin lamina can be approximated by a CUBIC CURVE – hence the use of the term spline in surface modelling. (See also B-SPLINE CURVE, CUBIC CURVE, and NURBS.)
[Bedi-89, Burger-89, Farin-88, Woodwark-86]

look-up table (LUT)
(1) An LUT can be a memory-based device frequently associated with FRAME STORES, containing colour intensities substituted for the values held in the FRAME STORE. (See also FRAME STORE and LOOK-UP TABLE ANIMATION.)
[Foley-90, Hearn-86, Rogers-85]
(2) An LUT can be a DATA STRUCTURE used in a programming environment used for storing an ordered set of data which can be retrieved by indexing any entry; this can also be implemented in hardware to store precomputed values for mathematical functions. (See also DATA STRUCTURE and GRAPHICAL DATA STRUCTURE.)
[Foley-90, Hearn-86, Rogers-85]

look-up table animation
Given a suitable image in the FRAME STORE, parts of the image can appear to move in a cyclic manner when the LOOK-UP TABLE entries are rotated – hence the name look-up table animation. (See also ANIMATION, COMPUTER ANIMATION, and FRAME STORE.)
[Foley-87]

low-level language

In computer language processing, a low-level language, such as an assembler language, has virtually a one-to-one correspondence between the mnemonics which form the language and with the machine code into which it is translated. (See also HIGH-LEVEL LANGUAGE.)

L-systems

L-systems as developed by Lindenmayer is a grammar that has been used for modelling plants – and consists of a set of productions (rules) that specify how an edge in a plant-like structure is to be replaced by some more complex element, at the same time preserving the integrity of the start and terminal nodes in the two structures. (See also HELIOTROPISM.)
[Prusinkiewicz-88a, Smith-84, Viennot-89]

luminance

Luminance is equivalent to the BRIGHTNESS component of a colour VIDEO SIGNAL and is represented by the letter *Y*, in the CMY acronym. Luminance is computed from

$$Y = 0.299\text{Red} + 0.587\text{Green} + 0.114\text{Blue}$$

The CCIR 601 digital standard allows 8 bits to encode the luminance channel which provides 256 levels of intensity, although this is not completely exploited by the standard. (See also CHROMINANCE, NTSC, PAL, and VIDEO SIGNAL.)
[Hearn-86, Hunt-75, Rogers-85]

luminosity

See BRIGHTNESS.

luminosity curve

A luminosity curve relates sensitivity to WAVELENGTH; this might be for the human eye or an electronic light detecting system. (See also BRIGHTNESS and LUMINANCE.)
[Gregory-86, Hunt-75]

LUT

See LOOK-UP TABLE.

LZW compression

LZW is an acronym for Lempel-Ziv and Welch, which is a data compression algorithm with applications for IMAGE COMPRESSION. Some images can be compressed by a factor of 50% or even 90% in some cases. The algorithm detects strings of pixel patterns which are referenced within a string table which itself is processed as though it were part of the image. (See also CELL ENCODING, IMAGE COMPRESSION, NAPLPS, and RUN-LENGTH ENCODING.)
[Welch-84]

m

Mach band

Ernst Mach discovered that the human visual system emphasizes intensity changes occurring at a boundary, causing a banding effect now named after him. These Mach bands can be very obvious when GOURAUD SHADING is applied to objects, where insufficient polygons are used to model areas of high curvature. (See also GOURAUD SHADING.)

[Burger-89, Gregory-86, Hearn-86, Rogers-85]

Mandelbrot set

The original Mandelbrot set displays graphically a map of the rate at which a point z_0 moves towards infinity under the repeated application of a mapping. Consider, for example, the mapping function

$$z \rightarrow z^2 + c$$

where z and c are COMPLEX NUMBERS, and $z_0 = 0$ is the initial value of z. If $c = x + \boldsymbol{i}y$, then the x and y terms can be used to address a plane forming the Mandelbrot set. The image is formed by choosing values for x and y from given limits, say for example $-2.25 \leq x \leq 0.75$ and $-1.5 \leq y \leq 1.5$, and by iterating the above mapping function until one of two conditions arises. If during the iterations the magnitude of z exceeds 10, say, the point $[x, y]$ is assigned a colour depending upon the number of iterations. But if z does not exceed 10, even after 200 iterations, then the point $[x, y]$ is assigned some background colour. The delicate FRACTAL boundary separating unstable values of c from the stable set encloses the Mandelbrot set. See Figure M-1. (See also FRACTAL and JULIA SET.)

[Mandelbrot-77, Mandelbrot-83, Peitgen-86, Peitgen-88]

mapping

A mapping is a transformation taking points or sets of points to other points or sets of points. The relevance of mapping in computer graphics is best illustrated in its use in the mapping of planar TEXTURE MAPS onto non-planar surfaces. Here a geometric process is required to perform a mapping procedure such that points on the surface have a unique point on the texture map. Similarly, a mapping procedure is also required to distort a 2-D geographical map into a 3-D spherical surface, which is a convenient way of modelling the world.

[Glassner-89, Rogers-85]

marching cubes

The marching cubes algorithm is used for creating triangular models of constant density surfaces from 3-D medical data. The algorithm employs a DIVIDE AND CONQUER strategy to locate a surface in a logical cube constructed from eight pixels from two adjacent data slices. As soon as the surface has been identified, it 'marches' on to the next until the volume has been processed. (See also CROSS-SECTION RENDERING, THRESHOLD RENDERING, VOLUME SHADER, and VOLUMETRIC RENDERING.)

[Lorensen-87]

Markov algorithm

A Markov algorithm, as distinct from a MARKOV PROCESS, is concerned with the transformation of strings of symbols and functions by recognizing the first occurrence of a string and replacing it by another. As an aid to this process it employs a set of productions (rules expressing how one string replaces another) which must be searched systematically.

[Korfhage-66, Markov-61, Monne-81]

Markov process

A Markov process describes a system with n states in which the probabilities are specified for passing from state to state in each time period. The key property for a Markov process is that the probabilities are constant from time period to time period. The system can be described by an $(n \times n)$ MATRIX P where the element $P_{i,j}$ is the conditional probability of passing from state i to state j. In computer graphics, Markov processes are related

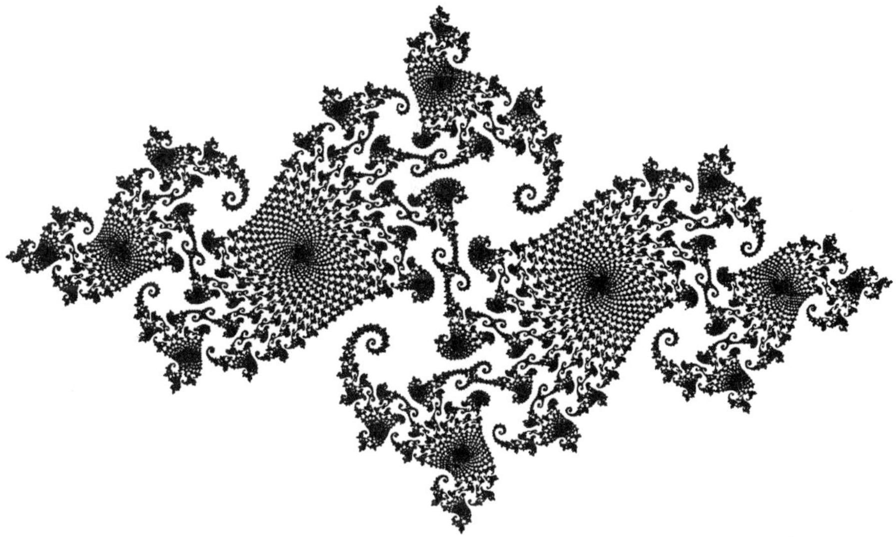

Figure M-1 *The black area of this image is the Mandelbrot set, named after Benoit Mandelbrot who discovered it in 1980. Adrien Douady and John Hamal Hubbard have proved that the set is connected; no part is disconnected from the main body. (Courtesy: Dietmar Saupe.)*

to ITERATED FUNCTION SYSTEMS. (See also ITERATED FUNCTION SYSTEMS.)
[Horn-90]

master coordinate space

An INSTANCE is defined in master coordinate space, and with the aid of INSTANCE TRANSFORMS becomes part of some image HIERARCHY. For example, the icon for an electrical resistance will have a graphical description in master coordinate space, and will be instanced in various orientations and scales in a WORLD COORDINATE SPACE, which itself becomes mapped onto a NORMALIZED DEVICE COORDINATE space. See Figure I-3. (See also DEVICE COORDINATE SYSTEM, EYE COORDINATE SYSTEM, NORMALIZED DEVICE COORDINATES, PHYSICAL DEVICE COORDINATES, and WORLD COORDINATE SPACE.)
[Burger-89, Foley-90, Hearn-86]

material editing

Material editing is a feature of an interactive system enabling a user to create and modify physical attributes assigned to objects such as texture, bumpiness or displacement.

matrix

In computer graphics, a matrix is used to define linear transformations such as scaling, rotation, shearing and translation. For example, the following matrix is used to rotate a shape about the origin by ø when using 2-D Cartesian coordinates

$$[x', y'] = [x, y]\begin{bmatrix} \cos(ø) & \sin(ø) \\ -\sin(ø) & \cos(ø) \end{bmatrix}$$

In general, a (3 x 3) matrix operating upon 2-D HOMOGE-

NEOUS COORDINATES can be represented by

$$[x', y', 1] = [x, y, 1] \left[\begin{array}{cc|c} a & b & g \\ c & d & h \\ \hline e & f & s \end{array}\right]$$

where *a, b, c,* and *d* cause scaling, rotation and shearing operations, *e* and *f* produce translation, *s* is the global homogeneous scaling factor and *g* and *h* control projection. (See also MATRIX OPERATION.)
[Burger-89, Gasson-83, Rogers-89, Stevenson-74]

matrix operation

Transformations such as translation, rotation, shear and scale have a matrix definition which permits the design of elegant algorithms, and also allows an integrated approach to implement these features in hardware. Matrix notation should be interpreted as a convenient method of summarizing a number of related mathematical operations. For example, the following family of equations contain some obvious typographical duplication:

$$X = 3t^2 + 2t + 1$$
$$Y = 4t^2 + 3t + 5$$
$$Z = 5t^2 + t + 2$$

The matrix notation permits the above operations to be condensed into

$$[X, Y, Z] = [t^2, t, 1] \begin{bmatrix} 3 & 4 & 5 \\ 2 & 3 & 1 \\ 1 & 5 & 2 \end{bmatrix}$$

which is much more elegant and compact. (See also AFFINE TRANSFORMATION, CONCATENATION, HOMOGENEOUS COORDINATES, INVERSE MATRIX, ROTATION MATRIX, SCALING MATRIX, TRANSLATION MATRIX, and TRANSPOSE MATRIX.)
[Burger-89, Gasson-83, Rogers-89, Stevenson-74]

matte

(1) Matte means dull.

(2) A matte is an opaque shape (stencil) used to isolate a portion of an image. This is often found in PAINT SYSTEMS and video animation techniques where part of an image needs to be isolated. (See also COMPOSITING and PAINT SYSTEM.)

MCGA

MCGA is an acronym for Multi-Color Graphics Array which is a built-in display adaptor for IBM's PS/2 models 25 and 30 computers, and provides a resolution of 640 by 480 pixels with 16 colours. (See also CGA, EGA, HDA, HGC, MDA, PVA, SUPER VGA and VGA.)

MDA

MDA is an acronym for Monochrome Display Adaptor originally developed by IBM to provide 80 columns by 25 rows of text and character-size symbols, with a 9 x 14 character matrix. (See also CGA, EGA, HDA, HGC, MCGA, PVA, SUPER VGA and VGA.)

mean

In the context of a FREQUENCY DISTRIBUTION, the mean is the centre point of a symmetric distribution such as a GAUSSIAN DISTRIBUTION; but for a skew distribution, it identifies the line containing the centre of gravity of the shape. (See also AVERAGE, FREQUENCY DISTRIBUTION, and GAUSSIAN DISTRIBUTION.)

mean deviation

The mean deviation of a FREQUENCY DISTRIBUTION is a measure of the average deviation from the arithmetic mean. It is expressed as

$$\text{mean deviation} = \frac{1}{n} \sum_{i=1}^{n} |(x_i - \bar{x})|$$

where n is the number of samples, $\bar{x}$ is the arithmetic mean, and x_i is any member of the distribution.
(See also AVERAGE, FREQUENCY DISTRIBUTION, STANDARD DEVIATION, and VARIANCE.)

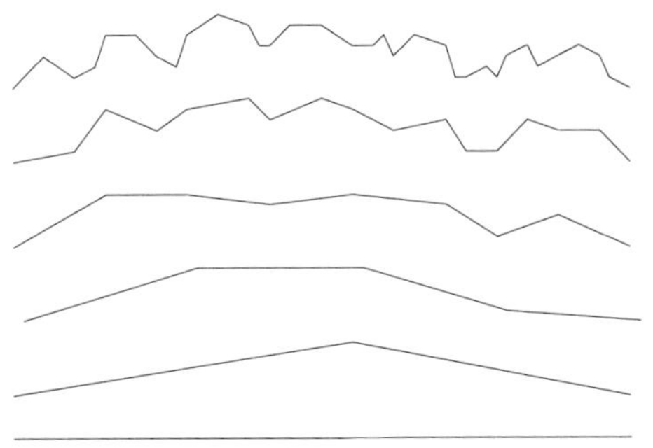

Figure M-2 *Midpoint displacement consists of repeatedly dividing line segments in two and moving the midpoint by some random amount. In this illustration the original bottom line has started to look fractal-like after 5 applications of this procedure.*

median

The median is the midpoint of some 2-D graph such as the position of the maximum point of a GAUSSIAN DISTRIBUTION. (See also AVERAGE, MEAN, MEAN DEVIATION, STANDARD DEVIATION, and VARIANCE.)

menu

A menu is a choice of actions presented to a user in a tabular form within an interactive computer system. The menu may be displayed upon a screen or attached to a data tablet, and the user selects a choice, perhaps using a mouse or stylus, and confirms or cancels the action. (See also HIERARCHICAL MENU, HUMAN–COMPUTER INTERACTION, ICONS, POP-UP MENU, PULL-DOWN MENU, USER INTERFACE, and WIMP ENVIRONMENT.)
[Burger-89]

metafile

A metafile in computer graphics generally stores low-level device independent picture commands. (See also DEVICE INDEPENDENT, DISPLAY LIST, and DISPLAY FILE.)
[Foley-90, Hearn-86, ISO-87g, ISO-88b]

microfacets

In REFLECTANCE MODELS that simulate the behaviour of specular reflections upon rough surfaces, the concept of microfacets is incorporated with a GAUSSIAN DISTRIBUTION controlling their orientation. This enables FRESNEL EFFECTS to be simulated, resulting in realistic images of metallic surfaces. (See also FRESNEL EFFECT, GAUSSIAN DISTRIBUTION, RAY TRACING, REFLECTANCE MODEL, SHADING MODEL, SPECULAR REFLECTION, and TORRANCE–SPARROW SHADING MODEL.)
[Cook-82b, Glassner-89, Rogers-85, Torrance-67]

micropolygon

The REYES renderer is built around the idea of a micropolygon which is a quadrilateral with approximately $^1/2$ pixel sides. This simplifies ANTI-ALIASING and the addressing of TEXTURE MAPS. (See also REYES.)
[Cook-87]

midpoint displacement

Midpoint displacement is a FRACTAL modelling technique where the midpoint of a 2-D line segment or a 3-D surface element is displaced by a Gaussian random offset. New lines or surface elements are repeatedly displaced until sufficient detail has been achieved. The VARIANCE of the offset must be scaled correctly during successive iterations. See Figure M-2. (See also FOURIER FILTERING, FOURIER FRACTAL, FRACTAL, FRACTAL CURVE, FRACTAL GEOMETRY, FRACTAL NOISE, and FRACTAL SURFACE.)
[Burger-89, Hearn-86, Magnenat-Thalmann-87b, Peitgen-88]

MIMD

MIMD is an acronym for Multiple-Instruction Multiple-Data – and describes multiple processor systems which function without the synchronizing clock pulses associated with SIMD machines. An array of TRANSPUTERS would be described as a MIMD architecture. (See also SIMD and TRANSPUTER.)
[Dew-89]

minimax test
The minimax test refers to a procedure that determines the minimum and maximum EXTENTS of a 2-D shape or 3-D object. (See also BOUNDING VOLUME and EXTENTS.)
[Foley-90, Rogers-85]

mip maps
Lance Williams coined the term 'mip maps' which are a hierarchical set of filtered texture maps developed to reduce the time spent in ANTI-ALIASING during TEXTURE MAPPING operations. The acronym 'mip' is from the Latin phrase *multum in parvo* meaning 'many things in a small place'. The mip maps are intended to be applied to surfaces viewed at different distances, and for any given distance two of the nested maps are selected and a linearly interpolated texture value is computed. (See also ANTI-ALIASING, TEXTURE MAP, and TEXTURE MAPPING.)
[Williams-83]

MIPS
MIPS is an acronym for Millions of Instructions Per Second – and computer graphics systems never have enough.

modelling
Modelling is a variety of disparate techniques used for representing structures within a computer graphics system. It addresses the representation of faceted objects, SCULPTURED SURFACES, molecules, FREE FORM SURFACES and natural phenomena. (See also BOUNDARY REPRESENTATION, CONSTRUCTIVE SOLID GEOMETRY, FREE FORM SURFACES, GEOMETRIC MODELLING, MOLECULAR MODELLING, NATURAL PHENOMENA MODELLING, PARTICLE SYSTEM, SCULPTURED SURFACES, SOFT OBJECTS, SOLIDS MODELLING, TERRAIN MODELLING, and WIRE FRAME.)
[Farin-88, Hearn-86, Woodwark-86]

model sheets
In traditional animation model sheets are used to illustrate a character from different angles and in a variety of poses; these become reference graphics for all the animators associated with a project. (See also ANIMATION, BAR SHEETS, FRAME, and STORYBOARD.)
[White-86]

moiré patterns
Moiré patterns are a moving wave-like effect often caused by interfering regular patterns such as repetitive texture displayed upon a raster device. They are very obvious on domestic television sets when a broadcast image contains a moving patterned material. (See also ALIASING, ANTI-ALIASING, ARTIFACT, FILTERING, and JAGGIES.)

molecular modelling
Molecular modelling is performed upon a computer graphics system to model atomic and molecular structures; such systems are able to display a graphical interpretation of atomic and molecular concepts such as atomic positions, electron bonds, equipotential fields and molecular orientations.
[Max-83, Max-88, Porter-79, Staudhammer-78]

monitor
A monitor is a raster display device capable of accepting video signals direct from video equipment or a computer FRAME STORE, where the signals might be RGB or COMPOSITE VIDEO. (See also BEAM PENETRATION CRT, CALLIGRAPHIC DISPLAY, CATHODE RAY TUBE, FRAME STORE, HIGH-RESOLUTION DISPLAY, MULTI-SCANNING MONITOR, and SHADOW-MASK COLOUR CRT.)
[Hearn-86]

monochrome
Black and white photography and television are monochrome as they exploit various levels of grey to represent an image, but there is no implication that grey is the only colour that may be used. (See also ACHROMATIC LIGHT and CHROMATIC LIGHT.)
[Hunt-75]

monomial basis
The monomial basis employs the monomials $t^0, t^1, t^2, \ldots, t^n$

as the basis for specifying polynomial WEIGHTING FUNCTIONS. For example, given four CONTROL POINTS $\boldsymbol{P}_0$, $\boldsymbol{P}_1$, $\boldsymbol{P}_2$ and $\boldsymbol{P}_3$, the BERNSTEIN BASIS FUNCTIONS are expressed in a polynomial form by the following

$$\boldsymbol{P}(t) = [\boldsymbol{P}_0, \boldsymbol{P}_1, \boldsymbol{P}_2, \boldsymbol{P}_3] \begin{bmatrix} (1-t)^3 \\ (1-t)^2\, 3t \\ (1-t)\ \ 3t^2 \\ t^3 \end{bmatrix}$$

This can be rewritten employing a monomial basis as

$$\boldsymbol{P}(t) = [\boldsymbol{P}_0, \boldsymbol{P}_1, \boldsymbol{P}_2, \boldsymbol{P}_3] \begin{bmatrix} -1 & 3 & -3 & 1 \\ 3 & -6 & 3 & 0 \\ -3 & 3 & 0 & 0 \\ 1 & 0 & 0 & 0 \end{bmatrix} \begin{bmatrix} t^3 \\ t^2 \\ t^1 \\ t^0 \end{bmatrix}$$

The monomial basis is also known as the POWER BASIS. (See also BASIS FUNCTION, BERNSTEIN BASIS FUNCTION, CONTROL POINTS, PARAMETRIC POLYNOMIAL, and RATIONAL POLYNOMIAL)
[Farin-88]

Monte-Carlo method
Monte-Carlo methods imply the use of random numbers within an algorithm, as used in STOCHASTIC SAMPLING.
[Halton-70]

motion blur
The idea of motion blur is based upon the observation that, when moving objects are recorded upon film, they will leave a blurred image because of the finite exposure time. RAY TRACING provides an excellent environment to implement this effect. (See also STOCHASTIC SAMPLING.)
[Burger-89, Glassner-88, Glassner-89, Max-85, Potmesil-83]

mouse
A mouse is a pointing device used in interactive computer graphics systems to control the screen's cursor. It generally consists of a small box capable of fitting into the user's palm who moves it over a flat horizontal surface. Fitted to the device are one or more buttons that can be used to create an EVENT signal. It operates in RELATIVE COORDINATES as it may be lifted away from its working surface and repositioned without affecting the cursor's position. The mouse is simply brushed over some surface, and its relative movement is conveyed to the system. (See also WIMP ENVIRONMENT.)
[Burger-89, Hearn-86]

multi-scanning monitor
A multi-scanning monitor is capable of adjusting to different scan rates, which is useful when it has to work with a variety of different graphics boards having different video standards. (See also BEAM PENETRATION CRT, CALLIGRAPHIC DISPLAY, CATHODE RAY TUBE, COLOUR MONITOR, HORIZONTAL SCAN FREQUENCY, MONITOR, REFRESH CRT, REFRESH RATE, SHADOW-MASK COLOUR CRT, and VIDEO SIGNAL.)

Munsell colour system
Munsell developed a colour system to order colours in terms of their HUE, VALUE and CHROMA levels. This was the first attempt at organizing colour into some coherent system, and has been extended with the introduction of computer graphics with the HSV COLOUR MODEL. (See also CHROMA, COLOUR, COLOUR MODEL, COLOUR SPACE, COMPLEMENTARY COLOUR, HLS COLOUR MODEL, HSV COLOUR MODEL, HUE, HUE CIRCLE, LIGHTNESS, PURITY, RGB COLOUR MODEL, SATURATION, and VALUE.)
[Boynton-79, Munsell-41]

n

NAPLPS

NAPLPS is an acronym for North American Presentation-Level Protocol Syntax, which is a shape-defined format for describing an image as a series of geometric shapes and patterns. As NAPLPS relies upon a set of predefined shapes, its application is limited, especially for encoding scanned photographs that do not exhibit regular patterns. (See also CELL ENCODING, IMAGE COMPRESSION, LZW COMPRESSION, and RUN-LENGTH ENCODING.)

natural phenomena modelling

When it comes to the modelling of natural phenomena such as fire, water, mist, waves and trees, the use of polygons, surface patches and CSG are unable to support the level of detail and geometric complexity associated with these structures. This has seen the introduction of techniques such as FRACTALS, ITERATED FUNCTION SYSTEMS, SOLID TEXTURE, HYPERTEXTURE, PARTICLE SYSTEMS, VOXELS and FOURIER NOISE, to resolve some very difficult modelling problems. (See also FOURIER FRACTAL, FRACTAL, FRACTAL GEOMETRY, FRACTIONAL BROWNIAN MOTION, HELIOTROPISM, HYPERTEXTURE, ITERATED FUNCTION SYSTEMS, L-SYSTEMS, PARTICLE SYSTEM, SOFT OBJECTS, and SOLID TEXTURE.)
[Blinn-82, Csuri-83, Fournier-82, Fournier-86, Gardner-85, Kajiya-89, Mastin-87, Max-86, Oppenheimer-86, Peachey-86, Weil- 86]

NDC

See NORMALIZED DEVICE COORDINATES.

near plane

See FRONT CLIPPING PLANE.

n-gon

An n-gon is an equilateral polygon with *n* sides.

1/f noise

See FRACTAL NOISE.

noise

Noise generally describes any undesirable signal introduced into a system: this may be random in nature or even an unwanted secondary signal. However, in computer graphics noise is frequently used to describe a data set whose values are totally random and is used for shape and surface geometry. It also describes a visual artifact resulting from STOCHASTIC SAMPLING in ANTI-ALIASING techniques. (See also BROWNIAN MOTION, FOURIER FILTERING, FOURIER FRACTAL, FRACTAL NOISE, FRACTIONAL BROWNIAN MOTION, and WHITE NOISE.)
[Peitgen-88]

non-linear transformation

A non-linear transformation such as bending, perspective, spherical, twisting or FREE FORM DEFORMATION does not preserve geometric properties such as area, length, angles and volume. (See also AFFINE TRANSFORMATION, FREE FORM DEFORMATION, LINEAR TRANSFORMATION, MATRIX OPERATION, NON-RIGID TRANSFORMATION, PERSPECTIVE PROJECTION, SHEAR MATRIX, and RIGID TRANSFORMATION.)
[Rogers-89, Stevenson-74]

non-rigid transformation

A non-rigid transformation will subject a shape or object to distortion and deformation as found in FREE FORM DEFORMATION and the PERSPECTIVE PROJECTION. (See also FREE FORM DEFORMATION, MATRIX OPERATION, NON-LINEAR TRANSFORMATION, PERSPECTIVE PROJECTION, RIGID TRANSFORMATION, and SHEAR MATRIX.)
[Rogers-89, Stevenson-74, Terzopoulos-88a]

normal

The term normal is either used to imply an ORTHOGONAL relationship or is synonymous with SURFACE NORMAL. See Figure F-1. (See also AVERAGE NORMAL, FACET NORMAL, NORMALIZATION, NORMAL VECTOR, SURFACE NORMAL, UNIT VECTOR, and VECTOR.)
[Gasson-83, Hearn-86, MacBeath-64, Rogers-85, Rogers-89]

normal distribution

See GAUSSIAN DISTRIBUTION.

normalization

Normalization refers to the process of adjusting a vector's magnitude to unity. For example, a vector **V** (where $|\mathbf{V}| \neq 0$) can be normalized to a UNIT VECTOR by the following operation:

$$\mathbf{V}' = \frac{\mathbf{V}}{\sqrt{(\mathbf{V} \bullet \mathbf{V})}}$$

(See also SCALAR PRODUCT, UNIT VECTOR, VECTOR, and VECTOR PRODUCT.)
[Burger-89, Hearn-86, MacBeath-64]

normalized device coordinates (NDC)

Normalized device coordinates are logical coordinates associated with a generic display device, but independent of any physical characteristics of the device. The coordinates range from 0 to 1 in each dimension (of which there are usually at least 3), which enables them to be converted to PHYSICAL DEVICE COORDINATES with a simple MAPPING function. (See also DEVICE COORDINATE SYSTEM, PHYSICAL DEVICE COORDINATES, and SCREEN COORDINATES.)
[Burger-89, Foley-90]

normal vector

For planar surfaces, a normal vector is ORTHOGONAL to the surface and its components are expressed in the plane equation's coefficients, or can be derived from the VECTOR PRODUCT of two suitable edges. For non-planar polygons there is no single normal vector and only an AVERAGE NORMAL can be derived, but if the polygon was triangulated a normal vector would exist for each triangular facet. See Figure F-1. (See also AVERAGE NORMAL, FACET NORMAL, NORMAL, NORMALIZATION, ORTHOGONAL, UNIT VECTOR, VECTOR, and VECTOR PRODUCT.)
[Burger-89, Foley-90, Hearn-86, Rogers-85, Rogers-89]

normal vector interpolation

See PHONG SHADING.

NTSC

NTSC is an acronym for the National Television Systems Committee, who defined the American television video standard. The refresh rate is 59.94 Hz (fields/second) providing a picture update rate of 29.97 Hz (frames/second), whilst the horizontal scan frequency is 15.734 kHz giving 262.5 lines/field, although they are not all seen. (See also PAL, SECAM, and VIDEO SIGNAL.)
[De Fanti-87, Hunt-75, Rogers-85]

NURBS

NURBS is an acronym for Non-Uniform Rational B-Splines which describe a class of B-SPLINE having the following features. The *Non-Uniform* aspect relates to the values of the KNOTS which are allowed to have non-integer values; this overcomes problems caused by clustered CONTROL POINTS. The *Rational* feature refers to the use of a pair of polynomials – where one is divided by the other – for the BASIS FUNCTIONS; this allows NURBS to accurately describe arcs and ellipses. (See also APPROXIMATING SPLINE, BASIS FUNCTION, BERNSTEIN BASIS FUNCTION, BETA SPLINE, B-SPLINE CURVE, B-SPLINE SURFACE PATCH, CATMULL–ROM SPLINE, CONTROL POINTS, INTERPOLATING SPLINE, KNOT, KNOT VECTOR, PARAMETRIC POLYNOMIAL, POLYNOMIAL, RATIONAL POLYNOMIAL, and SPLINE.)
[Farin-88, Shantz-88]

Nyquist limit

When a complex signal is regularly sampled and a reconstructed signal is made from these samples, the reconstruction will be identical to the original signal if the latter does not contain any frequency components greater than the Nyquist limit; this limit is half the sampling frequency. If the signal exceeds this limit, the high-frequency components will appear as a low-frequency 'alias' in the reconstruction. (See also ALIASING, ANTI-ALIASING, ARTIFACT, CONVOLUTION, CONVOLUTION FILTER, CONVOLUTION THEOREM, FILTER, FILTERING, FOURIER TRANSFORM, FOURIER WAVEFORM ANALYSIS, FREQUENCY DOMAIN, INVERSE FOURIER TRANSFORM, JAGGIES, OVERSAMPLING, POINT SAMPLING, SAMPLING, SINC FILTER, SPATIAL ALIASING, SPATIAL DOMAIN, STOCHASTIC SAMPLING, and UNIFORM SAMPLING.)
[Blinn-89a, Blinn-89b, Blinn-89c, Gonzalez-87, Pratt-78]

O

object buffer

The object buffer is a technique for accelerating RAY TRACING calculations – and exploits the use of a conventional RENDERER to create a pixel image, not in the form of pixel intensities, but in the form of the nearest objects for each pixel. This buffer of object references can then be exploited by the RAY TRACING algorithm to identify the first object intersecting the EYE RAY. (See also LIGHT BUFFER, PARAMETERIZED RAY TRACING, RAY TRACING, RENDERER, and Z-BUFFER.)

[Glassner-89]

object-oriented programming

Object-oriented programming provides an environment where the major ideas of a problem area become fundamental objects in a program. Applied to a 3-D computer graphics environment, geometric objects retain their individuality as programming entities – and through suitable commands they are assigned attributes and new geometric states that are retained within local DATA STRUCTURES. Each object type can be assigned not only attributes but code, which can be effected when corresponding messages are initiated. Hierarchically linked objects can exploit the feature of 'inheritance' found in object-oriented programming, whereby all elements inherit attributes that have been assigned to higher levels within the structure. Object-oriented languages include C++, Object-Pascal, Neon, OOPC, Objective-C, Orient 84, Smalltalk and ASE. (See also C++, LISP, and SMALLTALK.)

[Steele-89, Youssef-86]

object space

Object space refers to the 3-D space associated with the descriptions of objects and light sources that are under investigation. (See also IMAGE SPACE, IMAGE SPACE ALGORITHMS, and OBJECT SPACE ALGORITHMS.)

[Burger-89, Foley-90, Hearn-86, Rogers-85]

object space algorithms

Object space algorithms are normally associated with HIDDEN-LINE REMOVAL HIDDEN-SURFACE REMOVAL, and rendering procedures that compute the final image from the geometrical relationships in the object's space; RAY TRACING is a natural example. (See also AREA SUBDIVISION ALGORITHMS, DEPTH SORT ALGORITHM, HIDDEN-LINE REMOVAL, HIDDEN-SURFACE REMOVAL, IMAGE SPACE ALGORITHM, RADIOSITY, and RAY TRACING.)

[Burger-89, Foley-90, Glassner-89, Hearn-86, Rogers-85]

oblique projection

Two examples of oblique parallel projection are CABINET and CAVALIER as they have the PROJECTION PLANE normal to a principal axis, but the direction of projection is not perpendicular to the PROJECTION PLANE; this ensures that parallelism of lines is preserved, but angles are not. (See also AXONOMETRIC ORTHOGRAPHIC PROJECTION, CABINET PROJECTION, CAVALIER PROJECTION, ISOMETRIC PROJECTION, ORTHOGRAPHIC PROJECTION, PARALLEL PROJECTION, PROJECTION, and PROJECTION PLANE.)

[Burger-89, Foley-90, Gasson-83, Hearn-86, Rogers-89]

observer

The observer is the name given to a pseudo 3-D eye existing within a computer graphics environment. It is located within the WORLD COORDINATE SYSTEM with an EYE POINT and AIM POINT, from which it is possible to calculate the observed view. (See also AIM POINT, EYE COORDINATE SYSTEM, EYE POINT, IMAGE SPACE, LINE OF SIGHT, PICTURE PLANE, VIEWING PYRAMID, VIEW VECTOR, VIEWING PYRAMID, and WORLD COORDINATE SPACE.)

[Burger-89, Foley-90, Hearn-86, Rogers-89]

obtuse angle

An obtuse angle is an angle between 90° and 180°.

octahedron

An octahedron is a PLATONIC OBJECT constructed from eight EQUILATERAL TRIANGLES. (See also CUBE, DODECAHEDRON, ICOSAHEDRON, PLATONIC OBJECTS, and TETRAHEDRON.)

[Critchlow-69, Gasson-83]

octree
An octree is a 3-D space partitioning strategy where a volume is recursively divided into a hierarchical organization of octants. A tree structure is used to reference the subdivided octants, which is also capable of indicating empty or void regions and enables it to be used as a modelling scheme. See Figure O-1. (See also DATA STRUCTURE, G-OCTREE, G-QUADTREE, GRAPHICAL DATA STRUCTURE, and QUADTREE.)
[Burger-89, Carlbom-85, Doctor-81, Hearn-86, Pavlidis-82, Yamaguchi-84]

off-line
An off-line activity is performed prior to the execution of a process which requires use of the data produced by the off-line activity. For example, the creation of DELTA FORM-FACTORS or BSP data can be computed off-line in advance of their use within an algorithm. (See also ON-LINE.)

on-line
An on-line activity is performed with the assistance of the computer engaged in the current task, e.g. sorting polygons into priority sequence for a REAL-TIME display system. (See also OFF-LINE.)

opacity
Opacity is an attribute associated with a surface describing its efficacy at absorbing light – and is the opposite of TRANSPARENCY. (See also AREA PROPERTIES, ATTRIBUTES, COLOUR ATTRIBUTES, OPACITY MAPPING, OPAQUE SURFACE, TRANSLUCENT SURFACE, TRANSLUCENCY, and TRANSPARENCY.)

opacity map
An opacity map is a table or matrix of numerical values representing the OPACITY levels to be applied to a surface during rendering. The map may be produced synthetically or as the result of a previous rendering process. For example, a sphere could be rendered in isolation from other objects and the pixel intensities retained to form an opacity map. When this map is used in another rendering process, it can be used to control the opacity of the sphere to allow potentially invisible background objects to become visible. (See also BUMP MAP, OPACITY, OPACITY MAPPING, and TEXTURE MAP.)

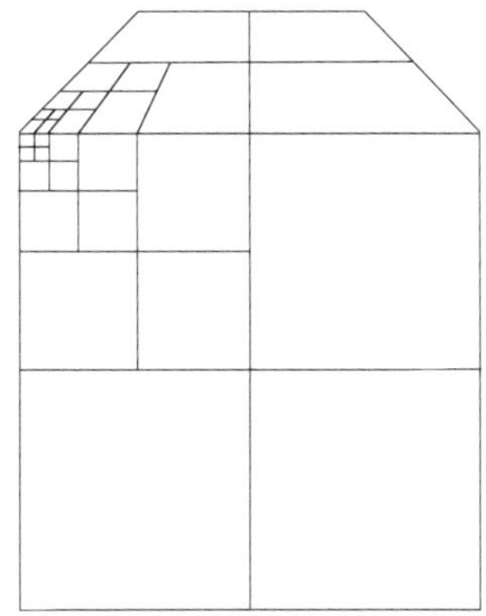

Figure O-1 *The octree partitioning strategy recursively divides a volume of space into eight equal cuboids: this allows a tree structure to be used to identify those voxels containing data or those which are empty. This method of encoding volumetric data is extremely useful in medical imaging.*

opacity mapping
Opacity mapping is a rendering feature where an OPACITY MAP is used to modulate the OPACITY of a surface to reveal underlying detail; this enables transparent objects to be simulated. (See also ENVIRONMENT MAPPING, OPACITY, OPACITY MAP, and TEXTURE MAPPING.)

opaque surface
Even though most computer graphics surfaces are opaque, the majority of RENDERERS do not prevent light sources from illuminating surfaces that are masked by

other opaque surfaces. However, RAY TRACING and RADIOSITY do ensure that surfaces in shadow are rendered correctly. (See also AREA PROPERTIES, GLOBAL ILLUMINATION MODEL, ILLUMINATION MODEL, OBJECT BUFFER, RADIOSITY, RAY TRACING, SHADOWS, SHADOW VOLUME, and TRANSPARENT SURFACE.)
[Burger-89]

orbit
An orbit is a sequence of points in some space generated by a function describing a DYNAMICAL SYSTEM. Some are predictable in that they might converge to zero or infinity, whilst others are chaotic and defy description. Certain QUADRATIC DYNAMICAL SYSTEMS have been used to create computer images based upon orbit plots. (See also CHAOS THEORY, CHAOTIC BEHAVIOUR, DYNAMICAL SYSTEMS, ITERATED FUNCTION SYSTEMS, MANDELBROT SET, and JULIA SETS.)
[Devaney-86, Peitgen-86, Peitgen-88]

ordered dither
Ordered dither is a DITHERING technique similar to HALFTONING for producing shaded images on BI-LEVEL DISPLAY devices. (See also DITHERING and HALFTONING.)
[Bayer-73, Burger-89, Hearn-86, Rogers-85]

orthogonal
Orthogonal means at right angles to some datum: for example, each axis in a 3-D Cartesian system of axes is orthogonal to the other two.
[Gasson-83]

orthogonal matrix
An orthogonal matrix has all of its CHARACTERISTIC ROOTS equal to unity; this is found in rotation matrices whose columns are mutually orthogonal UNIT VECTORS. The INVERSE MATRIX is simply the TRANSPOSE MATRIX. This relationship is exploited in REAL-TIME IMAGE GENERATORS. (See also CHARACTERISTIC ROOTS, CONCATENATION, MATRIX, MATRIX OPERATION, ORTHOGONAL, ROTATION MATRIX, TRANSPOSE MATRIX, and UNIT VECTOR.)
[Stevenson-74]

orthographic projection
An orthographic projection is a PARALLEL PROJECTION where the direction of projection is perpendicular to the PROJECTION PLANE. (See also AXONOMETRIC ORTHOGRAPHIC PROJECTION, CABINET PROJECTION, CAVALIER PROJECTION, ISOMETRIC PROJECTION, OBLIQUE PROJECTION, PARALLEL PROJECTION, PERSPECTIVE PROJECTION, and PROJECTION.)
[Burger-89, Foley-90, Gasson-83, Rogers-89]

Ostwald colour system
See HLS COLOUR MODEL.

out point
An edit operation is defined by two points identifying the IN POINT and the out point. (See also 4-FIELD SEQUENCE, 8-FIELD SEQUENCE, and IN POINT.)

output pipeline
The output pipeline identifies a data pathway between computational elements or procedures within a computer graphics system, starting where the application program transforms internal data into WORLD COORDINATES and then EYE COORDINATES, which in turn become transformed into NORMALIZED DEVICE COORDINATES and finally PHYSICAL DEVICE COORDINATES. (See also NORMALIZED DEVICE COORDINATES, PHYSICAL DEVICE COORDINATES, and WORLD COORDINATE SPACE.)
[Burger-89, Foley-90]

output primitives
The graphical entities available within display systems, such as arc and circle generation and line types are collectively known as output primitives.

Overhauser curve
An Overhauser curve is used to draw a curve through a set of points by first connecting PARABOLAS through consecutively overlapping sets of three points and then linearly blending together the overlapping segments to produce a smooth curve. (See also APPROXIMATING SPLINE, BLENDING FUNCTION, and LINEAR INTERPOLATION.)
[Brewer-77, Burger-89, Overhauser-68, Woodwark-86]

overlay plane

An overlay plane is a separate memory plane storing an image that can be superimposed upon the main image held in a FRAME STORE. (See also FRAME STORE.)

oversampling

In computer graphics, oversampling is a strategy for reducing ALIASING by taking extra sample points at each pixel; although some improvement is detected this cannot be an approach that will totally eliminate ALIASING. (See also ADAPTIVE SAMPLING, ALIASING, ANTI-ALIASING, FILTER, FILTERING, FOURIER WAVEFORM ANALYSIS, JAGGIES, NYQUIST LIMIT, POINT SAMPLING, SAMPLING, SPATIAL ALIASING, STOCHASTIC SAMPLING, and UNIFORM SAMPLING.)
[Blinn-89a, Glassner-89]

page description language (PDL)

A page description language describes page layouts in the form of codes referencing attributes such as line thickness, orientation, italic, colour fill and font size. (See also DESK-TOP PUBLISHING and POSTSCRIPT.)

painter's algorithm

One of the tasks of a RENDERER is to ensure that objects are correctly ordered in space and so perform HIDDEN-SURFACE REMOVAL – and a simple way of achieving this is to sort the objects into a Z-DEPTH sequence and render them into a FRAME STORE starting with the most distant ones and progressing towards the nearest. The painter's algorithm, which is also known as the DEPTH SORT ALGORITHM, operates in this manner. A consequence of this algorithm is that it is unable to cope with interpenetrating objects and ANTI-ALIASING. (See also A-BUFFER, HIDDEN-SURFACE REMOVAL, OBJECT SPACE ALGORITHMS, SCAN-LINE ALGORITHM, Z-BUFFER ALGORITHM, and ZZ-BUFFER.)
[Burger-89, Foley-90, Hearn-86, Rogers-85]

paint system

A paint system is an interactive computer graphics environment that allows a user to develop a coloured image upon a screen using actions and features of traditional painting. A paint system should be capable of providing colour selection and mixing, different brush sizes, cut and paste, different paint modes, pattern generation, compositing and mattes.
[Burger-89, Hearn-86, Quantel-81, Smith-78b, Smith-79, Strassmann-86]

PAL

PAL is an acronym for Phase Alternation Line and describes the UK television video standard. The vertical scan frequency is 50 Hz (fields/second) providing a picture update rate of 25 Hz (frames/second), whilst the horizontal scan frequency is 15.625 kHz and corresponds to 312.5 lines/field, although they are not all seen. (See also NTSC, SECAM, and VIDEO SIGNAL.)
[De Fanti-87, Hunt-75]

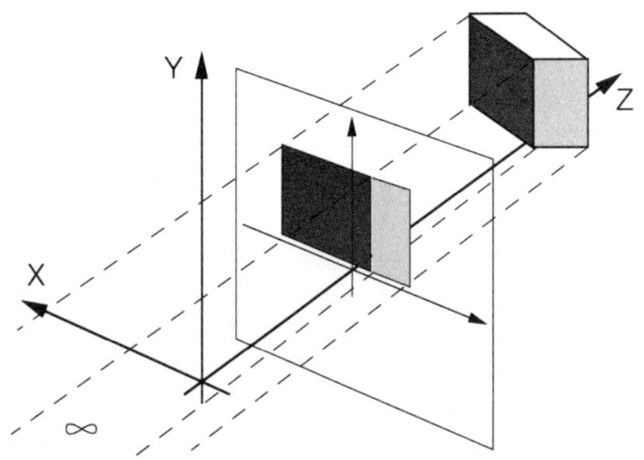

Figure P-1 *In the parallel projection the centre of projection is effectively at infinity; this makes the lines of projection parallel with the z-axis. In this example, the projection plane is orthogonal with the direction of projection.*

palette
Computer graphics systems with 24-bit LOOK-UP TABLES associated with 8-bit frame stores provide a total palette of 16.7 million colours, but only 256 are actively available; for the entire palette to be displayed a 24-bit frame store is required. (See also BYTE and FRAME STORE.)
[Burger-89]

panning
Panning is the process of moving a camera or viewpoint horizontally or vertically across a scene. (See also ZOOM.)
[Burger-89, Hearn-86, White-86]

parallax
Parallax is the horizontal displacement seen when an object is viewed from two offset positions and is exploited by the human binocular visual system to compute depth information. STEREOSCOPIC DISPLAYS exploit this phenomenon to display realistic 3-D scenes. (See also DEPTH CUES, STEREOPSIS, and STEREOSCOPIC DISPLAY.)
[Boynton-79, Gregory-86]

parallel
Parallel lines and planes remain a constant distance apart. (See also AFFINE TRANSFORMATION and PARALLEL PROJECTION.)
[Gasson-83]

parallel projection
There are two types of parallel projection: orthographic and oblique. The ORTHOGRAPHIC PROJECTION has the direction of the projection ORTHOGONAL to the PROJECTION PLANE, whilst the OBLIQUE PROJECTION retains the parallel projected lines, but they are oblique to the PROJECTION PLANE. See Figure P-1. (See also AXONOMETRIC ORTHOGRAPHIC PROJECTION, CABINET PROJECTION, CAVALIER PROJECTION, ISOMETRIC PROJECTION, OBLIQUE PROJECTION, ORTHOGRAPHIC PROJECTION, PARALLEL PROJECTION, PERSPECTIVE PROJECTION, and PROJECTION.)
[Burger-89, Foley-90, Gasson-83, Hearn-86, Rogers-89]

parallel rendering
To reduce the time spent rendering images, it is sometimes possible to use a multi-processor computer; this process is known as parallel rendering. (See also DISTRIBUTED RENDERING, MIMD and SIMD.)
[Cleary-86, Dew-89, Potmesil-89, Torborg-87]

parameter
A parameter is a variable used for controlling the value of a mathematical function. This might be found in the basis functions employed in curve definition or be a value that is used to control a sequence of animation. (See also PARAMETER SPACE, PARAMETRIC CURVE, PARAMETRIC EQUATION, and PARAMETRIC POLYNOMIAL.)
[Bowyer-83, Gasson-83, Hearn-86, Rogers-85]

parameterization
Parameterization refers to the substitution of a set of explicit PARAMETRIC EQUATIONS to replace a mathematical form which, perhaps, describes a relationship in general implicit terms. For example, a plane is expressed

implicitly by the equation

$$ax + by + cz + d = 0$$

but this has a parametric equivalent as

$$\begin{bmatrix} x \\ y \\ z \end{bmatrix} = u \begin{bmatrix} x_u \\ y_u \\ z_u \end{bmatrix} + v \begin{bmatrix} x_v \\ y_v \\ z_v \end{bmatrix} + \begin{bmatrix} x_0 \\ y_0 \\ z_0 \end{bmatrix}$$

where $[x_u, y_u, z_u]$ and $[x_v, y_v, z_v]$ are two non-parallel vectors on the plane, and $[x_0, y_0, z_0]$ is any point on the plane. Both forms have their merits and applications. (See also ALGEBRAIC SURFACE, EXPLICIT SURFACE, IMPLICIT SURFACE, PARAMETER, PARAMETER SPACE, PARAMETRIC EQUATION, and PLANE EQUATION.)
[Bowyer-83, Glassner-89, Rogers-89]

parameterized ray tracing
Parameterized ray tracing removes the need to ray trace a scene if the geometry is unchanged and only surface properties, colours and lighting values have been altered. The technique employs a parametric expression for each pixel which explicitly references the surfaces hit by a ray, together with its reflected and refracted secondary and higher order components. (See also RAY TRACING.)
[Sequin-89]

parameter space
A parameter space refers to the SPATIAL DOMAIN where parameters belonging to some parametric process can be organized and manipulated. For example, the 3-D coordinates for a BÉZIER SURFACE PATCH can be developed from values assigned to a pair of parameters – and whilst the patch description occurs in OBJECT SPACE, the parametric formulation occurs in parameter space. (See also MAPPING, PARAMETRIC CURVE, PARAMETRIC EQUATION, and PARAMETRIC POLYNOMIAL.)
[Burger-89, Foley-90, Gasson-83, Hearn-86, Rogers-89]

parametric bicubic surface
See BICUBIC PATCH.

parametric cubic curve
The following PARAMETRIC POLYNOMIALS are an example of a parametric cubic curve:

$$x = 2t + 3t^3$$
$$y = t + 2t^3$$

where the X- and Y-components are computed individually from two cubic equations expressed as polynomials in t. (See also PARAMETRIC CURVE, PARAMETRIC EQUATION, PARAMETRIC POLYNOMIAL, and POLYNOMIAL.)
[Bowyer-83, Burger-89, Hearn-86, Rogers-89, Woodwark-86]

parametric curve
A parametric curve is defined by coordinates derived from functions sharing some common parameter. For example, a parametric arc can be generated by the two functions

$$x = \text{radius.cos}(t)$$
$$y = \text{radius.sin}(t)$$

where t is a parameter varying between given limits. (See also PARAMETER, PARAMETRIC EQUATION, and PARAMETRIC POLYNOMIAL.)
[Bowyer-83, Burger-89, Gasson-83, Hearn-86, Rogers-89]

parametric equation
A parametric equation expresses a relationship between a variable and a parameter not directly related to the system being numerically simulated. For example, Bézier and B-spline techniques employ PARAMETRIC POLYNOMIALS to compute the individual coordinates of a curve using an independent parameter, which is generally allowed to range between 0 and 1. This parametric formulation provides a convenient mechanism for simultaneously gen-

erating all the coordinates from one or two parameter values. (See also BÉZIER CURVE, B-SPLINE CURVE, PARAMETER, PARAMETER SPACE, PARAMETRIC CURVE, and PARAMETRIC POLYNOMIAL.)
[Bowyer-83, Burger-89, Gasson-83, Hearn-86, Rogers-89, Woodwark- 86]

parametric polynomial

A parametric polynomial is an algebraic expression of MONOMIAL terms of different powers, where the term is a parameter used to control the final value. For example, the following is a parametric polynomial:

$$x = 2 + t + 3t^2 + 4t^3$$

They are useful in surface patch definition and BLENDING FUNCTIONS. (See also BLENDING FUNCTION, MONOMIAL BASIS, PARAMETER, and PARAMETRIC CURVE.)
[Bowyer-83, Foley-90, Hearn-86, Rogers-89, Woodwark-86]

parametric surface patch

A parametric surface patch such as Bézier, B-spline, Coons and Ferguson have their geometry defined by coordinates derived from two functions sharing some common parameter. In general, two parameters which take on values between 0 and 1 are substituted into relevant BASIS FUNCTIONS which in turn are used to weight a matrix of geometric CONTROL POINTS. (See also BÉZIER SURFACE PATCH, BICUBIC PATCH, BIPARAMETRIC PATCH, B-SPLINE SURFACE PATCH, CARTESIAN PRODUCT PATCH, COONS PATCH, FERGUSON PATCH, HERMITE PATCH, PARAMETER, PATCH, and QUADRATIC SURFACE PATCH.)
[Bowyer-83, Farin-88, Gasson-83, Hearn-86, Rogers-89, Woodwark-86]

particle system

A powerful technique used for modelling natural phenomena is that of particle systems, where discrete particles are controlled by numerical values representing their position, size, velocity, colour, life-time, birth time etc. In this way it is possible to mimic effects such as water, rain, fire and smoke. (See also HYPERTEXTURE, NATURAL PHENOMENA MODELLING, and SOFT OBJECTS.)
[Burger-89, Magnenat-Thalmann-86, Reeves-83, Reeves-85, Rogers-85]

PASCAL

PASCAL is a high-level programming language popular in educational institutes for the teaching of structured programming.
[Grogono-80]

patch

A patch is a portion of a surface whose geometry is defined parametrically such that slope CONTINUITY is preserved at the boundaries; this enables a number of patches to be organized to form a continuous surface description. It is also synonymous with SURFACE PATCH. See Figure B-4. (See also BÉZIER SURFACE PATCH, B-SPLINE SURFACE PATCH, CONTINUITY, COONS PATCH, FERGUSON PATCH, HERMITE PATCH, and PARAMETRIC SURFACE PATCH.)
[Bohm-84, Burger-89, Farin-88, Rogers-89, Woodwark-86]

patched surface

A patched surface is a continuous surface constructed from a number of individual patches which have common continuity attributes at their boundaries. (See also BÉZIER SURFACE PATCH, B-SPLINE SURFACE PATCH, CONTINUITY, COONS PATCH, FERGUSON PATCH, and HERMITE PATCH.)
[Bohm-84, Burger-89, Farin-88, Gasson-83, Hearn-86, Rogers-89, Woodwark-86]

PDES

See PRODUCT DATA EXCHANGE SPECIFICATION.

PDL

See PAGE DESCRIPTION LANGUAGE.

Peano curve

In 1890, Peano published a paper on a SPACE FILLING CURVE

which now bears his name; it is a regular space filling curve which, given a matrix of points, will visit every point only once. Such curves can be used for distributing errors in rendering algorithms and for IMAGE COMPRESSION algorithms and for television. See Figure P-2. (See also FRACTAL, FRACTAL CURVE, FRACTAL DIMENSION, and SPACE FILLING CURVES.)
[Peano-90]

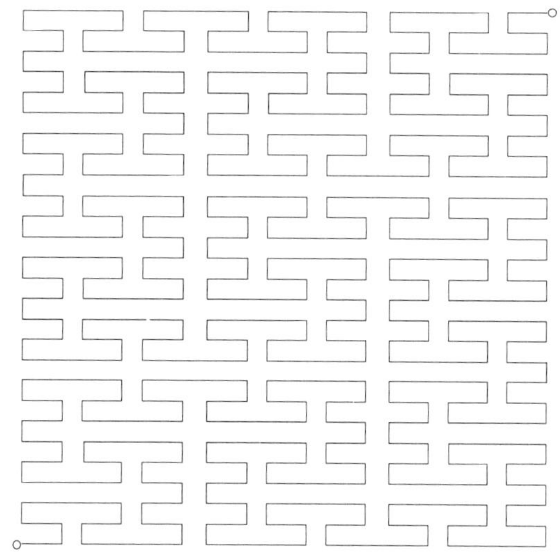

Figure P-2 *This Peano curve starts at the bottom left-hand corner and finishes at the top right-hand corner visiting every matrix point. In this example, the basic shape is that of the letter 'S' which can be confirmed by examining the first five line segments.*

pel
See PIXEL.

pencil tracing
Pencil tracing is a variant of RAY TRACING where a pencil or bundle of rays is processed using paraxial approximation theory; the latter is a technique employed in the design of optical and electromagnetic systems. (See also RAY TRACING.)
[Glassner-88, Shinya-87]

pentagon
A pentagon is a five-sided regular POLYGON.
[Gasson-83]

penumbra
Penumbra is the blurred border of a shadow caused by multiple diffuse reflections or a DISTRIBUTED LIGHT SOURCE, such as the sun. (See also LIGHT BUFFER, RAY TRACING, and SHADOW VOLUME.)
[Glassner-89]

perimeter
The perimeter of a boundary is its total linear distance, which is a concept taught at school alongside familiar aspects of Euclidean geometry; however, the concept of perimeter takes on strange properties when one is dealing with FRACTALS. Theoretically, a FRACTAL CURVE has an infinite perimeter whilst having a finite area; in practice, a relaxed FRACTAL in the form of a coastline still behaves strangely in that its perimeter depends upon the scale of the measuring device. In fact, if one plots a graph of the perimeter against the different measuring scales (using log–log axes), the slope measures the FRACTAL DIMENSION of the curve. (See also FRACTAL, FRACTAL DIMENSION, and FRACTAL CURVE.)
[Mandelbrot-77, Mandelbrot-82, Peitgen-86, Peitgen-88]

perpendicular
Perpendicular means at right angles to a line or surface.
[Gasson-83]

persistence
(1) Persistence is a phosphor's ability to continue glowing after it is no longer being excited.
[Hunt-75]
(2) Persistence is the retina's ability to remain excited

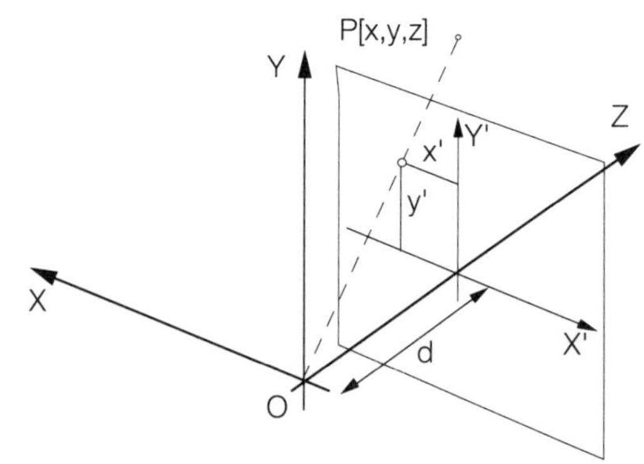

Figure P-3 *A perspective projection is captured by identifying points on the projection plane intersected by the projection lines – and the transformed coordinates of P are*
x' = -dx/z and y' = dy/z

when it has been stimulated, creating an after vision effect, and also related to the eye's FUSION FREQUENCY. (See also FLICKER, FUSION FREQUENCY, and REFRESH RATE.)
[Boynton-79, Gregory-86, Hearn-86]

perspective foreshortening
The size reduction as an object recedes from an observer is known as perspective foreshortening, and varies inversely as the distance of the object from the CENTRE OF PROJECTION. (See also PERSPECTIVE PROJECTION.)
[Burger-89, Foley-90, Gasson-83, Rogers-89]

perspective projection
A perspective projection creates an effect similar to the operation of a PINHOLE CAMERA, whereby the size of an object is dependent upon its distance from the observer. Generally, a point is located behind the PROJECTION PLANE, called the CENTRE OF PROJECTION; points on objects are then traced to this position, and where projection lines intersect the PROJECTION PLANE a perspective projection is formed. The further the object is from the observer, the smaller its projected image. See Figure P-3. (See also CENTRE OF PROJECTION, LINE OF PROJECTION, LINE OF SIGHT, OBSERVER, PICTURE PLANE, PINHOLE CAMERA, PROJECTION, PROJECTION PLANE, and VIEWING PYRAMID.)
[Burger-89, Foley-90, Gasson-83, Hearn-86, Rogers-89]

perspective transformation
A perspective transformation is used to create a PERSPECTIVE PROJECTION by projecting points in OBJECT SPACE onto some PICTURE PLANE and it can be represented by a (4 x 4) MATRIX. (See also MATRIX OPERATION, OBJECT SPACE, and PERSPECTIVE PROJECTION.)
[Rogers-89]

PHIGS
PHIGS is an acronym for Programmers Hierarchical Interactive Graphics System which is a graphics standard, like GKS, but extends into the more advanced aspects of computer graphics such as REAL-TIME and interactive systems. There are no windowing tools. PHIGS+ are extensions that address the area of SURFACE PATCHES, shading, lighting and DEPTH CUEING. (See also CORE, GKS and GKS-3D.)
[Burger-89, Hearn-86, ISO-87c, ISO-87f, Shuey-86]

PHIGS+
PHIGS+ includes extensions to PHIGS that address the capabilities of high-performance workstations in the areas of REAL-TIME interaction, lighting, shading, depth cueing and surface primitives. (See also PHIGS.)
[van Dam-88]

Phong shading
In 1973 Bui Tuong Phong submitted his doctoral thesis *Illumination for Computer Generated Images* and revealed a SHADING MODEL which incorporated a term to compute SPECULAR REFLECTIONS. This term can be stated simply as

$$I_p K_s \cos^g (\varnothing)$$

where I_p is the colour intensity of a point LIGHT SOURCE; K_s

is a term introduced to control the specular highlight and is independent of the surface colour, ø is the angle between the VIEW VECTOR and the reflected ray from the LIGHT SOURCE and *g* is a gloss term controlling the size of the specular highlight. The SHADING MODEL has to be applied at every pixel, perhaps on a scan-line basis, over the entire surface being rendered, as a new value of ø is required for each pixel; as ø depends upon the SURFACE NORMAL, the latter can be interpolated from two edge normal vectors. This is why Phong shading is sometimes referred to as a NORMAL-VECTOR INTERPOLATION scheme. The gloss term *g* controls the size of the specular highlight, with large values (50 – 100) creating the impression of a shiny surface. Low values create the effect of rough plastic and produce a smeared reflection. (See also CONSTANT SHADING, COSINE SHADING, COOK–TORRANCE SHADING, GOURAUD SHADING, NORMAL VECTOR, RADIOSITY, RAY TRACING, REFLECTANCE MODEL, RENDERER, RENDERING EQUATION, RENDERMAN, REYES, SURFACE NORMAL, TORRANCE–SPARROW SHADING MODEL, and VIEW VECTOR.)
[Bishop-86, Burger-89, Foley-90, Hearn-86, Phong-73, Rogers-85]

phosphor
A phosphor is a substance which when excited by an electron beam radiates light of a certain colour. In television CRTs, patterns of red, green and blue phosphor dots or stripes are used to form the coloured image by a scanning electron beam under the control of a VIDEO SIGNAL; when these colours are integrated by the eye a wide range of colour sensations are created. (See also BEAM PENETRATION CRT, CALLIGRAPHIC DISPLAY, CATHODE RAY TUBE, GAMMA CORRECTION, FLICKER, PERSISTENCE, REFRESH CRT, and SHADOW-MASK COLOUR CRT.)
[Hearn-86, Hunt-75, Rogers-89]

photorealism
Although many applications for computer graphics only require simple representations of 3-D structures, photorealism is the quest of some researchers to create images that are indistinguishable from photographs of real-world scenes. (See also GLOBAL ILLUMINATION MODEL, RADIOSITY, RAY TRACING, and RENDERMAN.)
[Amanatides-87]

physical device coordinates
Physical device coordinates are the actual physical coordinates associated with a device. These would be real coordinates upon a plotter, or pixel addresses on a display screen.
[Burger-89, Foley-90, Hearn-86, Rogers-85]

pick device
A pick device is an input device such as a LIGHT PEN or data tablet STYLUS for identifying graphic elements upon a display screen. (See also JOYSTICK, LIGHT PEN, MOUSE, STYLUS, and TRACKBALL.)
[Hearn-86]

picture plane
The picture plane is the projection plane in projections such as parallel and perspective, and is the basis for algorithms in resolving shading and HIDDEN-SURFACE REMOVAL calculations. See Figure P-3. (See also OBLIQUE PROJECTION, PARALLEL PROJECTION, PROJECTION, PROJECTION PLANE, and PERSPECTIVE PROJECTION.)
[Burger-89, Foley-90, Rogers-85]

picture processing
See IMAGE PROCESSING.

piecewise curves
A DIVIDE AND CONQUER approach is used to describe complex curves by constructing them from discrete curve segments containing slope CONTINUITY properties at their boundaries. Such piecewise curves may have their individual segments defined using a Bézier or B-spline basis, and the continuity property guarantees that the curve joins are completely invisible. (See also BÉZIER CURVE, B-SPLINE CURVE, CONTINUITY, HERMITE CURVE, and PARAMETRIC CUBIC CURVE.)
[Farin-88, Gasson-83, Rogers-89, Woodwark-86]

pinhole camera
In a pinhole camera, a small hole on one side of a light-tight box, allows light rays to impinge upon a photographic film on the opposite side of the box. This simple model is very similar to the ideas used in computer graphics systems to create a PERSPECTIVE PROJECTION. (See also LINE OF PROJECTION, PERSPECTIVE PROJECTION, and VIEWING PYRAMID.)

pitch
Pitch is a rotational movement about a horizontal axis ORTHOGONAL to the facing direction, and is normally used in conjunction with ROLL and YAW to define the attitude of an object or OBSERVER. (See also ROLL and YAW.)
[Gasson-83]

pixel
A pixel is the smallest picture element addressable upon a display screen. The term PEL is also used, but pixel has a wider usage.
[Hearn-86, Rogers-85]

pixel averaging
A simple FILTERING technique is that of pixel averaging, where an image is first created to a high resolution and then averaged to a final lower resolution. This is equivalent to using a box-reconstruction FILTER. (See also ANTI-ALIASING, FILTERING, NYQUIST LIMIT, OVERSAMPLING, POINT SAMPLING, SPATIAL ALIASING, and UNIFORM SAMPLING.)
[Gonzalez-87, Pavlidis-82, Pratt-78, Rogers-85]

pixel footprint
A pixel's footprint refers to its shape when it is projected back onto some surface during a PERSPECTIVE PROJECTION operation. It is frequently used in TEXTURE MAPPING to identify the area of the TEXTURE MAP impacting upon the current pixel. (See also INVERSE PERSPECTIVE MAPPING, PERSPECTIVE PROJECTION, and TEXTURE MAPPING.)

pixellate
Some PAINT SYSTEMS offer a pixellation effect which creates a mosaic effect on an image.

Pixel-planes
Henry Fuchs *et al.* at the University of North Carolina at Chapel Hill have developed a hardware rendering system called Pixel-planes. It operates by manipulating equations describing surfaces on an incremental basis, and by broadcasting commands in parallel it obtains near REAL-TIME operation. (See also FORWARD DIFFERENCES.)
[Fuchs-85]

planar
Planar is synonymous with flat, but formally it is a surface property defined by a PLANE EQUATION. A feature of planar surfaces is that every point on the surface shares a common SURFACE NORMAL. (See also PLANE EQUATION and SURFACE NORMAL.)
[Burger-89, Gasson-83, Hearn-86, Rogers-89]

plane equation
A plane equation can be expressed as

$$ax + by + cz + d = 0$$

where *a, b, c* and *d* are constants peculiar to the given plane. Points on the plane satisfy the above relationship, whereas points on one side of the plane produce a negative result (rather than zero) and points on the opposite side produce positive values. (See also HALF SPACE and IMPLICIT SURFACE.)
[Burger-89, Foley-90, Gasson-83, Hearn-83, Rogers-85, Rogers-89]

Platonic objects
There are five Platonic objects – TETRAHEDRON, CUBE, OCTAHEDRON, ICOSAHEDRON and the DODECAHEDRON – which are the only objects that can be constructed entirely from

one particular regular polygon. This proof is based upon the relationship between vertices, edges and faces summarized by EULER'S RULE.
[Blinn-87b, Critchlow-69, Gasson-83]

plotter
A plotter is a graphics peripheral for creating images from lines or dots. Basically there are two types: X–Y PLOTTERS which recreate an image by moving a pen over a drawing surface, and ELECTROSTATIC PLOTTERS which create an image from patterns of small dots. (See also ELECTROPHOTOGRAPHIC PLOTTER, ELECTROSTATIC PLOTTER, FLATBED PLOTTER, INK JET PLOTTER, and X–Y PLOTTER.)
[Hearn-86, Rogers-89]

point light source
A point light source radiates light equally in all directions and is the simplest light source to implement. It requires a position and a colour intensity, which is normally expressed in terms of three fractional values for the ADDITIVE PRIMARY COLOURS. (See also DIRECTIONAL LIGHT SOURCE, DISTRIBUTED LIGHT SOURCE, and SPOT LIGHT.)
[Burger-89, Foley-90, Glassner-89, Hearn-86, Rogers-85]

point sampling
Point sampling is the process of deriving a pixel's intensity by SAMPLING an internally stored scene at one position on the pixel, perhaps the pixel's centre. This UNIFORM SAMPLING causes ALIASING artifacts such as jagged edges, which is why other SAMPLING techniques have evolved to improve picture quality. (See also ADAPTIVE SAMPLING, ALIASING, ANTI-ALIASING, BED-OF-NAILS, FILTER, FILTERING, JAGGIES, NYQUIST LIMIT, OVERSAMPLING, SAMPLING, SPATIAL ALIASING, STOCHASTIC SAMPLING, and UNIFORM SAMPLING.)
[Blinn-89a, Glassner-89, Hearn-86]

point-spread function
In FILTERING, a point-spread function is a weighting function also known as an impulse response, which is a filter's response to a finite impulse and describes the filter shape used for ANTI-ALIASING. Typical filters include BOX, TENT, GAUSSIAN and SINC. (See also ALIASING, ANTI-ALIASING, BARTLETT FILTER, BOX FILTER, CONVOLUTION, CONVOLUTION FILTER, FILTER, FILTERING, FOURIER TRANSFORM, FOURIER WAVEFORM ANALYSIS, GAUSSIAN FILTER, NYQUIST LIMIT, SINC FILTER, TENT FILTER, and BASIS FUNCTION.)
[Blinn-89a, Blinn-89b]

point vector
The components of a point vector are the perpendicular projections of a point to the axes. (See also CARTESIAN COORDINATES and VECTOR.)

Poisson disk distribution
In the SPATIAL DOMAIN, a Poisson disk distribution is a non-uniform distribution with the restriction that no two samples are closer than a specified distance. The human eye appears to have such a distribution of receptors outside the regular structure of the fovea; this accounts for the eye's ability to generate NOISE rather than ALIASING artifacts in this zone. In the FREQUENCY DOMAIN the Poisson disk distribution consists of a central spike (the d.c. component), standing on a plateau of noise which extends beyond the NYQUIST LIMIT. (See also GAUSSIAN DISTRIBUTION.)
[Glassner-89, Gregory-86]

Poisson distribution
A Poisson distribution is a FREQUENCY DISTRIBUTION for describing discrete events that occur randomly within space or time. For example, blood cells on a microscope slide exhibit a Poisson spatial distribution for the cell count in different, but similar, areas. The distribution is used to describe the probability of some event occurring a number of times; therefore the probabilities should sum to unity. The expression describing such a distribution is

$$1 = e^{-z}(1 + z + \frac{z^2}{2!} + \frac{z^3}{3!} + \frac{z^4}{4!} + \frac{z^5}{5!} \ldots\ldots)$$

where z is the expected or average number of occurrences of an event, and the probability of observing the

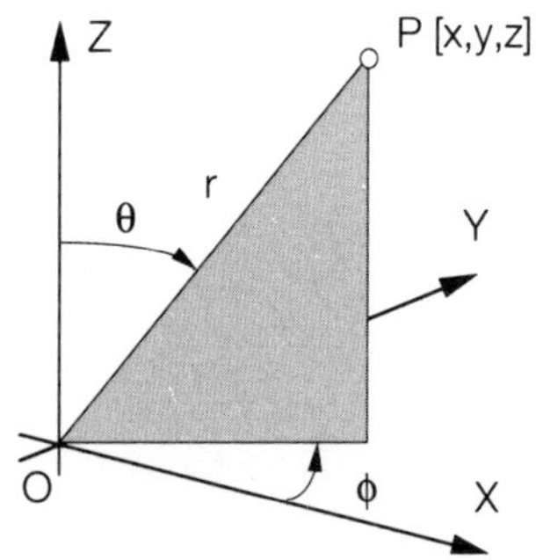

Figure P-4 *Whilst P has Cartesian coordinates [x, y, z], its spherical polar coordinates are specified in terms of the radius r and the two angles: θ and ϕ.*

occurrence of 0, 1, 2, 3, 4 etc. events is given by the individual terms of the expression. The Poisson distribution should only be applied in situations where the expectation *z* is reasonably constant from trial to trial. A feature of the distribution is that the mean value *z* is equal to its VARIANCE, so that the STANDARD DEVIATION will be equal to the square root of *z*.

Poisson faulting

In the generation of FRACTIONAL BROWNIAN MOTION, Poisson faulting applies Gaussian random displacements (faults or steps) to a surface (planar or spherical) at Poisson distributed intervals. Voss uses this technique to create fractal planets. (See also FRACTAL GEOMETRY, FRACTIONAL BROWNIAN MOTION, POISSON DISK DISTRIBUTION, and STOCHASTIC MODELLING.)
[Mandelbrot-82, Musgrave-89]

polar coordinates

Polar coordinates are a system for locating a point in space using radial measurements and angles rather than the offset measurements used in Cartesian notation. See Figure P-4. (See also AREA COORDINATES and CARTESIAN COORDINATES.)
[Gasson-83]

polling

Polling is the process of investigating the status of a device. For example, a system might poll an input device to assess its status, which, if it changes, means that an EVENT is created for the resident graphics package to resolve.

polygon

A polygon is a figure formed by a closed chain of straight line segments. They may be REGULAR, IRREGULAR, CONVEX or CONCAVE or have holes, and are fundamental building blocks for many modelling schemes. (See also ANTI-CLOCKWISE POLYGON, CLOCKWISE POLYGON, CONCAVE POLYGON, CONVEX POLYGON, IRREGULAR POLYGON, N-GON, RE-ENTRANT POLYGON, and REGULAR POLYGON.)
[Hearn-86, Rogers-85, Rogers-89]

polygonal mesh

A polygonal mesh is a structure formed from a family of interlocking polygons.
[Hearn-86]

polygon rasterization

Polygon rasterization is the process of converting a polygon into a RASTER format which is then suitable for HIDDEN-SURFACE REMOVAL, perhaps using a Z-BUFFER.
[Burger-89, Foley-90, Pineda-88, Rogers-85]

polyhedron

A polyhedron is a multi-faceted solid object constructed from polygons. (See also PLATONIC OBJECTS.)
[Gasson-83]

polynomial

A monomial term in mathematics describes a quantity raised to any power; thus a polynomial represents a sequence of such terms. For example:

$ax^2 + bx + c$

is a polynomial in x. PARAMETRIC POLYNOMIALS play an important role in curve and surface definition. (See also BLENDING FUNCTION, PARAMETRIC POLYNOMIAL, and RATIONAL POLYNOMIAL.)
[Rogers-89]

polynomial weighting function
See BASIS FUNCTION.

pop-up menu
A pop-up menu literally 'pops up' on the screen when a specific task is requested and disappears after a menu item has been selected. (See also MENU, PULL-DOWN MENU, and WIMP ENVIRONMENT).
[Burger-89, Hearn-86]

portable
Portable software can be supposedly transferred to various processing systems and still function correctly – and standards such as GKS and PHIGS assist in increasing portability by removing its dependencey upon computer graphics hardware. (See also DEVICE DEPENDENT, DEVICE INDEPENDENT, GKS, and PHIGS.)
[Burger-89]

post-production
Post-production encompasses all the procedures needed to integrate the many individual sequences that go to make up the final piece of video graphics; these include compositing, editing, video effects, dissolves, and soundtrack.

PostScript
PostScript is a PAGE DESCRIPTION LANGUAGE for defining text and graphics in a machine independent format.

power basis
See MONOMIAL BASIS.

preroll
Preroll is the process of rewinding a videotape machine to ensure that when it is started it has the correct operational speed when an edit point is obtained.

primary colours
A primary colour implies that it is pure in the sense that it is not the product of a mixing process. Experiments have shown that the ADDITIVE PRIMARY COLOURS: red, green and blue, in the form of lights, are capable of creating a wide range of other colours when mixed in different proportions. Thomas Young (1773–1829) gave the name 'principal colours' initially to red, yellow and blue, but revised this to red, green and violet. Today it is generally accepted that the three primary colours are due to the nature of the human retina, which appears to contain cones sensitive to three portions of the visible spectrum. The SUBTRACTIVE PRIMARY COLOURS cyan, magenta and yellow form the basis of printing processes where coloured pigments absorb incident light and reflect a proportion based upon their density. However, these three coloured pigments must be augmented by black for high-quality printing. See Figure A-1. (See also CMY COLOUR MODEL, CMYK, COLOUR, COLOUR MODEL, COLOUR SPACE, GREY COMPONENT REPLACEMENT, SUBTRACTIVE COLOUR MIXING, and SUBTRACTIVE PRIMARY COLOURS.)
[Hearn-86, Hunt-75, Rogers-85]

primitive
A primitive is a graphical entity such as a line, circle, cube or sphere which can be used for constructing more complex structures.
[Hearn-86]

probabilistic ray tracing
See DISTRIBUTED RAY TRACING.

procedural animation
Rule-based animation, or procedural animation, involves some algorithmic procedure to describe how an animation sequence proceeds. Examples include a swinging

pendulum, a rotating wheel, wave motion or fractal mist. (See also ANIMATION, BEHAVIOURAL ANIMATION, CHARACTER ANIMATION, COMPUTER ANIMATION, DISPLACEMENT ANIMATION, GOAL-ORIENTED ANIMATION, KEY-FRAME ANIMATION, and RIGID-BODY ANIMATION.)
[Green-88]

procedural texture
Texture generated by functions rather than from TEXTURE MAPS is called procedural texture. Such functions exploit NOISE, LOOK-UP TABLES and filtered random numbers to provide an algorithmic basis for creating texture detail. (See also HYPERTEXTURE, ITERATED FUNCTION SYSTEMS, NOISE, SOLID NOISE, SOLID TEXTURE, TEXEL, TEXTURE MAP, and TEXTURE MAPPING.)
[Perlin-85]

product data exchange specification (PDES)
Like IGES, PDES provides a standard for the exchange of data between CAD systems. (See also IGES.)

program
A program is an organized sequence of computer instructions.

progressive radiosity
Progressive radiosity is an iterative strategy for computing FORM-FACTORS in a RADIOSITY environment. The algorithm selects the surface with the greatest reflected and/or emitted energy and computes the FORM-FACTORS between this and the other surfaces; these FORM-FACTORS are then used to increment the radiosity of each element. The algorithm continues until a steady-state condition is obtained. (See also FORM-FACTOR, RADIOSITY, and RAY TRACING.)
[Arvo-86, Baum-89, Chattopadhyay-87, Cohen-88, Greenberg-89, Shao-88, Wallace-89]

projection
A projection is a mathematical technique for converting a system of *n*-dimensional points into an $(n - 1)$-dimensional space. In computer graphics systems, projections (especially perspective) are used to transform 3-D coordinates into 2-D points upon a PROJECTION PLANE. (See also AXONOMETRIC ORTHOGRAPHIC PROJECTION, ISOMETRIC PROJECTION, OBLIQUE PROJECTION, ORTHOGRAPHIC PROJECTION, PARALLEL PROJECTION, and PERSPECTIVE PROJECTION.)
[Burger-89, Foley-90, Gasson-83, Hearn-86, Rogers-89]

projection plane
A projection plane is a PLANAR surface, generally ORTHOGONAL to a principal 3-D axis, which enables points of intersection to be calculated where lines connect object vertices to a CENTRE OF PROJECTION. In computing a PERSPECTIVE PROJECTION, the projection plane is equivalent to the PICTURE PLANE. See Figure P-3. (See also OBLIQUE PROJECTION, PARALLEL PROJECTION, PERSPECTIVE PROJECTION, and PROJECTION.)
[Burger-89, Foley-90, Gasson-83, Hearn-86, Rogers-89]

pseudo-colouring
Pseudo-colouring or false-colouring refers to the substitution of levels stored in a FRAME STORE by colours held in a LOOK-UP TABLE. This is frequently employed in IMAGE PROCESSING for clarifying detail in satellite and medical images.
[Ware-88]

pseudo display file
A pseudo display file is a device-independent DISPLAY FILE which can be used for driving a variety of different display devices. (See also DISPLAY FILE and DISPLAY LIST.)
[Hearn-86]

pull-down menu
A pull-down menu is activated by selecting a system feature normally displayed as ICONS or words upon a screen; on selection, the menu is exposed or 'pulled down' to reveal further actions available to the user. Once the menu action has been selected the menu is removed. (See also

HUMAN–COMPUTER INTERACTION, MENU, POP-UP MENU, and WIMP ENVIRONMENT.)

purity

When colours are mixed additively, equal amounts of red, green and blue create a level of white light; the term purity is a measure of how much a colour has been desaturated by this white component. A totally saturated colour means that there is no white light at all, which implies that the colour can be matched by one or two of the ADDITIVE PRIMARY COLOURS. (See also ADDITIVE PRIMARY COLOURS, CHROMA, COLOUR, COLOUR MODEL, COLOUR SPACE, HUE, LIGHTNESS, and VALUE.)
[Hearn-86, Hunt-75, Rogers-85]

PVA

PVA is an acronym for Professional Video Adaptor which is a video graphics board with a resolution of 1280 x 800 interlaced, and 1280 x 400 non-interlaced. (See also CGA, EGA, HDA, HGC, MCGA, MDA, SUPER VGA, and VGA.)

q

quadratic

A quadratic equation is a POLYNOMIAL which has no terms with a power greater than two.
[Bowyer-83]

quadratic shading

Conventional GOURAUD SHADING linearly interpolates colour values along a raster, whereas quadratic shading employs a QUADRATIC interpolant. This has the advantage of disguising the MACH BANDS caused by the intensity gradients that can occur at edges. (See also GOURAUD SHADING, PHONG SHADING, SHADING, and SHADING MODEL.)

quadratic surface patch

A quadratic surface patch is a SURFACE PATCH description which relies upon second-order equations to identify points upon the surface, as employed, for example, in quadratic BÉZIER SURFACE PATCHES. (See also BÉZIER SURFACE PATCH, B-SPLINE SURFACE PATCH, NURBS, PARAMETRIC SURFACE PATCH, PATCH, and PATCHED SURFACE.)
[Cendes-87, Farin-88, Miller-88b, Rogers-85, Woodwark-86]

quadrilateral

A quadrilateral is a four-sided figure.

quadtree

Like an octree which recursively partitions a 3-D volume of space into octants, a quadtree recursively partitions a 2-D area of space into quadrants. This enables any point within this area to be defined in terms of a sequence of numbers representing the partition numbers containing the point as the space is repeatedly divided. Quadtrees provide a hierarchical mechanism for storing pixel images – and many new algorithms have been created for their manipulation and processing. See Figure Q-1. (See also DATA STRUCTURE, G-QUADTREE, GRAPHICAL DATA STRUCTURE, HIERARCHY, and OCTREE.)
[Hearn-86, Kaufman-89, Miller-89]

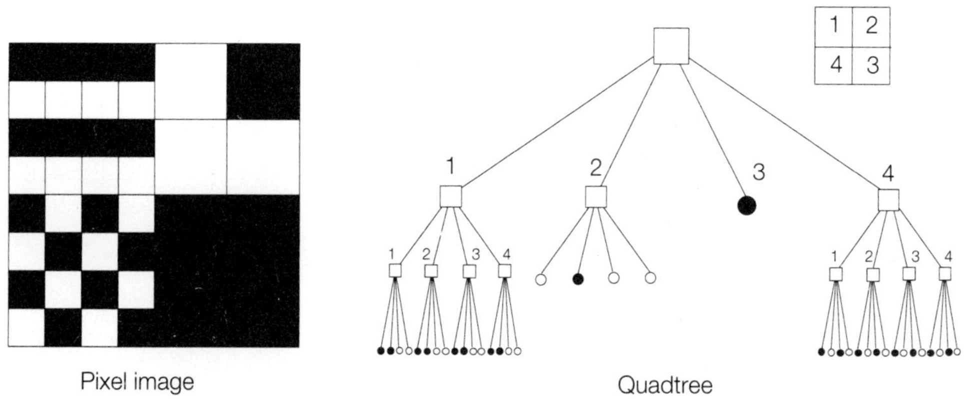

Figure Q-1 *The quadtree partitioning strategy recursively divides an area into four equal parts: this allows a tree structure to identify those quadrants storing information and those remaining empty. In the above illustration the pixel image on the left can be represented by the quadtree on the right. The top-right legend shows the numbering sequence given to the divided areas. Note that the division process is continued only if there are data stored at a lower level. In this example, the third quadrant at the first level is completely black and further division is unnecessary.*

quantizing
Quantizing is the process of SAMPLING a continuous signal into discrete levels.

quartic surface
A quartic surface is defined by a fourth-degree equation in three variables, such as a torus.

quaternions
Quaternions are an extension of the notion of COMPLEX NUMBERS and are used in computer graphics to resolve the problems encountered when EULER ANGLES are used to control the rotation of objects and the observer. Where three Euler attitude angles are used to define a rotation, quaternions employ four parameters, three imaginary and one real as follows

$$q = a\mathbf{i} + b\mathbf{j} + c\mathbf{k} + d$$

where

$$\mathbf{i}^2 = \mathbf{j}^2 = \mathbf{k}^2 = -1$$
$$\mathbf{ij} = \mathbf{k},\ \mathbf{jk} = \mathbf{i},\ \mathbf{ki} = \mathbf{j}$$
$$\mathbf{ij} = -\mathbf{ji},\ \mathbf{jk} = -\mathbf{kj},\ \mathbf{ki} = -\mathbf{ik}$$

[Burger-89, Hart-89, Shoemake-85]

radian

A radian is an angular measurement where, by definition, 2π radians are equivalent to 360°: this means that one radian equals approximately 57.296°.

radiosity

Radiosity is an ILLUMINATION MODEL used for computing surface light intensities resulting from multiple diffuse reflections. The algorithm requires that surfaces are divided into small patches, and for those that are visible to other patches FORM-FACTORS are needed to express the fractional amount of light leaving one patch and arriving at another. These are computed from a set of simultaneous equations using reflectivity coefficients, areas, patch radiosity and emission values. The equations can be solved using the Gauss–Siedel method, which converges rapidly to a steady-state solution. From these intensities, entire surfaces may be rendered by linearly interpolating the light levels between the small patches: naturally this implies that the accuracy of the final image depends upon using sufficient patches; unfortunately, the computation increases in a square law. Once the FORM-FACTORS have been computed, any view of the 3-D environment can be taken, as the lighting levels are view-independent. This technique produces very realistic images, even without SPECULAR REFLECTIONS. (See also DELTA FORM-FACTORS, DIFFUSE REFLECTION, FORM-FACTOR, ILLUMINATION MODEL, and PROGRESSIVE RADIOSITY.)
[Baum-89, Cohen-86, Cohen-88, Greenberg-89, Immel-86, Rushmeier- 87, Sillion-89, Wallace-87, Wallace-89]

ramification matrix

A ramification MATRIX is used in the generation of random binary trees that exhibit the fractal property of SELF-SIMILARITY. (See also FRACTAL.)
[Viennot-89]

random

Random implies without order – and in computer graphics random processes frequently employ pseudo-random number generators, or LOOK-UP TABLES storing random numbers, to implement STOCHASTIC algorithms. (See also DETERMINSITIC and STOCHASTIC.)

raster

A raster refers to one line of pixels drawn upon a CRT. The horizontal resolution of the raster depends upon the quality of the monitor and the bandwidth of the original signal source. (See also CATHODE RAY TUBE, FIELD, FRAME, INTERLACING, MONITOR, RASTER SCANNING, and REFRESH CRT.)
[Hearn-86, Rogers-85]

raster computer graphics

Raster computer graphics encompasses those techniques associated with the display of images upon pixel-based devices. This would include images developed within a FRAME STORE as well as high-resolution film-based images. In the early days of computer graphics – before the evolution of raster displays – images were created upon calligraphic devices such as VECTOR DISPLAYS and STORAGE TUBES; today, the industry is dominated by raster technology. (See also CALLIGRAPHIC DISPLAY, FRAME STORE, and SCAN-LINE ALGORITHM.)
[Gharachorloo-89]

raster coordinate system

The raster coordinate system is the method of addressing pixels upon a CRT.
(See also CATHODE RAY TUBE and RASTER.)
[Rogers-85]

raster display

A raster display is a display device employing a RASTER SCANNING refresh system. (See also CATHODE RAY TUBE, COLOUR MONITOR, and RASTER SCANNING.)
[Burger-89, Foley-90, Hearn-86, Rogers-85]

rasterizing

See SCAN CONVERSION.

RasterOps

RasterOps or raster operations refer to operations per-

formed upon bitmaps in a FRAME STORE. For example, a zoom facility can be implemented by replicating pixels an integer number of times; thus a four-times zoom could be effected by converting an (n x n) pixel area into a ($4n$ x $4n$) pixel area substituting a (4 x 4) pixel block for every original pixel. (See also BI-LEVEL DISPLAY, BIT-BLT, BIT MAPPING, and BLITTER.)
[Burger-89, Foley-90]

raster scanning
An image is maintained upon a REFRESH CRT by raster scanning, where a scanning spot is initially positioned at the top-left hand corner of the screen and is stroked across from left to right to produce one RASTER of information. At the end of each RASTER, the beam intensity is suppressed whilst the spot is repositioned beneath the previous left-hand point, and the next raster is produced. When the beam reaches the bottom of the screen, it is again blanked off whilst a vertical retrace is made to the original starting point. Generally, computer graphics raster displays are non-interlaced, whereas television systems employ two interlaced FIELDS to keep the overall system FLICKER and BANDWIDTH to a minimum. (See also CATHODE RAY TUBE, FIELD, FLICKER, FRAME, INTERLACING, PAL, NTSC, REFRESH RATE, and SECAM.)
[Burger-89, Foley-90, Hearn-86, Hunt-75, Rogers-85, Rogers-89]

rational
A rational number can be represented by a ratio of two whole numbers. For example, 0.25 is rational, as it can be represented by $\frac{1}{4}$; however, the square-root of 2 (approximately 1.4142) is irrational, as it cannot be expressed as the ratio of two whole numbers, which also implies that its accuracy presents problems when it is stored within a computer. RATIONAL POLYNOMIALS also exhibit rather special properties, and are used in NURBS for curve and surface patch definition. (See also NURBS and RATIONAL POLYNOMIAL.)
[Dantzig-30]

rational polynomial
Whereas simple polynomials can only approximate certain curves such as an arc, rational polynomials (which are expressed as the ratio of two polynomials) can produce a precise shape, hence their use in NURBS. (See also NURBS and POLYNOMIAL.)
[Bohm-84, Farin-88, Piegl-87b, Piegl-89, Woodwark-86]

ray casting
Ray casting is a hidden-surface detection strategy generally associated with rendering CSG objects. Like RAY TRACING, the algorithm involves casting rays into the OBJECT SPACE to identify the nearest surface for every pixel; but whereas RAY TRACING traces back the multiple reflections and refractions that might have occurred, ray casting uses the nearest intersection for rendering purposes. (See also CONSTRUCTIVE SOLID GEOMETRY and RAY TRACING.)
[Glassner-88]

ray intersection point
In RAY TRACING a ray intersection point identifies where a cast ray intersects with a surface in OBJECT SPACE. The shortest of these rays identifies the first visible surface. (See also RAY CASTING, RAY INTERSECTION TREE and RAY TRACING.)
[Glassner-88]

ray intersection tree
In ray tracing, the ray intersection tree stores the hierarchy of rays transmitted and reflected for one sample point. The maximum possible depth of the tree is determined by the user and controls the number of secondary reflections and refractions in the rendered image. The tree is traversed by an algorithm which computes the impact that the rays have on the intensity of the sampled point. (See also ADAPTIVE TREE-DEPTH CONTROL and RAY TRACING.)
[Glassner-89, Goldsmith-87]

ray tracing
In essence, the ray tracing algorithm traces the origins of the singular light ray which arrives through the centre

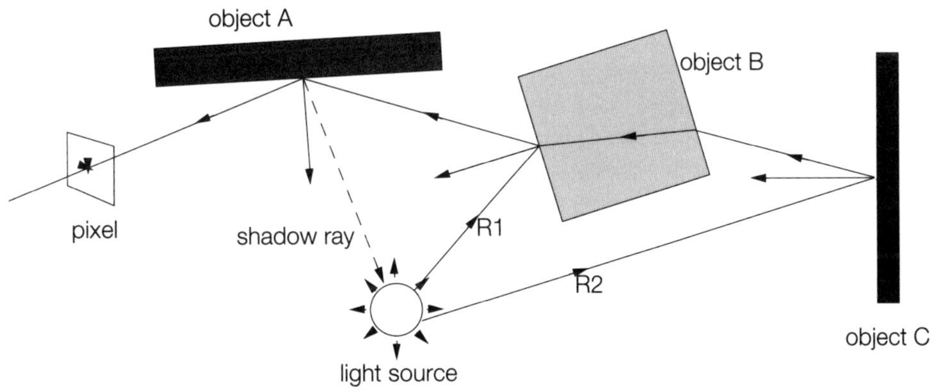

Figure R-1 *Ray tracing attempts to discover the optical origins and object intersections of light rays contributing to the colour value of a single pixel. By tracing back the specular reflective and transmissive paths of light in the above diagram, one discovers that ray R1 reflects off object B, then object A and into the pixel's centre point, whilst ray R2 reflects from object C, is refracted by object B and follows the same path as R1 into the pixel. Shadow testing can be achieved by sending out a shadow feeler ray; for example, if a shadow test is made at the point of incidence on object A, the ray would not intersect with any surface on its journey to the light source, therefore it cannot be in shadow.*

of a pixel. To achieve this, a ray is cast back into the OBJECT SPACE to discover whether it emanated directly from a LIGHT SOURCE, was reflected by a surface, or was refracted by some transmissive medium. This optical approach to light permits the realistic rendering of shadows, DEPTH OF FIELD, MOTION BLUR, reflections and refractions. See Figure R-1. (See also ADAPTIVE TREE-DEPTH CONTROL, BACKWARD RAY TRACING, BEAM TRACING, CONE TRACING, DEPTH OF FIELD, DISTRIBUTED RAY TRACING, FORWARD RAY TRACING, LIGHT BUFFER, MOTION BLUR, OBJECT BUFFER, OBJECT SPACE, PARAMETERIZED RAY TRACING, PENCIL TRACING, PENUMBRA, RAY INTERSECTION TREE, SHADOW RAY, SHADOWS, and STOCHASTIC RAY TRACING.)
[Burger-89, Glassner-89, Hart-89, Hearn-86, Kajiya-82, Kajiya-83, Kajiya-84, Kalra-89, Kay-79a, Kay-86, Rogers-85, Roth-82, Sequin-89, Ward-88, Youssef -86]

real image
A real image, as opposed to a VIRTUAL IMAGE, is one that can be captured upon a screen, whereas a virtual image can only be observed by being brought into focus on the retina (itself acting as a screen). (See also VIRTUAL IMAGE.)
[Jenkins-76]

real-time
The term 'real-time' implies that a computer system is capable of reacting in the user's own time domain, so that there is no observable delay between a user command and a computer response. Therefore, true real-time computer graphics systems must be capable of generating new images without introducing any degree of hesitation. Such systems do exist, normally in the form of workstations capable of displaying vectors at very high speed, but fully rendered colour scenes containing

approximately 500 polygons still require a dedicated IMAGE GENERATOR. However, even these devices introduce a small latency of about 50 milliseconds, which is just tolerable. (See also IMAGE GENERATOR and PIXEL-PLANES.)
[Fuchs-83, Romney-68, Watkins-70]

recursive algorithm
(1) See RECURSIVE ALGORITHM.
(2) A recursive algorithm references itself as part of its strategy in solving a problem. Certain problems such as factorial calculations, BERNSTEIN BASIS FUNCTIONS, B-SPLINE BLENDING FUNCTIONS, and DIVIDE AND CONQUER algorithms enable a recursive or an iterative strategy to be employed. Although the recursive approach is generally compact and apparently elegant, it is not necessarily computationally efficient.
[Burger-89, Woodwark-86]

re-entrant polygon
The edges of a re-entrant polygon can mutually intersect themselves, but as they have no practical application they can cause problems for systems not expecting them.

reflectance mapping
See ENVIRONMENT MAPPING.

reflectance model
A reflectance model is a basis upon which reflection calculations are made. Such models include diffuse (Gouraud), specular (Phong) and microfaceted (Blinn). (See also AMBIENT LIGHT, BIDIRECTIONAL REFLECTANCE, COOK–TORRANCE SHADING, DIFFUSE REFLECTION, GLOBAL ILLUMINATION MODEL, GOURAUD SHADING, ILLUMINATION MODEL, LAMBERT'S COSINE LAW, MICROFACET, PHONG SHADING, RADIOSITY, RAY TRACING, RENDERING EQUATION, SHADING MODEL, SNELL'S LAW, SPECULAR REFLECTION, and TORRANCE–SPARROW SHADING MODEL.)
[Bahar-87, Buckalew-89, Cook-82a, Cook-82b, Kajiya-85, Rogers-85]

reflection coefficient
When a surface is illuminated, some light will be absorbed and possibly transmitted, whilst the rest is reflected away from the surface. In reality this process of absorption, transmission and reflection is a function of WAVELENGTH – and even the most sophisticated ILLUMINATION MODELS can only approximate this behaviour. Simple REFLECTANCE MODELS attempt to simulate such phenomena by associating reflection coefficients with surfaces for the red, green and blue light components – so that the reflected light can be easily computed by multiplying the same colour components of a LIGHT SOURCE by this fractional value. Reflection coefficients are required for the ambient, diffuse and specular light components, although the latter is used only to control the specularity of the surface. (See also AMBIENT REFLECTION COEFFICIENT, DIFFUSE REFLECTION COEFFICIENT, and SPECULAR REFLECTION COEFFICIENT.)
[Burger-89, Foley-90, Hearn-86, Rogers-85, Rogers-89]

reflection of light
The reflection of light is summarized by two laws: the first law of reflection states that the incident ray, the reflected ray and the surface normal at the point of incidence all lie in the same plane; the second law states that the ANGLE OF REFLECTION equals the ANGLE OF INCIDENCE. These laws form the basis for ILLUMINATION MODELS in computer graphics. See Figure A-3. (See also ANGLE OF INCIDENCE, ANGLE OF REFLECTION, REFLECTANCE MODEL, REFLECTION COEFFICIENT, REFLECTION VECTOR, SURFACE NORMAL, and VECTOR.)
[Burger-89, Glassner-89, Hearn-86, Jenkins-76, Rogers-86]

reflection vector
A reflection vector identifies the direction of a reflected light ray away from a surface. It would be needed in computing SPECULAR REFLECTIONS and RAY TRACING calculations. See Figure A-3. (See also ANGLE OF INCIDENCE, ANGLE OF REFLECTION, RAY TRACING, REFLECTION OF LIGHT, SPECULAR REFLECTION, and VECTOR.)
[Burger-89, Foley-90, Glassner-89, Hearn-86, Rogers-85]

refraction of light

Refraction is the change of direction of light when it moves from one medium to another and undergoes a speed change. This occurs when light moves, for example, between air, glass or water. The change in direction is quantified by a WAVELENGTH dependent quantity called the REFRACTIVE INDEX. A RAY TRACING environment provides an ideal framework for simulating these effects. See Figure A-3. (See also ANGLE OF REFRACTION, REFRACTIVE INDEX, SPECULAR TRANSMISSION, and TOTAL INTERNAL REFLECTION.)

[Burger-89, Glassner-89, Hearn-86, Jenkins-76, Kay-79a, Rogers-85]

refractive index

The refractive index of a medium is the ratio

$$\frac{\sin(\alpha_i)}{\sin(\alpha_r)}$$

where α_i is the angle of incidence and α_r is the angle of refraction. The refractive index is a measure of how much light is diverted from its normal straight path, and can be simulated in RAY TRACING. (See also ANGLE OF INCIDENCE, ANGLE OF REFRACTION, RAY TRACING, and SINE.)

[Hearn-86, Jenkins-76, Rogers-85]

refresh buffer

See FRAME STORE.

refresh CRT

A refresh CRT is a display device such as a television or computer graphics workstation, which maintains its image by repeatedly refreshing FIELDS or FRAMES of raster information. (See also BEAM PENETRATION CRT, CALLIGRAPHIC DISPLAY, CATHODE RAY TUBE, COLOUR MONITOR, FIELD, FLYBACK, FRAME, FUSION FREQUENCY, HIGH-RESOLUTION DISPLAY, INTERLACING, MONITOR, MULTI-SCANNING MONITOR, RASTER, SHADOW-MASK COLOUR CRT, and STEREOSCOPIC DISPLAY.)

[Hearn-86, Hunt-75, Rogers-85]

refresh rate

The refresh rate is the frequency with which a raster display is refreshed. PAL television is 50 Hz (fields/second) and NTSC is 59.94 Hz (fields/second), whilst many computer graphics workstations exceed 60Hz (frames/second). The reason for the unusual value for the NTSC refresh rate is that at 60 Hz unacceptable levels of interference arise within the encoded signal. (See also CATHODE RAY TUBE, FIELD, FLICKER, FRAME, FUSION FREQUENCY, HORIZONTAL SCAN FREQUENCY, INTERLACING, NTSC, PAL, PERSISTENCE, PHOSPHOR, RASTER DISPLAY, SECAM, UPDATE RATE, and VIDEO FREQUENCY.)

[Hearn-86, Hunt-75, Rogers-85]

region filling

See AREA INFILL.

regular polygon

A regular polygon has sides of equal length, and equal angles subtended to its centre point. (See also ANTICLOCKWISE POLYGON, CLOCKWISE POLYGON, CONCAVE POLYGON, CONVEX POLYGON, IRREGULAR POLYGON, and RE-ENTRANT POLYGON.)

[Gasson-83]

relative coordinates

Relative coordinates are physical measurements locating a point in space relative to some convenient arbitrary system of axes. (See also ABSOLUTE COORDINATES, CARTESIAN COORDINATES, DEVICE COORDINATE SYSTEM, NORMALIZED DEVICE COORDINATES, PHYSICAL DEVICE COORDINATES, SCREEN COORDINATES, and WORLD COORDINATE SPACE.)

[Burger-89, Foley-90, Rogers-89]

remote-sensing

Satellite and aerial imaging are examples of data gathering processes termed remote sensing, which can provide excellent sources of data for TERRAIN MODELLING. (See also TERRAIN MODELLING.)

renderer
A renderer is a program for creating a shaded synthetic image based upon 3-D geometric descriptions, surface attributes and an ILLUMINATION MODEL. The final image will be spatially correct in that surfaces are ordered correctly from the observer, and the surfaces will appear illuminated within the scope of the illumination model. Surfaces may be enhanced with texture or reflections; shadows and penumbrae may be computed from the LIGHT SOURCES; and the image may be filtered to minimize any artifacts introduced by associated hardware limitations. A number of algorithms have evolved over recent years, but RADIOSITY and RAY TRACING have been associated with some of the most realistic images to date. (See also A-BUFFER, ATTRIBUTES, COOK–TORRANCE SHADING, CROSS- SECTION RENDERING, DISTRIBUTED RENDERING, GOURAUD SHADING, ILLUMINATION MODEL, PARALLEL RENDERING, PHONG SHADING, RADIOSITY, RAY TRACING, RENDERING EQUATION, RENDERMAN, REYES, THRESHOLD RENDERING, TORRANCE–SPARROW SHADING MODEL, and VOLUMETRIC RENDERING.)
[Burger-89, Hearn-86, Foley-90]

rendering equation
Kajiya's rendering equation is an integral equation which in his words 'states that the transport intensity of light from one surface point to another is simply the sum of the emitted light and the total light intensity which is scattered toward the latter point from all other surface points'. This seems very similar to the RADIOSITY approach, but Kajiya's equation does address the reflectance properties of surfaces.
[Kajiya-86, Wallace-87]

rendering pipeline
The rendering pipeline identifies the logical pathway in a computer graphics system associated with the calculations for illumination, shading, depth cueing and pseudo colouring.

RenderMan
Pixar's RenderMan product is a powerful interface specification between 3-D modelling and photorealistic rendering techniques. It is the most ambitious project, so far, to tackle the problems of defining software routines to handle everything from quadratic surface modelling tools to the rendering of particle systems.
[Upstill-90]

resistive sheet tablet
Some digitizing tablets employ sheets of conductive and resistive materials separated by a small distance to provide a mechanism for generating coordinates. The resistive material has a voltage applied in one coordinate direction so that, when a stylus tip presses the two layers together, the voltage at that point is transferred to the conducting surface and the point is decoded. By incorporating two sheets, the X- and Y-coordinates can be created. (See also DIGITIZER, GRAPHICS TABLET, and TOUCH TABLET.)
[Ward-87]

resolution
(1) Resolution is a measure of a system's ability to display fine detail accurately. For example, a raster display is concerned with the physical number of lines and pixels visible on a screen, whereas a laser printer is assessed by how many dots/inch can be printed.
(2) Where digital encoding is involved, the resolution of the system will be controlled by the number of bits available for the digital code.
[Burger-89, Hearn-86, Rogers-86]

response time
The system response time is the elapsed time between initiating an event and the system's reaction. On single-user workstations the response time is virtually instantaneous, but multi-user computers can still give rise to delays of one or more seconds, which can be intolerable in interactive computer graphics. (See also REAL-TIME.)
[Foley-90]

reverse video
See INVERSE VIDEO.

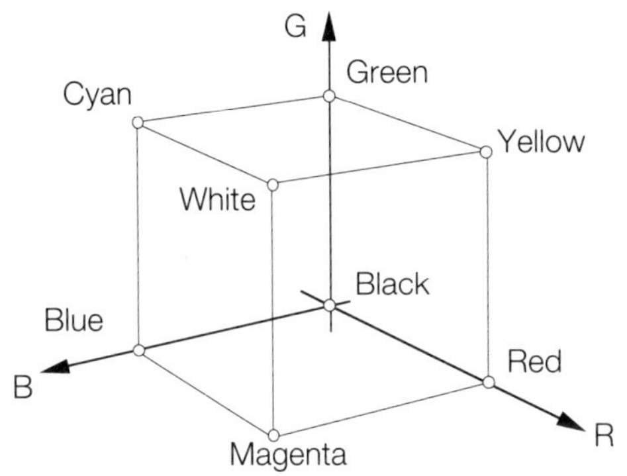

Figure R-2 *The RGB colour space is a unit cube where colour can be specified in terms of its primary colour components. Although it is useful in visualizing additive colour mixing, it cannot assist in visualizing related families of hue or saturation.*

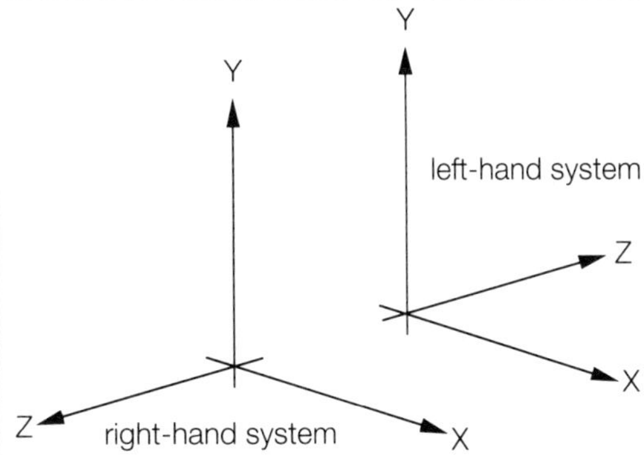

Figure R-3 *The majority of computer graphics algorithms employ a right-handed system of Cartesian axes, but one can move from one system to the other simply by reversing the direction of any one axis.*

Reyes
The Reyes rendering system is a software package whose name is derived from the claim that it 'Renders Everything You Ever Saw'.
[Cook-87]

RGB
RGB is an acronym for Red, Green and Blue, the ADDITIVE PRIMARY COLOURS.
[Burger-89, Foley-90, Hearn-86, Hunt-75, Rogers-85]

RGB colour model
The RGB colour model employs a colour space consisting of a 3-D set of Cartesian axes labelled red, green and blue; then if each primary colour has a range of 0 to 1, a unit cube defines the gamut of possible colours. Although this model is central to computer graphics for colour manipulation, it conceptually offers very little at the interactive interface, where one tends to use the HSV COLOR MODEL, with, perhaps, the added control of mixing individually the red, green and blue components. See Figure R-2. (See also COLOUR MODEL, COLOUR SPACE, HLS COLOUR MODEL, HSV COLOUR MODEL, and MUNSELL COLOUR SYSTEM.)
[Burger-89, Foley-90, Hearn-86, Hunt-75, Rogers-85]

right-handed axes
Cartesian axes can be formed with a left- or right-handed configuration: the latter would have one's right-hand thumb aligned with the X-axis, the first finger with the Y-axis and the middle finger with the Z-axis. One must be careful when undertaking transformations between right- and left-handed systems, as sign changes can occur. See Figure R-3. (See also LEFT-HANDED AXES.)
[Gasson-83]

rigid-body animation
Rigid-body animation is concerned with the modelling and animation of rigid bodies physically interacting with one another over a period of time. Such simulations prevent bodies from inter-penetrating by using Newtonian dynamics to calculate forces that determine their future positions, velocities and accelerations. One assumption concerning rigid bodies is that they do not change shape

or volume. (See also COLLISION DETECTION, DYNAMIC CONSTRAINTS, ELASTICALLY DEFORMABLE OBJECTS, FORWARD DYNAMICS, FORWARD KINEMATICS, GOAL-ORIENTED ANIMATION, INVERSE DYNAMICS PROCEDURAL ANIMATION, and RIGID TRANSFORMATION.)
[Armstrong-85, Baraff-89, Hahn-88, Moore-88]

rigid-body transformation
See RIGID TRANSFORMATION.

rigid transformation
A rigid transformation preserves the geometric integrity of shapes and objects. Examples are rotation, translation and scaling. (See also AFFINE TRANSFORMATION, LINEAR TRANSFORMATION, and RIGID-BODY ANIMATION.)

RLE
See RUN-LENGTH ENCODING.

roll
Roll is a rotational movement about an axis parallel to the facing direction and is normally used in conjunction with PITCH and YAW. (See also PITCH and YAW.)
[Gasson-83]

rotation matrix
Matrices provide a powerful mechanism for describing geometric transformations, and the rotation matrix enables single vertices to be rotated about a point or axis by a specified angle. In the homogeneous form this will be a 3 x 3 matrix for 2-D rotations, and a 4 x 4 matrix for 3-D rotations. (See also HOMOGENEOUS COORDINATES, TRANSLATION MATRIX, and SCALING MATRIX.)
[Burger-89, Foley-90, Gasson-83, Hearn-86, Rogers-89]

rubberbanding
Rubberbanding refers to an interaction technique used in interactive computer graphics in which a 'rubber-band' in the form of a line-segment is displayed between some fixed point on the display and a point which is being interactively moved or selected.
[Hearn-86]

rule-based animation
See PROCEDURAL ANIMATION.

ruled surface
See LOFTED SURFACE.

run-length encoding (RLE)
Run-length encoding exploits line coherence in image compaction, whereby identical consecutive pixels on a raster enable the compacted form to be specified in terms of the starting pixel, the number of consecutive pixels and the pixel colour. Obviously the technique is only efficient where an image contains spans of consistent colours. (See also CELL ENCODING, IMAGE COMPRESSION, LZW COMPRESSION, and NAPLPS.)
[Hearn-86, Laws-75]

S

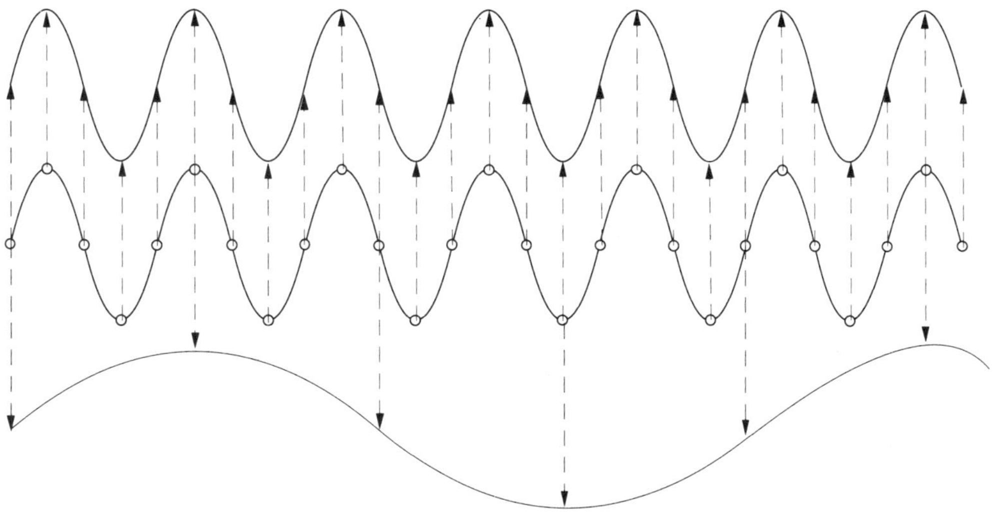

Figure S-1 *If the centre waveform is ampled as indicated, it is possible to reconstruct it as shown in the top waveform, but if it is sampled at a much lower frequency, the reconstructed waveform is of a lower frequency. This false reconstruction is called an 'alias' of the original and is obviously caused by undersampling. In raster computer graphics a similar phenomenon occurs when a complex scene is incorrectly sampled; such aliasing artifacts appear as jagged polygon edges.*

sampling
Sampling is the process of investigating the status of some system at different points in time or space. Raster images are derived by sampling the SPACE DOMAIN associated with geometric descriptions of images and objects. As the sampling rate is dominated by the resolution of the graphics hardware, ALIASING problems inevitably arise when very fine detail (geometric or texture) is processed. Similarly, when a swinging or rotating element is sampled in the TIME DOMAIN, the video refresh rate forms a limit that can cause TEMPORAL ALIASING such as 'wagon wheels', i.e. wheels that appear to go backwards. See Figure S-1. (See also ADAPTIVE SAMPLING, ALIASING, ANTI-ALIASING, FILTERING, FOURIER WAVEFORM ANALYSIS, NYQUIST LIMIT, OVER-SAMPLING, POINT SAMPLING, SPATIAL ALIASING, STOCHASTIC SAMPLING, TEMPORAL ALIASING, and UNIFORM SAMPLING.)
[Blinn-89a, Glassner-88, Hearn-86, Rogers-85]

saturation
Saturation relates to the PURITY of coloured light in terms of the white light component and the remaining colour component. For example, a fully-saturated colour can only be formed from one or any two of the ADDITIVE PRIMARY COLOURS, because if three colours are employed, the colour will be diluted by the component of white light created by equal amounts of red, green and blue light. (See also ADDITIVE COLOUR MIXING, ADDITIVE PRIMARY COLOURS, CHROMA, DOMINANT WAVELENGTH, HLS, HSV, HUE, PURITY, and VALUE.)
[Burger-89, Foley-90, Hearn-86, Munsell-41, Rogers-85]

scalar
A scalar value is a quantity which has magnitude, but no direction. A scalar variable is a scalar value which varies

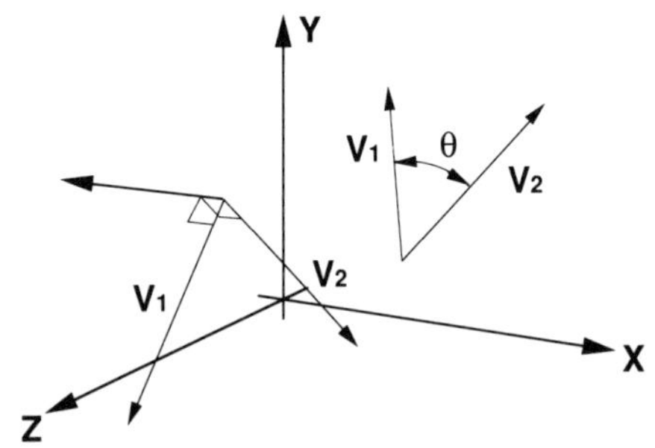

Figure S-2 *Given two vectors V_1 and V_2, the scalar product (or dot product) operation reveals the cosine of the enclosed angle, whilst the vector product (or cross product) creates a third vector orthogonal to the plane containing the original vectors.*

with some other parameters (usually time). (See also VECTOR.)

scalar product

A frequently used operation in computer graphics algorithms is the scalar product, which reveals the cosine of the angle between two vectors. It can be used to identify back faces by investigating the sign of the scalar product of a FACET NORMAL and the EYE VECTOR to that facet. For example, if ***p*** and ***q*** are defined as follows

$$\mathbf{p} = a\mathbf{i} + b\mathbf{j} + c\mathbf{k}$$
$$\mathbf{q} = d\mathbf{i} + e\mathbf{j} + f\mathbf{k}$$

then the scalar product ***p•q*** is

$$\mathbf{p}\bullet\mathbf{q} = ad + be + cf$$

and

$$\mathbf{p}\bullet\mathbf{q} = |\mathbf{p}|\,|\mathbf{q}|\cos(\theta)$$

where θ is the angle between ***p*** and ***q***. This is also known as the DOT PRODUCT. See Figure S-2. (See also VECTOR PRODUCT.)

[Gasson-83, Rogers-89]

scaling matrix

A scaling operation multiplies the dimensions of an object along each axis and can be represented as a scaling matrix. Generally, the scaling operation is relative to the current origin, but by translating an off-centre object back to the origin, scaling and applying a reverse translation, the scaling operation can be relative to any desired point. This entire operation can be CONCATENATED into one homogeneous matrix. (See also AFFINE TRANSFORMATION, HOMOGENEOUS COORDINATES, MATRIX OPERATION, ROTATION MATRIX, and TRANSLATION MATRIX.)

[Burger-89, Foley-90, Gasson-83, Hearn-86, Rogers-89]

scan conversion

Scan conversion is the process of converting the boundary representation of a shape into a pixel format; such techniques are employed for creating circles, ellipses and arcs, and also for converting vector definitions of images into a raster format for electrostatic plotters. (See also DDA, POLYGON RASTERIZATION and SCAN-LINE COHERENCE.)

[Dunlavey-83, Gasson-83, Gharachorloo-89, Hearn-86, Hersch-87, Kaufman-87, Pineda-88, Rogers-89, Wu-89]

scan-line

A scan-line is a horizontal line of pixels forming one RASTER.

scan-line algorithm

A scan-line algorithm proceeds on a RASTER scan-line by scan-line in a certain order. (See also A-BUFFER, DISTRIBUTED RENDERING, PARALLEL RENDERING, RADIOSITY, RAY TRACING, and RENDERER.)

[Atherton-83, Blinn-78b, Bouknight-69, Clark-79, Hamlin-77, Hearn-86, Lane-79, Lane-80, Max-90a, Rogers-85, Watkins-70, Whitted-78, Wylie-67]

scan-line coherence
Scan-line coherence describes a characteristic of raster scan graphics where adjacent pixels are likely to be similar, which can be exploited by algorithms. (See also AREA COHERENCE, COHERENCE, DEPTH COHERENCE, and EDGE COHERENCE.)
[Burger-89, Foley-90, Hearn-86, Rogers-85]

scanner
A scanner is an input device capable of scanning a monochrome or coloured piece of artwork and converting it into a pixel format for storage within a computer system. (See also DIGITIZER.)

scientific visualization
Scientific visualization is concerned with the use of computer graphics to visualize multi-dimensional data associated with scientific projects as an aid to its understanding and interpretation. Typical examples include the visualization of electric forces within electron clouds; chemical and molecular reactions, liquid flow, aerodynamics, cloud formation, weather, and chaotic reactions.
[Papathomas-88, Robertson-85, Sabella-88, Upson-86, Upson-89]

screen coordinates
Screen coordinates is an addressing scheme for referencing pixels on a screen. These coordinates are used when converting eye coordinates into a screen image. (See also DEVICE COORDINATE SYSTEM, EYE COORDINATE SYSTEM, NORMALIZED DEVICE COORDINATES, PHYSICAL DEVICE COORDINATES, and WORLD COORDINATE SPACE.)
[Burger-89, Foley-90, Gasson-83, Hearn-86]

scroll
Scroll is a graphical operation in which an image (often text) is moved (scrolled) up or down on a screen.

sculptured surfaces
Complex surface forms constructed from patches and blends are referred to as sculptured surfaces.
[Farin-88, Woodwark-86]

SECAM
SECAM is an acronym for Système Electronique Couleur Avec Mémoire (a system for electronic colour with memory) and is a colour video encoding system used in France, the USSR and some other eastern countries. It, like PAL, displays 625 lines at 50 Hz. (See also NTSC, PAL, and VIDEO SIGNAL.)
[Hunt-75]

selective erase
The past technology of STORAGE TUBES could not handle selective erasure, where a portion of an image is modified without redrawing the entire image. With the advent of RASTER COMPUTER GRAPHICS, where images are stored to individual pixels, selective erasure is now a vital feature of menu-driven systems. (See also CATHODE RAY TUBE, FRAME STORE, and STORAGE TUBE.)

self affinity
In the world of fractals, self affinity is a property applied to certain FRACTALS, which are not self-similar. It refers to the independent re-scaling of more than one parameter that must be applied to certain fractal-like shapes to keep them statistically invariant when the spatial scale is varied. FRACTALS based upon FRACTIONAL BROWNIAN MOTION requires such scaling. Many structures described by IFSs are also self-affine in that they are defined usually in terms of AFFINE mappings. (See also AFFINE, FRACTAL, FRACTAL GEOMETRY, FRACTIONAL BROWNIAN MOTION, ITERATED FUNCTION SYSTEMS, and SELF-SIMILARITY.)
[Peitgen-88]

self-similarity
Self-similarity is a property normally associated with FRACTALS which exhibit consistent features under various levels of spatial scale. Actually, 'similar' means invariant under a 'similitude', where the latter term is a mapping which scales all distances by some fixed amount, e.g. rotation, global scaling and reflection. This characteristic has been exploited to model apparently complex forms recursively, e.g. ferns, grasses and other similar plant

forms. (See also COLLAGE THEOREM, FRACTAL, FRACTAL DIMENSION, FRACTIONAL BROWNIAN MOTION, and ITERATED FUNCTION SYSTEMS.)
[Mandelbrot-77, Mandelbrot-82, Oppenheimer-86, Peitgen-88]

series
(1) **Animation:** A series is an ordered sequence of images creating an IMAGE SEQUENCE.
(2) **Mathematics**: A series is an infinite sequence of terms which may or may not converge towards some value. They can be used, for example, to evaluate trigonometric functions in computer programs.

set-theoretic modelling
See CONSTRUCTIVE SOLID GEOMETRY.

shading
Shading refers to the rendering stage of synthetic image generation where a RENDERER computes the final pixel intensities transferred to a frame store. To achieve this it requires access to surface geometry, surface attributes, the associated REFLECTANCE MODEL and an ILLUMINATION MODEL. (See also COOK–TORRANCE SHADING, COSINE SHADING, CROSS-SECTION RENDERING, GOURAUD SHADING, ILLUMINATION MODEL, PHONG SHADING, RADIOSITY, RAY TRACING, REFLECTANCE MODEL, RENDERER, RENDERMAN, REYES, TORRANCE–SPARROW SHADING MODEL, and VOLUMETRIC RENDERING.)
[Burger-89, Foley-90, Hearn-86, Lorig-86, Rogers-85]

shading model
A shading model is synonymous with ILLUMINATION MODEL and defines the rules used to compute illumination levels in rendering.
[Burger-89, Foley-90, Hearn-86, Kajiya-86, Rogers-85]

shadow-mask colour CRT
A shadow-mask colour CRT incorporates a thin plate positioned immediately behind the screen; this contains a regular pattern of holes allowing the impinging red, green and blue electron beams to be directed upon the correct triad of colour phosphors. (See also BEAM PENETRATION CRT, CALLIGRAPHIC DISPLAY, CATHODE RAY TUBE, MULTISCANNING MONITOR, and REFRESH CRT.)
[Hearn-86]

shadow ray
In RAY TRACING, a shadow ray or *feeler ray* is formed at a RAY INTERSECTION POINT to see whether it is directly illuminated by a light source. The shadow ray is a ray cast to the active light sources – and if this intersects with an OPAQUE surface, then the associated light source cannot be illuminating the original RAY INTERSECTION POINT. The LIGHT BUFFER can also be used to speed up these calculations. See Figure R-1. (See also LIGHT BUFFER, RAY INTERSECTION POINT, RAY TRACING, and SHADOW VOLUME.)
[Glassner-88]

shadows
Even though shadows occur naturally, they are not a natural result of the rendering process and require special attention and considerable computation. However, the algorithms used for their creation include AREA SUBDIVISION ALGORITHMS, RADIOSITY, RAY TRACING, SHADOW VOLUMES, Z-BUFFER and the ZZ-BUFFER.
[Atherton-78a, Atherton-78b, Brotman-84, Chin-89, Crow-77, Glassner-89, Hearn-86, Hourcade-85, Max-86, Rogers-85, Williams-78]

shadow volume
A shadow volume is a volume of space associated with a light source and an object. It is constructed by developing projection lines from a light source to the SILHOUETTE EDGES of the object to define a projected volume behind the object in shadow. Any polygon totally or partially within this shadow volume will be shadowed.
[Bergeron-86, Chin-89, Crow-77, Nishita-87]

shear
The term shear is a special case of the AFFINE mapping which may be visualized by imagining an object to be composed of an infinity of layers parallel to some fixed

surface, and by then sliding each layer a distance proportional to its distance from the fixed surface. It can be represented as a MATRIX OPERATION and is a useful feature in modelling and animation. (See also AFFINE, MATRIX OPERATION and SHEAR MATRIX.)
[Gasson-83, Hearn-86, Rogers-89]

shear matrix
A shear or skew matrix is an AFFINE TRANSFORMATION which distorts a shape but preserves parallel lines. (See also ROTATION MATRIX, SCALING MATRIX, and TRANSLATION MATRIX.)
[Gasson-83, Hearn-86, Rogers-89]

silhouette edge
The boundary shape of an object, or its silhouette edge, is a projected view of a 3-D object. Its identification plays an important part in some HIDDEN-LINE REMOVAL algorithms.
[Rogers-85]

SIMD
SIMD is an acronym for Single-Instruction Multiple-Data. It is associated with a computer processor architecture where a large number of processors execute synchronously the same instruction stream upon their seperate and independent sets of data. Consequently SIMD has applications in areas where large data bases have to be examined sequentially, for example in DNA matching and IMAGE PROCESSING. (See also MIMD.)
[Dew-89]

sinc filter
A sinc filter is the perfect filter shape for removing unwanted high-frequency detail and is based upon the sinc function

$$\text{sinc}(x) = \frac{\sin(\pi x)}{\pi x}$$

Unfortunately, it is infinitely wide and cannot be implemented in this theoretical form; however, by using the process of 'windowing', a central portion can be effectively isolated, which begins to approximate to an ideal square wave FOURIER TRANSFORM. See Figure S-3. (See also BARTLETT FILTER, BASIS FUNCTION, BOX FILTER, CONVOLUTION FILTER, FILTER, FILTERING, FOURIER TRANSFORM, GAUSSIAN FILTER, and TENT FILTER.)
[Blinn-89a]

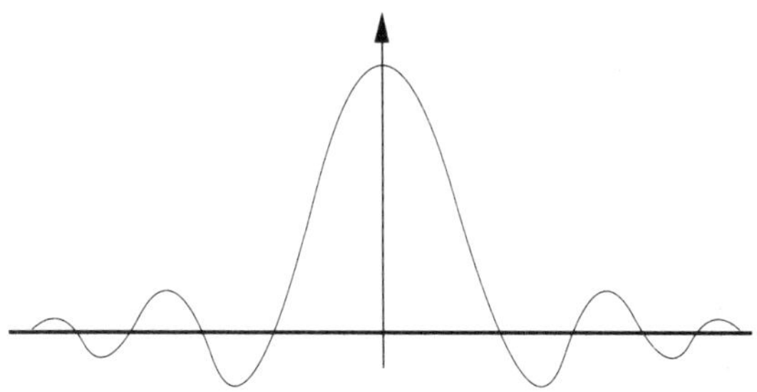

Figure S-3 *The above waveform is an approximation of the sinc function which is symmetric about the vertical axis and extends to infinity. It is the ideal filter for filtering raster images to ensure that frequencies above the Nyquist limit are removed without attenuating any low-frequency components.*

sinc function
See SINC FILTER.

sine
In the context of right-angled triangles, the sine of an angle is the ratio of the opposite edge over the hypotenuse. (See also COSINE and TANGENT.)

sine function
The sine function generates a sinusoidal waveform and can be derived from a knowledge of the COSINE using

$$\sin^2(\theta) + \cos^2(\theta) = 1$$

singular matrix
A singular matrix has a zero DETERMINANT. (See also DETERMINANT, INVERSE MATRIX and MATRIX.)

sliders
In interactive computer graphics systems, sliders refer to graphical slider controls displayed on a screen to control a variable parameter. (See also HUMAN–COMPUTER INTERACTION, ICON, MENU, and USER INTERFACE.)
[Chen-88]

slow in/slow out
In traditional animation slow in/slow out relates to the spacing of drawings in an animated sequence, and ultimately influences the degree of attack or hesitation incorporated into a movement. The terms are also synonymous with CUSHIONING and EASING. (See also BLENDING FUNCTIONS, CUSHIONING, and EASING.)
[Lasseter-87, White-86]

Smalltalk
Smalltalk is an OBJECT-ORIENTED PROGRAMMING language developed at the Xerox PARC and is available in various implementations for Macs, IBM compatibles and the Acorn Archimedes. (See also C++ and OBJECT-ORIENTED PROGRAMMING.)

SMPTE
SMPTE is an acronym for the Society of Motion Picture and Television Engineers, which is a United States organization coordinating recommendations for standards for their industry.

SMPTE time code
SMPTE time code is a signal recorded onto videotape for every FRAME showing the elapsed time in hours, minutes, seconds together with the frame count. (See also DROP-FRAME TIME CODE, 4-FIELD SEQUENCE, 8-FIELD SEQUENCE, TIME CODE, and VIDEO SIGNAL.)

snapping
Many interactive drawing systems include a snapping feature where the user can determine the resolution at the point where data are collected. The input graphics screen is effectively covered by a regular matrix of points fixed to some desired spacing, and as points are input, say with a stylus or mouse, their position will be aligned to the nearest matrix position, which is called snapping and also called ‘gravity’.
[Bier-86a]

Snell’s law
Snell’s law states that when light crosses the boundary of two transmissive media

$$n_i \sin(\theta_i) = n_t \sin(\theta_t)$$

where n_i and n_t are the refractive indices for the incident and transmissive media respectively, and θ_i and θ_t are the angles of incidence and refraction respectively at the point of intersection. This model is easily implemented into a RAY TRACING environment. (See also ANGLE OF INCIDENCE, ANGLE OF REFRACTION, FRESNEL EFFECT, RAY TRACING, REFRACTION OF LIGHT, and REFRACTIVE INDEX.)
[Glassner-89, Jenkins-76]

soft objects
Soft objects describe a class of spongy structures that are modelled from surfaces of constant value from a scalar field. These fields are initially built from a series of points which possess an energy or field value. By computing equipotential surfaces, a wide range of ‘blobs’ can be formed and rendered. (See also FRACTALS.)
[Wyvill-86, Wyvill-87]

solid angle
Where conventional angles measure a linear angular rotation in space, a solid angle measures a 3-D subtended angle formed by a surface to a point in units of STERADIANS. By definition, there are 4π steradians formed by a unit sphere to its centre. Solid angles arise in illumination calculations, especially in RADIOSITY. (See also STERADIAN.)
[Gasson-83]

solid modelling
Solid modelling are modelling schemes for describing 3-D objects containing sufficient geometric detail that a numerically controlled machine can be used for their creation. Also, physical properties such as weight, volume, surface area, centre of gravity etc. may be computed. These schemes include BOUNDARY REPRESENTATION and SET-THEORETIC MODELLING. (See also BOUNDARY REPRESENTATION and CONSTRUCTIVE SOLID GEOMETRY.)
[Hearn-86]

solid noise
Procedural texture employs solid noise functions that generate random values at points in space. (See also HYPERTEXTURE, PROCEDURAL TEXTURE, SOLID TEXTURE, and STOCHASTIC DEFORMATION.)
[Lewis-89]

solid texture
Solid texture is generated by procedures capable of assigning texture modulations to a volume of space. When such a volume is associated with a 3-D object, the texture can be effectively mapped onto any exposed surface, giving the impression that the object is constructed from a textured material. (See also HYPERTEXTURE, SOLID NOISE, and TEXTURE MAPPING.).
[Lewis-89, Peachey-85, Perlin-85, Wyvill-87]

space filling curves
In the late nineteenth century Peano and Hilbert formalized the description of space filling curves, and unknowingly became entwined in the development of FRACTALS. Their curves are theoretically capable of covering completely an area with an infinite length but finite area. Practically, they have been used in IMAGE COMPRESSION, rendering and even proposed as a mechanism for broadcasting variable resolution images. See Figure P-2. (See also FRACTALS and ITERATED FUNCTION SYSTEMS.)
[Hilbert-91, Peano-90, Sierpinski-12]

spacers
In animation spacers are blank frames used to set the location of other frames in COMPOSITING.

span
When a polygon is being processed by a SCAN-LINE ALGORITHM it is divided into spans which represent the polygon's EXTENT for the relevant rasters; the spans for one RASTER are then sorted horizontally before being rendered.
[Rogers-85]

spatial aliasing
Spatial aliasing occurs in computer graphics when a geometric description of a shape is sampled at a spatial resolution incompatible with its highest detail. This SAMPLING rate is governed by the pixel resolution of the FRAME STORE, and causes the familiar jagged edges on polygonal shapes. It can also occur whenever an image, such as a TEXTURE MAP, is sampled incorrectly, giving rise to unwanted flickering artifacts. Although increasing the sampling rate reduces the ALIASING artifacts, FILTERING out the unwanted information in the first place and perhaps introducing NOISE rather than regular ARTIFACTS is more effective. (See also ADAPTIVE SAMPLING, ALIASING, ANTI-ALIASING, ARTIFACT, FILTERING, NOISE, NYQUIST LIMIT, OVERSAMPLING, PIXEL AVERAGING, POINT SAMPLING, SAMPLING, STOCHASTIC SAMPLING, TEMPORAL ALIASING, and UNIFORM SAMPLING.)
[Blinn-89a, Blinn-89b, Glassner-88, Glassner-89, Hearn-86, Rogers-85]

spatial coherence
See AREA COHERENCE.

spatial domain
In FOURIER WAVEFORM ANALYSIS the spatial domain refers to the real space having a physical spatial dimension, and in ANTI-ALIASING schemes pixel filter shapes such as BOX, TENT or SINC are shapes in the spatial domain, as opposed to their FOURIER TRANSFORMS in the FREQUENCY DOMAIN. (See also FOURIER WAVEFORM ANALYSIS, FREQUENCY DOMAIN, and INVERSE FOURIER TRANSFORM.)
[Blinn-89a, Blinn-89b, Gonzalez-87, Pratt-78]

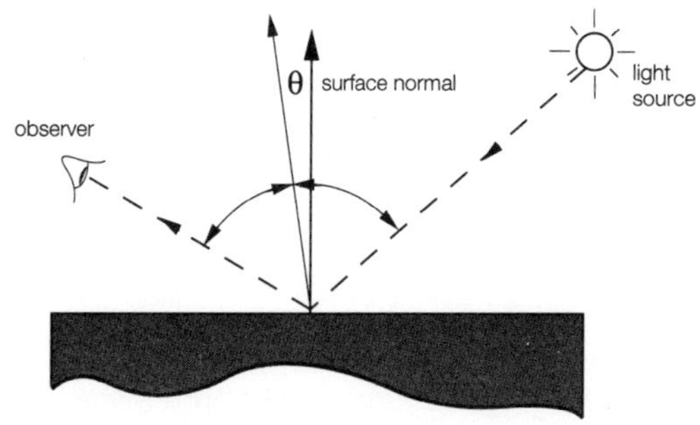

Figure S-4 *In this illustration, if the observer is positioned such that the angle of incidence equals the angle of reflection, a specular reflection is seen. But although the observer is off-axis, the angular deviation from the surface normal can be used to spread the highlight, as in Phong shading.*

spatial interpolation
Spatial interpolation is a FILTERING technique applied to a single digital video frame, used by digital effects systems to increase or decrease the spatial resolution of an image.

spectral colour
A spectral colour is a pure colour dominated by light of one WAVELENGTH. (See also COLOUR and WAVELENGTH.)
[Boynton-79, Gregory-86, Hunt-75]

spectral energy
The spectral energy response curve relates the radiant energy of a light source to WAVELENGTH and reveals how a light source influences the colour of its environment.
[Hunt-75]

spectral synthesis
See FOURIER FILTERING.

specularity
Specularity is synonymous with 'shininess'. (See also GLOSS COEFFICIENT.)

specular reflection
A specular reflection is the reflection of a light source seen by an observer on a reflective surface and is implemented in PHONG SHADING. See Figure S-4. (See also ANGLE OF REFLECTION, COOK–TORRANCE SHADING, FRESNEL EFFECT, GLOSS COEFFICIENT, PHONG SHADING, REFLECTION OF LIGHT, SPECULAR REFLECTION COEFFICIENT, and TORRANCE–SPARROW SHADING MODEL.)
[Burger-89, Foley-90, Glassner-88, Hearn-86, Rogers-85]

specular reflection coefficient
In the specular reflection model, initially proposed by Phong, the specular reflection coefficient is a fractional value used to modulate the intensity of the SPECULAR REFLECTION. In reality, the intensity and colour of specular reflections depends upon the micro-geometry of the illuminated surface, but simple shading models frequently employ a specular reflection coefficient, chosen to create a realistic effect. (See also AMBIENT REFLECTION COEFFICIENT, DIFFUSE REFLECTION COEFFICIENT, PHONG SHADING, and SPECULAR REFLECTION.)
[Burger-89, Foley-90, Glassner-88, Hearn-86, Rogers-85]

specular transmission
Specular transmission relates to the transmission of light through a medium where ray paths obey SNELL'S LAW, i.e. they are transmitted but in a direction related to the incident angle and the refractive indices of the two materials. (See also ANGLE OF INCIDENCE, ANGLE OF REFRACTION, DIFFUSE TRANSMISSION, FRESNEL EFFECT, REFRACTION OF LIGHT, and SNELL'S LAW.)
[Glassner-88, Jenkins-76]

sphere of influence
A sphere of influence implies that some action only operates up to some critical radius, as found in BEHAVIOURAL ANIMATION where an object is only influenced by other objects within a given sphere of influence. (See also BOUNDING SPHERE.)

spline
(1) Historically, a spline is a flexible lath fixed and weighted at set intervals to create a smooth curve and was employed in the ship construction industry.
(2) In the world of computer graphics the physical properties of a spline are simulated using functions that guarantee slope CONTINUITY, and they form the basis of curve and surface modelling. There are many schemes for creating such curves, perhaps the most popular being BETA-SPLINE, B-SPLINE, CATMULL–ROM SPLINE, and the CARDINAL SPLINE. (See also APPROXIMATING SPLINE, BETA SPLINE, B-SPLINE CURVE, CATMULL-ROM SPLINE, INTERPOLATING SPLINE, and NURBS.)
[Bohm-84, Burger-89, Farin-88, Hearn-86, Rogers-89, Woodwark-86]

spot light
A spot light is a light source capable of illuminating a scene within a restricted angular cone. (See also DARK LIGHT, DIRECTIONAL LIGHT SOURCE, DISTRIBUTED LIGHT SOURCE, LIGHT SOURCE, LIGHT SOURCE DIRECTION, and POINT LIGHT SOURCE.)

spot size
In CRT technology, the spot size is the diameter of the focused electron beam, and is relevant to the final perceived resolution of the image. (See also BEAM PENETRATION CRT, CATHODE RAY TUBE, and PHOSPHOR.)
[Hunt-75]

spread angle
The spread angle is the angular spread of a SPOT LIGHT. (See also SPOT LIGHT.)

sprite
A sprite is a group of pixel values or BIT MAP which can be dynamically mapped into a video FRAME STORE to produce animation effects exploited in video games often under hardware control.

standard deviation
The standard deviation of a FREQUENCY DISTRIBUTION is a measure of the distribution's dispersion and is computed by

$$s = \sqrt{\text{VARIANCE}}$$

$$\text{where variance} = \frac{1}{n}\sum_{i=1}^{n}(x_i - \overline{x})^2$$

where n is the number of samples,
$\overline{x}$ is the average,
and x_i is a sample variable.

stencil
See MATTE and ALPHA CHANNEL.

STEP
STEP is an acronym for Standard for the Exchange of Product Model Data proposed by DIN. STEP is attempting to unify data exchange standards at an international level and is addressing areas such as maintenance and analysis rules, as well as the conventional aspects of CAD modelling. (See also CGM and IGES.)

steradian
A steradian is a unit of measure for SOLID ANGLES. (See also SOLID ANGLE.)

stereopsis
Stereopsis is the depth cue created by binocular vision, and provides the human visual system with two different views of the physical world which assist the brain in rapidly constructing an accurate 3-D interpretation. (See also DEPTH PERCEPTION, PARALLAX, and STEREOSCOPIC DISPLAY.)
[Boynton-79, Hearn-86, Rogers-85]

stereoscopic display
With the increasing amount of 3-D work being undertaken with computer graphics, stereoscopic displays are providing a powerful aid to visualizing and manipulating 3-D structures. They create an illusion of 3-D depth by

projecting a pair of images to a viewer with the aid of devices such as vari-focal mirrors, liquid crystal shutters, polarization displays and dual CRTs. For example, with the liquid crystal shutter approach, a monochrome monitor can be driven to display two alternate images that conventionally make up the red and green images in 3-D systems. Over the screen are placed two red and green dichroic polarizers, orthogonally polarized, followed by an LCD cell. When a voltage is applied across the cell, the crystals in the solution are aligned perpendicular to the glass plates of the cell, making it transparent. When the voltage is removed, the crystals relax in a shearing motion that shifts the phase by 90°; by alternating this voltage in time with the REFRESH RATE, the viewer will see alternating red and green images which, with the aid of a pair of passive red and green glasses, are converted into a 3-D image. (See also DEPTH PERCEPTION, PARALLAX, and STEREOPSIS.)
[Hearn-86, Hodges-85, Rogers-89]

stochastic
Stochastic is synonymous with random processes and plays an increasing role in computer graphics algorithms. Such techniques are found in SAMPLING strategies in RAY TRACING and FRACTALS. (See also DETERMINISTIC, ITERATED FUNCTION SYSTEMS, STOCHASTIC DEFORMATION, STOCHASTIC RAY TRACING, and STOCHASTIC SAMPLING.)

stochastic deformation
Stochastic deformation is a modelling technique employing a vector-valued SOLID NOISE function to deform a 3-D model by disturbing its vertices. The SOLID NOISE function generates three STOCHASTIC values forming a vector field, which ultimately can modulate surface geometry. (See also NOISE, SOLID NOISE, STOCHASTIC, and VECTOR.)
[Lewis-89]

stochastic modelling
Stochastic modelling involves the use of random procedures in modelling complex 3-D structures such as sea spray, stochastic branching in tree growth, fractal terrains and clouds. These techniques include POISSON FAULTING, FOURIER FILTERING and MIDPOINT DISPLACEMENT. (See also FOURIER FILTERING, FRACTAL GEOMETRY, MIDPOINT DISPLACEMENT, and POISSON FAULTING.)
[Demko-85, Fournier-82, Fournier-85, Mandelbrot-68, Mandelbrot-75, Mandelbrot-82, Oppenheimer-86, Smith-84, Voss-83, Voss-85]

stochastic ray tracing
Stochastic ray tracing is an ANTI-ALIASING strategy using STOCHASTIC SAMPLING in RAY TRACING. (See also ALIASING, ANTI-ALIASING, NOISE, OVERSAMPLING, POINT SAMPLING, RAY TRACING, SAMPLING, STOCHASTIC, and STOCHASTIC SAMPLING.)
[Glassner-89]

stochastic sampling
When the IMAGE SPACE is uniformly sampled at pixel centres, ALIASING occurs if the scene contains frequency elements above the NYQUIST LIMIT. Stochastic sampling sub-samples the image space at appropriate, non-uniformly spaced locations, and frequencies above the NYQUIST LIMIT do not appear as a recognizable low-frequency alias but as uniform WHITE NOISE of the correct average intensity. (See also ADAPTIVE SAMPLING, ALIASING, ANTI-ALIASING, FILTERING, NOISE, NYQUIST LIMIT, and OVERSAMPLING.)
[Dippe-85, Glassner-89, Pixar-87, Purgathofer-86]

storage tube
Early computer graphics systems depended heavily upon storage tubes, where text and graphics were displayed calligraphically upon a monochrome screen (normally green). The image was formed by using a conventional electron beam to draw an image onto an intermediate storage element behind the phosphor screen; this information was then used to control a secondary electron flow to the display phosphor. Perhaps its greatest weakness was its inability to erase selective areas of the screen. (See also BEAM PENETRATION CRT, CALLIGRAPHIC DISPLAY, CATHODE RAY TUBE, REFRESH CRT, and SELECTIVE ERASE.)

storyboard
A storyboard is a collection of drawings illustrating key images within an animation sequence. Storyboards are a vital means of communication between designer and animator, as they provide a simple mechanism for expressing concepts such as scale, pace, perspective, dynamics, timings, scene changes etc. (See also BAR SHEETS and MODEL SHEETS.)
[White-86]

strobing
Strobing is an effect seen in animated images containing elements which are apparently moving very fast, with the result that the human visual system registers a 'pulsating' or strobing effect which may make the image jump or appear as a double exposure.
[Glassner-88]

stroke display
See CALLIGRAPHIC DISPLAY.

stylus
A stylus is a hand-held pen used in conjunction with a tablet or digitizer; it normally incorporates a positional sensing coil and a switch to initiate an event in the associated computer. Although many systems still require the pen to be connected via a cable to its control unit, cordless styli are being manufactured that operate with an infrared channel. (See also DIGITIZER and GRAPHICS TABLET.)
[Hearn-86]

subroutine
One aid in the design of large computer programs is to construct a suite of subroutines that perform a useful function which, perhaps, is required elsewhere within the system. This design methodology has the advantage of dividing a project between many analysts, who can design, implement, test and document small convenient portions of code. (See also OBJECT-ORIENTED PROGRAMMING.)

subtractive colour mixing
Where additive colour mixing is used to create colour additively from light sources, subtractive colour mixing is the process where printed colours are created by allowing overlayed colour separations of cyan, magenta, yellow and black pigments to subtract colours from any incident light. (See also ADDITIVE COLOUR MIXING and SUBTRACTIVE PRIMARY COLOURS.)
[Foley-90, Hearn-86, Hunt-75]

subtractive primary colours
The subtractive primary colours are cyan, magenta and yellow, and they are referred to as subtractive because in any printing process coloured pigments, when illuminated, absorb certain portions of the spectrum and reflect others, thus subtracting colour from the incident light. See Figure A-1. (See also ADDITIVE PRIMARY COLOURS, CMYK, and SUBTRACTIVE COLOUR MIXING.)
[Foley-90, Hearn-86, Hunt-75]

super VGA
Super VGA is an extension of the VGA graphics board and offers a RESOLUTION of 800 x 600 compared with VGA's limit of 640 x 480. (See also CGA, EGA, HDA, HGC, MCGA, MDA, PVA, and VGA.)

surface normal
A surface normal is a NORMAL VECTOR at a particular point on a surface; this definition anticipates its association with any type of surface from a simple PLANAR surface to a B-SPLINE SURFACE PATCH where the surface normal changes continuously over the patch. Where the surface is planar, the surface normal is synonymous with FACET NORMAL. However, surface normals are not always well-defined, as found in some FRACTAL surfaces. (See also AVERAGE NORMAL, FACET NORMAL, and NORMAL VECTOR.)
[Burger-89, Foley-90, Gasson-83, Hearn-86, Rogers-85, Rogers-89]

surface of revolution
See SWEPT SURFACE.

surface patch
A very powerful technique for constructing complex surfaces is to divide them into simple elements called surface patches; these individually can be numerically modelled using popular techniques such as BÉZIER, B-SPLINE, NURBS and COONS. The reason for this approach is that it is virtually impossible to describe mathematically the free form surfaces required by CAD systems. Consequently, the DIVIDE AND CONQUER strategy suggested that if a small element of the surface could be described, and that there were methods of ensuring surface CONTINUITY over the patch boundaries, very complex surface descriptions would be possible. See Figure B-4. (See also BÉZIER SURFACE PATCH, B-SPLINE SURFACE PATCH, CARTESIAN PRODUCT PATCH, CONTINUITY, COONS PATCH, FERGUSON PATCH, HERMITE PATCH, NURBS, PARAMETRIC SURFACE PATCH, and PATCHED SURFACE.)
[Bohm-84, Farin-88, Hearn-86, Rogers-89, Woodwark-86]

surface shadowing
Surface shadowing concerns the calculation of shadows created by the oblique illumination of HEIGHT FIELDS. (See also HEIGHT FIELD and SHADOW VOLUME.)
[Robertson-89]

surrounding polygon
In DIVIDE AND CONQUER display algorithms, a surrounding polygon encloses a reference window, and represents one of the possible conditions in the space division process. (See also CONTAINED POLYGON, DISJOINT POLYGON, INTERSECTING POLYGON, and WARNOCK ALGORITHM.)
[Rogers-85, Warnock-68]

swept surface
A swept surface is a 3-D surface formed by rotating a 2-D contour about an axis. Each point on the contour generates a polygon corner on the swept surface, and the final number of polygons is determined by the number of steps through which the contour is rotated. Swept surfaces are a powerful, yet simple, modelling scheme for creating symmetric objects such as bottles, glasses, columns, chess pieces, spheres etc. (See also BOUNDARY REPRESENTATION and EXTRUDING.)
[Hearn-86, Piegl-87a]

sync
Sync refers to the electronic synchronizing pulses used in video systems to control the frame generation rates. (See also COMPOSITE, NTSC, PAL, SECAM, and VIDEO SIGNAL.)

sync generator
A sync generator is an electronic device providing a source of SYNC signals to synchronize a collection of video components. (See also SYNC and VIDEO SIGNAL.)

synchronous
The term synchronous implies that a process is in step with some other process. For example, in a SIMD computer architecture, the individual processors execute the same instruction synchronously upon different data sets. (See also SIMD.)
[DEW-89]

t

tablet
A tablet is a small active surface used as a DIGITIZER in conjunction with a STYLUS, but size restricts its application to the input of small drawings. (See also DIGITIZER.)
[Hearn-86]

tangent
In the context of right-angled triangles, the tangent of an angle is the ratio of the vertical height over the horizontal base. It is also represented by

$$\tan(\theta) = \frac{\sin(\theta)}{\cos(\theta)}$$

teapot
In 1975 Martin Newell produced a 3-D teapot constructed from BÉZIER SURFACE PATCHES and it has now acquired a rather special status within the computer graphics community as a modelling icon.
[Crow-87]

temporal aliasing
Temporal aliasing occurs when the sampling rate in the time domain is insufficient to detect spatial changes caused by moving objects. The most obvious example of temporal aliasing is found in films and television programmes depicting rotating wheels, for at certain speeds the spokes appear to be rotating contrary to the direction of motion. This is caused when the sampling rate of the camera is insufficient to register the rapid motion of the wheel's structure. In computer graphics, temporal aliasing arises in similar circumstances and can be used to effect in animation where it is called MOTION BLUR. (See also MOTION BLUR and SPATIAL ALIASING.)
[Burger-89, Glassner-89, Korein-83]

temporal interpolation
Temporal interpolation is used as a motion smoothing technique where points in space on successive time frames are interpolated.

tensor
In computer graphics, a tensor is a mathematical object with well-defined properties for handling transformations that are independent of a coordinate system. Tensors are generally associated with surface modelling where they are found in the form of a MATRIX of elements the elements of which are not SCALAR quantities but VECTORS.

tent filter
A tent filter is a simple filter used in ANTI-ALIASING with a WEIGHTING FUNCTION the shape of an isosceles triangular tent centred over a pixel but overlapping neighbouring pixels by one half of a pixel. Because of this wide base, pixels at the edge of the image must still be bordered by one further pixel for the filtering to be complete. Although it is slightly more effective than the BOX FILTER, it still suffers from similar drawbacks.
[Blinn-89a]

terrain modelling
Terrain modelling is concerned with the creation of 3-D surface descriptions of geographical terrain. This can be accomplished through the use of stereoscopic satellite images, DIGITAL ELEVATION MODELS (DEMs), aerial/satellite images, shape from shading strategies and FRACTAL techniques. The French SPOT satellite provides an excellent method of data capture as it is positioned in a near polar orbit at an altitude of 823 km. Consequently it is able to cover the entire earth's surface once every 26 days. Its sun-synchronous orbit means that it crosses the equator at 1030 GMT every day; thus a pair of images can be compared with a time difference of 26 days. Its resolution is 6000 x 6000 covering an area of 60 km x 60 km, with a single pixel covering 100 square metres.
[Dungan-79, Kaneda-89, Marshall-80, Miller-86]

tessellation
A tessellation is a spatial organization of regular shapes or objects.
[Critchlow-69, Gasson-83]

tetrahedron
A tetrahedron is a PLATONIC OBJECT constructed from four EQUILATERAL TRIANGLES. (See also CUBE, DODECAHEDRON, ICOSAHEDRON, OCTAHEDRON, and PLATONIC OBJECTS.)
[Critchlow-69, Gasson-83]

texel
In two dimensions, a texel is the smallest addressable element of a TEXTURE MAP; but in three dimensions it may be the smallest addressable element of a 3-D texture map in which both parameters of a ILLUMINATION MODEL and surface geometry such as normal and tangent vector values are stored.
[Blinn-82, Kajiya-84, Kajiya-89]

text mode
In raster graphics, the text mode restricts characters to pixel blocks, say 8 by 8 pixels. These areas can then reference permanent character definitions held in ROM, or disk-loaded character maps stored in RAM.
[Burger-89, Hearn-86]

texture map
A texture map is a 2-D pattern of pixel intensities, derived synthetically procedurally or input from an external image, for use as a surface decoration using a TEXTURE MAPPING algorithm. (See also BUMP MAP, HYPERTEXTURE, MAPPING, MIP MAPS, PROCEDURAL TEXTURE, SOLID NOISE, SOLID TEXTURE, and TEXTURE MAPPING.)
[Blinn-76]

texture mapping
Texture mapping is the process of substituting detail stored within a reference source of texture (map) onto a surface having any arbitrary orientation. The mapping procedure can incorporate an ILLUMINATION MODEL and the effects of perspective, and can involve ANTI-ALIASING techniques to filter possible high-frequency detail. (See also BUMP MAPPING, DISPLACEMENT MAPPING, ENVIRONMENT MAPPING, and OPACITY MAPPING.)
[Bier-86b, Blinn-76, Burger-89, Carey-85, Crow-84, Fiume-87, Glassner-86, Oka-87, Samek-86, Smith-87]

thermal printer
A thermal printer is a multi-pass printing machine, somewhat similar to an electrostatic printer, and in the printing process paper is heated with a pattern of pixel dots and pressed against sheets of coloured wax which melts and sticks to the paper.

three-space
The term three-space is synonymous with 3-D space. (See also TWO-SPACE.)

threshold rendering
In medical imaging, threshold rendering is used to realize synthetic images from VOXEL data sets derived from computer-aided tomography (CAT) scanners. This data includes an associated density attribute which can be selected to create a threshold at which the RENDERER considers the VOXEL to be visible. By varying this level, it is possible to render interior views or isolate a particular portion of the volume. (See also CROSS-SECTION RENDERING, G-OCTREE, and VOLUMETRIC RENDERING.)
[Sabella-88]

TIFF
TIFF is an acronym for Tag Image File Format, which is a common format developed by Aldous and Microsoft for scanner vendors and DESK-TOP PUBLISHING software.

time code
Video tapes can be formatted with a time code identifying the elapsed hours, minutes, seconds and frames. (See also SMPTE TIME CODE.)

tint-build
A tint-build is a colour 'built' by combining percentages of two or more CMYK colours.

Torrance–Sparrow shading model
Although the PHONG SHADING model is used to reveal specular highlights on reflective surfaces, it is not very effective at handling metallic surfaces which, although they can be highly reflective, possess surface properties that require special attention. The Torrance–Sparrow shading model incorporates the optical behaviour of rough surfaces by assuming that they are covered by V shaped microfacets having a GAUSSIAN DISTRIBUTION of depth and orientation. The facets can be self-shadowing and cause light dispersion depending on the incident wavelength. The model is sensitive to the material properties of the illuminated object, its roughness factor, its orientation and the wavelength of the incident light. (See also COOK–TORRANCE SHADING, COSINE SHADING, GLOBAL ILLUMINATION MODEL, GOURAUD SHADING, PHONG SHADING, RADIOSITY, RAY TRACING, RENDERING EQUATION, REYES, and SHADING MODEL.)
[Blinn-77, Burger-89, Cook-82a, Cook-82b, Foley-90, Rogers-85, Torrance-67]

total internal reflection
Total internal reflection is a phenomenon associated with optical boundaries between two media having different refractive indices. If, for example, a light ray is travelling through glass towards a boundary into air, when the angle of incidence exceeds a CRITICAL ANGLE it will be reflected back into the glass. For an ANGLE OF INCIDENCE less than this critical angle, the light ray escapes into the air. RAY TRACING can simulate this effect. (See also CRITICAL ANGLE, REFRACTIVE INDEX, and SPECULAR TRANSMISSION.)
[Glassner-89, Jenkins-76]

touch screens
Some display devices incorporate touch screens whereby a user may touch a physical zone of the active surface and the position is detected. Such screens play an important role in HUMAN–COMPUTER INTERACTION. (See also HUMAN–COMPUTER INTERACTION.)
[Hearn-86]

touch tablet
A touch tablet is a touch-sensitive surface providing absolute CURSOR control and MOUSE emulation. (See also HUMAN–COMPUTER INTERACTION and TOUCH SCREEN.)
[Buxton-85, Hearn-86]

trackball
A trackball is an interactive device consisting of an exposed (yet constrained) free rolling ball which can be brushed by the user to control the screen CURSOR or any other system parameter adjusted at the workstation interface. (See also CURSOR-CONTROL KEYS, JOYSTICK, LIGHT PEN, MOUSE, STYLUS, TOUCH SCREENS, and TOUCH TABLET.)
[Hearn-86]

transformation
In computer graphics, as in mathematics, the idea of a transformation is used to perform some mathematical operation upon one or more CARTESIAN COORDINATES. In this context, a transformation is closely linked with a MATRIX which succinctly describes transformations such as translation, scaling and rotation. (See also AFFINE TRANSFORMATION, HOMOGENEOUS COORDINATES, LINEAR TRANSFORMATION, MATRIX OPERATION, NON-LINEAR TRANSFORMATION, NON-RIGID TRANSFORMATION, and RIGID TRANSFORMATION.)
[Burger-89, Gasson-83, Hearn-86, Rogers-89, Stevenson-74]

translation matrix
A translation displaces a shape or object by specified distances, whilst preserving all other geometric properties and relationships. It can be implemented in a MATRIX form using HOMOGENEOUS COORDINATES. (See also HOMOGENEOUS TRANSFORMATION, ROTATION, SCALING, and SHEAR.)
[Burger-89, Gasson-83, Hearn-86, Rogers-89]

translucency
Translucency describes a property associated with materials which, whilst transmitting light, destroy any coherence associated with the incident light. This prop-

erty is found in certain plastics and glass, where surface features and the internal structure causes the transmitted light to be coloured and randomly scattered. (See also OPACITY, TRANSLUCENT SURFACE, and TRANSPARENCY.)
[Burger-89, Glassner-89, Rogers-85]

translucent surface
A translucent surface transmits, refracts and reflects light without preserving any incident coherence. Frosted glass and some plastics exhibit such diffuse transmission caused by surface irregularities and internal composition. (See also OPAQUE SURFACE and TRANSPARENT SURFACE.)
[Glassner-90, Rogers-85]

transparency
Transparency is an attribute assigned to objects to mimic the transmissive qualities of substances such as glass. The degree of transparency is controlled by a transparency coefficient associated with an object. Although it can be simulated very easily in RAY TRACING, the A-BUFFER and the ZZ-BUFFER, it is unfortunate that it cannot be handled by the ubiquitous Z-BUFFER. (See also OPACITY and TRANSLUCENCY.)
[Burger-89, Foley-90, Glassner-89, Hearn-86, Kay-79a, Kay-79b, Mammen-89, Rogers-85]

transparency coefficient
A transparency coefficient is a fractional value associated to an object controlling the amount of incident light transmitted by the surface.
[Burger-89, Foley-90, Glassner-89, Hearn-86, Rogers-85]

transparent surface
A transparent surface is a surface that will transmit any incident light, as determined by a TRANSPARENCY COEFFICIENT. (See also OPAQUE SURFACE and TRANSLUCENT SURFACE.)
[Burger-89, Foley-90, Hearn-86, Glassner-89, Rogers-85]

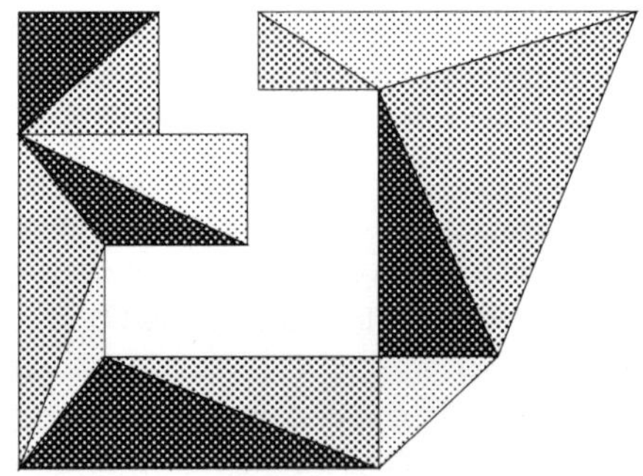

Figure T-1 *Any 2-D shape can be transformed into a mesh of triangles as shown above, although there can be many solutions to the problem. Similarly, a parametric surface patch can also be triangulated so that it may be rendered using polygonal shading techniques.*

transpose matrix
In MATRIX notation a transpose matrix is formed by reflecting every element about a line joining the top-left element with the bottom-right element. For example, given the MATRIX A

$$\text{where } A = \begin{bmatrix} a & b & c \\ d & e & f \\ g & h & i \end{bmatrix}$$

$$\text{then } A^T = \begin{bmatrix} a & d & g \\ b & e & h \\ c & f & i \end{bmatrix}$$

where A^T is the transpose of A. It is used as part of the INVERSE MATRIX operation and also to simplify MATRIX nomenclature. (See also HOMOGENEOUS COORDINATES, INVERSE MATRIX, MATRIX, and ORTHOGONAL MATRIX.)
[Gasson-83, Stevenson-74]

Transputer
Developed by Inmos, the Transputer was the first computer fabricated upon a single chip. Its communication

links allow it to be configured into multi-processor MIMD networks, and there are many commercial products incorporating one or more Transputers. (See also MIMD.)
[Dew-89]

triangle
A triangle is a three-sided POLYGON – and apart from it being the simplest form of POLYGON, its most useful attribute is that it is always PLANAR. (See also EQUILATERAL TRIANGLE and ISOSCELES TRIANGLE.)

triangle processor
A triangle processor is a VLSI device dedicated to the rasterizing of 3-D triangles. It can also compute the Z-DEPTH for every pixel so that it can operate with a Z-BUFFER. (See also GEOMETRY ENGINE and PIXEL-PLANES.)
[Deering-88]

triangular patch
Whilst a familiar patch definition is square or rectangular, it is possible to form complex surfaces from triangular patches where each triangle defines, for example, a BÉZIER SURFACE PATCH. (See also BÉZIER SURFACE PATCH, BICUBIC PATCH, BIPARAMETRIC PATCH, B-SPLINE SURFACE PATCH, CARTESIAN PRODUCT PATCH, COONS PATCH, FERGUSON PATCH, HERMITE PATCH, NURBS, PARAMETRIC SURFACE PATCH, QUADRATIC SURFACE PATCH, and SURFACE PATCH.)
[Bohm-84, Farin-88, Sablonniere-85]

triangulation
Triangles are essential to model building as they are the simplest planar shape, and planarity is extremely important in the context of shading. Consequently, a method of rendering SURFACE PATCHES is to employ triangulation to degenerate the surface into a mesh of triangles, which can be rendered individually. See Figure T-1.
[Burger-89, Gasson-83, Herzen-87, Wordenweber-83]

Trichromatic colour system
The Trichromatic colour system is a *three-colour* approach for creating colours from the primary colours, using either the additive or subtractive systems. (See also ADDITIVE COLOUR MIXING, SUBTRACTIVE COLOUR MIXING, and TRI-STIMULOUS THEORY.)
[Gregory-86, Hunt-75]

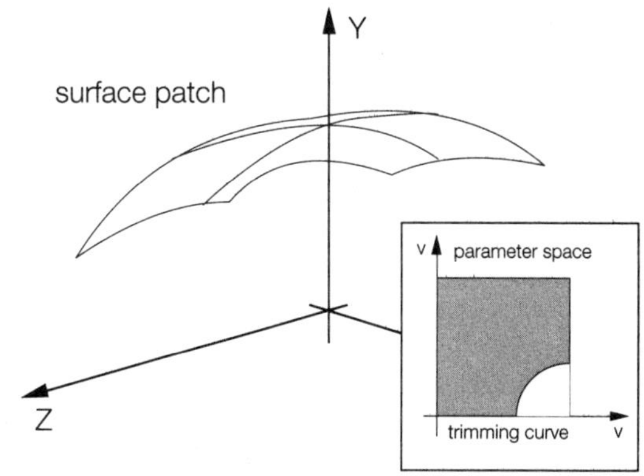

Figure T-2 *By incorporating a trimming curve as shown in the inset drawing, the parametric surface patch can be assigned a 3-D form that would otherwise be difficult to specify.*

trimmed surface
A trimmed surface describes a SURFACE PATCH which has been cut to some desired shape using TRIMMING CURVES. See Figure T-2. (See also PARAMETRIC SURFACE PATCH, SURFACE PATCH, and TRIMMING CURVE.)
[Casale-87, Crocker-87a, Farin-88, Rockwood-89, Shantz-88]

trimming curve
A trimming curve is a curve in PARAMETER SPACE which when mapped onto a PARAMETRIC SURFACE PATCH creates the required surface outline. See Figure T-2. (See also PARAMETER SPACE, PARAMETRIC PATCH, SURFACE PATCH, and TRIMMED SURFACE.)
[Casale-87, Crocker-87a, Farin-88, Rockwood-89, Shantz-88]

trimming loop

A trimming loop is a sequence of trimming curves connected in head to tail fashion to form a closed loop. Trimming curves are not permitted to intersect, as they would create spatial anomalies. (See also PARAMETRIC PATCH, SURFACE PATCH, TRIMMED SURFACE, and TRIMMING CURVE.)
[Casale-87, Crocker-87a, Farin-88, Rockwood-89, Shantz-88]

tri-stimulus theory

The tri-stimulus theory is a widely held and experimentally sound theory based upon the existence of three types of colour receptors in the retina, called cones, which are sensitive to three portions of the visible spectrum, dominated by the hues red, green and blue. This theory is extended to the operation of colour television and colour computer graphics, where individual colour components for red, green and blue are maintained in separate memory planes forming a FRAME STORE. (See also ADDITIVE COLOUR MIXING, ADDITIVE PRIMARY COLOURS, CIE PRIMARIES, COLOUR, PRIMARY COLOURS, and TRICHROMATIC COLOUR SYSTEM.)
[Boynton-79, Gregory-86, Hearn-86, Hunt-75, Rogers-85]

truncation

Truncation refers to the removal of low-order bits on digital video systems, leading to possible unwanted visual artifacts.

TTL

TTL is an acronym for Transistor–Transistor Logic and refers to integrated circuits capable of short distance connections, perhaps between neighbouring racks. (See also ECL.)

turtle graphics

A turtle is a small plotting device which can be controlled in REAL-TIME by a microcomputer, and its images are plotted as line drawings upon sheets of paper laid upon the floor.

twisted facet

Generally, polygons are assumed to be PLANAR, but unfortunately this is not always the case. Occasions arise when twisted facets – whose edges do not all lie in the same plane – can give rise to shading artifacts when the facet or a light source moves. A compromise to avoid such problems is to triangulate the surface, or assign a global facet normal.
[Rogers-85, Rogers-89]

twist vectors

Twist vectors are associated with the definition of a Hermite SURFACE PATCH where four twist vectors are used to control the degree of 'twist' applied to the corners. (See also FERGUSON PATCH and HERMITE PATCH.)
[Farin-88, Woodwark-86]

two-space

The term two-space is synonymous with 2-D space. (See also THREE-SPACE.)

undo facility

An undo facility enables an interactive user to 'undo' the last command issued and return to an earlier status. This is an extremely useful feature in a PAINT SYSTEM or a drawing package; however, it is not possible to 'undo' all operations without effort. (See also HUMAN–COMPUTER INTERACTION.)

uniform sampling

When an image is created by sampling the IMAGE SPACE at the centre of each pixel, the sampling is uniform. STOCHASTIC SAMPLING avoids the ALIASING artifacts caused by uniform sampling by selecting several random positions at each pixel, and although aliasing still occurs, it appears as NOISE. SEE FIGURE S-1. (SEE ALSO ADAPTIVE SAMPLING, ALIASING, ANTI-ALIASING, FILTERING, NYQUIST LIMIT, OVERSAMPLING, POINT SAMPLING, and STOCHASTIC SAMPLING.)

[Glassner-89]

unimodal

Unimodal implies that a FREQUENCY DISTRIBUTION has one central maximum near the centre of the distribution, as in a GAUSSIAN DISTRIBUTION. (See also FREQUENCY DISTRIBUTION and GAUSSIAN DISTRIBUTION.)

unit vector

Although VECTORS encode magnitude and direction, computer graphics algorithms tend to concentrate on their directional handling capacities; consequently, the idea of a unit vector where the magnitude is scaled to unity is a useful form. As an example, if vector **v** is a unit vector, then

$$\boldsymbol{v} = a\boldsymbol{i} + b\boldsymbol{j} + c\boldsymbol{k}$$

$$\text{and} \quad |\boldsymbol{v}| = \sqrt{(a^2 + b^2 + c^2)} = 1$$

Unit vectors must be treated with great care, especially in DOT PRODUCT operations where

$$\boldsymbol{v}_1 \bullet \boldsymbol{v}_2 = |\boldsymbol{v}_1||\boldsymbol{v}_2|\cos(\theta)$$

where θ is the enclosed angle. When $\boldsymbol{v}_1$ and $\boldsymbol{v}_2$ are unit vectors, this simplifies to

$$\boldsymbol{v}_1 \bullet \boldsymbol{v}_2 = \cos(\theta)$$

But one must be sure that this unity is always preserved when using the latter expression, as unpredictable results will occur. (See also VECTOR PRODUCT and NORMALIZATION.)

[Burger-89, Gasson-83, Rogers-89]

UNIX

UNIX is an operating system developed at Bell Laboratories in the early seventies by Ken Thompson. In 1983 AT&T released UNIX System V which was accepted as the industry standard.

unpainting

Some PAINT SYSTEMS have an unpainting facility that allows a limited number of recent paint actions to be cancelled: effectively the system responds by 'unpainting' the current image. Naturally, this implies that, whilst the user is painting, the system must be recording user actions in the event of the unpainting facility being activated. (See also UNDO FACILITY.)

update rate

The update rate defines the rate at which a display system is modified with new image detail, as opposed to the REFRESH RATE which governs the frequency at which the stored image is displayed. In REAL-TIME systems the update rate must be maintained to create the illusion of continuity. (See also ANIMATION, FLICKER, FUSION FREQUENCY, and REAL-TIME.)

[Rogers-85]

user interface

The user interface is a communication specification defining how a user interacts with a computer system. In the context of an interactive computer graphics system, this will encompass the graphical concepts being manipulated, the command instructions, methods of interaction such as MENUS and PICK DEVICES, system

response signals and the graphical layout of the display screen for communication purposes. (See also HUMAN–COMPUTER INTERACTION, REAL-TIME, and WIMP ENVIRONMENT.)
[Hearn-86]

uv-coordinates
In mapping operations, uv-coordinates are generally associated with a rectangular SPACE DOMAIN that can be mapped onto some arbitrary surface. This might be in TEXTURE MAPPING where a pixel's footprint is projected onto the TEXTURE MAP to derive the TEXEL addresses expressed as uv-coordinates.
[Hearn-86]

value

The MUNSELL COLOUR SYSTEM value is equivalent to the term LIGHTNESS; this system employs three parameters to define any colour: HUE, CHROMA and value. (See also COLOUR SPACE, COLOUR MODEL, CHROMA, HUE, and MUNSELL COLOUR SYSTEM.)
[Burger-89, Hearn-86, Munsell-41, Rogers-85]

vanishing point

In a PERSPECTIVE PROJECTION certain lines will appear to converge at some distant point called a vanishing point, and a single cube can produce one, two or three vanishing points depending on the orientation of the observer with the cube. See Figure V-1. (See also PERSPECTIVE PROJECTION, PROJECTION, and PROJECTION PLANE.)
[Burger-89, Gasson-83, Hearn-86, Rogers-89]

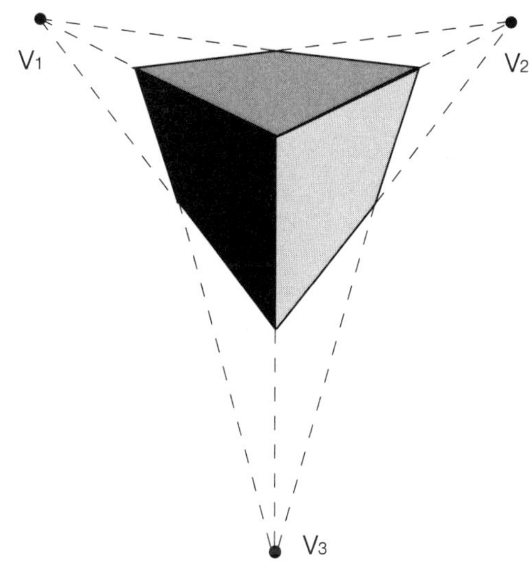

Figure V-1 *In this 3-point perspective drawing the three vanishing points V_1, V_2 and V_3 identify three points at infinity where families of parallel lines appear to converge. This is an automatic feature of the perspective projection.*

variance

Variance, like STANDARD DEVIATION, is a feature of a frequency distribution and is defined as follows

$$\frac{1}{n}\sum_{i=1}^{n}(x_i - \overline{x})^2$$

where n is the number of samples, $\overline{x}$ is the average and x_i is a sample variable. Variance is the square of the STANDARD DEVIATION of a sample or set of data. (See also AVERAGE, FREQUENCY DISTRIBUTION, GAUSSIAN DISTRIBUTION, MEAN DEVIATION, POISSON DISTRIBUTION, and STANDARD DEVIATION.)

V-buffer

In VOLUMETRIC RENDERING the V-buffer is used for resolving visibility problems and functions by partitioning the OBJECT SPACE containing the data into cells; these are then processed by starting with those cells intersecting a plane between the observer and the data, and the plane is moved progressively into the data set. During the processing, a SCAN-LINE analysis is made of the data using opacity, shading and texture detail. (See also HIDDEN-SURFACE REMOVAL and VOLUMETRIC RENDERING.)
[Upson-88]

VDU

See VISUAL DISPLAY UNIT.

vector

Unlike a SCALAR quantity, vectors encode quantities composed of two or more components. For example, a 3-D force has magnitude and direction: these can be encoded into three values where the direction is represented by three components in a CARTESIAN COORDINATE system and the force is represented by the length of the resultant line. Vectors can be created from the CARTESIAN COORDINATES defining computer graphics models, which also allows one to determine the orientation and lengths of edges. Furthermore, the vector operations SCALAR PRODUCT and VECTOR PRODUCT allow one to determine the enclosed angle between two vectors, and a third vector

ORTHOGONAL to any two distinct vectors. (See also CARTESIAN COORDINATES, NORMAL VECTOR, POINT VECTOR, SCALAR PRODUCT, UNIT VECTOR, and VECTOR PRODUCT.)
[Burger-89, Gasson-83, Hearn-86, Rogers-89]

vector display
See CALLIGRAPHIC DISPLAY.

vector graphics
Historically, the term vector graphics described images constructed from sequences of arbitrarily drawn straight lines, as produced by FLATBED PLOTTERS and CALLIGRAPHIC DISPLAYS. However, with the introduction of RASTER GRAPHICS, vector graphic images now exploit a technology that manipulates pixels rather than lines. Nevertheless, the term is still part of the computer graphics scene. (See also RASTER COMPUTER GRAPHICS.)

vector product
Given two distinct vectors, the vector product operation creates a third vector ORTHOGONAL to the plane containing the original vectors. In computer graphics, this operation can be used to create a SURFACE NORMAL from two edges of a FACET. Given two vectors $\boldsymbol{p}$ and $\boldsymbol{q}$:

$$\boldsymbol{p} = a\boldsymbol{i} + b\boldsymbol{j} + c\boldsymbol{k}$$
$$\boldsymbol{q} = d\boldsymbol{i} + e\boldsymbol{j} + f\boldsymbol{k}$$

then the vector product $\boldsymbol{p}\times\boldsymbol{q}$ is given by

$$\boldsymbol{p}\times\boldsymbol{q} = (bf - ce)\boldsymbol{i} + (cd - af)\boldsymbol{j} + (ae - bd)\boldsymbol{k}$$

This operation is also known as the CROSS PRODUCT. (See also SCALAR PRODUCT.)
[Burger-89, Gasson-83, Rogers-89]

vertex
A vertex only requires two or three coordinates for its definition, but from this fundamental building block are constructed edges, facets, polygons and polyhedra. The relationship between vertices, edges and facets is summarized by EULER'S RULE.
[Rogers-89]

vertex colour
As colour is represented numerically within a computer graphics environment, it means that it can be interpolated like any other quantity – hence the term vertex colour describes a situation when colour values can be assigned to vertices of an object and interpolated to achieve an unusual surface finish across a FACET. (See also GOURAUD SHADING.)

vertex normal
A vertex normal is an ORTHOGONAL UNIT VECTOR associated with a vertex, perhaps derived from the edges belonging to the facet sharing the vertex. (See also AVERAGE NORMAL, NORMAL, NORMALIZATION, NORMAL VECTOR, SURFACE NORMAL, and UNIT VECTOR.)
[Gasson-83, Rogers-89]

vertical blanking interval
The blank portion of a video signal allowing the electron beams to be retraced to the top of a new FIELD or FRAME is called the vertical blanking interval. (See also FIELD, FRAME, INTERLACING, VERTICAL RETRACE, and VIDEO SIGNAL.)

vertical interval time code
A vertical interval time code is a SMPTE TIME CODE inserted in the VERTICAL BLANKING INTERVAL. (See also TIME CODE.)

vertical resolution
In CRT displays, vertical resolution refers to the number of RASTERS stroked across in one FRAME. NTSC television has 525, PAL television has 625 and some computer graphics workstations have 1024 lines. Other devices such as plotters and LCD screens etc. also have an associated vertical resolution.
[Hearn-86]

vertical retrace
See FLYBACK.

VGA
VGA is an acronym for Video Graphics Array developed

by IBM for the PS/2 computer. Its standard resolution is 640 x 480 but it can be extended to 1024 x 768. It can display 256 colours from a palette of 256K. (See also CGA, EGA, HDA, HGC, MCGA, MDA, PVA, and SUPER VGA.)

video bandwidth
See BANDWIDTH.

video buffer
See FRAME STORE.

video disk
A video disk is a digital storage device holding raster images which can be retrieved at video rates with the aid of a laser-driven playback unit. They are conventionally used for storing film and television programmes, but the same technology is employed for audio compact disk and CD-ROM.

video frequency
The video frequency refers to the modulation frequency applied to a CRT's beam during a raster stroke: it controls the number of pixels displayed on the RASTER and is also known as the DOT-CLOCK FREQUENCY.

video look-up table
See LOOK-UP TABLE.

video mixing
Video mixing is the process of combining two or more video channels to create special effects such as wipes, COMPOSITING, keying and cross mixes. (See also ALPHA CHANNEL, CHROMA KEYING, COMPOSITING, DIGITAL CHROMA KEYING, DIGITAL MIXING, KEYING, MATTE, POST-PRODUCTION, and VIDEO SIGNAL.)

video RAM
See VRAM.

video signal
A video signal encodes the CHROMINANCE and LUMINANCE information of a raster image together with the synchronization pulses controlling the display device. The three television standards are NTSC, PAL and SECAM. (See also CHROMINANCE, COMPOSITE, HDTV, LUMINANCE, NTSC, PAL, and SECAM.)

viewing pyramid
Because of the rectangular nature of display screens, the field of vision of the OBSERVER becomes a viewing pyramid, with the observer located at the pyramid's apex and the BACK CLIPPING PLANE forming its base. Object definitions within the viewing pyramid will be visible, with all other external artifacts invisible, having been removed by a clipping process. See Figure C-5. (See also CLIPPING, DEPTH CLIPPING, FRUSTUM, OBSERVER, and PICTURE PLANE.)
[Burger-89, Foley-90, Hearn-86, Rogers-89]

view plane
See PICTURE PLANE.

viewport
A viewport is a rectangular area of a display screen which receives the contents of a mapped window. A graphics system must allow a user to establish such an area anywhere upon the screen and perform the correct mapping from the window to the viewport, even when they may have different ASPECT RATIOS.
[Hearn-86, Rogers-89]

view vector
A view vector establishes the orientation of the observer and can be defined by the position of the observer using the EYE POINT and AIM POINT. Other methods are possible but, ultimately, sufficient information is required to orient the observer's frame of reference in WORLD COORDINATE SPACE. (See also AIM POINT, EYE POINT, LINE OF PROJECTION, LINE OF SIGHT, OBSERVER, PICTURE PLANE, and VECTOR.)
[Hearn-86]

view volume
See VIEWING PYRAMID.

virtual image
Unlike a REAL IMAGE, a virtual image can be seen but not projected upon a screen; it is formed upon the retina which forms a screen. As an example, consider the reflection seen in a spherical mirror: it appears to be behind the mirror and cannot be directly projected upon some surface.
[Jenkins-76]

virtual reality
Users of REAL-TIME computer graphics workstations are able to manipulate a virtual world in the form of images; these might be representing the atoms of a molecular structure, an interior design for a new building, or even an animation sequence for advertising. But this virtual world still remains physically inaccessible to the user. However, technology is now available that permits the user to interact with this virtual world. Systems such as VPL's EyePhone, which is a colour stereo display system worn on the user's head, provides a realistic 3-D image. The step into the virtual reality is made by tracking the user's head movements and using this to control the perspective view seen by the user. This means that the user can walk physically about an empty room and see a computer-generated virtual reality. (See also DATAGLOVE and HUMAN–COMPUTER INTERACTION.)

visual acuity
Visual acuity refers to the eye's ability to resolve detail, and is specified in terms of an angular measurement relative to the eye. In normal lighting conditions this is about 4 minutes of arc, but as light levels fall and 'gloom' sets in, it increases to 6 minutes of arc.
[Boynton-79, Rogers-85]

visual display unit (VDU)
A visual display unit is a display terminal connected to a computer for the presentation of information.

visual programming
Conventionally, programs are designed by assembling sequences of instructions, but visual programming explores other methods using tables and graphical forms that aid in the process of controlling logical processes.
[Haeberli-88, Myers-86]

VLSI
VLSI is an acronym for Very Large-Scale Integration and relates to the technology of manufacturing in semiconducting materials, electronic circuits for processing DIGITAL SIGNALS, e.g. processors and related memory units. (See also ASIC and GEOMETRY ENGINE.)

volumetric rendering
Volumetric data, perhaps derived from a computer simulation or from a medical imaging system, employs volumetric rendering to create 3-D scenes from the numerical SCALAR or VECTOR values. (See also CROSS-SECTION RENDERING, G-OCTREE, and VOXEL.)
[Drebin-88, Levoy-88, Upson-88]

voxel
A voxel is a volume of space and represents the 3-D equivalent of a pixel. If a display has N by N pixels, one can imagine the space behind the screen extending a further N pixels, creating in all $N \times N \times N$ voxel elements. (See also G-OCTREE, OCTREE, and QUADTREE.)
[Hearn-86, Kaufman-88, Kaufman-89]

voxel space automata
Ned Greene introduced the term voxel space automata to describe a class of growth processes that sense and react to their voxel environment.
[Greene-89, Kaufman-89]

VRAM
VRAM is an acronym for Video RAM, which are chips used for FRAME STORES as they offer higher speed than conventional RAM chips, and have two input–output ports or buses which allow the memory to be updated whilst their contents are being displayed.

W

walk-through
The term walk-through is generally used in computer graphics systems employed for architectural applications, where the computer's 'eye' dynamically traces a path equivalent to a 'walk-through' in the modelled scene. (See also COMPUTER ANIMATION and REAL-TIME.)

Warnock algorithm
In 1968 John Warnock demonstrated a hidden-line/surface algorithm which exploited AREA COHERENCE within a DIVIDE AND CONQUER strategy. It works in IMAGE SPACE by recursively dividing up four equal windows into smaller similar elements, and stops dividing when the polygon in question is disjoint, contained by or intersects or is surrounded by the current window. See Figure A-4. (See also CONTAINED POLYGON, DISJOINT POLYGON, DIVIDE AND CONQUER, HIDDEN-LINE REMOVAL, HIDDEN-SURFACE REMOVAL, IMAGE SPACE, and INTERSECTING POLYGON)
[Burger-89, Rogers-85, Warnock-68]

wavelength
Wavelength of a sinusoidal waveform is the distance between two similar points on the shape.
[Burger-89, Hearn-86, Jenkins-76]

weighting function
See BASIS FUNCTION.

Weiler–Atherton algorithm
Weiler and Atherton developed a technique which could be applied to CLIPPING and HIDDEN-LINE REMOVAL: in clipping it can be used to clip one polygon against another, where both polygons can be concave and contain holes, and in HIDDEN-LINE REMOVAL occulted edges are removed by clipping polygon boundaries in OBJECT SPACE by other occulting polygons. (See also CLIPPING, COHEN–SUTHERLAND ALGORITHM, DEPTH CLIPPING, HIDDEN-LINE REMOVAL, and HIDDEN-SURFACE REMOVAL.)
[Rogers-85, Weiler-77]

white light
The sensation of white light occurs when the eye receives radiant energy with a wide range of frequencies, as found in sunlight. In the RGB COLOUR MODEL, white light is created when equal amounts of red, green and blue light are mixed together. See Figure A-1. (See also ADDITIVE COLOUR MIXING, CHROMATIC LIGHT, ILLUMINANT C, and RGB COLOUR MODEL.)
[Boynton-79, Burger-89, Gregory-86]

white noise
White noise describes a random signal that has no bias to any one frequency component. (See also FOURIER FRACTAL, FRACTAL GEOMETRY, and FRACTAL NOISE.)
[Peitgen-88]

WIMP environment
A WIMP environment describes a computer graphics system that provides users with WINDOWS, ICONS, MENUS and pointing devices. (See also ICONS, MENU, MOUSE, PULL-DOWN MENU, USER INTERFACE, and WINDOW.)

window
(1) A window is a rectangular zone of a display screen where a user may activate a computer process and perhaps produce graphics whilst simultaneously working with other similar processes. The user has control over the position and size of the window with the interaction of a MOUSE. (See also WIMP ENVIRONMENT.)
[Hearn-86, Hopgood-85, Rogers-89]
(2) A window can also be a rectangular region in the EYE COORDINATE SYSTEM defining the minimum and maximum X- and Y-coordinates isolating a specific area of interest. This window will then be mapped onto a VIEWPORT for display. (See also EYE COORDINATE SYSTEM and VIEWPORT.)
[Foley-90, Hearn-86, Myers-88, Rhoden-89, Rogers-85]

winged-edge data structure
The BOUNDARY REPRESENTATION scheme for modelling polyhedra must ensure that geometric integrity is preserved

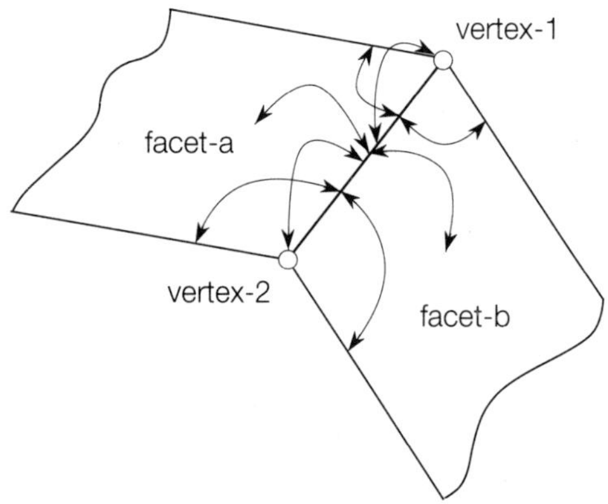

Figure W-1 *In the winged-edge data structure, pointers are maintained to provide links between facets and the shared edge, vertices and their associated edge and the partitioning edge with the edges joining at its ends. These links are shown diagrammatically above.*

not only when a structure is formed, but when it is edited. The winged-edge data structure is employed in modellers to maintain this data during its manipulation by a system of two-way pointers interconnecting any edge with its associated end vertices, neighbouring faces and edges. Although the structure maintains essential data to conserve EULER'S RULE, geometric inconsistencies can still arise with CONCAVE POLYGONS. See Figure W-1. (See also BOUNDARY REPRESENTATION, DATA STRUCTURE, EULER'S RULE, and GRAPHICAL DATA STRUCTURE.)
[Woodwark-86]

wipe
In animation, the term wipe is used to describe the introduction of a new image(s) by sliding one out and introducing another. (See also CROSS-DISSOLVE.)

wire frame
The term wire frame is used to describe a view of a 3-D object, where all edges are drawn, producing a 'see-through' wire-like image. (See also DEPTH CUES and HIDDEN-LINE REMOVAL.)
[Burger-89, Hearn-86]

workstation
A workstation is a configuration of a processor, screen, keyboard and local disk-storage, all of which are generally connected to a local area network (LAN). A user will be able to undertake all the standard tasks of program development, compilation and execution without being influenced by other users. Central disk-storage is accessed through the LAN and a file-server.
[Burger-89]

world coordinate space
The world coordinate space is a reference space for constructing 3-D models, light sources, an observer and any trajectories employed for animation purposes. To obtain a rendered view of any scene, world coordinates must be transformed into the EYE COORDINATE SYSTEM to provide the necessary geometric features for HIDDEN-SURFACE REMOVAL and illumination. See Figure E-2. (See also ABSOLUTE COORDINATES, CARTESIAN COORDINATES, EYE COORDINATE SYSTEM, and SCREEN COORDINATES.)
[Burger-89, Foley-90, Hearn-86, Rogers-89]

wraparound
Wraparound is an effect where image detail removed by a CLIPPING or windowing operation reappears on the opposite edge of the display device, creating the impression that it has been completely 'wrapped around'.
[Hearn-86]

wrapping
Any mathematical operation for distorting an image to follow the surface contour of a reference object involves wrapping operations. Relatively simple trigonometric

functions are sufficient to wrap vector images onto cylinders, cones and spheres, but more complex TEXTURE MAPPING algorithms are required to wrap pixel images because of the ensuing problems of ALIASING. (See also TEXTURE MAPPING.)
[Glassner-89]

WYSIWYG
WYSIWYG is an acronym for 'What You See Is What You Get', a popular description for computer systems that supposedly always display upon the screen an accurate replica of what will eventually be transferred to hard-copy: this is almost never true. (See also HUMAN–COMPUTER INTERACTION and WIMP ENVIRONMENT.)

X-coordinate
The X-coordinate of a point is a linear measurement along the X-axis from the origin to the point. See Figure C-1. (See also CARTESIAN COORDINATES.)

X Windows
X Windows is a DEVICE INDEPENDENT graphics standard for controlling WINDOWS within a distributed environment. It provides programmers with a software toolkit to implement window systems and display 2-D graphics. (See also DEVICE INDEPENDENT, USER INTERFACE, WIMP ENVIRONMENT, and WINDOW.)
[Burger-89, Nye-87, Scheifler-88]

X-Y plotter
An X–Y plotter is a graph plotter (flat, drum, belt etc.) which recreates line drawings, or is capable of cutting plastic masks, from X- and Y-coordinates supplied by some computer system. (See also ELECTROPHOTOGRAPHIC PLOTTER, FLATBED PLOTTER, and INK JET PLOTTER.)
[Hearn-86, Rogers-89]

y

yaw

Yaw is a rotational movement about a vertical axis and is normally used in conjunction with ROLL and PITCH to orient an object or OBSERVER. (See also PITCH and ROLL.)
[Gasson-83]

Y-coordinate

The Y-coordinate of a point is a linear measurement along the Y-axis from the origin to the point. See Figure C-1. (See also CARTESIAN COORDINATES.)

YIQ

YIQ is a COLOUR MODEL used in NTSC television signals where the 'Y' component represents LUMINANCE, and 'I' and 'Q' are colour differences encoding RGB. The values for YIQ can be derived from RGB using the following matrix

$$\begin{bmatrix} Y \\ I \\ Q \end{bmatrix} = \begin{bmatrix} 0.299 & 0.587 & 0.114 \\ 0.596 & -0.274 & -0.322 \\ 0.211 & -0.522 & 0.311 \end{bmatrix} \begin{bmatrix} R \\ G \\ B \end{bmatrix}$$

(See also COLOUR MODEL, NTSC, RGB, and YUV.)
[Hunt-75]

yon clipping plane

See BACK CLIPPING PLANE.

YUV

YUV is a COLOUR MODEL used in PAL television signals; 'Y' is the LUMINANCE component whilst 'U' and 'V' are the scaled and filtered colour difference signals used to modulate the subcarrier for the CHROMINANCE signal. (See also COLOUR MODEL, NTSC, RGB, and YIQ.)
[Hunt-75]

Z

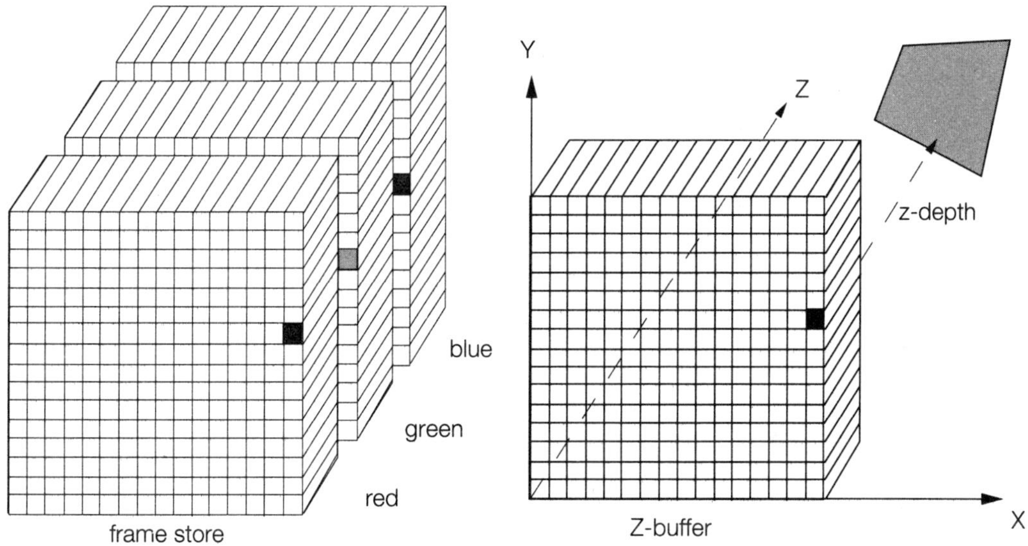

Figure Z-1 *The Z-buffer algorithm operates in conjunction with a frame store shown on the left and a Z-buffer shown on the right, where for each pixel element of the store, the Z-buffer maintains the z-depth of the closest facet. This strategy allows facets to be rendered in a random sequence and resolves the visible and invisible portions of intersecting objects.*

Z-buffer
A Z-buffer is a memory buffer normally built into graphics workstations, which stores for every pixel in an image Z-DEPTH values in EYE COORDINATE SPACE of the nearest surface. (See also Z-BUFFER ALGORITHM and ZZ-BUFFER.)
[Burger-89, Foley-90, Hearn-86, Rogers-85]

Z-buffer algorithm
The Z-buffer algorithm is a HIDDEN-SURFACE REMOVAL algorithm which, with the aid of a Z-BUFFER, can create a correctly occulted scene from a random sequence of surfaces. Initially the Z-buffer, which will always store the Z-DEPTH of the nearest surface for a pixel, is set to high values. For every rendered surface, the z-depth in eye coordinates is computed for every affected pixel; if this depth is less than, or equal to, that currently held in the Z-buffer, the FRAME STORE receives the rendered intensity level while the Z-buffer is updated. If the depth is greater than the current Z-buffer value, the surface is effectively occulted for this pixel and is ignored. Although the algorithm has an elegant and simple hardware implementation, it does suffer from an inability to cope with ANTI-ALIASING and TRANSPARENCY; nevertheless, it is extremely popular for general-purpose computer graphics WORKSTATIONS. See Figure Z-1. (See also A-BUFFER, DEPTH SORT ALGORITHM, EYE COORDINATE SPACE, HIDDEN-SURFACE REMOVAL, Z-BUFFER, Z-DEPTH, and ZZ-BUFFER.)
[Burger-89, Dyer-87, Foley-90, Hearn-86, Okino-84, Rogers-85]

Z-coordinate
The Z-coordinate of a point is a linear measurement along the Z-axis from the origin to the point. See Figure C-1. (See also CARTESIAN COORDINATES.)

z-depth

When WORLD COORDINATES are transformed to EYE COORDINATE SPACE, the observer is generally positioned at the origin directed along the positive Z-axis. The Z-coordinates of objects then represent the z-depths from the observer, which are used in the Z-BUFFER ALGORITHM and DEPTH SORT ALGORITHMS to resolve HIDDEN-SURFACE REMOVAL. (See also DEPTH-SORT ALGORITHM, EYE COORDINATE SPACE, PAINTER'S ALGORITHM, and Z-BUFFER ALGORITHM.)

zoom

Zoom is a facility in computer graphics systems whereby the user may enlarge or decrease the size of part of an image by 'zooming' in or out relative to some specified point. This may be a hardware feature, and if so will generally provide a REAL-TIME response. (See also PANNING.)
[Burger-89, Hearn-86]

ZZ-buffer

The ZZ-buffer is a HIDDEN-SURFACE REMOVAL algorithm based upon the Z-BUFFER ALGORITHM but overcomes the latter's difficulties in handling TRANSPARENT SURFACES and ANTI-ALIASING. Basically, the algorithm operates by partitioning up the IMAGE SPACE into small rectangular cells, and for each cell, lists of polygons are created that impact upon the area. Whenever an opaque surface completely masks a cell – and is also closer than any previous polygon – the polygon list (which is maintained in z-range sequence) is deleted, as these polygons are no longer visible. Other partially overlapping polygons and transparent surfaces are placed in their relevant positions. Once every polygon has been processed, the lists are resolved and rendered. The algorithm lends itself to shadows, penumbrae, DEPTH OF FIELD effects, and STOCHASTIC SAMPLING. (See also A-BUFFER and Z-BUFFER ALGORITHM.)
[Salesin-89]

Abram-85 Abram, Greg, and Westover, Lee, 'Efficient Alias-free Rendering using Bit-masks and Look-up Tables',*Computer Graphics,* Vol. 19, No. 3, pp. 53–59, July 1985 (Proc. SIGGRAPH 85).
Amanatides-84 Amanatides, John, 'Ray Tracing with Cones', *Computer Graphics*, Vol. 18, No. 3, pp. 129–135, July 1984 (Proc. SIGGRAPH 84).
Amanatides-87 Amanatides, John, 'Realism in Computer Graphics: A Survey', *IEEE, CG&A,* Vol. 7, No. 1, pp. 44–56, January 1987.
Ammeraal-86 Ammeraal, Leendert, *Programming Principles in Computer Graphics*, Wiley, New York, 1986.
ANSI-88 ANSI, 'Metafile for the Storage and Transfer of Picture Description Information, Addendum 3 (CGM)', ANSI X3H3/88-55, 1988.
Armstrong-85 Armstrong, William W., and Green, Mark W., 'The Dynamics of Articulated Rigid Bodies for the Purposes of Animation', *Proc. of Graphics Interface '85,* Canadian Information Processing Society, Toronto, Ontario, pp. 407–415, May 1985.
Arvo-86 Arvo, James, 'Backwards Ray Tracing', *Developments in Ray Tracing,* Vol. 12, SIGGRAPH Course Notes, 1986.
Atherton-78a Atherton, Peter R., 'Polygon Shadow Generation with Application to Solar Lights', Master's thesis, Cornell University, 1978.
Atherton-78b Atherton, Peter R., Weiler, Kevin, and Greenberg, Donald, 'Polygon Shadow Generation', *Computer Graphics*, Vol. 12, No. 3, pp. 275–281, 1978 (Proc. SIGGRAPH 78).
Atherton-83 Atherton, Peter R., 'A Scan-line Hidden Surface Removal Procedure for Constructive Solid Geometry', *Computer Graphics*, Vol. 17, No. 3, pp. 73–82, July 1983 (Proc. SIGGRAPH 83).

Badler-87 Badler, Norman I., Manoochehri, Kamran H., and Walters, Graham, 'Articulated Figure Positioning by Multiple Constraints', *IEEE, CG&A,* Vol. 7, No. 6, pp. 28–38, June 1987.
Bahar-87 Bahar, Ezekiel, and Chakrabarti, Swapan, 'Full-wave Theory applied to Computer-aided Graphics for 3D Objects', *IEEE, CG&A,* Vol. 7, No. 7, pp. 46–60, July 1987.
Baraff-89 Baraff, David, 'Analytical Methods for Dynamic Simulation of Non-penetrating Rigid Bodies', *Computer Graphics,* Vol. 23, No. 3, pp. 223–232, July 1989 (Proc. SIGGRAPH 89).
Barnsley-85 Barnsley, Michael F., Ervin, V., Hardin, D., and Lancaster, J., 'Solution of an Inverse Problem for Fractals and Other Sets', *Proc. National Academy of Sciences, USA*, Vol. 83, April 1985.
Barnsley-88 Barnsley, Michael F., Jacquin, Arnaud, Malassenet, Francois, Reuter, Laurie, and Sloan, Alan D., 'Harnessing Chaos for Image Synthesis', *Computer Graphics,* Vol. 22, No. 4, pp. 131–140, August 1988 (Proc. SIGGRAPH 88).
Barnsley-89 Barnsley, Michael F., *Fractals Everywhere,* Academic Press, San Francisco, 1989.
Barrett-87 Barrett, A. N., and Mackay, A. L., *Spatial Structure and the Microcomputer*, Macmillan, London, 1987.
Barry-88 Barry, Phillip, and Goldman, Ronald N., 'A Recursive Evaluation Algorithm for a Class of Catmull–Rom Splines', *Computer Graphics,* Vol. 22, No. 4, pp. 199–204, August 1988 (Proc. SIGGRAPH 88).
Barsky-81 Barsky, Brian A., 'The Beta-spline A Local Representation Based on Shape Parameters and Fundamental Geometric Measures', Doctoral dissertation, Department of Computer Science, University of Utah, 1981.
Barsky-88 Barsky, Brian A., *Computer Graphics and Geometric Modelling using Beta-splines,* Springer Verlag, Berlin, 1988.
Barsky-90 Barsky, Brian A. and DeRose, Tony D., 'Geometric Continuity of Parametric Curves: Construction of Geometrically Continuous Splines', *IEEE, CG&A,* Vol. 10, No. 1, pp. 60–68, January 1990.
Barzel-87 Barzel, Ronen, and Barr, Alan H., *Dynamic Constraints, Topics in Physically Based Modelling, Course Notes,* Vol. 16, 1987, SIGGRAPH.

Barzel-88 Barzel, Ronen, and Barr, Alan H., 'A Modelling System Based On Dynamic Constraints', *Computer Graphics*, Vol. 22, No. 4, pp. 179–188, August 1988 (Proc. SIGGRAPH 88).
Baum-89 Baum, Daniel R., Rushmeier, Holly E., and Winget, James M., 'Improving Radiosity Solutions Through the Use of Analytically Determined Form-factors', *Computer Graphics*, Vol. 23, No. 3, pp. 325–334, July 1989 (Proc. SIGGRAPH 89).
Bayer-73 Bayer, B. E., 'An Optimum Method for Two-level Rendition of Continuous Tone Pictures', *Int. Conf. on Communications, Conf. Record,* pp. 2611–15, 1973.
Bedi-89 Bedi, S., and Vickers, G. W., 'Surface Lofting and Smoothing with Skeletal-lines', *Computer Aided Geometric Design,* Vol. 6, No. 2, pp. 87–96, May 1989.
Bergeron-78 Bergeron, R. D., Bono, P. R., and Foley, J. D., 'Graphics Programming Using the Core System', *Computing Surveys,* Vol. 10, pp. 389–443, 1978.
Bergeron-86 Bergeron, P., 'A General Version of Crow's Shadow Volumes', *IEEE, CG&A,* Vol. 6, No. 9, pp. 17–28, 1986.
Bergman-86 Bergman, Larry, *et al*. 'Image Rendering by Adaptive Refinement', *Computer Graphics,* Vol. 20, No. 4, pp. 29–37, August 1986 (Proc. SIGGRAPH 86).
Bézier-73 Bézier, Pierre, 'UNISURF system principles, programme, language', *Computer Languages for Numerical Control*, (ed. Hatvany, J.) North-Holland, Amsterdam, pp. 417–426, (Proc. PROLAMAT 73 Conference, Budapest), 1973.
Bier-86a Bier, Eric Allan, 'Snap-dragging', *Computer Graphics*, Vol. 20, No. 4, pp. 233–240, August 1986 (Proc. SIGGRAPH 86).
Bier-86b Bier, Eric Allan, and Sloan, K. R., 'Two-part Texture Mappings', *IEEE, CG&A,* Vol. 6, No. 9, pp. 40–53, 1986.
Bishop-86 Bishop, Gary, and Weimer, David M., 'Fast Phong Shading', *Computer Graphics,* Vol. 20, No. 4, pp. 103–106, August 1986 (Proc. SIGGRAPH 86).
Blinn-76 Blinn, James F., and Newell, Martin E., 'Texture and Reflection in Computer Generated Images', *CACM,* Vol. 19, pp. 542–547, 1976.
Blinn-77 Blinn, James F., 'Models of Light Reflection for Computer Synthesized Pictures', *Computer Graphics,* Vol. 11, No. 2, pp. 192–198, 1977 (Proc. SIGGRAPH 77).
Blinn-78a Blinn, James F., and Newell, M. E., 'Clipping Using Homogeneous Coordinates', *Computer Graphics*, Vol. 12, No. 3, pp. 245–251, 1978 (Proc. SIGGRAPH 78).
Blinn-78b Blinn, James F., 'A Scan Line Algorithm for the Computer Display of Parametrically Defined Surfaces', *Computer Graphics,* Vol. 12, 1978 (supplement to Proc. SIGGRAPH 78).
Blinn-78c Blinn, James F., 'Simulation of Wrinkled Surfaces', *Computer Graphics*, Vol. 12, No. 3, pp. 286–292, 1978 (Proc. SIGGRAPH 78).
Blinn-82 Blinn, James F., 'Light Reflection Functions for Simulation of Clouds and Dusty Surfaces', *Computer Graphics*, Vol. 16, No. 3, pp. 21–29, 1982 (Proc. SIGGRAPH 82).
Blinn-87a Blinn, James F., 'Nested Transformations and Blobby Man', *IEEE, CG&A,* Vol. 7, No. 10, pp. 59–65, October 1987.
Blinn-87b Blinn, James F., 'Platonic Solids', *IEEE, CG&A,* Vol. 7, No. 11, pp. 62–66, November 1987.
Blinn-89a Blinn, James F., 'Return of the Jaggy', *IEEE, CG&A*, Vol. 9, No. 2, pp. 82–89, March 1989.
Blinn-89b Blinn, James F., 'Dirty Pixels', *IEEE, CG&A*, Vol. 9, No. 4, pp. 100–105, July 1989.
Blinn-89c Blinn, James F., 'What We Need Around Here Is More Aliasing',*IEEE, CG&A,* Vol. 9, No. 1, pp. 75–79, January 1989.
Blinn-90 Blinn, James F., 'Tirage Tables', *IEEE, CG&A,* Vol. 10, No. 1, pp. 70–75, January 1990.
Bohm-84 Bohm, Wolfgang, Farin, Gerald, and Kahmann, Jurgen, 'A Survey of Curve and Surface Methods in CAGD', *Computer Aided Geometric*

Design, North-Holland, Amsterdam, Vol. 1, pp. 1–60, 1984.

Bono-87 Bono, P. R., and Herman, I., (eds), *GKS Theory and Practice*, Springer-Verlag, Berlin, 1987.

Bouknight-69 Bouknight, W. J., 'An Improved Procedure for Generation of Half-tone Computer Graphics Representations', University of Illinois Coordinated Science Lab. Tech. Rep. R- 432, 1969.

Bowyer-83 Bowyer, Adrian, and Woodwark, John, *A Programmer's Geometry,* Butterworths, London, 1983.

Boynton-79 Boynton, Robert M., *Human Colour Vision*, Holt, Rinehart and Winston, New York, 1979.

Bresenham-65 Bresenham, J. E., 'Algorithm for Computer Control of a Digital Plotter', *IBM Systems Journal,* Vol. 4, pp. 25–30, 1965.

Bresenham-77 Bresenham, J. E., 'A Linear Algorithm for Incremental Digital Display of Circular Arcs', *CACM*, Vol. 20, pp. 100–106, 1977.

Bresenham-87 Bresenham, Jack E., 'Ambiguities in Incremental Line Rastering', *IEEE, CG&A,* Vol. 7, No. 5, pp. 31–43, May 1987.

Brewer-77 Brewer, J. A., and Anderson, D. C., 'Visual Interaction with Overhauser Curves and Surfaces', *Computer Graphics*, Vol. 1, No. 2, pp. 132–137, 1977 (Proc. SIGGRAPH 77).

Brigham-74 Brigham, E. Oran, *The Fast Fourier Transform,* Prentice-Hall, Englewood Cliffs, NJ, 1974.

Brotman-84 Brotman, Lynne Shapior, and Badler, N. I., 'Generating Soft Shadows with a Depth Buffer Algorithm', *IEEE, CG&A,* Vol. 4, No. 10, pp. 5–12, 1984.

Brotman-88 Brotman, Lynne Shapior, and Netravali, Arun N., 'Motion Interpolation by Optimal Control', *Computer Graphics,* Vol. 22, No. 4, pp. 309–315, August 1988 (Proc. SIGGRAPH 88).

Bruderlin-89 Bruderlin, Armin, and Calvert, Thomas W., 'Goal-directed, Dynamic Animation of Human Walking', *Computer Graphics,* Vol. 23, No. 3, pp. 233–242, July 1989 (Proc. SIGGRAPH 89).

Bu-87 Bu, J., and Deprettere, E. F., 'A VLSI Algorithm for Computing Form-factors in Radiative Transfer Computer Image Synthesis', *Computer Graphics 1987*, (ed. Kuni, T. L.), Springer-Verlag, Tokyo, pp. 181–193, 1987.

Buckalew-89 Buckalew, Chris, and Fussell, Donald, 'Illumination Networks: Fast Realistic Rendering with General Reflectance Functions', *Computer Graphics*, Vol. 23, No. 3, pp. 89–98, July 1989 (Proc. SIGGRAPH 89).

Burger-89 Burger, Peter, and Gillies, Duncan, *Interactive Computer Graphics*, Addison-Wesley, Reading, MA,1989.

Buxton-85 Buxton, William, Hill, Ralph, and Rowley, Peter, 'Issues and Techniques in Touch-sensitive Tablet Input', *Computer Graphics*, Vol. 19, No. 3, pp. 215–224, July 1985 (Proc. SIGGRAPH 85).

Cabral-87 Cabral, Brian, Max, Nelson, and Springmeyer, Rebecca, 'Bidirectional Reflection Functions from Surface Bump Maps', *Computer Graphics*, Vol. 21, No. 4, pp. 273–281, July 1987 (Proc. SIGGRAPH 87).

Campbell-86 Campbell, Graham, DeFanti, Thomas A., *et al.*, 'Two Bit/Pixel Full Colour Encoding', *Computer Graphics*, Vol. 20, No. 4, pp. 215–223, August 1986 (Proc. SIGGRAPH 86).

Carey-85 Carey, R. J., and Greenberg, D. P., 'Textures for Realistic Image Synthesis', *Computers and Graphics,* Vol. 9, No. 2, pp. 125–138, 1985.

Carlbom-85 Carlbom, I., Chakravarty, I., and Vanderschel, D., 'A Hierarchical Data Structure for Representing the Spatial Decomposition of 3-D Objects', *IEEE, CG&A*, Vol. 5, No. 4, pp. 24–31, 1985.

Carpenter-80 Carpenter, Loren C., 'Computer Rendering of Fractal Curves and Surfaces', pp. 1–8, August 1980 (supplement to Proc. SIGGRAPH 80).

Carpenter-84 Carpenter, Loren C., 'The A-buffer, an Antialiased Hidden Surface Method', *Computer Graphics*, Vol. 18, No. 3, pp. 103–108, July 1984.

Casale-87 Casale, Malcolm S., 'Free-form Solid Modelling with Trimmed Surface Patches', *IEEE, CG&A,* Vol. 7, No. 1, pp. 33–43, January 1987.

Catmull-74a Catmull, Edwin, 'A Subdivision Algorithm for Computer Display of Curved Surfaces', Doctoral thesis, University of Utah, December 1974.

Catmull-74b Catmull, Edwin, and Rom, Raphael, 'A Class of Local Interpolating Splines', *Computer Aided Geometric Design,* Academic Press, San Francisco, pp. 317–326, 1974.

Catmull-75 Catmull, Edwin, 'Computer Display of Curved Surfaces', *Proc. IEEE Conf. Computer Graphics Pattern Recognition and Data Structures,* p. 11, May 1975.

Catmull-79 Catmull, Edwin, 'Tutorial on Compensation Tables', *Computer Graphics*, Vol. 13, pp. 1–7, 1979 (Proc. SIGGRAPH 79).

Cendes-87 Cendes, Zoltan J., and Wong, Steven H., 'C1 Quadratic Interpolation Over Arbitrary Point Sets', *IEEE, CG&A*, Vol. 7, No. 11, pp. 8–16, November 1987.

Chadwick-89 Chadwick, John E., Haumann, David R., and Parent, Richard E., 'Layered Construction for Deformable Animated Characters', *Computer Graphics*, Vol. 23, No. 3, pp. 243–252, July 1989 (Proc. SIGGRAPH 89).

Chang-89 Chang, Sheue-Ling, Shantz, Michael, and Rocchetti, Robert, 'Rendering Cubic Curves and Surfaces with Integer Adaptive Forward Differencing', *Computer Graphics*, Vol. 23, No. 3, pp. 157–166, July 1989 (Proc. SIGGRAPH 89).

Chattopadhyay-87 Chattopadhyay, Subdeb, and Fujimoto, Akira, 'Bi-directional Ray Tracing', *Computer Graphics, Proc. of CG International '87,* Springer-Verlag, Tokyo, 1987.

Chen-87 Chen, Y. C., 'Lens Effect on Synthetic Image Generation Based on Light Particle Theory', *Computer Graphics 1987*, (ed. Kuni, T. L.), Springer-Verlag, Tokyo, pp. 347–366, 1987.

Chin-89 Chin, Norman, and Feiner, Steven, 'Near Real-time Shadow Generation Using BSP Trees', *Computer Graphics*, Vol. 23, No. 3, pp. 99–106, July 1989 (Proc. SIGGRAPH 89).

Chiyokura-86 Chiyokura, Hiroaki, 'Localized Surface Interpolation Method for Irregular Meshes', *Advanced Computer Graphics*, Springer-Verlag, Tokyo, pp. 3–19, 1986.

Chiyokura-87 Chiyokura, Hiroaki, 'An Extended Rounding Operation for Modeling Solids with Free-form Surfaces', *IEEE, CG&A*, Vol. 7, No. 12, pp. 27–36, December 1987.

Clark-79 Clark, James H., 'A Fast Scan-line Algorithm for Rendering Parametric Surfaces', *Computer Graphics,* Vol. 13, 1979 (supplement to Proc. SIIGRAPH 79).

Clark-82 Clark, James H., 'The Geometry Engine A VLSI Geometry System for Graphics', *Computer Graphics*, Vol. 16, pp. 127–133, 1982 (Proc. SIGGRAPH 82).

Cleary-86 Cleary, J., *et al.,* 'Multiprocessor Ray Tracing', *Computer Graphics Forum,* Vol. 5, No. 1, pp. 3–12, 1986.

Cohen-85 Cohen, Michael F., and Greenberg, Donald P., 'The Hemi-cube: A Radiosity Solution for Complex Environments', *Computer Graphics,* Vol. 19, No. 3, pp. 31–40, July 1985 (Proc. SIGGRAPH 85).

Cohen-86 Cohen, M. F., and Greenberg, D. P., 'An Efficient Radiosity Approach for Realistic Image Synthesis', *IEEE, CG&A,* Vol. 6, No. 3, pp. 26–35, 1986.

Cohen-88 Cohen, M. F., Chen, S. E., Wallace, J. R., and Greenberg, D. P., 'A Progressive Refinement Approach to Fast Radiosity Image Generation', *Computer Graphics*, Vol. 22, No. 4, pp. 75–84, 1988 (Proc. SIGGRAPH 88).

Cole-87 Cole, A. J., 'Compaction Techniques for Raster Scan Graphics using Space-filling Curves', *Computer Journal,* Vol. 30, No. 1, pp. 87–92, 1987.

Comninos-89 Comninos, Peter P., 'Fast Free-form Deformation of Polyhedral Data', *Proc. CG-89, London,* Blenheim-Online, London, pp. 225-241, 1989.

Cook-82a Cook, Robert L., 'A Reflection Model for Realistic Image Synthesis', Master's thesis, Cornell University, 1982.

Cook-82b Cook, Robert L., and Torrance, K. E., 'A Reflectance Model for Computer Graphics', *ACM Trans. Graphics,* Vol. 1, pp. 7–24, 1982.
Cook-84 Cook, R. L., Porter, T., and Carpenter, L., 'Distributed Ray Tracing', *Computer Graphics,* Vol. 18, No. 3, pp. 137–145, July 1984 (Proc. SIGGRAPH 84).
Cook-86 Cook, Robert L., 'Practical Aspects of Distributed Ray Tracing', SIGGRAPH '86 Developments in Ray Tracing Seminar Notes, August 1986.
Cook-87 Cook, Robert L., Carpenter, Loren, and Catmull, Edwin, 'The Reyes Image Rendering Architecture', *Computer Graphics*, Vol. 21, No. 4, pp. 95–102, July 1987 (Proc. SIGGRAPH 87).
Coons-67 Coons, S. A., and Herzog, B., 'Surfaces for Computer-aided Aircraft Design', *Proc. AIAA 4th Annual Meeting and Technical Display Conf. Anaheim,* 1967, (AIAA Paper 67–895).
Critchlow-69 Critchlow, Keith, *Order in Space,* Thames and Hudson, New York, 1969.
Crocker-87a Crocker, Gary A., and Reinke, William F., 'Boundary Evaluation of Non-convex Primitives to Produce Parametric Trimmed Surfaces', *Computer Graphics,* Vol. 21, No. 4, pp. 129–136, July 1987 (Proc. SIGGRAPH 87).
Crocker-87b Crocker, Gary A., 'Screen-area Coherence for Interactive Scanline Display Algorithms', *IEEE, CG&A*, Vol. 7, No. 9, pp. 11–17, September 1987.
Crow-77 Crow, Franklin C., 'Shadow Algorithms for Computer Graphics', *Computer Graphics*, Vol. 11, No. 3, pp. 242–248, July 1977 (Proc. SIGGRAPH 77).
Crow-81 Crow, Franklin C., 'A Comparison of Antialiasing Techniques', *IEEE, CG&A,* Vol. 1, pp. 40–47, 1981.
Crow-84 Crow, Franklin C., 'Summed-area Tables for Texture Mapping', *Computer Graphics*, Vol. 18, No. 3, pp. 207–212, July 1984 (Proc. SIGGRAPH 84).
Crow-86 Crow, Franklin C., 'Advanced Image Synthesis: Anti-aliasing', *Advances in Computer Graphics*, (eds Enderle, I. G., Grave, M., and Lillehagen, F.) Springer-Verlag, Berlin, pp. 419–440, 1986.
Crow-87 Crow, Franklin C., 'The Origins of the Teapot', *IEEE, CG&A*, Vol. 7, No. 1, pp. 8–19, 1987.
Csuri-83 Csuri, C. A., 'Panel The Simulation of Natural Phenomena', *Computer Graphics*, Vol. 17, pp. 137–139, July 1983 (Proc. SIGGRAPH 83).
Cyrus-78 Cyrus, M., and Beck, J., 'Generalized Two- and Three-dimensional Clipping', *Computers & Graphics,* Vol. 3, pp. 23–28, 1978.

Dai-89 Dai, F., 'Collision-free Motion of an Articulated Kinematic Chain in a Dynamic Environment', *IEEE, CG&A,* Vol. 9, No. 4, pp. 70–74, July 1989.
Dantzig-30 Dantzig, Tobias, *Number: The Language of Science*, Free Press, New York, 1930.
Deering-88 Deering, M., Winner, S., Schediwy, B., Duffy, C., and Hunt, N., 'The Triangle Processor and Normal Vector Shader A VLSI System for High Performance Graphics', *Computer Graphics,* Vol. 22, No. 4, pp. 21–30, August 1988 (Proc. SIGGRAPH 88).
DeFanti-87 DeFanti, Tom, and Sandin, Dan, 'The Usable Intersection of PC Graphics and NTSC Video Recording', *IEEE, CG&A,* Vol. 7, No. 10, pp. 50–58, October 1987.
Demko-85 Demko, S., Hodges, L., and Naylor, B., 'Construction of Fractal Objects with Iterated Function Systems', *Computer Graphics,* Vol. 19, No. 3, pp. 271–278, July 1985 (Proc. SIGGRAPH 85).
Devai-87 Devai, F., 'An Intersection-Sensitive Hidden-Surface Algorithm', *Proc. Eurographics 87,* North-Holland, Amsterdam, 1987.
Devaney-86 Devaney, R. L., *An Introduction to Chaotic Dynamical Systems,* Benjamin Cummings, Menlo Park, CA, 1986.
Dew-89 Dew, P. M., Earnshaw, R. A., and Heywood, T. R., (eds), *Parallel Processing for Computer Vision and Display,* Addison-Wesley, London, 1989.
Dippe-84 Dippe, Mark A. Z., and Swensen, J., 'An Adaptive Subdivision Algorithm and Parallel

Architecture for Realistic Image Synthesis', *Computer Graphics*, Vol. 18, No. 3, pp. 149–158, July 1984 (Proc. SIGGRAPH 84).

Dippe-85 Dippe, Mark A. Z., and Wold, Erling Henry, 'Antialiasing Through Stochastic Sampling', *Computer Graphics*, Vol. 19, No. 3, pp. 69–78, July 1985 (Proc. SIGGRAPH 85).

Dobkin-88 Dobkin, David, Guibas, Leonidas, Hershberger, John, and Snoeyink, Jack, 'An Efficient Algorithm for Finding the CSG Representation of a Simple Polygon', *Computer Graphics*, Vol. 22, No. 4, pp. 31–40, August 1988 (Proc. SIGGRAPH 88).

Doctor-81 Doctor, L. J., and Torborg, J. G., 'Display Techniques for Octree-encoded Objects', *IEEE, CG&A*, Vol. 1, No. 3, pp. 29–38, 1981.

Doros-79 Doros, M., 'Algorithms for Generation of Discrete Circles, Rings and Disks', *Computer Graphics and Image Processing,* Vol. 10, pp. 366–371, 1979.

Drebin-88 Drebin, Robert A., Carpenter, Loren, and Hanrahan, Pat, 'Volume Rendering', *Computer Graphics,* Vol. 22, No. 4, pp. 65–74, August 1988 (Proc. SIGGRAPH 88).

Duff-85 Duff, Tom, 'Compositing 3-D Rendered Images', *Computer Graphics,* Vol. 19, No. 3, pp. 41–44, July 1985 (Proc. SIGGRAPH 85).

Dungan-79 Dungan, W., 'A Terrain and Cloud Computer Image Generation Model', *Computer Graphics,* Vol. 13, pp. 143–150, 1979 (Proc. SIGGRAPH 79).

Dunlavey-83 Dunlavey, Michael R., 'Efficient Polygon-Filling Algorithms for Raster Displays', *ACM Trans. Graphics*, Vol. 2, pp. 264–273, 1983.

Dyer-87 Dyer, Scott, and Whitman, Scott, 'A Vectorized Scan-line Z-buffer Rendering Algorithm', *IEEE, CG&A,* Vol. 7, No. 7, pp. 34–45, July 1987.

Earnshaw-85 Earnshaw, R. A., (ed.), *Fundamental Algorithms for Computer Graphics,* Springer-Verlag, Berlin,1985.

Falconer-85 Falconer, K. J., *The Geometry of Fractal Sets*, Cambridge University Press, Cambridge, 1985.

Farin-85 Farin, Gerald, 'A Modified Clough–Tocher Interpolant', *Computer Aided Geometric Design*, Vol. 2, pp. 19–27, 1985.

Farin-88 Farin, Gerald, *Curves and Surfaces for Computer Aided Geometric Design,* Academic Press, New York, 1988.

Ferguson-64 Ferguson, J. C., 'Multivariate Curve Interpolation', *JACM*, Vol. 11, No. 2, pp. 221–228, 1964.

Fiume-87 Fiume, E., 'Conformal Texture Mapping', *Proc. Eurographics 87*, North-Holland, Amsterdam, 1987.

Fletcher-87 Fletcher, G. Yates, and McAllister, David, F., 'An Analysis of Tension Methods for Convexity-preserving Interpolation', *IEEE, CG&A*, Vol. 7, No. 8, pp. 7–14, August 1987.

Fletcher-90 Fletcher, G. Yates, and McAllister, David, F., 'Automatic Tension Adjustment for Interpolating Splines', *IEEE, CG&A,* Vol. 10, No. 1, pp. 10–17, 1990.

Floyd-75 Floyd, R., and Steinberg, L., 'An Adaptive Algorithm for Spatial Gray Scale', *Int. Symp. Dig. Tech. Pap*., pp. 36–37, 1975.

Foley-87 Foley, James D., and Kim, Won Chul, 'Image Composition via Lookup Table Manipulation', *IEEE, CG&A*, Vol. 7, No. 11, pp. 26–35, November 1987.

Foley-90 Foley, James, Van Dam, Andries, Feiner, Steven, and Hughes, John, *Computer Graphics: Principles and Practice*, 2nd Edn, Addison-Wesley, Reading, MA, 1990.

Forrest-72 Forrest, A. R., 'Interactive Interpolation and Approximation by Bézier Polynomials', *Computer Journal,* Vol. 15, No. 1, pp. 71–79, 1972.

Forrest-85 Forrest, A. R., 'Antialiasing in Practice', *Fundamental Algorithms for Computer Graphics,* (ed. Earnshaw, R. A.) Springer-Verlag, Berlin, pp. 113–134, 1985.

Forsey-88 Forsey, David R., and Bartels, Richard H., 'Hierarchical B-spline Refinement', *Computer*

Graphics, Vol. 22, No. 4, pp. 205–212, August 1988 (Proc. SIGGRAPH 88)

Fournier-82 Fournier, Alain, Fussell, Don, and Carpenter, Loren, 'Computer Rendering of Stochastic Models', *CACM*, Vol. 25, No. 6, pp. 371–384, June 1982.

Fournier-85 Fournier, Alain, and Milligan, T., 'Frame Buffer Algorithms for Stochastic Models', *IEEE, CG&A*, Vol. 5, No. 10, pp. 40–46, 1985.

Fournier-86 Fournier, Alain, 'A Simple Model of Ocean Waves', *Computer Graphics*, Vol. 20, No. 4, pp. 75–84, August 1986 (Proc. SIGGRAPH 86).

Fournier-88 Fournier, Alain, and Fiume, Eugene, 'Constant-time Filtering with Space-variant Kernels', *Computer Graphics*, Vol. 22, No. 4, pp. 229–238, August 1988 (Proc. SIGGRAPH 88).

Fuchs-83 Fuchs, H., Abram, G. D., and Grant, E. D., 'Near Real-time Shaded Display of Rigid Objects', *Computer Graphics,* Vol. 17, pp. 65–72, July 1983 (Proc. SIGGRAPH 83).

Fuchs-85 Fuchs, Henry, Goldfeather, Jack, *et al.*, 'Fast Spheres, Shadows, Textures, Transparencies, and Image Enhancements in Pixel-planes', *Computer Graphics,* Vol. 19, No. 3, pp. 111–120, July 1985 (Proc. SIGGRAPH 85).

Gangnet-82 Gangnet, M., Perny, D., and Coueignoux, P., 'Perspective Mapping of Planar Textures', *Proc. Eurographics 82,* North-Holland, Amsterdam, pp. 115–123, 1982.

Gardner-85 Gardner, Geoffrey Y., 'Visual Simulation of Clouds', *Computer Graphics*, Vol. 19, No. 3, pp. 297–303, July 1985 (Proc. SIGGRAPH 85).

Gasson-83 Gasson, Peter C., *Geometry of Spatial Forms,* Ellis Horwood, Chichester, 1983.

Gharachorloo-89 Gharachorloo, Nader, Gupta, Satish, Sproull, Robert F., and Sutherland, Ivan E., 'A Characterization of Ten Rasterization Techniques', *Computer Graphics,* Vol. 23, No. 3, pp. 355–368, July 1989 (Proc. SIGGRAPH 89).

Girard-85 Girard, Michael, and Maciejewski, A. A., 'Computational Modelling for the Computer Animation of Legged Figures', *Computer Graphics,* Vol. 19, No. 3, pp. 263–270, July 1985 (Proc. SIGGRAPH 85).

Girard-87 Girard, Michael, 'Interactive Design of 3D Computer-animated Legged Animal Motion', *IEEE, CG&A*, Vol. 7, No. 6, pp. 39–51, June 1987.

Glassner-86 Glassner, Andrew S., 'Adaptive Precision in Texture Mapping', *Computer Graphics*, Vol. 20, No. 4, pp. 297–306, August 1986 (Proc. SIGGRAPH 86).

Glassner-88 Glassner, Andrew S., 'Spacetime Ray Tracing for Animation', *IEEE, CG&A,* Vol. 8, No. 2, pp. 60–70, March 1988.

Glassner-89 Glassner, Andrew S., (ed.) *An Introduction to Ray Tracing,* Academic Press, New York, 1989.

Gleick-87 Gleick, J., *Chaos, Making a New Science,* Viking, New York, 1987.

Goldfeather-86 Goldfeather, Jack, Hultquist, Jeff P. M., and Fuchs, Henry, 'Fast Constructive Solid Geometry Display in the Pixel-powers Graphics System', *Computer Graphics*, Vol. 20, No. 4, pp. 107–116, August 1986 (Proc. SIGGRAPH 86).

Goldfeather-89 Goldfeather, Jack, and College, Carleton, 'Near Real-time CSG Rendering Using Tree Normalization and Geometric Pruning', *IEEE, CG&A,* Vol. 9, No. 3, pp. 20-28, March 1989.

Goldsmith-87 Goldsmith, Jeffrey, and Salmon, John, 'Automatic Creation of Object Hierarchies for Ray Tracing', *IEEE, CG&A,* Vol. 7, No. 5, pp. 14–20, May 1987.

Gonska-83 Gonska, H., and Meier, J., 'A Bibliography on Approximation of Functions by Bernstein Type Operators', (eds Schumaker, L., and Chui, K.), *Approximation Theory IV*, Academic Press, New York, 1983.

Gonzalez-87 Gonzalez, Rafael C., and Wintz, Paul, *Digital Image Processing,* Addison-Wesley, Reading, MA, 1987.

Goodman-86 Goodman, Tim, and Unsworth, Keith, 'Manipulating Shape and Producing Geometric

Continuity in Beta-spline Curves', *IEEE, CG&A*, Vol. 6, No. 2, pp. 50–56, 1986.

Gouraud-71 Gouraud, H., 'Computer Display of Curved Surfaces', Doctoral thesis, University of Utah, 1971; also *IEEE Trans.* Vol. C-20, pp. 623–628, 1971.

Gourret-89 Gourret, Jean-Paul, Thalmann, Nadia Magrenat, and Thalmann, Daniel, 'Simulation of Object and Human Skin Deformations in a Grasping Task', *Computer Graphics,* Vol. 23, No. 3, pp. 21–30, July 1989 (Proc. SIGGRAPH 89).

Grabowski-87 Grabowski, H., and Glatz, R., 'IGES Model Comparison System: A Tool for Testing and Validating IGES Processors', *IEEE, CG&A*, Vol. 7, No. 11, pp. 47–57, November 1987.

Grant-85 Grant, Charles W., 'Integrated Analytical Spatial and Temporal Anti-aliasing for Polyhedra in 4-space,' *Computer Graphics,* Vol. 19, No. 3, pp. 79-84, July 1985 (Proc. SIGGRAPH 85).

Green-88 Green, Mark, and Sun, Hanqui, 'A Language and System for Procedural Modeling and Motion', *IEEE, CG&A*, Vol. 8, No. 6, pp. 52–64, November 1988.

Greene-89 Greene, Ned, 'Voxel Space Automata: Modelling with Stochastic Growth Processes in Voxel Space', *Computer Graphics*, Vol. 23, No. 3, pp. 175–184, July 1989 (Proc. SIGGRAPH 89).

Gregory-86 Gregory, R. L., *Eye and Brain: the psychology of seeing*, Weidenfeld and Nicolson, London, 1986.

Grogono-80 Grogono, Peter, *Programming in PASCAL,* Addison-Wesley, Reading, MA, 1980.

Greenberg-89 Greenberg, Donald, Cohen, Michael, Hall, Roy, Rushmeier, Holly, and Wallace, John, 'Radiosity', Course Notes, SIGGRAPH 89, 1989.

Gupta-81 Gupta, Satish, and Sproull, Robert F., 'Filtering Edges for Gray-scale Displays', *Computer Graphics*, Vol. 15, pp. 1–6, 1981 (Proc. SIGGRAPH 81).

Haeberli-88 Haeberli, Paul E., 'ConMan: A Visual Programming Language for Interactive Graphics', *Computer Graphics*, Vol. 22, No. 4, pp. 103–111, August 1988 (Proc. SIGGRAPH 88).

Hahn-88 Hahn, James K., 'Realistic Animation of Rigid Bodies', *Computer Graphics*, Vol. 22, No. 4, pp. 299–308, August 1988 (Proc. SIGGRAPH 88).

Haines-86 Haines, E. A., and Greenberg, D. P., 'The Light Buffer: a Shadow Testing Accelerator', *IEEE, CG&A,* Vol. 6, No. 9, pp. 6–16, September 1986.

Hall-86 Hall, R., 'A Characterization of Illumination Models and Shading Techniques', *The Visual Computer*, Vol. 2, No. 5, pp. 268–277, 1986.

Halton-70 Halton, J. H., 'A Retrospective and Prospective Survey of the Monte-Carlo Method', *SIAM Review,* Vol. 12, No. 1, January 1970.

Hamlin-77 Hamlin, G., and Gear, C., 'Raster-scan Hidden Surface Algorithm Techniques', *Computer Graphics*, Vol. 11, pp. 206–213, July 1977 (Proc. SIGGRAPH 77).

Hart-89 Hart, John C., Sandin, Daniel J., and Kauffman, Louis H., 'Ray Tracing Deterministic 3-D Fractals', *Computer Graphics*, Vol. 23, No. 3, pp. 289–296, July 1989 (Proc. SIGGRAPH 89).

Hausner-65 Hausner, Melvin, *A Vector Space Approach to Geometry,* Prentice-Hall, Englewood Cliffs, NJ, 1965.

Hearn-86 Hearn, Donald, and Baker, M. Pauline, *Computer Graphics,* Prentice-Hall, Englewood Cliffs, NJ, 1986.

Heckbert-84 Heckbert, Paul S., and Hanrahan, P., 'Beam Tracing Polygonal Objects', *Computer Graphics,* Vol. 18, No. 3, pp. 119–127, July 1984 (Proc. SIGGRAPH 84).

Heckbert-86a Heckbert, Paul S., 'Filtering by Repeated Integration', *Computer Graphics,* Vol. 20, No. 4, pp. 315–321, August 1986 (Proc. SIGGRAPH 86).

Heckbert-86b Heckbert, Paul S., 'Survey of Texture Mapping', *IEEE, CG&A,* Vol. 6, No. 11, pp. 56–67, 1986.

Hedgley-82 Hedgley, David R. Jr., 'A General Solution to the Hidden-line Problem', NASA Ref. Pub.

1085, March 1982.

Herman-85 Herman, I., Reviczky, J., and Tolnay-Knefely, T., 'A Concept for a GKS Machine', *Proc. Eurographics 85*, North-Holland, Amsterdam, 1985.

Hersch-87 Hersch, Roger D., 'Character Generation under Grid Constraints', *Computer Graphics*, Vol. 21, No. 4, pp. 243–252, July 1987 (Proc. SIGGRAPH 87).

Herzen-87 Herzen, Brian Von, and Barr, Alan H., 'Accurate Triangulations of Deformed, Intersecting Surfaces', *Computer Graphics*, Vol. 21, No. 4, pp. 103–110, July 1987 (Proc. SIGGRAPH 87).

Hilbert-91 Hilbert, D., 'Ueber Stetige Abildung einer Linie auf ein Flachenstuck,' *Mathematische Annalen,* Vol. 38, pp. 459–460, 1891.

Hodges-85 Hodges, L. F., and McAllister, D. F., 'Technology and Techniques for Stereoscopic Display of Computer Generated Images', *IEEE, CG&A*, Vol. 5, No. 9, pp. 38–45, 1985.

Hopgood-85 Hopgood, F. R. A., Duce, D. A., Fielding, E. V. C., Robinson, K., and Williams, A. S. (eds), *Methodology of Window Management. Proc. of an Alvey Workshop,* Springer-Verlag, Berlin, 1985.

Hopgood-86 Hopgood, F. R. A., Duce, D. A., Gallop, J. R., and Sutcliffe, D. C., *Introduction to the Graphical Kernel System (GKS)*, 2nd edn, Academic Press, New York, 1986.

Horn-76 Horn, B. K. P., 'Circle Generators for Display Devices', *Computer Graphics and Image Processing,* Vol. 5, pp. 280–288, 1976.

Horn-90 Horn, Alastair N., 'Iterated Function Systems, the Parallel Progressive Synthesis of Fractal Tiling Structures and their Applications to *Computer Graphics*', D. Phil. Thesis, Oxford University, 1990.

Hourcade-83 Hourcade, J. C., and Nicolas, A., 'Inverse Perspective Mapping in Scanline Order onto Non-planar Quadrilaterals', *Proc. Eurographics 83,* North-Holland, Amsterdam, pp. 309–319, 1983.

Hourcade-85 Hourcade, J. C., and Nicolas, A., 'Algorithms for Antialiased Cast Shadows', *Computers & Graphics,* Vol. 9, No. 3, pp. 259–265, 1985.

Hunt-75 Hunt, R. W. G., *The Reproduction of Colour in Photography, Printing and Television,* Fountain Press, Tolworth, 1975.

Ikanage-86 Ikanage, M., 'Caustics and Specular Reflection Models for Spherical Objects and Lenses', *The Visual Computer*, Vol. 2, No. 6, pp. 379–383, 1986.

Immel-86 Immel, David S., Cohen, Michael F., and Greenberg, Donald P., 'A Radiosity Method for Non-diffuse Environments', *Computer Graphics*, Vol. 20, No. 4, pp. 133–142, August 1986 (Proc. SIGGRAPH 86).

Isaacs-87 Isaacs, Paul M., and Cohen, Michael F., 'Controlling Dynamic Simulation with Kinematic Constraints, Behaviour Functions and Inverse Dynamics', *Computer Graphics*, Vol. 21, No. 4, pp. 215–224, July 1987 (Proc. SIGGRAPH 87).

ISO-85 ISO, 'Graphical Kernel System (GKS), Functional Description', ISO 7942 – 1985, DIN 66252, EN 27942, 1985/86.

ISO-87a ISO, 'Metafile for Transfer and Storage of Picture Description Information (CGM)', ISO 8632/1–4, 1987.

ISO-87b ISO, 'Graphical Kernel System for Three Dimensions (GKS-3D), Functional Description', ISO/IEC DIS 8805, 1987.

ISO-87c ISO, 'Programmer's Hierarchical Interactive Graphics System (PHIGS), Functional Description', ISO/IEC DIS 9592, 1987.

ISO-87d ISO, 'GKS Language Bindings', ISO 8651/1–3, DIN 66292, 1987.

ISO-87e ISO, 'GKS-3D Language Bindings', ISO/IEC DP 8806, 1987.

ISO-87f ISO, 'PHIGS Language Bindings', ISO/IEC DP 9593, 1987.

ISO-87g ISO, 'Metafile for Transfer and Storage of Picture Description Information, Addendum 1, Functional Specification', ISO DPAD 8632–1, 1987.

ISO-88a ISO/IEC, 'Interfacing Techniques for Dialogues with Graphical Devices (Computer Graphics Interfaces, CGI), Functional Specification', ISO/IEC DP

9636/1–6, April 1988.
ISO-88b ISO/IEC, 'Metafile for the Storage and Transfer of Picture Description Information, Addendum 2, Functional Specification', ISO/IEC JTC1/SC24 N23, 1988.

Jansen-84 Jansen, F. W., 'Data Structures for Ray Tracing', *Computer-Aided Design and Geometry,* North-Holland, Amsterdam, pp. 57–73, 1984.
Jassen-83 Jassen, Terry L., 'A Simple Efficient Hidden Line Algorithm', *Computers & Structures,* Vol. 17, No. 4, pp. 563–571, 1983.
Jenkins-76 Jenkins, Francis A., and White, Harvey E., *Fundamentals of Optics,* McGraw-Hill, New York, 1976.
Joblove-78 Joblove, George H., and Greenberg, Donald, 'Color Spaces for Computer Graphics', *Computer Graphics*, Vol. 12, pp. 20–25, 1978 (Proc. SIGGRAPH 78).
Joe-87 Joe, Barry, 'Discrete Beta Splines', *Computer Graphics*, Vol. 21, No. 4, pp. 137–144, July 1987 (Proc. SIGGRAPH 87).
Julia-18 Julia, Gaston, 'Sur l'itération des fonctions rationnelles,' *Journal de Math. Pure et Appl*. Vol. 8, pp. 47–245, 1918.

Kajiya-82 Kajiya, James T., 'Ray Tracing Parametric Patches', *Computer Graphics,* Vol. 16, pp. 245–254, 1982 (Proc. SIGGRAPH 82).
Kajiya-83 Kajiya, James T., 'New Techniques for Ray Tracing Procedurally Defined Objects', *Computer Graphics,* Vol. 17, No. 3, pp. 91–102, July 1983 (Proc. SIGGRAPH 83).
Kajiya-84 Kajiya, James T., 'Ray Tracing Volume Densities', *Computer Graphics*, Vol. 18, No. 3, pp. 165–174, 1984 (Proc. SIGGRAPH 84).
Kajiya-85 Kajiya, James T., 'Anisotropic Reflection Models', *Computer Graphics*, Vol. 19, No. 3, July 1985 (Proc. SIGGRAPH 85).
Kajiya-86 Kajiya, James T., 'The Rendering Equation', *Computer Graphics,* Vol. 20, No. 4, pp. 143–150, August 1986 (Proc. SIGGRAPH 86).
Kajiya-89 Kajiya, James T., and Kay, Timothy, 'Rendering Fur with Three Dimensional Textures', *Computer Graphics,* Vol. 23, No. 3, pp. 271–280, July 1989 (SIGGRAPH 89).
Kalra-89 Kalra, Devendra, and Barr, Alan H., 'Guaranteed Ray Intersections with Implicit Surfaces', *Computer Graphics*, Vol. 23, No. 3, pp. 297–306, July 1989 (Proc. SIGGRAPH 89).
Kaneda-89 Kaneda, Kazufumi, Kato, Fujiwa, Nakamae, Eihachiro, Nishita, Tomoyuki, and Tanaka, Hideo, 'Three-dimensional Terrain Modelling and Display for Environmental Assessment', *Computer Graphics,* Vol. 23, No. 3, pp. 207–214, July 1989 (Proc. SIGGRAPH 89).
Kaufman-87 Kaufman, Arie, 'Efficient Algorithms for 3D Scan-conversion of Parametric Curves, Surfaces, and Volumes', *Computer Graphics*, Vol. 21, No. 4, pp. 171–179, July 1987 (Proc. SIGGRAPH 87).
Kaufman-88 Kaufman, Arie, and Bakalash, Reuven, 'Memory and Processing Architecture for 3D Voxel-based Imagery', *IEEE, CG&A,* Vol. 8, No. 6, pp. 10–23, November 1988.
Kaufman-89 Kaufman, Arie, and Bandopadhay, Amit, 'Forest of Quadtrees: An Object Representation for 3D Graphics', pp. 221–234, *Proc. Eurographics 89*, *Hamburg,* North Holland, Amsterdam, 1989.
Kay-79a Kay, Douglas S., 'Transparency, Refraction and Ray Tracing for Computer Synthesized Images', Master's thesis, Program of Computer Graphics, Cornell University, January 1979.
Kay-79b Kay, Douglas S., and Greenberg, Donald, 'Transparency for Computer Synthesized Images', *Computer Graphics*, Vol. 13, pp. 158–164, 1979 (Proc. SIGGRAPH 79).
Kay-86 Kay, Timothy L., 'Ray Tracing Complex Scenes', *Computer Graphics*, Vol. 20, No. 4, pp. 269–278, August 1986 (Proc. SIGGRAPH 86).
Kelley-88 Kelley, Alex D., Malin, M. C., and Nielson, G. M., 'Terrain Simulation Using a Model of Stream Erosion', *Computer Graphics*, Vol. 22, No. 4, pp.

263–268, August 1988 (Proc. SIGGRAPH 88).
Kernighan-78 Kernighan, Brian W., and Ritchie, Dennis M., *The C Programming Language,* Prentice-Hall, Englewood Cliffs, NJ, 1978.
Kessner-85 Kessner, L. R. A., Peters, F. J., and van Lierop, M. L. P., (eds), *Data Structures for Raster Graphics,* Proc. of a Workshop held at Steensel, Springer-Verlag, Berlin, 1985.
Kirk-87 Kirk, D. B., 'The Simulation of Natural Features Using Cone Tracing', *The Visual Computer,* Vol. 3, No. 2, pp. 63–71, 1987.
Koch-06 Koch, H. von, 'An Elementary Geometric Method for Studying Some Questions in the Theory of Planar Curves', *Acta Mthematica,* Vol. 30, pp. 145–174, 1906.
Kochan-86 Kochan, D. (ed.), *CAM: Developments in Computer-integrated Manufacturing*, Springer-Verlag, Berlin, 1986.
Korein-83 Korein, J., and Badler, V. R., 'Temporal Anti-aliasing in Computer Generated Animation', *Computer Graphics*, Vol. 17, pp. 377–388, July 1983 (Proc. SIGGRAPH 83).
Korkhage-66 Korfage, Robert R., *Logic and Algorithms,* Wiley, New York, 1966.
Kornfeld-87 Kornfeld, Cary, 'The Image Prism: A Device for Rotating and Mirroring Bitmap Images', *IEEE, CG&A*, Vol. 7, No. 5, pp. 21–30, May 1987.
Kuni-83 Kuni, T. L. (ed.), *Computer Graphics, Proc. InterGraphics '83*, Springer-Verlag, Berlin,1983.

Laidlaw-86 Laidlaw, David H., Trumbore, W. Benjamin, and Hughes, John F., 'Constructive Solid Geometry for Polyhedral Objects', *Computer Graphics,* Vol. 20, No. 4, pp. 161–170, August 1986 (Proc. SIGGRAPH 86).
Lane-79 Lane, J. M., and Carpenter, L. C., 'A Generalized Scan Line Algorithm for the Computer Display of Parametrically Defined Surfaces', *Computer Graphics and Image Processing*, Vol. 11, pp. 290–297, 1979.
Lane-80 Lane, J. M., Carpenter, L. C., Whitted, T., and Blinn, J. F., 'Scan Line Methods for Displaying Parametrically Defined Surfaces', *CACM*, Vol. 23, pp. 23–34, 1980.
Lasseter-87 Lasseter, John, 'Principles of Traditional Animation Applied to 3D Computer Animation', *Computer Graphics*, Vol. 21, No. 4, pp. 35–44, July 1987 (Proc. SIGGRAPH 87).
Laws-75 Laws, B. A., 'A Gray-scale Graphic Processor Using Run-length Encoding', *Proc. IEEE Conf. Computer Graphics, Pattern Recognition, Data Structures*, pp. 7–10, May 1975.
Lee-85 Lee, R. A., Redner, R. A., and Uselton, S. P., 'Statistically Optimized Sampling for Distributed Ray Tracing', *Computer Graphics*, Vol. 19, No. 3, pp. 61–67, July 1985 (Proc. SIGGRAPH 85).
Lee-87 Lee, Y. C., 'Machine Understanding of CSG: Extraction and Unification of Manufacturing Features', *IEEE, CG&A,* Vol. 7, No. 1, pp. 20–32, January 1987.
Levoy-88 Levoy, Marc, 'Display of Surfaces from Volume Data', *IEEE, CG&A*, Vol. 8, No. 3, pp. 29–37, May 1988.
Lewis-89 Lewis, J. P., 'Algorithms for Solid Noise Synthesis', *Computer Graphics*, Vol. 23, No. 3, pp. 263–270, July 1989 (Proc. SIGGRAPH 89).
Liang-83 Liang, You-Dong, and Barsky, Brian, 'An Analysis and Algorithm for Polygon Clipping', *CACM*, Vol. 26, pp. 868–877, 1983.
Lien-87 Lien, Sheue-Ling, Shantz, Michael, and Pratt, Vaughan, 'Adaptive Forward Differencing for Rendering Curves and Surfaces', *Computer Graphics,* Vol. 21, No. 4, pp. 111–118, July 1987 (Proc. SIGGRAPH 87).
Lim-87 Lim, H. L., 'Fast Hidden Surface Removal Through Structural Analysis and Representation of Objects and Their Contours', *Computer Graphics 1987* (ed. Kuni, T. L.), Springer-Verlag, Tokyo, pp. 75–88, 1987.
Lindbloom-89 Lindbloom, Bruce J., 'Accurate Color Reproduction for Computer Graphics Applications', *Computer Graphics*, Vol. 23, No. 3, pp. 117–126, July 1989 (Proc. SIGGRAPH 89).

Lorensen-87 Lorensen, William E., and Cline, Harvey E., 'Marching Cubes: A High Resolution 3D Surface Construction Algorithm', *Computer Graphics*, Vol. 21, No. 4, pp. 163–169, July 1987 (Proc. SIGGRAPH 87).

Lorig-86 Lorig, G., 'Advanced Image Synthesis: Shading', *Advances in Computer Graphics*, (eds Enderle, I. G., Grave, M., and Lillehagen, F.), Springer-Verlag, Berlin, pp. 441–456, 1986.

MacBeath-64 MacBeath, A. M., *Elementary Vector Algebra*, Oxford University Press, Oxford, 1964.

Magnenat-Thalmann-85 Magnenat-Thalmann, Nadia, and Thalmann, Daniel, *Computer Animation,* Springer-Verlag, Berlin,1985.

Magnenat-Thalmann-86 Magnenat-Thalmann, Nadia, Thalmann, Daniel, and Bland, S., 'The Integration of Particle and Polygon Rendering Using an A-buffer Algorithm', *Proc. Eurographics 86,* North-Holland, Amsterdam, pp. 161–169, 1986.

Magnenat-Thalmann-87a Magnenat-Thalmann, Nadia, and Thalmann, Daniel, 'An Indexed Bibliography on Image Synthesis', *IEEE, CG&A*, Vol. 7, No. 8, pp. 27–38, August 1987.

Magnenat-Thalmann-87b Magnenat-Thalmann, Nadia, *et al.*, 'A Geometric Study of Parameters for the Recursive Midpoint Subdivision', *Computer Graphics 1987*, (ed. Kuni, T. L.), Springer-Verlag, Tokyo, pp. 45–55, 1987.

Mammen-89 Mammen, Abraham, 'Transparency and Antialiasing Algorithms Implemented with the Virtual Pixel Maps Technique', *IEEE, CG&A*, Vol. 9, No. 4, pp. 43–55, July 1989.

Mandelbrot-68 Mandelbrot, Benoit, and van Ness, J., 'Fractional Brownian Motions, Fractional Noises and Applications', *SIAM Review*, Vol. 10, No. 4, pp. 422–437, 1968.

Mandelbrot-75 Mandelbrot, Benoit, 'Stochastic Models of the Earth's Relief, the Shape and Fractal Dimension of Coastlines, and the Number Area Rule for Islands', *Proc. National Academy of Sciences, USA,* Vol. 72, No. 10, pp. 2825–2828, 1975.

Mandelbrot-77 Mandelbrot, B., *Fractals Form, Chance, and Dimension*, W.H. Freeman, San Francisco, 1977.

Mandelbrot-82 Mandelbrot, Benoit, *The Fractal Geometry of Nature,* W.H. Freeman, New York, 1982.

Mao-87 Mao, Xiaoyang, Kunii, L., Fujishiro, Issei, and Noma, Tsukasa, 'Hierarchical Representations of 2D/3D Gray-scale Images and their 2D/3D Two-way Conversion', *IEEE, CG&A,* Vol. 7, No. 12, pp. 37–44, December 1987.

Markov-61 Markov, A. A., *Theory of Algorithms,* Israel Program for Scientific Translations, Jerusalem, 1961.

Marshall-80 Marshall, R., Wilson, R., and Carlson, Wayne, 'Procedural Models for Generating Three-dimensional Terrain', *Computer Graphics,* Vol. 14, pp. 154–162, July 1980 (Proc. SIGGRAPH 80).

Mastin-87 Mastin, Gary A., Watterberg, Peter A., and Mareda, John F., 'Fourier Synthesis of Ocean Scenes', *IEEE, CG&A*, Vol. 7, No. 3, pp. 16–23, March 1987.

Max-83 Max, Nelson L., 'Computer Representation of Molecular Surfaces', *IEEE, CG&A*, Vol. 3, No. 5, pp. 21–29, 1983.

Max-85 Max, Nelson L., and Lerner, Douglas M., 'A Two-and-a-Half-D Motion-Blur Algorithm', *Computer Graphics*, Vol. 19, No. 3, pp. 85–93, July 1985 (Proc. SIGGRAPH 85).

Max-86 Max, Nelson L., 'Atmospheric Illumination and Shadows', *Computer Graphics,* Vol. 20, No. 4, pp. 117–124, August 1986 (Proc. SIGGRAPH 86).

Max-88 Max, Nelson L., and Getzoff, Elizabeth D., 'Spherical Harmonic Molecular Surfaces', *IEEE, CG&A*, Vol. 8, No. 4, pp. 42–50, July 1988.

Max-90 Max, Nelson L., 'Antialiasing Scan-line Data', *IEEE, CG&A,* Vol. 10, No. 1, pp. 18–30, January 1990.

Meyer-80 Meyer, Gary W., and Greenberg, Donald, 'Perceptual Color Spaces for Computer Graphics', *Computer Graphics*, Vol. 14, pp. 254–261, August

1980 (Proc. SIGGRAPH 80).
Meyer-88 Meyer, Gary W., and Greenberg, Donald P., 'Color-defective Vision and Computer Graphics Displays', *IEEE, CG&A,* Vol. 8, No. 5, pp. 28–40, September 1988.
Middleditch-85 Middleditch, Alan E., 'Blend Surfaces for Set Theoretic Volume Modelling Systems', *Computer Graphics*, Vol. 19, No. 3, pp. 161–170, July 1985 (Proc. SIGGRAPH 85).
Middleton-52 Middleton, W. E. Knowles, *Vision through the Atmosphere*, University of Toronto Press, Toronto, 1952.
Miller-86 Miller, G. S. P., 'The Definition and Rendering of Terrain Maps', *Computer Graphics,* Vol. 20, No. 4, pp. 39–48, August 1986 (Proc. SIGGRAPH 86).
Miller-88a Miller, Gavin S. P., 'The Motion Dynamics of Snakes and Worms', *Computer Graphics,* Vol. 22, No. 4, pp. 169–178, August 1988 (Proc. SIGGRAPH 88).
Miller-88b Miller, James, R., 'Analysis of Quadratic-surface Based Solid Models', *IEEE, CG&A*, Vol. 8, No. 1, pp. 28–42, January 1988.
Miller-89 Miller, James R., 'Architectural Issues in Solid Modelers', *IEEE, CG&A*, Vol. 9, No. 5, pp. 72–87, 1989.
Mirolo-89 Mirolo, Claudio, and Pagello, Enrico, 'A Solid Modelling System for Robot Action Planning', *IEEE, CG&A,* Vol. 9, No. 1, pp. 55–69, July 1989.
Monne-81 Monne, J., Schmitt, F., and Massaloux, D., 'Bidimensional Texture Synthesis by Markov Chains', *Computer Graphics and Image Processing*, Vol. 17, pp. 1–23, 1981.
Moore-88 Moore, Matthew, and Wilhelms, Jane, 'Collision Detection and Response for Computer Animation', *Computer Graphics,* Vol. 22, No. 4, pp. 289–298, August 1988 (Proc. SIGGRAPH 88).
Mumford-88 Mumford, A., and Skall, M., *CGM and the Real World,* Springer-Verlag, Berlin, 1988.
Mumford-89 Mumford, Anne M., 'CG-on File', *Proc. Computer Graphics '89, London,* pp. 349-357, November 1989, Blenheim-Online, London.
Munsell-41 Munsell, A. H., *A Color Notation,* 9th edn, Munsell Color Company, Baltimore, MD, 1941.
Musgrave-89 Musgrave, F. Kenton, Kolb, Craig E., and Mace, Robert S., 'The Synthesis and Rendering of Eroded Fractal Terrains', *Computer Graphics,* Vol. 23, No. 3, pp. 41–50, July 1989 (Proc. SIGGRAPH 89).
Myers-75 Myers, A. J., 'An Efficient Visible Surface Program', Report to the NSF, Ohio State University Computer Graphics Research Group, July 1975.
Myers-86 Myers, Brad A., 'What are Visual Programming, Programming by Example, and Program Visualization?', *Proc. of Graphics Interface 1986.*
Myers-88 Myers, Brad, 'A Taxonomy of Window Manager User Interfaces', *IEEE, CG&A*, Vol. 8, No. 5, pp. 65–84, September 1988.

Naiman-87 Naiman, Avi, and Fournier, Alain, 'Rectangular Convolution for Fast Filtering of Characters', *Computer Graphics*, Vol. 21, No. 4, pp. 233–242, July 1987 (Proc. SIGGRAPH 87).
Nakamae-86 Nakamae, Eihachiro Nakamae, Harada Koichi, and Ishizaki, Takao, 'A Montage Method: The Overlaying of the Computer Generated Images onto a Background Photograph', *Computer Graphics,* Vol. 20, No. 4, pp. 207–214, August 1986 (Proc. SIGGRAPH 86).
Nakamae-89 Nakamae, Eihachiro, Ishizaki, Takao, Nishita, Tomoyuki, and Takita, Shinichi, 'Compositing 3D Images with Antialiasing and Various Shading Effects', *IEEE, CG&A*, Vol. 9, No. 2, pp. 21–29, March 1989.
Newell-72 Newell, M. E., Newell, R. G., and Sancha, T. L., 'A Solution to the Hidden Surface Problem', *Proc. ACM Annual Conf., Boston, August 1972,* pp. 443–450.
Newman-79 Newman, W. M., and Sproull, R. F., *Principles of Interactive Computer Graphics,* 2nd edn, McGraw-Hill, New York, 1979.
Nicholl-87 Nicholl, Tina M., Lee, D. T., and Nicholl,

Robin A., 'An Efficient New Algorithm for 2-D Line Clipping: its Development and Analysis', *Computer Graphics*, Vol. 21, No. 4, pp. 253–262, July 1987 (Proc. SIGGRAPH 87).

Nishita-87 Nishita, Tomoyuki, 'A Shading Model for Atmospheric Scattering Considering Luminous Intensity Distribution of Light Sources', *Computer Graphics,* Vol. 21, No. 4, pp. 303–310, July 1987 (Proc. SIGGRAPH 87).

Nye-87 Nye, Adrian, *The X Window System,* Programming Manual for Version 11, Release 1, Vol. 1, O'Reilly & Associates,1987.

Oka-87 Oka, Masaaki, Tsutui, Kyoya, Ohba, Akio, Kurauchi, Yoshitaka, and Tago, Takashi, 'Real-time Manipulation of Texture-mapped Surfaces', *Computer Graphics*, Vol. 21, No. 4, pp. 181–188, July 1987 (Proc. SIGGRAPH 87).

Okino-84 Okino, N., Kakazu, Y., and Morimoto, M., 'Extended Depth Buffer Algorithms for Hidden-Surface Visualization', *IEEE, CG&A,* Vol. 4, No. 5, pp. 79–88, 1984.

Oppenheim-75 Oppenheim, A. V., and Schafer, R. W., *Digital Signal Processing*, Prentice-Hall, Englewood Cliffs, NJ, 1975.

Oppenheimer-86 Oppenheimer, Peter E., 'Real Time Design and Animation of Fractal Plants and Trees', *Computer Graphics,* Vol. 20, No. 4, pp. 55–64, August 1986 (Proc. SIGGRAPH 86).

Ostwald-31 Ostwald, N., *Colour Science*, Vols I and II, Winsor & Winsor, London, 1931.

Overhauser-68 Overhauser, A. W., 'Analytic Definition of Curves and Surfaces by Parabolic Blending', Ford Motor Company Scientific Laboratories Technical Report SL68-40.

Overington-76 Overington, Ian, *Vision and Acquisition,* Pentech Press, 1976.

Painter-89 Painter, James, and Sloan, Kenneth, 'Antialiased Ray Tracing by Adaptive Progressive Refinement', *Computer Graphics*, Vol. 23, No. 3, pp. 281–288, July 1989 (Proc. SIGGRAPH 89).

Papathomas-88 Papathomas, T. V., Schiavone, J. A., and Julesz, B., 'Application of Computer Graphics to the Visualization of Meteorological Data', *Computer Graphics,* Vol. 22, No. 4, pp. 327–334, August 1988 (Proc. SIGGRAPH 88).

Pavlidis-82 Pavlidis, Theo, *Algorithms for Graphics and Image Processing,* Computer Science Press, Rockville, MD, 1982.

Peachey-85 Peachey, Darwyn R., 'Solid Texturing of Complex Surfaces', *Computer Graphics,* Vol. 19, No. 3, pp. 279–286, July 1985 (Proc. SIGGRAPH 85).

Peachey-86 Peachey, Darwyn R., 'Modeling Waves and Surf', *Computer Graphics,* Vol. 20, No. 4, pp. 65–74, August 1986 (Proc. SIGGRAPH 86).

Peano-90 Peano, G., 'Sur une courbe, qui remplit toute une aire plaine', *Mathematische Annalen,* Vol. 36, pp. 157–160, 1890.

Peitgen-86 Peitgen, Heinz-Otto, and Richter, Peter H., *The Beauty of Fractals,* Springer-Verlag, Berlin,1986.

Peitgen-88 Peitgen, Heinz-Otto, and Saupe, Dietmar, (eds), *The Science of Fractal Images*, Springer-Verlag, New York, 1988.

Pentland-89 Pentland, Alex, and Williams, John, 'Good Vibrations: Modal Dynamics for Graphics and Animation', *Computer Graphics*, Vol. 23, No. 3, pp. 215–222, July 1989 (Proc. SIGGRAPH 89).

Perlin-85 Perlin, Ken, 'An Image Synthesizer', *Computer Graphics,* Vol. 19, No. 3, pp. 287–296, July 1985 (Proc. SIGGRAPH 85).

Perlin-89 Perlin, Ken, and Hoffert, Eric M., 'Hypertexture', *Computer Graphics,* Vol. 23, No. 3, pp. 253–262, July 1989 (Proc. SIGGRAPH 89).

Phong-73 Phong, Bui-Tuong, 'Illumination for Computer Generated Images', Doctoral thesis, University of Utah, 1973; also in *CACM*, Vol. 18, pp. 311–317, 1973.

Piegl-87a Piegl, L., 'Infinite Control Points – A Method for Representing Surfaces of Revolution Using Boundary Data', *IEEE, CG&A*, Vol. 7, No. 3, pp. 45–55,

March 1987.
Piegl-87b Piegl, L., 'Interactive Data Interpolation by Rational Bézier Curves', *IEEE, CG&A,* Vol. 7, No. 4, pp. 45–61, April 1987.
Piegl-89 Piegl, Leslie, and Tiller, Wayne, 'A Menagerie of Rational B-spline Circles', *IEEE, CG&A*, Vol. 9, No. 5, pp. 48–56, September 1989.
Pineda-88 Pineda, Juan, 'A Parallel Algorithm for Polygon Rasterization', *Computer Graphics,* Vol. 22, No. 4, pp. 17–20, August 1988 (Proc. SIGGRAPH 88)
Pins-89 Pins, Markus, and Hild, Hermann, 'Variations on a Dither Algorithm', *Proc. Eurographics 89, Hamburg*, North Holland, Amsterdam, pp. 381–392, 1989.
Pirsch-83 Pirsch, P., and Netravali, A. N., 'Transmission of Gray Level Images by Multilevel Dither Techniques', *Computer Graphics,* Vol. 7, pp. 31–44, 1983.
Pitteway-67 Pitteway, M. L. V., 'Algorithm for Drawing Ellipses or Hyperbolas with a Digital Plotter', *Computer Journal,* Vol. 10, pp. 282–289, 1967.
Pixar-87 Pixar Inc., 'Pseudo-random point sampling techniques in computer graphics', UK Patent GB 2,177,577 A, 1987.
Platt-88 Platt, John C., and Barr, Alan H., 'Constraint Methods for Flexible Models', *Computer Graphics*, Vol. 22, No. 4, pp. 279–288, August 1988 (Proc. SIGGRAPH 88).
Porter-79 Porter, T., 'The Shaded Surface Display of Large Molecules', *Computer Graphics,* Vol. 13, pp. 234-236, 1979 (Proc. SIGGRAPH 79).
Porter-84 Porter, T., and Duff, T., 'Compositing Digital Images', *Computer Graphics*, Vol. 18, No. 3, pp. 253–259, 1984 (Proc. SIGGRAPH 84).
Potmesil-81 Potmesil, Michael, and Chakravarty, I., 'A Lens and Aperture Camera Model for Synthetic Image Generation', *Computer Graphics*, Vol. 15, pp. 297–305, 1981 (Proc. SIGGRAPH 81).
Potmesil-82 Potmesil, Michael, and Chakravarty, I., 'Synthetic Image Generation with a Lens and Aperture Camera Model', *ACM Trans. Graphics*, Vol. 1, pp. 85–108, 1982.
Potmesil-83 Potmesil, Michael, and Chakravarty, I., 'Modelling Motion Blur in Computer-generated Images', *Computer Graphics,* Vol. 17, pp. 389–399, July 1983 (Proc. SIGGRAPH 83).
Potmesil-87 Potmesil, Michael, and Hoffert, Eric M., 'FRAMES: Software Tools for Modelling, Rendering and Animation of 3D Scenes', *Computer Graphics*, Vol. 21, No. 4, pp. 85–93, July 1987 (Proc. SIGGRAPH 87).
Potmesil-89 Potmesil, Michael, McMillan, Leonard, *et al.,* 'A Parallel Image Computer with a Distributed Frame Buffer: System Architecture and Programming', *Proc. Eurographics 89*, *Hamburg,* North-Holland, Amsterdam, pp. 197–220, 1989.
Pratt-78 Pratt, William K., *Digital Image Processing,* Wiley, London, 1978.
Preparata-85 Preparata, F. P., and Shamos, M. I., *Computational Geometry: An Introduction,* Springer-Verlag, Berlin, 1985.
Prusinkiewicz-88a Prusinkiewicz, Przemyslaw, Lindenmayer, Aristid, and Hanan, James, 'Development Models of Herbaceous Plants for Computer Imagery Purposes', *Computer Graphics*, Vol. 22, No. 4, pp. 141–150, August 1988 (Proc. SIGGRAPH 88).
Prusinkiewicz-88b Prusinkiewicz, Przemyslaw, and Sandness, Glenn, 'Koch Curves as Attractors and Repellers', *IEEE, CG&A,* Vol. 8, No. 6, pp. 26–40, November 1988.
Purgathofer-86 Purgathofer, W., 'A Statistical Method for Adaptive Stochastic Sampling', *Proc. Eurographics 86,* North-Holland, Amsterdam, pp. 145–152, 1986.

Quantel-81 Quantel Ltd., 'Video Image Creation', UK Patent GB 2,089,625B, 1981.

Reeves-81 Reeves, W., 'Inbetweening for Computer Animation using Moving Point Constraints', *Computer Graphics*, Vol. 15, No. 3, pp. 263–269, August 1981

(Proc. SIGGRAPH 81).
Reeves-83 Reeves, William T., 'Particle Systems – A Technique for Modelling a Class of Fuzzy Objects', *Computer Graphics*, Vol. 17, pp. 359-376, July 1983 (Proc. SIGGRAPH 83).
Reeves-85 Reeves, William T., 'Approximate and Probabilistic Algorithms for Shading and Rendering Structured Particle Systems', *Computer Graphics,* Vol. 19, No. 3, pp. 313–322, July 1985 (Proc. SIGGRAPH 85).
Reeves-87 Reeves, William T., Salesin, David H., and Cook, Robert L., 'Rendering Antialiased Shadows with Depth Maps', *Computer Graphics*, Vol. 21, No. 4, pp. 283–291, July 1987 (Proc. SIGGRAPH 87).
Rembold-86 Rembold, U., and Dillmann, R., (eds), *Computer-aided Design and Manufacturing*, Springer Verlag, Berlin, 1986.
Reynolds-87 Reynolds, Craig W., 'Flocks, Herds, and Schools: A Distributed Behavioural Model', *Computer Graphics*, Vol. 21, pp. 25–34, July 1987 (Proc. SIGGRAPH 87).
Rhoden-89 Rhoden, Desi, and Wilcox, Chris, 'Hardware Acceleration for Window Systems', *Computer Graphics*, Vol. 23, No. 3, pp. 61–67, July 1989 (Proc. SIGGRAPH 89).
Robertson-85 Robertson, Phillip K., and O'Callaghan, J. F., 'The Applications of Scene Synthesis Techniques to the Display of Multidimensional Data', *ACM Trans. Graphics,* Vol.4, No. 4, pp. 247–275, 1985.
Robertson-88 Robertson, Phillip K., 'Visualizing Color Gamuts: A User Interface for the Effective Use of Perceptual Color Spaces in Data Displays', *IEEE, CG&A,* Vol. 8, No. 5, pp. 50–64, September 1988.
Robertson-89 Robertson, Phillip K., 'Spatial Transformations for Rapid Scan-line Surface Shadowing', *IEEE, CG&A,* Vol. 9, No. 2, pp. 30–38, March 1989.
Rochester-87 University of Rochester, 'Computer Systems for Curve-solid Classification and Solid Modelling', USA Patent 4,649,498, 1987.
Rockwood-87 Rockwood, Alyn, 'A Generalized Scanning Technique for Display of Parametrically Defined Surfaces', *IEEE, CG&A,* Vol. 7, No. 8, pp. 15–26, August 1987.
Rockwood-89 Rockwood, Alyn, Heaton, Kurt, and Davis, Tom, 'Real-time Rendering of Trimmed Surfaces', *Computer Graphics*, Vol. 23, No. 3, pp. 107–116, July 1989 (Proc. SIGGRAPH 89).
Rogers-85 Rogers, David F., *Procedural Elements for Computer Graphics,* McGraw-Hill, New York, 1985.
Rogers-89 Rogers, David F., and Adams, J. Alan, *Mathematical Elements for Computer Graphics*, 2nd edn, McGraw-Hill, New York, 1989.
Romney-68 Romney, G. W., Watkins, G. S., and Evans, D. C., 'Real Time Display of Computer Generated Half-tone Perspective Pictures', *IFIP 1968,* North-Holland, Amsterdam, pp. 973–978, 1968.
Roth-82 Roth, Scott D., 'Ray Casting for Modelling Solids', *Computer Graphics and Image Processing,* Vol. 18, pp. 109–144, 1982.
Rubin-80 Rubin, S., and Whitted, T. A., 'À Three-dimensional Representation for Fast Rendering of Complex Scenes', *Computer Graphics*, Vol. 14, No. 3, pp. 110–116, July 1980 (Proc. SIGGRAPH 80).
Rushmeier-87 Rushmeier, Holly E., and Torrance, Kenneth E., 'The Zonal Method for Calculating Light Intensities in the Presence of a Participating Medium', *Computer Graphics,* Vol. 21, No. 4, pp. 293–302, July 1987 (Proc. SIGGRAPH 87).

Sabella-88 Sabella, Paolo, 'A Rendering Algorithm for Visualizing 3D Scalar Fields', *Computer Graphics*, Vol. 22, No. 4, pp. 51–58, August 1988 (Proc. SIGGRAPH 88).
Sablonnière-85 Sablonnière, Paul, 'Bernstein–Bézier Methods for the Construction of Bivariate Spline Approximants', *Computer Aided Geometric Design*, Vol. 2, pp. 29–36, 1985.
Salesin-89 Salesin, D., and Stolfi, J., 'The ZZ-Buffer: a Simple and Efficient Rendering Algorithm with Reliable Antialiasing', *Proc. ACM SIGGRAPH PIXIM 89*

Paris 2nd Conference, pp. 451–466, 1989.
Samek-86 Samek, M., Slean, C., and Weghorst, H., 'Texture Mapping and Distortion in Digital Graphics', *The Visual Computer,* Vol. 2, No. 5, pp. 313–321, 1986.
Samet-88a Samet, Hanan, and Webber, Robert E., 'Hierarchical Data Structures and Algorithms for Computer Graphics', *IEEE, CG&A*, Vol. 8, No. 3, pp. 48–68, May 1988.
Samet-88b Samet, Hanan, and Webber, Robert E., 'Hierarchical Data Structures and Algorithms for Computer Graphics', *IEEE, CG&A,* Vol. 8, No. 4, pp. 59–75, July 1988.
Schachter-83 Schachter, Bruce J., *Computer Image Generation*, Wiley, London, 1983.
Schafer-89 Schafer, Mark, 'Displacement Animation', *Proc. Computer Graphics '89,* pp. 197–216, November 1989, Blenheim-Online, London.
Scheifler-88 Scheifler, Robert W., 'X Window System Protocol, Release 2, X Version 11', MIT, Laboratory for Computer Science, 1988.
Schumacker-69 Schumacker, R. A., Brand, B., Gilliland, M., and Sharp, W., 'Study for Applying Computer Generated Images to Simulation', AFHRL-TR-69-14, Air Force Human Resources Laboratory, Wright-Patterson AFB, OH, September 1969.
Sederberg-86 Sederberg, Thomas W., and Parry, Scott R., 'Free-form Deformation of Solid Geometric Models', *Computer Graphics*, Vol. 20, No. 4, August 1986 (Proc. SIGGRAPH 86).
Segal-88 Segal, Mark, and Sequin, Carlo H., 'Partitioning Polyhedral Objects into Nonintersecting Parts', *IEEE, CG&A*, Vol. 8, No. 1, pp. 53–67, January 1988.
Sequin-89 Sequin, Carlo H., and Eliot, K. Smyrl, 'Parameterized Ray Tracing', *Computer Graphics,* Vol. 23, No. 3, pp. 307–314, July 1989 (Proc. SIGGRAPH 89).
Shantz-87 Shantz, Michael, and Lien, Sheue-Ling, 'Shading Bicubic Patches', *Computer Graphics*, Vol. 21, No. 4, pp. 189–196, July 1987 (Proc. SIGGRAPH 87).
Shantz-88 Shantz, Michael, and Chang, Sheue-Ling, 'Rendering Trimmed NURBS with Adaptive Forward Differencing', *Computer Graphics,* Vol. 22, No. 4, pp. 189–198, August 1988 (Proc. SIGGRAPH 88).
Shao-88 Shao, Min-Zhi, Peng, Qun-Sheng and Liang, You-Dong, 'A New Radiosity Approach by Procedural Refinements for Realistic Image Synthesis', *Computer Graphics*, Vol. 22, No. 4, pp. 93–101, August 1988 (Proc. SIGGRAPH 88).
Shapiro-60 Shapiro, H. S., and Silverman, R. A. 'Alias-free Sampling of Random Noise', *SIAM Journal*, Vol. 8, No. 2, pp. 225–248, June 1960.
Shinya-87 Shinya, Mikio, Takahashi, Tokiichiro, and Naito, Seiichiro, 'Principles and Applications of Pencil Tracing', *Computer Graphics*, Vol. 21, No. 4, pp. 45–54, July 1987 (Proc. SIGGRAPH 87).
Shirai-86 Shirai, Y., *Three-Dimensional Computer Vision*, Springer-Verlag, Berlin, 1986.
Shoemake-85 Shoemake, Ken, 'Animating Rotation with Quaternion Curves', *Computer Graphics*, Vol. 19, No. 3, pp. 245–254, July 1985 (Proc. SIGGRAPH 85).
Shuey-86 Shuey, D., Bailey, D., and Morrissey, T. P., 'PHIGS: A Standard, Dynamic, Interactive Graphics Interface', *IEEE, CG&A*, Vol. 6, No. 8, pp. 50–58, 1986.
Sierpinski-12 Sierpinski, W., 'Sur une nouvelle courbe qui remplit toute une aire plaine', *Bulletin Academie Sciences Cracovie, Series* A, pp. 462–478, 1912.
Sillion-89 Sillion, Francois, and Puech, Claude, 'A General Two-pass Method Integrating Specular and Diffuse Reflection', *Computer Graphics,* Vol. 23, No. 3, pp. 335–344, July 1989 (Proc. SIGGRAPH 89).
Singer-86 The Singer Company, 'Modular Digital Image Generator', US Patent 4,570,233, 1986.
Smith-78a Smith, Alvy Ray, 'Color Gamut Transformation Pairs', *Computer Graphics,* Vol. 12, pp. 12–19, 1978 (Proc. SIGGRAPH 78).
Smith-78b Smith, Alvy Ray, 'PAINT', Technical

Memo No. 7, New York Institute of Technology, 1978.
Smith-79 Smith, Alvy Ray, 'Tint Fill', *Computer Graphics*, Vol. 13, pp. 276–283, 1979.
Smith-83 Smith, Alvy Ray, 'Spline Tutorial Notes', Technical Memo No. 77, Computer Graphics Project, Lucasfilm, 1983.
Smith-84 Smith, Alvy Ray, 'Plants, Fractals and Formal Languages', *Computer Graphics*, Vol. 18, No. 3, pp. 1–10, July 1984 (Proc. SIGGRAPH 84).
Smith-85 Smith, Alvy Ray, 'Tutorial Notes: Introduction to Computer Animation', *Computer Graphics,* Vol. 19, pp. 112–123, July 1985 (Proc. SIGGRAPH 85).
Smith-87 Smith, Alvy Ray, 'Planar 2-pass Texture Mapping and Warping', *Computer Graphics,* Vol. 21, No. 4, pp. 263–272, July 1987 (Proc. SIGGRAPH 87).
Sproull-68 Sproull, Robert F., and Sutherland, Ivan E., 'A Clipping Divider', *1968 Fall Joint Computer Conference,* Thompson Books, Washington, DC, pp. 765–775, 1968.
Sproull-85 Sproull, R. F., Sutherland, W. R., and Ullner, M. K., *Device Independent Graphics,* McGraw-Hill, New York, 1985.
Standish-80 Standish, Thomas A., *Data Structures Techniques*, Addison-Wesley, Reading, MA, 1980.
Staudhammer-78 Staudhammer, J., 'On the Display of Space Filling Atomic Models in Real Time', *Computer Graphics*, Vol. 12, pp. 167–172, 1978 (Proc. SIGGRAPH 78).
Steele-89 Steele, Bruce, 'OOP Gets the Message Across', *Proc. CG-89, London,* pp. 207–216, Blenheim-0nline, London, 1989.
Stevenson-74 Stevenson, G., *An Introduction to Matrices, Sets and Groups*, Longman, Harlow, 1974.
Strassmann-86 Strassmann, Steve, 'Hairy Brushes', *Computer Graphics*, Vol. 20, No. 4, pp. 225–232, August 1986 (Proc. SIGGRAPH 86).
Suenaga-79 Suenaga, Y., Kamae, T., and Kobayashi, T., 'A High-speed Algorithm for the Generation of Straight Lines and Circular Arcs', *IEEE, Trans. Comput.*, Vol. C-28, pp. 728–736, 1979.
Sutherland-74a Sutherland, Ivan E., and Hodgman, Gary W., 'Reentrant Polygon Clipping', *CACM*, Vol. 17, pp. 32–42, 1974.
Sutherland-74b Sutherland, Ivan E., Sproull, Robert F., and Schumacker, R. A., 'A Characterization of Ten Hidden-surface Algorithms', *Computing Surveys*, Vol. 6, pp. 1–55, 1974.

Terzopoulos-87 Terzopoulos, Demetri, Platt, J., and Fleischer, K., 'Elastically Deformable Models', *Computer Graphics*, Vol. 21, No. 4, pp. 205–214, July 1987 (Proc. SIGGRAPH 87).
Terzopoulos-88a Terzopoulos, Demetri, and Fleischer, Kurt, 'Modelling Inelastic Deformation: Viscoelasticity, Plasticity, Fracture', *Computer Graphics,* Vol. 22, No. 4, pp. 269–278, August 1988 (Proc. SIGGRAPH 88).
Terzopoulos-88b Terzopoulos, Demetri, and Witkin, Andrew, 'Physically Based Models with Rigid and Deformable Components', *IEEE, CG&A,* Vol. 8, No. 6, pp. 41–51, November 1988.
Tezenas du Montcel-85 Tezenas du Montcel, B., and Nicolas, A., 'An Illumination Model for Ray-tracing', *Proc. Eurographics 85*, North-Holland, Amsterdam, pp. 63–75, 1985.
Thibault-87 Thibault, William C., and Naylor, Bruce F., 'Set Operations on Polyhedra Using Binary Space Partitioning Trees', *Computer Graphics*, Vol. 21, No. 4, pp. 153–162, July 1987 (Proc. SIGGRAPH 87).
Thiemann-89 Thiemann, Rolf, 'Visualisation of Digital Terrain Data', *Proc. Eurographics 89,* North-Holland, Amsterdam, pp. 173–195, 1989.
Torborg-87 Torborg, John G., 'A Parallel Processor Architecture for Graphics Arithmetic Operations', *Computer Graphics*, Vol. 21, No. 4, pp. 197–204, July 1987 (Proc. SIGGRAPH 87).
Torrance-67 Torrance, K. E., and Sparrow, E. M., 'Theory for Off-specular Reflection from Roughened Surfaces', *Journal of the Optical Society of America*, Vol. 57, pp. 1105–1114, 1967.

Upson-86 Upson, Craig, 'The Visualisation of Amorphous Phenomena', *The Visual Computer*, Vol. 2, No. 5, pp. 321–326, 1986.
Upson-88 Upson, Craig, 'V-Buffer: Visible Volume Rendering', *Computer Graphics*, Vol. 22, No. 4, pp. 59–64, August 1988 (Proc. SIGGRAPH 88).
Upson-89 Upson, Craig, *et al.,* 'The Application Visualization System: A Computational Environment for Scientific Visualization', *IEEE, CG&A,* Vol. 9, No. 4, pp. 30–42, July 1989.
Upstill-90 Upstill, Steve, *The RenderMan Companion,* Addison-Wesley, Reading, MA, 1990.

Van Dam-88 Van Dam, Andries, *et al.,* 'PHIGS+ Functional Description Revision 3.0', *Computer Graphics,* Vol. 22, No. 3, pp. 125-218, July 1988.
Verbeck-84 Verbeck, C. P., and Greenberg, D. P., 'A Comprehensive Light-source Description for Computer Graphics', *IEEE, CG&A,* Vol. 4, No. 7, pp. 66–75, 1984.
Viennot-89 Viennot, Xavier Gerard, Eyrolles, Geroges, Janey, Nicolas, and Arques, Didier, 'Combinatorial Analysis of Ramified Patterns and Computer Imagery of Trees', *Computer Graphics,* Vol. 23, No. 3, pp. 31–40, July 1989 (Proc. SIGGRAPH 89).
Vince-85 Vince, John A., *Computer Graphics for Graphic Designers*, Frances Pinter, London, 1985.
Vince-89 Vince, John A., 'The Art of Simulation', in *Computers in Art, Design and Animation,* pp. 235–245, Springer-Verlag, Berlin, 1989.
Voss-83 Voss, R. F., 'Fourier Synthesis of Gaussian Fractals 1/f Noises, Landscapes, and Flakes', in *State of the Art in Image Synthesis, Tutorial No. 10,* SIGGRAPH 1983, ACM, New York, 1983.
Voss-85 Voss, R. F., 'Random Fractal Forgeries', *Fundamental Algorithms for Computer Graphics*, (ed. Earnshaw, R. A.), Springer-Verlag, Berlin, pp. 805–836, 1985.

Walker-88 Walker, James S., 'Fourier Analysis', Oxford University Press, Oxford, 1988.
Wallace-87 Wallace, John R., Cohen, Michael F., and Greenberg, Donald P., 'A Two-pass Solution to the Rendering Equation: A Synthesis of Ray Tracing and Radiosity Methods', *Computer Graphics,* Vol. 21, No. 4, pp. 311–320, July 1987 (Proc. SIGGRAPH 87).
Wallace-89 Wallace, John R., Elmquist, Kells A., and Haines, Eric A., 'A Ray Tracing Algorithm for Progressive Radiosity', *Computer Graphics*, Vol. 23, No. 3, pp. 315–324, July 1989 (Proc. SIGGRAPH 89).
Ward-87 Ward, Jean Renard, and Phillips, Mark J., 'Digitizer Technology: Performance Charactersistics and the Effects on the User Interface', *IEEE, CG&A*, Vol. 7, No. 4, pp. 31–44, April 1987.
Ward-88 Ward, Gregory J., Rubinstein, Francis M., and Clear, Robert D., 'A Ray Tracing Solution for Diffuse Interreflection', *Computer Graphics*, Vol. 22, No. 4, pp. 85–92, August 1988 (Proc. SIGGRAPH 88).
Ware-88 Ware, Colin, 'Color Sequences for Univarate Maps: Theory, Experiments, and Principles', *IEEE, CG&A,* Vol. 8, No. 5, pp. 41–49, September 1988.
Warnock-68 Warnock, John E., 'A Hidden Line Algorithm for Halftone Picture Representation', University of Utah Computer Science Dept Rept. TR 4–5, May 1968, NTIS AD 761 995.
Warnock-69 Warnock, John E., 'A Hidden-surface Algorithm for Computer Generated Halftone Pictures', University of Utah Computer Science Dept Rept. TR 4–15, June 1969, NTIS AD 753 671.
Waters-87 Waters, Keith, 'A Muscle Model for Animating Three-dimensional Facial Expression', *Computer Graphics*, Vol. 21, No. 4, pp. 17–24, July 1987 (Proc. SIGGRAPH 87).
Watkins-70 Watkins, G. S., 'A Real-time Visible Surface Algorithm', University of Utah Computer Science Dept Tech. Rep. UTEC-CS-70-101, June 1970, NTIS AD 762 004.
Weeg-66 Weeg, G. P., and Reed, G. B., *Introduction to Numerical Analysis,* Blaisdell, 1966.
Weghorst-84 Weghorst, H., Hooper, G., and

Greenberg, D., 'Improved Computational Methods for Ray Tracing', *ACM Trans. Graphics*, Vol. 3, No. 1, pp. 52–69, January 1984.

Weil-86 Weil, Jerry, 'The Synthesis of Cloth Objects', *Computer Graphics*, Vol. 20, No. 4, pp. 49–54, August 1986 (Proc. SIGGRAPH 86).

Weiler-77 Weiler, K., and Atherton, P., 'Hidden Surface Removal Using Polygon Area Sorting', *Computer Graphics*, Vol. 11, pp. 214–222, July 1977 (Proc. SIGGRAPH 77).

Welch-84 Welch, Terry A., 'A Technique for High-performance Data Compression', *IEEE Computer*, Vol. 17, No. 6, June 1984.

White-86 White, Tony, *The Animator's Workbook,* Phaidon, Oxford, 1986.

Whitted-78 Whitted, T., 'A Scan-line Algorithm for Computer Display of Curved Surfaces', *Computer Graphics*, Vol. 12, 1978 (supplement to Proc. SIGGRAPH 78).

Whitted-79 Whitted, J. T., 'An Improved Illumination Model for Shaded Display', *CACM,* Vol. 23, pp. 343–349, 1979 (Proc. SIGGRAPH 79).

Wilhelms-85 Wilhelms, Jane, and Barsky, Brian, 'Using Dynamic Analysis to Animate Articulated Bodies such as Humans and Robots', *Graphics Interface,* 1985.

Wilhelms-87 Wilhelms, Jane, 'Using Dynamic Analysis for Realistic Animation of Articulated Bodies', *IEEE, CG&A*, Vol. 7, No. 6, pp. 12–27, June 1987.

Williams-78 Williams, Lance, 'Casting Curved Shadows on Curved Surfaces', *Computer Graphics*, Vol. 12, pp. 270–274, 1978 (Proc. SIGGRAPH 78).

Williams-83 Williams, Lance, 'Pyramidal Parametrics', *Computer Graphics*, Vol. 17, No. 3, pp. 1–11, July 1983 (Proc. SIGGRAPH 83).

Willis-87 Willis, P. J., 'Visual Simulation of Atmospheric Haze', *Computer Graphics,* Vol. 6, No. 1, pp. 35–41, July 1987 (Proc. SIGGRAPH 87).

Winston-84 Winston, Patrick Henry, and Horn, Berthold Klaus Paul, *LISP,* 2nd edn, Addison-Wesley, Reading, MA, 1984.

Witkin-88 Witkin, Andrew, and Kass, Michael, 'Spacetime Constraints', *Computer Graphics,* Vol. 22, No. 4, pp. 159–168, August 1988 (Proc. SIGGRAPH 88).

Woodwark-86 Woodwark, John, *Computing Shape,* Butterworths, London, 1986.

Woodwark-89 Woodwark, John, (ed.), *Geometric Reasoning,* Oxford Science Publications, Oxford, 1989.

Wordenweber-83 Wordenweber, B., 'Surface Triangulation for Picture Production', *IEEE, CG&A,* Vol. 3, No. 8, pp. 45–51, 1983.

Wu-89 Wu, Xiaolin, and Rokne, Jon G., 'Double-step Generation of Ellipses', *IEEE, CG&A*, Vol. 9, No. 4, pp. 56–69, July 1989.

Wylie-67 Wylie, C., Romney, G. W., Evans, D. C., and Erdahl, A. C., 'Halftone Perspective Drawings by Computer', *FJCC 1967*, Thompson, Washington, DC, pp. 49–58, 1967.

Wyvill-85 Wyvill, G., and Kunii, T. L., 'A Functional Model for Constructive Solid Geometry', *The Visual Computer*, Vol. 1, No. 1, pp. 3–14, 1985.

Wyvill-86 Wyvill, G., McPheeters, C., and Wyvill, B. L. M., 'Data Structure for Soft Objects', *The Visual Computer*, pp. 227–234, August 1986.

Wyvill-87 Wyvill, Geoff, and Wyvill, Brian, 'Solid Texturing of Soft Objects', *IEEE, CG&A,* Vol. 7, No. 12, pp. 20–26, December 1987.

Yamaguchi-84 Yamaguchi, K., Kuni, T. L., and Fujimura, K., 'Octree-related Data Structures and Algorithms', *IEEE, CG&A*, Vol. 4, No. 1, pp. 53–59, 1984.

Youssef-86 Youssef, S., 'A New Algorithm for Object Oriented Ray Tracing', *Computer Vision, Graphics and Image Processing,* Vol. 34, pp. 125–137, 1986.